Public *Speaking*

YOUR PATHWAY TO SUCCESS

Fermin Irigoyen

Skyline College

Kendall Hunt
publishing company

Kendall Hunt
publishing company

www.kendallhunt.com
Send all inquiries to:
4050 Westmark Drive
Dubuque, IA 52004-1840

ISBN 978-0-7575-6653-0

Printed in the United States of America
10 9 8 7 6 5 4 3

CONTENTS

FIVE PILLARS TO SUCCESSFUL PUBLIC SPEAKING

PILLAR ONE: PREPARATION FOR SUCCESS BEFORE HEADING TO THE PODIUM

PILLAR TWO: SPEECH PREPARATION: THE FOUNDATION TO SUCCESS

ABOUT THE AUTHOR

Professor Fermin Irigoyen is a tenured member of the Speech Communication faculty at Skyline College in San Bruno, California where he has taught since 1999. Fermin graduated from California State University, Hayward, now known as California State University, East Bay with a Bachelor's Degree in Speech Communication with a Minor in Business Administration. In addition, Fermin earned his Master's Degree in Speech Communication also from California State University, Hayward.

In addition, to teaching Speech Communication at Skyline College, Fermin worked as a news anchor/reporter for CNN affiliate KLIV am radio in San Jose, California. While working at KLIV Fermin covered the San Jose Sharks of the National Hockey League on their quest to the Stanley Cup. Fermin also produced and directed the documentary *Brothers,* that examined the interpersonal dynamics from three sets of brothers from the San Francisco Bay Area.

Professor Irigoyen is interested in hearing from you if you have any questions, comments, or concerns about *Public Speaking: Your Pathway to Success.* Professor Irigoyen may be contacted by email at: irigoyen@smccd.edu or through the mail at:

Skyline College
Language Arts Division
Fermin Irigoyen
3300 College Drive
San Bruno CA 94066

Pillar 1

Preparation for Success Before Heading to the Podium

Chapter 1

A Positive Mental Attitude: Your Gateway to Success in Public Speaking

A POSITIVE MENTAL ATTITUDE CAN LEAD YOU TO GREATNESS

On your pathway to success having a positive mental attitude is one of the strongest assets you possess. There are three areas where you have complete control on your pathway to success, your thoughts, the mental pictures you create, and your actions. These three points contribute to how you go through any given situation, and your public speaking experience is no different. It is your responsibility to create a dynamic public speaking experience for yourself and your audience. Proficiency in public speaking will advance you in your formal education, and in your chosen profession.

Embrace the Process of Learning a New Skill

Public speaking is one of the more valuable skills you can develop to be a more marketable and attractive leader in your given field. Since public speaking is a new skill you will be learning, you are about to enjoy a new voyage toward a valuable destination—success. Throughout this text, *Public Speaking: Your Pathway to Success*, you will learn theories and concepts that will help guide you in your new public speaking skill. However, you will need to turn the corner from just learning the theories to actually starting to deliver speeches in order to gain the experience you need to hone your craft. Anytime you learn a new skill you will encounter four different stages of development. Communication scholars Wackman, Miller, and Nunnally discuss these four distinct stages of learning a new skill in their 1976 book *Student Workbook: Increasing Awareness and Communication Skills*. According to their typology, as a beginning public speaker, you first will experience beginning awareness, then transition into awkwardness, followed by skillfulness, and lastly integration.

When learning a new skill, **beginning awareness** occurs when you learn that there is a specialized and more authoritative way of doing something. In the world of public speaking you will begin to learn that delivering a speech is more than just standing up in front of a group of people to randomly express your thoughts. You will learn that public speaking is a skill and there is a formal preparation process *before* heading to the podium. Moreover, you will begin to see that many of the fears about public speaking one may have can be overcome with specific preparation strategies. You will learn about those strategies throughout this textbook.

Anytime you learn something new, your initial attempts may be **awkward** and uneasy. This happens to beginning public speakers as they learn how to use a speaker's outline, correctly cite their sources orally, implement findings from an audience analysis survey, and maintain eye contact with their audience while standing at a podium. Doing all of these actions at once throws many beginning public speakers for a temporary loop. The gap between randomly talking in front of an audience and preparing a formal public address is large, but with a positive mental attitude and strong skill-set you can progressively fill that gap. With diligent practice and a good attitude you can move from this phase into the skillfulness phase of learning a new skill.

The **skillfulness phase** of your development allows you to handle yourself well enough to do the task, but you are still thinking about the appropriate actions to do the task. For example, while delivering your speech you are thinking "I need more eye contact here," "slow your rate of speech here," "stress this point with hand gestures." The point is you are up at the podium delivering a speech but you are still thinking about what needs to be done. As time goes on and you garner more public speaking experience you will begin to deliver speeches while implementing the necessary actions without thinking of the mechanics of public speaking, and the process will become instinctual.

The last stage in the skill development process is the **integration stage.** During this phase you are delivering a speech, and all of those thoughts you had of doing particular actions during the skillfulness stage will come naturally and automatically, so your focus now is on delivering a well-thought-out address for your audience.

Anytime you are learning any new skill, remember these four distinct phases in your development. Oftentimes the reason people do not succeed is not because they lack talent or skill, it is because they quit too early in their learning process. Keeping these four stages in mind will give you the perspective to confidently weather the turbulent storms of learning any new skill. In short, your voyage through these different stages in your public speaking learning experience may be bumpy, but a positive and persistent mental attitude will navigate you towards a valuable and rewarding new skill that will enhance your status in any organization.

Goal Setting

It is important for you to actively set goals for public speaking. Goal setting is fundamental to success regardless of your desired profession or objective. Ask yourself, "What do I want to accomplish in my public speaking course?" "What do I want to be able to do as a result of my public speaking experience?" "How can I develop the necessary skill-set to deliver my acceptance of the employee of the year award?" By asking these questions you are now able to articulate your end goal of what you need to be able to do as a result of your public speaking class. This goal setting exercise will work with anything you would like to accomplish. One thing to keep in mind about goals and the direction of your life is that you may not be able to arrive at the desired destination in an instance but you can surely change the direction towards your desired outcome on a dime.

You must be realistic as to what you can achieve in a beginning semester of public speaking. For example, if your goal is to be a client for the Washington Speaker's Bureau earning over $150,000 per speech by the end of the semester, and you have never delivered a speech before, you may want to lower your bar. However, building your skills to deliver a 10-minute persuasive speech is well within your grasp; especially if you have never delivered a speech before.

Ideally any goal that you establish should be measurable (minutes, number of orally cited sources, number of people in the audience), and have a deadline (a specific day and time). The goal must be stated specifically, because hazy goals turn out hazy outcomes. A sensible practice when establishing and writing a goal down is to do some action towards the attainment of that goal immediately, to build momentum towards that goal. For example, if your goal is to "deliver a 10-minute persuasive speech to the student council on their October 28th meeting" you would immediately call the student council and get placed on their October 28th agenda. This will create urgency and focus to prepare for your October 28th presentation. Moreover, after documenting your goal, a brief description as to why you want to achieve this goal will anchor your commitment towards your objective.

Once you have those goals documented, perhaps also on a 3x5 card for easy access, review those goals at least twice a day. The best times for reviewing your goals would be when waking up in the morning and before going to bed at night. Remember in the morning you want to create a purpose so that at night you can relish in its achievement.

Once you have documented your goals and why you want to achieve them, and allocated time to review your goals, it is now time to develop action plans to achieve your goals. Action towards your goals makes your aspirations a reality. Winston Churchill was known to have stickers placed on his memos saying "Action this Day," and through his actions Churchill became a prominent figure in world history. So clearly document the necessary actions for you to achieve your public speaking goals.

The fun begins when you establish goals for yourself, because you can be sure that roadblocks and barriers will visit you on your pathway to success. For example, when establishing a goal thoughts now turn to "boy I'm going to have to stay late at the library," or "I now have to get my computer fixed so I can work on my outline." Essentially you begin to create reasons why you should not attempt to deliver that speech at the student council meeting or the campus ministry group. It is good to address these doubts head-on and write them out on paper, so that now you can confront and overcome those limiting beliefs analytically and not emotionally.

Creating a goal is your way of stepping out of your comfort zone, and when we do step out of our normal terrain uncertainty creeps in and with uncertainty comes the emotion of fear. Fear is the biggest emotion to overcome in public speaking. It is a normal emotion in public speaking, so welcome fear and use it to your advantage. Throughout the textbook you will learn specific strategies to overcome your public speaking fear.

In pursuit of worthy goals life sometimes gets in the way and that derails us from our progress. For example, your computer breaks down while drafting your outline or your roommate decides to clean the apartment and throws your textbook in the dumpster, or you come down with a case of laryngitis on the day you are scheduled to deliver your speech. Again welcome these funny life instances and do your best to think ahead and anticipate life and prepare for those unfortunate life experiences. That is why the sage advice of starting your speech preparation early usually off-sets many of these "last minute" derailments in achieving your public speaking goals.

Accomplishing big goals in your life requires you to grow and become a bigger person. Goals force us to grow and stretch, and developing public speaking goals will require you to stretch your skill-set and comfort zone. Sometimes we are afraid of growth, because growth means change, but the only constant in life is change—so embrace the empowering process of transforming your life and skill-set. Take the time to establish those public speaking and life goals and get busy making those goals real and tangible, but of course do not stop at the achievement of a particular goal, because there are more goals with your name written on them.

In short, write down the goals that you want to achieve. Next write a short description as to why you want to achieve your particular goal, what you would miss if you did not achieve this goal, and what you would gain from the achievement of the goal. Third, revisit your written goals and your "why" description at least twice a day. Fourth, think about how you can surround yourself with the appropriate people who can help you attain your goal. By consistently referring to your written goals you will have that extra nudge to take the appropriate action to meet your desired results. On your pathway to success, you will learn that it is not what you take on that matters, but what you accomplish at the end of the day.

Visualization

One way to create the best public speaking experience for yourself is through the process of **visualization.** Take the time to close your eyes and visualize yourself delivering a high-quality speech, and allow those images to be absorbed by your subconscious mind. Picture yourself standing in front of your audience to receive their applause as you get ready to say your opening line of your introduction. Visualize yourself in the venue (this may be your classroom), picture the color of the walls, the seating arrangements, the scents that distinguish the particular venue, the sounds of the acoustics of the room, the sound of your fluid delivery, the feel of your outline in your hands when you turn the page, and the taste of a well done speech for your audience. The more you can visualize your speech by capturing all of your senses in a movie format, the more real your public speaking experience can become. Our minds have a difficult time distinguishing something that we have imagined from reality. So spend time visualizing your success beforehand, so that by the time you are at the podium, in your mind's eye this is an activity you have already done successfully. In short, through the visualization process, you have already experienced delivering your speech. This is a success strategy that combats nervousness, stage fright, and strengthens your confidence.

In conjunction with the process of visualization you can create written affirmations to support your efforts at delivering a successful speech. For example, "I am delivering an engaging speech to inform

Visualizing your success at the podium will lead to a
better public speaking experience
Source: Shutterstock © Gabriel Moisa

that is well prepared, well researched, and well delivered." When crafting an affirmation, here are some tips that will make the process a useful one. Start with "I am," affirm what you want and *not* what you do not want, and keep it short and precise. If you have your affirmations on a 3 x 5 card, you can refer to them throughout the day to keep your positive vision front and center in your mind. Furthermore, with your positive affirmation in hand you can now *believe* that you have already delivered an engaging speech to inform that was well prepared, well researched, and well delivered.

Another added-value characteristic of the visualization and affirmation process is that it creates positive expectations of yourself and the presentation of your public address. Unfortunately, negative thoughts and emotions drive many beginning public speakers. Common thoughts from beginning public speakers are, "Boy, I hope I don't blow this," "My audience is really going to laugh at me when I stumble on my words," "I feel like a fraud delivering a speech about this topic." As you can see, with thoughts like this, of course you are not going to come across as confident or competent in your message. You must head to the podium *believing* in yourself, and your message, and if you do not you can bet your audience will not either. As we said earlier, you have 100% control of your thoughts and believing in yourself is a choice.

As you develop a positive mental attitude, the word "can't," must be eliminated from your vocabulary. The word can't is a paralyzing self-limiting belief that will make your public speaking experience more challenging. Let us think about this mindset, "I can't deliver a speech without embarrassing myself." Here you are communicating feelings of self-doubt and that self-doubt will be communicated to your audience nonverbally. Now, let us substitute the "can't" with "I don't know how" and see how that changes your approach and thinking towards public speaking. "I don't know how to deliver a speech without embarrassing myself," communicates an openness to yourself to learn the appropriate techniques of public speaking so you do not embarrass yourself. By saying "I don't know how," you are communicating a proactive quality and the willingness to make the necessary improvements to fill a skill gap. Conversely, "I can't" communicates passivity and an attitude of unwillingness to deliver a speech without embarrassing yourself. When preparing to learn about the basic principles of public speaking be mindful of the language you are telling yourself, because those words lead to self-fulfilling prophecies.

A **self-fulfilling prophecy** happens when one's expectations of an event affect the person's behavior in that given event. For example, when you get your assignment for your first speech, and in your mind you have already told yourself that you will do terribly on the assignment because you "can't do public speaking," that will lead you to inaction during the preparation phase of developing your speech. The day finally comes when it is your turn to deliver your speech and you bomb. In your mind you are saying "I told you I couldn't do public speaking." At the beginning of the process you made up your mind that you would not do well, and presto, you did exactly what you told yourself once the assignment was handed out. In short, if you see yourself as capable and competent to complete the given assignment you will find yourself achieving your public speaking goal.

There are four phases to a self-fulfilling prophecy:

1. Clutching onto an expectation for yourself or others
2. Acting in harmony with that expectation
3. The expectation becomes realized
4. The original expectation is supported and strengthened

So to help you in the mental aspect of delivering a well-thought-out address, first "be" the proficient public speaker, then "do" the necessary tasks required to be a proficient public speaker, and soon you will "have" everything come together on your pathway to success as a public speaker.

Enthusiasm is the Fuel to a Positive Mental Attitude

Thomas Fuller, a chaplain to King Charles II of England said, "The real difference between men is energy. A strong will, a settled purpose, and invincible determination can accomplish almost anything; and in this lies the distinction between great men and little men." Enthusiasm is a must in public speaking. Obviously enthusiasm is a characteristic that is needed at the podium, but it is even more important during the preparation process. Your enthusiastic effort during the preparation process carries and builds to the time you deliver your speech. The enthusiasm you demonstrate in the research phase will attract library staff to want to help you. When conducting your audience analysis survey your enthusiasm will be sensed by those who are filling out your survey, and they will oftentimes give you a more thoughtful response to your questions. When delivering your speech, enthusiasm will create a likeability factor and your audience will be more inclined to give you their complete and undivided attention. The more you demonstrate interest in your speech, the more your audience will want to listen to your message. No one wants to listen to someone who comes across like they are simply going through the motions, so have some enthusiasm. Give the full preparation process of delivering your speech your best effort, and do not settle for being average. You know what happens to the person sitting in the middle of the road? They get run over, so do not be road kill! In short, your enthusiasm for your topic, your audience, and the work behind the scenes is contagious. Enthusiasm and passion will defeat talent any day.

Modeling Successful Public Speakers

One of the easiest ways to develop the confidence that will contribute to a positive mental attitude is modeling other successful public speakers. Anthony Robbins is quoted as saying "success leaves clues," and in order to be a successful public speaker it is a good idea to observe the numerous outstanding public speakers in world history. One outstanding Web site that contains many of the world's most famous speeches may be found at www.americanrhetoric.com/. By watching world-class speeches, you will be able to see how top notch public speakers deliver their message, frame their emotional appeals, organize their thoughts, and present themselves as leaders. When studying other public speakers you want to look for traits you can implement in your public-speaking skill-set and that can help you become a better public speaker.

Conversely, watching speeches by those whose talent and skills may not lie in public speaking can also give you tips as to what *not* to do. The bottom line is if you get into the routine of watching speeches, doing this analytical activity will give you insights and put you on a track to becoming a competent and confident public speaker. Understanding what not to do is often as significant as learning what to do.

What do the following prominent public speakers have in common? Mahatma Ghandi, Dr. Martin Luther King Jr., Ronald Reagan, John F. Kennedy, Franklin Delano Roosevelt, Bill Clinton, Richard Nixon, Russell H. Conwell, Winston Churchill, Nelson Mandela, Susan B. Anthony, Woodrow Wilson, Dwight Eisenhower, Ben Franklin, Abraham Lincoln, Patrick Henry, Plato, Aristotle, Al Gore, Steve Jobs, Theodore Roosevelt, Lou Gehrig, Lance Armstrong, Jack Welch, Lee Iacocca, Dr. Norman Vincent Peale, Billy Graham, Dr. Robert H. Schuller, Angelina Jolie, Napoleon Hill, Dale Carnegie, John D. Rockefeller, Mother Teresa, César Chávez, Tom Peters, Steven Covey, and Warren Bennis.

All of these people use public speaking as a means to influence the world in causes bigger than themselves. The skill of public speaking is a valuable tool that can be used to influence society and or your respective communities. By modeling these difference makers you can develop your public speaking skills to become a difference maker yourself. In the grand scheme of life, how do you plan to use your newly acquired public speaking skills to influence the world in which you live?

Time Management

When you think about the most precious commodity on the face of the world, time is at the top of the list. Yet we waste minutes every day and over a lifetime we waste productive years that could have accomplished great things. We will be learning about very influential people in world history who used public speaking to impact the world we know today. The one thing we have in common with the most influential people in the world is that all of us have 1,440 minutes in a day, which comes out to 525,600 minutes in a year (except for leap years), so you can tack on another 1,440 minutes. Unfortunately in the realm of beginning public speaking, many students do not maximize their daily 1,440 minutes to the fullest and demonstrate the fruits of their poor time management at the podium in front of an audience.

Not having a clear purpose of what your desired outcome is in a given day is a sure way to waste time. Arguably one of the world's greatest boxers in history, Muhammad Ali, woke up every morning with the purpose to be the "Greatest" and took the necessary actions to make that happen. Ali had this to say about time, "Don't count the days, and make the days count." The same can be said about public speakers preparing for their speeches, have a clear purpose as to what you hope to accomplish. If you start the day with purpose you will end the day with achievements. Focused thinking about delivering your best possible speech will remove the unnecessary distractions and intellectual clutter so that you can concentrate on creating a well-thought-out public address. If you do not know what your end goal is, how will you ever accomplish your noble pursuits?

When time is used wisely, it can create solutions to problems, innovate new products or services, and acquire knowledge which will lead to higher capacities for achievement. Having a strong sense of urgency in using your time wisely is important in preparing for a speech, so START EARLY! In addition, urgency creates energy, and energy leads to action and productivity, so use this to your advantage. By procrastinating and poorly utilizing your time you are simply suspending success. Now, does putting off success make any sense?

One way to maximize your time is to create deadlines for yourself, like "in the next 30 minutes I will select a topic and write a specific purpose for my upcoming persuasive speech." While doing this activity you will have a timer that will count down from 30 minutes to 00:00. This will create urgency but it is also a tool to maintain your focus on a given task in the preparation process; and when you complete these tasks, slowly but surely you will go from selecting a topic all the way through the practicing of your delivery phase in your speech preparation. Maintaining your focus on your speech preparation will help you ignore those silly distractions that can erase your allotted 1,440 minutes in a day on your way to greatness.

In order to use your time wisely, you will have to learn to say the word "no." When preparing for your speech assignments your undivided attention and focus are needed to prepare a sound public address. Also, saying "no" to these time-robbers like your cell phone, text messaging, video games, and email/web surfing

Source: Shutterstock © PeppPic

activities while preparing for your speech will keep you focused and in a position to be fully prepared for your upcoming speech. Moreover, by saying "no" to other fun activities such as frat parties, athletic events, hanging out with friends, and nights at the club, you are saying "yes" to your success and your individual achievement towards your given goals, such as earning an "A" in your public speaking course.

The Preparation Process

"The more you sweat in peace, the less you bleed in war."
— GENERAL GEORGE S. PATTON, JR. (AMERICAN GENERAL, 1885–1945)

Having a positive mental attitude will help your time management for the preparation for your upcoming public address. The keys to maximizing your time are staying focused on your objective of delivering a sound public address and starting the process early. The speech preparation process consists of 13 steps, and one of the best ways to maximize the preparation process is to create a timeline for the completion of each of these steps. One of the common flaws in beginning public speakers is they do not give themselves an adequate amount of time to complete each of these steps thoroughly. You do not want to rush through the process, but to methodically work through the steps so give yourself the best opportunity to succeed.

Step 1: Select a topic

Step 2: Determine a general purpose

Step 3: Formulate your specific purpose

Step 4: Document a central idea that accurately reflects the main points of the speech

Step 5: Conduct an audience analysis survey

Step 6: Research your topic using the library, the Internet, and field studies

Step 7: Support your ideas using examples, statistics, and testimony

Step 8: Organize the body of your speech

Step 9: Create a catchy introduction and conclusion

Step 10: Develop and proofread a preparation and speaker's outline of your speech

Step 11: Analyze the word choice in your speech, refine and edit

Step 12: Implement appropriate visual aids that reinforce and add value to your message

Step 13: Practice your delivery

Each of these steps is discussed in greater detail throughout the textbook. You can become a good public speaker by following the principles set forth in *Public Speaking: Your Pathway to Success*. Achieving the goal of becoming a competent and confident public speaker will require you to grow out of your comfort zones so enjoy the ride down your pathway to success and take action now!

Summary: Creating a Positive Mental Attitude towards the Power of Public Speaking

On your pathway to success, public speaking is a skill that will distinguish you as a competent member of an organization and community. Whenever you learn a new skill you will go through four distinct phases in your learning development: beginning awareness, awkwardness, skillfulness, and integration. One of the primary reasons people do not succeed in mastering a new skill is that they do not allow themselves to go through the entire process, and quit too early in the game.

Establishing clear goals in your public speaking development is a sure way to measure your progress. Learning the basics of establishing goals is a transferable skill that may be applied to the various aspects of your personal development. First, set up a realistic destination you would like to reach, yet one that will stretch your current skill-set. Next, write out your goals on paper and make sure your goals are measurable and have a deadline. Next develop the appropriate actions that will get you to your destination. Finally, refer to your written goals at least twice a day to keep you on track and reinforce the goals' importance in your daily activities.

After you have a set of clearly written goals, the additional practice of visualization will help you realize those goals. It is important to spend some quiet time alone visualizing yourself delivering a successful speech for your audience before you actually deliver your speech for your class. When visualizing yourself delivering your speech think about yourself enthusiastically presenting your materials, and while visualizing be sure to tap into your five senses: seeing, tasting, hearing, touching, and smelling. Because you will more than likely be delivering your speech in the same room in which you are taking your class, creating a movie-like vision will be much easier for you. In addition to the visualization process, writing down encouraging affirmations will keep your positive mental attitude anchored on a successful speech.

Modeling prominent and successful public speakers is a fantastic way to help you make progress on your quest to becoming a flourishing public speaker. By studying the greats you can pick up specific characteristics that you may want to include in your public speaking style. Modeling is a proven activity to get you to where you want to go in a shorter amount of time.

Time is the most precious commodity we have and maximizing your preparation time will help you shine while you are at the podium delivering your speech. The key with managing your time is to start early and set up a schedule of what needs to get done and when it needs to be completed. During your time scheduling, give yourself extra time for the practice of your delivery before heading to the podium. An unfortunate pitfall with beginning public speakers is to procrastinate and short change themselves in practicing. There is nothing more heartbreaking than preparing a well-written and supported speech and not having practiced your delivery, so it comes across as if you are delivering your speech for the first time in front of your audience. Procrastination is merely postponing your success, so why wait to succeed?

Capitalizing on the preparation process is one of the surest ways to be fully prepared for your speech and will translate into more confidence in your message. The preparation phase is the building blocks to successful public speaking and attacking each step enthusiastically and with a positive mental attitude will create a successful public speaking address experience for yourself and your audience. Each of the steps in the preparation process will be discussed thoroughly in the following chapters of the text.

On your pathway to success having a positive mental attitude will take you places, and the skill-set of public speaking can lead you to greatness.

Name: _____

True-False

1. T F During the integration stage you handle yourself well enough to do the task but you are still thinking about the appropriate actions to do the task.

2. T F By asking yourself "What do I want to accomplish in my public speaking course" will help you articulate an end goal as a result of your public speaking course.

3. T F You should review your goals at least twice a day.

4. T F The more you can visualize your speech by capturing all of your senses in a movie format, the less real your public speaking experience will become.

5. T F Watching poor public speakers will only hurt your development as a beginning public speaker.

6. T F "The more you sweat in peace, the less you bleed in war," was quoted by General H. Norman Schwarzkopf.

Multiple Choice

7. All of these steps are involved when learning to perform a new skill except:

    a. Awareness
    b. Attentiveness
    c. Awkwardness
    d. Skillfulness
    e. Integration

8. Which of the following is *not* a phase to the self-fulfilling prophecy

    a. Clutching onto an expectation for yourself or others
    b. Acting in harmony with that expectation
    c. Visualize the harmony of your subconscious mind
    d. The expectation becomes realized
    e. The original expectation is supported and strengthened

9. By watching world-class speeches you should be able to do the following except:

    a. How top notch public speakers deliver their message
    b. Frame their emotional appeals
    c. Organize their thoughts
    d. Observe audience reaction
    e. Present themselves as leaders

10. There are _____ minutes in a day.

    a. 14,440
    b. 1,440
    c. 144,440
    d. 4,140
    e. 41,140

11. _____ is a proven activity to get you to where you want to go in a shorter amount of time.

   a. Modus operandi
   b. Maneuvering
   c. Mimicking
   d. Modeling
   e. Manipulating

12. The three areas where you have complete control over on your pathway to success are:

   a. Your thoughts, the mental channels in the subconscious you create, and your reactions
   b. Creating a dynamic public speaking experience, the advancement of your education, and professional actions
   c. Public speaking situations, your actions, and the preparation process
   d. Your thoughts, the mental pictures you create, and your actions
   e. Goal setting, visualization, and positive mental attitude

13. When phrasing an affirmation on a 3 × 5 card which term would you start the affirmation:

   a. "I hope,"
   b. "I will,"
   c. "I am,"
   d. "I can't,"
   e. "My audience,"

Essay

14. Please list the 13 steps in the preparation process.

15. Describe the benefits of being enthusiastic in both your speech preparation and the actual delivery of your speech.

Chapter 2

Strategies to Combat Your Stage Fright

"According to most studies, people's number one fear is public speaking. Number two is death. Death is number two. Does that sound right? This means to the average person, if you go to a funeral, you're better off in the casket than doing the eulogy."

—JERRY SEINFELD (COMEDIAN)

When asking college students "what worries you about public speaking," the common responses are:

"I'm afraid I will mess up and people will laugh at me."

"I am not comfortable with being in the center of attention."

"What if I forget what to say?"

"I'm going to make myself look silly if I make a mistake."

"I have never had to do this before."

"The audience will know more about the subject than I do."

"What if the audience does not agree with what I have to say?"

"I don't want to be judged by a bunch of strangers."

"The audience will totally know I'm nervous."

In a sense these college students are afraid of the unknown. As a critical thinker and a trained public speaker, it is your job to be able to identify the unknowns and turn those unknowns into knowns. For example, in response to "What if I forget what to say," you will learn how to create a speaker's outline that you will bring to the podium. If for whatever reason you forget what to say, all you have do is simply compose yourself, look down at your outline, and continue with your speech. In short, with your public speaking concerns will come strategies throughout the textbook that will help you breakthrough those concerns to become a competent and confident public speaker.

Public speaking gets a bad rap because we are often asked to deliver a speech with little or no training. This is similar to asking someone to learn to ride a bicycle in front of an audience of 30 people. Public speaking is a skill like riding a bicycle is a skill. Can you remember the first few times you were learning to ride a bike on two wheels, and you fell down? You simply got back on the bike and enjoyed many years on a bicycle. The same can be said about public speaking, it is a skill; so embrace the process and enjoy the ride.

The biggest fear with public speaking comes from the speaker's relationship with the audience. Remember, your audience members are real live human beings with thoughts and feelings like yourself, and they want to see you do well. Yet, many public speakers see the audience as an opponent and not a partner. Dale Carnegie had this to say about fear, "Inaction breeds doubt and fear. Action breeds confidence and courage. If you want to conquer fear, do not sit home and think about it. Go out and get busy." What Carnegie is trying to say is that you must be active in facing your fears. In this text you will learn strategies to overcome your fears such as how to complete an audience analysis survey *before* delivering your speech. The more we become familiar with something or somebody, the more at ease we become in the situation. The same is true regarding the speaker's relationship with the audience. Essentially, by taking steps to learn about the audience, you are taking the mystery out of who your audience members are and treating them like real people. In short, you are taking the invisible and making it visible, taking the abstract and making it concrete. For example suppose you are preparing for a speech to persuade about the dangers of smoking, and you are afraid to offend the members of your class, yet you do not know where they stand on the issue. Imagine now that you conducted an audience analysis survey and learned that 46% of the class smokes between 10 and 15 cigarettes a day. Now you are getting concrete information about your audience, as opposed to inaccurately guessing the class' smoking habits. Here you are taking the unknown and making it a known piece of valuable information, which bolsters your poise and confidence at the podium and makes your message more audience-focused.

There is a strong relationship between uncertainty and anxiety. The higher the uncertainty of the situation, the higher the anxiety one would experience in that given situation. So the lesson here is to minimize as many of the uncertainties as you can so that they become certainties. Going through the process of really examining and documenting your uncertainties and fears takes courage, but it is really a good process in being honest with yourself. On your pathway to success there will be many uncertain situations you will have to face, so learn to take the initiative of taking those uncertainties and turning them into something tangible and real. The more real something is, the less scary it becomes and more manageable it becomes to break through those self-limiting barriers. In short your focus must be on delivering a well-thought-out address for your audience, and not worrying about non-public speaking matters.

If you are feeling nervous before a speech consider yourself normal. Often times beginning public speakers feel guilty or even ashamed about being nervous before a speech, and that is a negative psychological association to have before a speech. Being nervous before a speech is an appropriate feeling to have, and it is those exact nervous feelings inside that bring out the best in world-renowned athletes, musicians, artists, lawyers, and business people before big events. It is important to note the distinction between facilitative and debilitative emotions. **Facilitative emotions** are feelings that spur you on to do good, positive, and inspiring things. Conversely, **debilitative emotions** paralyze competent people to underachieve. It will be your responsibility to harness that nervous energy to catapult yourself to do your best behind the podium.

By lowering the uncertainty of your upcoming public speaking experience will lower your anxiety during your speech.
Source: Shutterstock © John Bailey

The key to conquering potentially debilitative emotions of nervousness in public speaking is to practice delivering as many speeches as you can. Essentially, the more you do something, the more comfortable the experience will become, and from there you can focus on delivering a well-thought-out address as opposed to being self-conscious in front of an audience. In addition, the more you see your audience as real human beings and not a group of scary people, the less threatening your audience becomes.

A prominent tool to help you overcome your public speaking nervousness is to be thoroughly prepared to deliver your speech. In order to be properly prepared for an extemporaneous speech these essential steps need to be covered:

- selecting and narrowing of a topic

- writing a clear specific purpose

- having a precise central idea

- doing an accurate audience analysis, accumulating valid materials

- supporting your main ideas, creating an easy—to-follow organization

- using suitable language, writing a catchy introduction and conclusion

- making value-added visual aids, and learning practiced delivery

Moreover, selecting a topic you are familiar with will give an edge to combat nervousness. The stronger your command of the topic, the easier it will be for you to manage your nervousness. The proper preparation process sounds daunting, but through the duration of the text you will gain the tools to master each of these essential steps for your public speaking success.

Another tool you may use to overcome your nervousness is to visualize yourself delivering a successful speech. It is important to really see yourself, like in a movie, delivering a well-thought-out speech, and watching your audience really enjoying your public address. You have an advantage in the visualization tool, because more than likely the classroom you are taking your class in is the same room in which you will be delivering your speeches. This will allow you to see the sights of that window off to the left, the door off to the right, your teacher at the table in the center back row, the lovely photo of Paris on the back wall. In addition, knowing exactly what your audience looks like (your classmates) is a huge advantage in the visualization process.

In addition to visualization and being fully prepared for your speech, most of your nervousness is not visible. In the world of poker when a player has a royal flush, more than likely the player is excited, nervous, and adrenaline is coursing through the player's body. If all of those feelings were visible, the other players around the table would fold. As you stand at the podium, you may feel like you have the royal flush, but no one will know your hand.

Beginning public speakers need to have a realistic outlook as to what you can accomplish with your speech, which helps manage your nervousness. Unfortunately, many beginning public speakers expect perfection in their early speeches and apply too much pressure on themselves. If you were to ask professional speakers speaking for the Washington Speakers Bureau earning over $150,000 per speech, I am sure they would say they have not delivered the perfect speech. Embrace the fact that you are learning a new, powerful, and life-changing skill, so do not expect perfection. With that said, your audience will expect that you are fully prepared, and that you will deliver an enthusiastic message, both of which are doable for beginning public speakers.

Another tip in managing your nervousness is to spend a lot of time working on your introduction. Much like an Olympic sprinter getting off the blocks cleanly for a good race, a public speaker also wants to get off the blocks (your introduction) cleanly. Moreover, a good start will enable you to build that momentum throughout the body and conclusion of your speech. You will learn techniques in developing a captivating introduction that will lead you to delivering a sound presentation. A well-practiced and interesting introduction will allow you to maintain strong eye contact while immediately engaging your audience right at the start. Your audience will be supportive of you and your efforts, so engage them; they are your friends and not the enemy.

As you gain public speaking experience and confidence your focus will be more on delivering your message to your audience than it is on being self conscious about how you are being perceived by your audience members. Once that focus of attention is fully embodied, you will then turn the corner towards being a successful public speaker. This process takes time, so again embrace the lessons along the way to take you on your pathway to success.

BUILDING ON YOUR CURRENT CONVERSATIONAL SKILLS TO STRENGTHEN YOUR PUBLIC SPEAKING SKILLS

Think about your cell phone bills at the end of the month. Some bills come in at $60, $80, $125, and in some cases over $275. That is a lot of time devoted to conversing with others and, with all of that experience talking, key public speaking skills have been clearly developed in your conversational and communication style that are applicable to your public speaking growth.

With all of the numerous people you interact with, think about how you distinctly communicate with each of those people. For example, how you address your best friend of ten years would be different from how you interact with your parents, which would be different from how you interact with your co-workers,

Building on your everyday conversation skills will help develop your public speaking proficiency
Source: Shutterstock © Baudot

which would be different from how you interact with your boss. The message here is that you have customized your message to a "particular" audience, a skill and mindset imperative in public speaking. Public speaking is an audience-focused activity so your message, delivery, and appeals must be tailored to your specific audience.

Another area where similarities between your conversational skills and public speaking intersect is utilizing the power of stories to communicate your points. Think about the many stories you may have shared with your friends that contributed to a $275 cell phone bill. Was the telling of stories a key method for you communicating your ideas? If so, telling stories also works well in communicating your main points in the public speaking arena. One point to remember when telling a story is to make sure that the story you are telling truly reinforces and supports the idea you are trying to communicate with your audience. It is easy to get way off track when telling a story to the point where the speaker and listener cannot remember what the whole point of the story was in the first place. Among your friends that can be an entertaining and humorous way to spend time with each other, but in front of an audience, they will expect more from you the speaker. Moreover, how you organize your thoughts in a story or in a conversation plays a big role in how your audience will perceive you as a speaker and communicator. The same goes with developing a speech—the stronger your thoughts are organized, the more credible you sound, which will make the job of the listeners who are trying to follow your speech much easier. Again you want to make your message easy for your audience to follow along.

Lastly a key similarity between your current conversational skills and public speaking skills is the power of feedback and how that shapes our conversation. Feedback comes in two forms, verbal feedback and nonverbal feedback. In observing **nonverbal feedback** from your audience you will notice the audience members' postures in their seats, eye contact, facial expressions, and gestures. When chatting with your friends, **verbal feedback** would come in the form of probing questions, direct requests for clarification, or simply a response to what was asked by your conversational partner. Moreover, in your everyday conversation nonverbal messages would include eye contact, posture, facial expressions, gestures, paralanguage, and touch. It is important to note that you will not be receiving verbal feedback while delivering your speech.

Key Distinctions between Conversation Skills and Public Speaking Skills

In public speaking there are some distinct differences from the daily conversations you may have with family, friends, or work colleagues. More planning is needed in what you will say in a public speaking venue as opposed to a conversation with your friends. How often have you scripted your message that you will communicate with your family, friends, or employer? Unless it is a serious matter, our conversations come from the top of our heads. Yet in public speaking, careful consideration must be focused on your word choice, evidence, support, and emotional appeals.

Next, the amount of time you have to communicate a message is often limited in the public speaking engagement. With the different assignments or engagements you may encounter, there is usually a time limit designated for each speaker. Now think about if you had a friend who laid down the time rules for conversation. For example, we will both start off with a one minute opening statement, break for a minute, each will then have a rebuttal period for thirty seconds, and finally have two minutes to close the conversation. Simply put, our conversations are not that rigid in time, they simply flow between the participants; however, in public speaking there are time limits and requirements that must be abided by.

In your conversations with the people you interact with regularly, it may be common to hear many voiced pauses, like: "uhm," "uhrr," "like," and "kinda." In public speaking, those voiced pauses will detract from your believability and credibility with the members of your audience. In short, public speaking requires more formality in what your message is, and how you deliver that message. So other characteristics that are acceptable in conversation, but are not acceptable in public speaking, would be: playing with your hair or jewelry, slouching posture, and the use of slang language.

The Speech Communication Process

The world in which we live is driven by systems, and public speaking and communication are no different. Understanding how the speech communication process works will help you grasp how each of the parts of communication come together as one. The players in the speech communication process are: the speaker, the message, the channel, the receiver, the feedback, the environment, and communication interference. We will examine how these players influence you and your speech.

The **speaker** is the driver of the process. Without the speaker the process will not start and generate the momentum needed to move the speech communication system. As the driver of the process, your credibility, your delivery, your preparation, and your audience analysis will be evaluated and rest squarely on the speaker's shoulders.

The **message** is the point you want to communicate to your audience. During the outlining phase of your preparation process, you must evaluate whether the message you want to communicate is actually the message communicated to your audience. Spending time scrutinizing your message before heading to the podium will allow you to accomplish your given mission. An additional component that needs to be acknowledged is the congruency between your verbal message and your nonverbal message. Messages contain the verbal component (subject matter) and the nonverbal component (emotions and relational aspects to a message) and they must be in sync for your audience to believe in your message. For example if you tell someone, "I love you" but it is in a lethargic tone and delivered reluctantly your message will not be believable. Your audience will be attuned to the nonverbal aspect of your message (eye contact, facial expressions, gestures, vocal variety, and delivery pacing).

The **channel** is the means by which a message is communicated. The channel may come in many forms, such as the television, radio, Internet broadcast, telephone, or simply by your voice, which is the most common channel used in a public speaking course. The channel you use to communicate will influence things like your rate of speech, visual aids, and emotional appeals. For example, if you are using a microphone to deliver a speech and there is an echo you will need to account for the echo and slow your rate of speech so your audience has a chance to comprehend what you are saying.

The **receiver** or listener of your message would be your audience. The real challenge in human communication is that every one of us carries different life experiences, areas of intellectual expertise, interests, values, and beliefs. As a public speaker and communicator, our message needs to penetrate through all of those perceptual filters that our audience members may have. Think about a movie you have watched five or so times, your experience has likely been different each time you watched that movie. The first time you watched the movie you were probably grasping the characters, plot lines, and the sound track used in the movie. However, as you watch the movie time after time, you are now reciting lines, singing along to the music, and looking forward to climactic parts to the movie. Based on your experience of watching the movie numerous times, your experience has evolved, and now when someone talks about this particular movie with you, it needs to go through your new perceptual filters. As you can see the discussion would be quite different if you had the conversation about the movie with someone who has never seen the movie. As a speaker it is your obligation to learn about your audience to best match your message to meet the needs of the listener.

Feedback regularly occurs in two-way communication and is delivered back to the speaker both verbally and nonverbally. When delivering a speech, your audience will not be offering verbal feedback, but they will be providing you with nonverbal feedback. You will be observing how your audience is responding

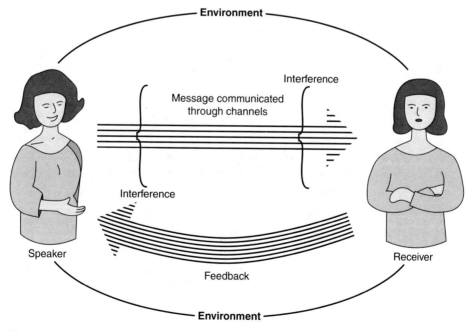

The Speech Communication Process

to your speech by how they are positioned in their seats, so if they are leaning forward at the edge of their chairs, it may be interpreted that they are interested in your message. Conversely, if your audience members are slouching in their chairs looking at the ceiling, this form of disconfirming communication may tell you that they are not engaged in your speech. A point to remember is that nonverbal communication is open to interpretation and is often very vague in its meaning.

Interference is anything that gets in the way of communication between the speaker and the listener. Interference or noise can come in many different forms, and from both the speaker and the audience. A speaker may become very self-conscious about delivering their speech and their focus may become about their nervousness and not about communicating their message to their audience. This leads to fidgeting and voiced pauses, a demonstration that the speaker is distracted. In your public speaking class interference may come from external sources. For example, think about the foot traffic outside your classroom that interferes with your teacher's lectures. Or if you happen to attend a college or university near an airport, the noise coming from the planes can serve as interference with a message. So in the case of the foot traffic it may be a good idea to close the door or post a sign saying "Quiet Please, Speeches in Progress." Be prepared ahead of time for potential interference so you can make the necessary seamless adjustments during your speech.

Another type of interference comes from your audience members. Unfortunately, many students forget to turn off their cell phones and other electronic devices before entering class and sometimes their phones ring with some sort of fancy ring tone, which can distract an entire class and take the attention away from the speaker's efforts. Another possible communication interference that may occur within your audience is if something like a bee starts flying around the classroom and pandemonium occurs. A more subtle form of interference is when your audience members are preoccupied with something going on in their lives and are deep in their own thoughts, and they are simply not listening to the speaker. In a sense the audience members are saying "my thoughts are more important than what you have to say in your speech." Life happens and as a speaker you have little to no control of your audience members' interference, so as a speaker get up to the podium, stay focused and do your best to wholeheartedly communicate your message. As a speaker you must be engaged in your message and do your best to meet the needs of the audience to keep the interest of the audience despite the numerous ways interference can detract from your speech.

The **environment** embodies all of the players involved in the speech communication process in addition to the time and place of the speech. Often times the time and place of a speech adds to the ambiance of the message. For example a commemorative speech for the fallen victims of the 9/11 attacks would lose its luster if were not delivered on September 11th in either Washington, D.C. or New York City. As you can see the environment and all of the players in the speech communication process contribute to the mood of the speech. Moreover, as a speaker you will need to make the necessary adjustments to your speech to best fit the situation. The sum of all of the parts in the speech communication process makes up the environment.

KNOWING THE ETHICAL RULES OF THE GAME

"Be prepared and be honest."
   —JOHN WOODEN (HEAD COACH, UCLA MEN'S BASKETBALL WITH 10 NCAA CHAMPIONSHIPS)

One of the most fundamental stages when putting together a speech is crafting your specific purpose. The specific purpose may be defined as "what you hope to accomplish in your speech." From there, the decision making process is easier for the rest of your speech development because you have the end goal in mind. With your carefully worded specific purpose, you can now ask yourself if the purpose of your speech is ethically sound. For example, say you crafted a specific purpose that says, "To persuade my audience to practice bungee jumping without a cord." Obviously, this is an extreme hypothetical example of someone who is unethically trying to do his/her audience harm. When crafting the purpose of your speech your goals must be ethically sound for the betterment of the audience's well-being.

As a public speaker you will find that you will form a relationship with your audience much like you would with a friend, and one of the foundations of any relationship is trust. Your audience must have no doubt in their minds that the speaker has their best interest at heart. Moreover, the audience will expect you to be honest in your words, and in the integrity of your evidence that you present to them. Think about the last time you lied to a friend or a friend lied to you, what was the consequence of that action to the relationship? Your relationship with the audience is similar, by not being truthful with your audience, that critical error will deteriorate the special connection between the speaker and the audience.

A speaker may demonstrate dishonesty in other ways such as through the manipulation of statistics. For example, say you were to conduct an in-class survey with about 25 students and you found out that 85% of the class purchased their public speaking textbooks online, and you take that information, run to your school newspaper and tell the editor that 85% of all students on campus purchased their textbooks online. In this example, you have manipulated your statistics, and not placed those findings in their appropriate context. Moreover, if you presented this information to the class that 85% of all students at the college purchased their textbooks online, then you would be misleading them while providing them an inaccurate picture of the online purchases of textbooks. The speaker has violated the speaker's obligation to provide his/her audience with accurate information. Once the audience learns how that statistic was derived, the audience will discount the speaker's ideas and evidence, not only for that speech presented then, but will also have a cynical eye for all future speeches presented by this specific speaker. In addition to the manipulation of statistics it is the responsibility of the speaker to verify the accuracy of information presented to the audience. While doing so, ask yourself, did you cite your sources accurately, and are the paraphrases and quotes documented properly for correctness?

Additional ethical rules that must be obeyed are the careless use of racist, sexist, and other demeaning language in public speaking. These principles also apply to religious beliefs, sexual orientations, and physical or mental disabilities. These forms of name calling and abusive language tactics have no place in public speaking. By using these unfortunate forms of language, you are announcing to your audience the caliber of your intellect and the lack of goodwill you have for your audience members. This strategy is a sure way to turn off an audience to the point of alienation. All members of your audience and society deserve to be treated with dignity and respect.

Another ethical guideline that must be followed is being completely prepared for your speech. The process of being prepared includes: selecting and narrowing a topic, crafting a specific purpose, having an accurate central idea, carefully compiling audience analyses, accumulating valid materials, using appropriate supporting materials, building a logical organization, using refined language, writing catchy introductions and conclusions, making value-added visual aids, and speaking with practiced delivery. It does not matter if you are delivering a speech to 2 people at the local community center on an early Sunday morning or to 12,000 screaming fans on a Friday night at Madison Square Garden in New York City. You owe it to yourself and to your audience to be thoroughly prepared to enthusiastically present a well-thought-out and worthwhile public address.

PLAGIARISM

Plagiarism may be defined as the unauthorized use or close imitation of the language and thoughts of another author and the representation of them as one's own original work. Plagiarism can get you in serious trouble, for example a teacher may give you an "F" for the assignment or the class, or worse, you may be expelled from your educational institution. Essentially, your teachers are interested in your ideas supported by sound evidence from reputable sources. Plagiarism comes in three forms: global plagiarism, patchwork plagiarism, and incremental plagiarism.

Global plagiarism is when a speaker takes a speech in its entirety from a single source and passes it off as his/her own. Global plagiarism is unfortunate because the speaker put no thought or effort into creating a sound public address that reflects his/her thoughts, feelings, and beliefs. In an academic setting, there is a spirit of exchanging ideas and concepts for intellectual growth and by carrying out global plagiarism you rob yourself and your classmates of that opportunity. **Patchwork plagiarism** occurs when the speaker directly takes materials from two or three sources verbatim, combines them, and then passes them off as his or her own work. **Incremental plagiarism** occurs when the speaker fails to give credit for particular parts of a speech that are borrowed in increments from other people.

A specific area that needs to be addressed with incremental plagiarism is the use of quotes and paraphrases. If you happen to quote somebody in your speech, make sure you attribute the quote to that person. For example, if you were delivering a speech about the importance of setting and achieving goals and you went on to say, "If you're bored with life, you don't get up every morning with a burning desire to do things; you don't have enough goals," even though you saw this was a direct quote from former Notre Dame football coach Lou Holtz that would be considered incremental plagiarism. In contrast, if you stated that same quote this way, you would be clear of incremental plagiarism because you stated where the quote came from: "A quote that captures the importance of goal setting was best said by former Notre Dame Football coach Lou Holtz, 'If you're bored with life, you don't get up every morning with a burning desire to do things; you don't have enough goals.'"

When paraphrasing text from a speech or some other written context, in a sense what you are doing is taking the originator's words and repackaging that message in your own words that are appropriate for your given audience. To appropriately paraphrase one's words is more than just taking the text and using your thesaurus to change the words. When you do that, the structure of the thought and sentence is still there; therefore, you would still need to give credit to the originator. When in doubt, the most prudent course of action when paraphrasing is to simply cite your source.

ETHICAL LISTENING

"Most of the successful people I've known are the ones who do more listening than talking."
—BERNARD M. BARUCH (AMERICAN ECONOMIST 1870–1965)

As public speakers your ethical responsibility is not only behind the podium but also as an audience member. Listening to another human is probably the most validating and confirming activity you can do for another person. Think about why sometimes we get upset or discouraged, often times it is because someone important to us is not listening to us. As a listener to speeches you carry a tremendous amount of influence on the success or failure of the speaker. In our context, in a college classroom, that power will impact your classmates who are, like you perhaps, trying to earn a college degree, learn

Audience members have an ethical obligation to
responsibly listen to the speaker
Source: Shutterstock © Dmitriy Shironosov

a valuable skill as a life-long learner, or exploring the possibility of becoming a Speech Communication major. The point that needs to be clear is to demonstrate compassion and empathy for your speaker who is probably nervous delivering his/her speech, because before you know it, it will be your turn at the podium.

As we learned in the speech communication process earlier in the chapter, a message is not a message from the speaker without a receiver, and in this case the receiver would be the audience. The key principles for ethical listening are to give your complete and undivided attention to the speaker, to avoid making quick unsubstantiated judgments about the speaker before listening to them, and to keep an open mind.

As an audience member, your complete and undivided attention is required regardless if your speaker is your teacher, your classmate, or your boss. By doing this you are communicating respect for the speaker and all of the effort he or she put in to delivering a well-reasoned and practiced public address. In the classroom setting paying attention to the main speaker sets the tone for a safe, supportive, and encouraging environment. By demonstrating these attitudes towards the main speaker, even perhaps your classmates, you are instilling confidence in them, and in turn the speaker will produce a stronger speech. Moreover, taking a public speaking course is fertile territory for learning. Not only will you be learning the techniques of public speaking from your instructor, you will be learning about subject matter that you may have never been exposed to in your previous learning experiences. Do not dismiss such a golden opportunity to learn about new topics, which will make you a more interesting person. Be a responsible listener.

An unfortunate characteristic of unethical listening is making a quick unsubstantiated judgment about the speaker or the topic based on inaccurate and sometimes silly perceptions. We have often seen or have even experienced first-hand when someone has made a snap judgment about somebody or something that is not accurate, only to find out later that they made a terrible mistake. It is mistakes like this that hurt relationships and dampen potential friendships. As a listener you have an obligation to honestly "hear out" what the speaker has to say without any prejudgments. If the speaker has honored his/her obligation to deliver an honest speech using reliable evidence from trustworthy sources, tailored his/her message to the audience, and has practiced his/her delivery, you have an obligation to listen. Once the speech is concluded, and you have paid attention to the speech in its entirety, then it is appropriate to make judgments about the speech in its proper context.

Finally, keeping an open mind when listening to a speech will help you become a better public speaker. An unethical public speaker may dismiss a speech because they may have an entirely different perspective on the subject matter being discussed. Again by not listening you are missing a golden opportunity to learn about the subject matter and the techniques used in the research and delivery of the speech. Watching and listening to other public speakers is a valuable way to improve your own public speaking skills, and you can only do that with an open mind. If your mind is closed, so will your chance to genuinely appreciate the talents, skills, and different flavors of other speakers. On your pathway to success, being a good listener allows you to empathize and support others, and those will be the same people to carry you across your particular finish line. World-renowned speaker Zig Ziglar said "You can have everything in life that you want if you will just help enough other people get what they want." In short being an ethical listener will enrich your life and the life of others.

Summary: Learning the Basic Skills and Ethical Rules of Public Speaking Will Help You Conquer Your Public Speaking Stage Fright

Greek philosopher Aristotle is quoted as saying, "Fear is pain arising from the anticipation of evil," and in combating your stage fright, take the time to understand what exactly you are afraid of or concerned with, and from there devise strategies to offset those fears. Essentially this will force you to become self-aware and take an active role in learning about your audience and yourself. Visualizing yourself delivering an effective speech is a powerful way to create a strong public speaking experience once you are at the podium. Moreover, the more you practice your speech—especially your introduction—the more likely you will be to start your speech off well, and have the ability to carry on the positive momentum.

Assisting you in the process of becoming more at ease with delivering speeches is to think about the skills you have acquired in your everyday conversation and apply them to public speaking. Customizing your message to a specific person or audience, using stories to illustrate your main points, and responding to your audience's feedback are qualities that are directly applicable between conversation and public speaking. In contrast, public speaking is more structured in organization and the use of time. In essence, your public speaking delivery requires more formality than in your everyday conversation.

Understanding the speech communication process will allow you to make more sense as to how your speech fits in the communication process. The major players in the speech communication process are the: speaker, message, channel, receiver, feedback, interference, and the environment.

Public speaking requires you to be ethical in the specific purpose of your message. Moreover as an ethical public speaker you must be honest in what you are telling your audience; have the audience's best interest at heart; not resort to racist, sexist, or demeaning language; and be fully prepared for every speech. You owe it to yourself and your audience to establish and maintain your personal integrity. Another matter to avoid in ethical public speaking is the use of plagiarism. There are three types of plagiarism to avoid: global, patchwork, and incremental. Your instructor and your audience want to hear what *you* have to say about your topic. Having a clear understanding between the distinction between a direct quote and paraphrasing will help you navigate through the plagiarism rules.

Because communication is a transaction there are ethical rules for the listener as an audience member. It is the listener's obligation to give the speaker their complete and undivided attention. By doing so, you are communicating confidence and respect to the speaker. Listening to the speaker will give you a wonderful opportunity to learn about a new subject matter and broaden your intellectual aptitude. Furthermore your responsibility also requires you to suspend all of your judgments about the speaker and the topic until after the speech, so keeping an open mind works to your advantage.

On your pathway to success overcoming your public speaking nervousness will take your career and professional development to new heights. To help you overcome nervousness, abide by the ethical rules discussed in this chapter and you will be on your pathway to success.

Name: _____

CHAPTER 2

True-False

1. T F Public speaking demands the same technique of delivery as ordinary conversation.
2. T F Most of the nervousness public speakers feel internally is not visible to their listeners.
3. T F The channel is the room in which speech communication takes place.
4. T F Debilitative emotions brings out the best emotions in a public speaking setting.
5. T F The nonverbal messages that listeners send back to speakers are called feedback.
6. T F Incremental plagiarism occurs when a speaker fails to give credit for particular parts of a speech that are borrowed.

Multiple Choice

7. The three kinds of plagiarism discussed in the text are
   a. valid plagiarism, incremental plagiarism, and necessary plagiarism.
   b. patchwork plagiarism, speech plagiarism, and global plagiarism.
   c. literary plagiarism, scientific plagiarism, and speech plagiarism.
   d. idea plagiarism, quotation plagiarism, and paraphrase plagiarism.
   e. global plagiarism, patchwork plagiarism, and incremental plagiarism.

8. Which of the following strategies is *least* likely to help you deal with nervousness in your speeches?
   a. thinking positively
   b. concentrating on your stage fright
   c. working especially hard on your introduction
   d. making eye contact with members of your audience
   e. using visual aids

9. When using the power of visualization as a strategy of managing stage fright, you should
   a. decrease the time necessary for preparing your speech.
   b. keep your mental pictures from becoming too vivid.
   c. focus on the positive aspects of your speech.
   d. all of the above.
   e. a and b only.

10. Global plagiarism occurs when a speaker
    a. bases his or her speech completely on foreign sources.
    b. fails to cite sources throughout the body of the speech.
    c. takes a speech entirely from a single source passes it off as her/his own.
    d. uses two or three sources and blends the information into a unified whole.
    e. bases the speech entirely on his or her personal experience.

11. A strategy for ethical listening is

    a. maintaining an open mind about the speakers ideas.
    b. judging the speaker on the basis of her or his prestige.
    c. taking accurate notes of what the speaker says.
    d. all of the above.
    e. a and c only.

12. On the first day of class Sandy heard her teacher's accent and immediately decided that she would not learn anything from this teacher. How did Sandy break a rule of ethical listening?

    a. Listening attentively.
    b. Avoid prejudging the speaker.
    c. Taking accurate notes.
    d. Supporting free speech.
    e. Avoid name-calling.

Essay

13. Explain two ways in which public speaking and conversation differ, and two ways in which they are similar.

14. Explain some strategies a public speaker can do to minimize the uncertainty of a public speaking situation.

Chapter 3

The Multicultural Component to Public Speaking

On your pathway to success, the world in which we live is getting smaller and smaller, and the need to be able to communicate with people from around the world is prevalent. Just with the existence of the Internet and social networking sites, we can communicate with people from around the world in a blink of an eye. Moreover, business is no longer limited to the boundaries of our national or state borders; in today's economy, business has gone global. There is an assumption now that all of us must be able to meet the global challenges set before us. Public speaking is a valuable skill that allows you to be in the forefront of your business or industry, and a polished public speaking skill-set can lead you and your company to millions—if not billions—of dollars. Speaking to a diverse audience has become commonplace and we are now in a stage in world history where we must demonstrate competency when interacting with people from around the world. In this chapter we will be examining general principles of intercultural communication to best meet the new and much needed communication across cultures competency.

Understanding the cultural dynamic of your audience will guide you to become a more competent public speaker
Source: Shutterstock © SVLumagraphica

By learning basic principles of multicultural communication, you will become a more effective public speaker because you will understand the cultural dynamics of your audience, as well as be a more receptive audience member yourself. Moreover, by being mindful of these multicultural principles you will put yourself in a place to be a difference maker while connecting with another human being on a global level. On your pathway to success, you will find that, no matter what field you work in, you are really in the people business. Whether you are selling computers, working shoulder to shoulder on a construction site, or assisting a sick patient at a hospital, being able to communicate effectively with people from around the world is a common denominator of all of these jobs. So as you read through this chapter, reflect on how understanding these multicultural communication principles will benefit you as a public speaker and a responsible audience member.

Worldview

Studying your **worldview** will allow you to see how you perceive the world and how that impacts the communication you may have with others, both as a public speaker and as an audience member. Each and every one of us carries a set of perceptual filters that influences how we interact with other people, and understanding your worldview and that of others will help you gain a stronger command of the communication process in its entirety. Our view of the world greatly shapes how we perceive people, places, things, and events. In their book *Cultural and Social Anthropology*, authors Edward Hoebel and Everett Frost define worldview as "the human being's inside view of the way things are colored, shaped, and arranged according to personal cultural preconceptions." Our worldview has an effect on all phases of our perception, including our thought process, attitudes, values, and beliefs. Your worldview is influenced by your daily habits and experiences ranging from, but not limited to, the language spoken in your home, the number of people in your family, the schools you attended, the time in history you were born, the climate you experience, the religions you are exposed to, to the foods you eat. All of these and more contribute to the worldview of people.

As a public speaker who is addressing a multicultural audience it is good to know how your worldview impacts your message, your word choice, your delivery, and your perception of your audience members. Furthermore, understanding how your audience sees the world will help you shape a more effective public address. The key here is to understand and accept that your audience may not see the world from your perspective, because they did not share your life experiences.

Ethnocentrism

If one takes the approach that one's ethnicity is the center of the universes and everyone else merely supports one's ethnicity, then one is demonstrating ethnocentrism. **Ethnocentrism** may be defined as "when one holds the mindset that one's own culture is superior to others'." Someone who is ethnocentric reasons that anyone who does not belong to his or her in-group is somehow wrong or even inferior. When ethnocentrism is taken to an extreme, it may cause a contentious relationship between the speaker and the audience. Public speaking is an audience-focused activity and in most contentious communication situations the flow of effective information stops. There are some advantages to ethnocentric rhetoric, such as using ethnocentrism to bring unity to a nation or a cultural group when an injection of national pride is needed. However, ethnocentric rhetoric may also be conflict-ridden and negative and lead to narrow-mindedness and antagonism.

As a public speaker you can avoid the negative effects of ethnocentrism by respecting the dignity of the values and beliefs of our multicultural society. You may not agree with others' values and beliefs, but the demonstration of respect of those values and beliefs will go a long way. By signifying respect for the diversity of your audience, you will create a more open line of communication between the speaker and the audience. Therefore, as a speaker, minimizing any potential hostility will increase the probability of your message being received by your audience.

As an audience member being aware of your own ethnocentrism is a step in the right direction in understanding the message of your public speaker. Ethnocentric behavior as an audience member may get in the way of listening to your speaker. Hence, it is your responsibility to be respectful of the speaker and his or her efforts and to listen graciously to their message regardless of the speaker's cultural background. As the world's borders become less divisive, an ethnocentric listener must be mindful not to snub speakers from different locales, based on the speaker's physical appearance, pronunciation of words, or approach to delivering his or her message.

Stereotyping

Stereotyping is categorizing individuals according to a set of characteristics assumed to belong to all members of a group. Categories of stereotyping may include race, age, gender, occupation, religion, disability, socio-economic status, educational level, and region of residence. In the perceptual process of stereotyping, we search for far-off actions that sustain our inaccurate viewpoints. One accurate way to avoid stereotyping is to go through the practice of decategorization. **Decategorization** is the process of treating the person as an individual instead of assuming that they possess the same characteristics as every other member of the group to which you have assigned them. When analyzing your audience before delivering your speech, the objective is to gather accurate information on the make-up of your audience instead of relying on assumptions. Furthermore, when learning about your speaker, take the time to accurately learn about the speaker's biography instead of making inaccurate assumptions about the speaker's background based on their appearance or the subject matter of their speech.

The Work of Geert Hofstede

Understanding the work of Dutch researcher Geert Hofstede can give you a glimpse into the multicultural dynamics of the speaker and your audience in our diverse society. Between 1967 and 1973 researcher Geert Hofstede conducted a study that spanned more than 70 countries showing national and regional cultural categories that affect the manners of societies and organizations. Hofstede's work can be studied in greater detail in his book, *Culture's Consequences: International Differences in Work-Related Values* Hofstede's research yielded four themes:

1. Individualism versus Collectivism

2. Power Distance

3. Masculinity

4. Uncertainty Avoidance

Individualism and Collectivism

When discussing the multicultural component of public speaking, it would be a mistake to assume that everyone from a particular culture fits the characteristics described by Hofstede's study. However, highlighting the characteristics of those studied in Hofstede's research can give a hint as to the distinctions of people from around the world. A nuanced use of his categories can help you communicate more effectively, do a better job of reaching your audiences, and understand your speaker more accurately when you are in the audience yourself.

Hofstede's first category divided countries into individualistic and collectivist cultures. According to his research, those countries on the individualism end of the spectrum would include: the United States of America, Australia, Great Britain, Canada, and the Netherlands. Conversely those countries listed on the collectivist end of the spectrum would include Venezuela, Colombia, Pakistan, Japan, and the territory of Hong Kong.

People in countries representing the **individualistic** category see their own personal goals as being more important than the goals of a particular group. An "I" philosophy is prevalent in their behavior and thought. In short, people in the individualistic cultures look out for number one, and place their own goals and needs above a group, or membership objectives. For example, we see this when employees hop from one job to another job for their own professional advancement as opposed to staying at one company for a long time, which would demonstrate loyalty and commitment to a particular company or group. Moreover, those in the individualistic cultures thrive on competition and the achievement of personal goals, as opposed to cooperation, and the attainment of group goals and a group's purpose. Furthermore, individual initiative with little collaboration of others is rewarded in the individualistic culture. The spirit of the individualistic culture was captured by a quote from the French philosopher Michel de Montaigne during the French Renaissance, "It is an absolute perfection to know how to get the very most out of one's individuality."

In the **collectivist** culture, the group's goals are more important than those of the individual. A "we" philosophy is the driver of behavior and thought. In the collectivist culture there is a strong distinction between the members of the in-group (families, organizations, or groups) and members of the out-group (those not in the family, organization, or group). There is a stronger sense of loyalty to the hierarchy and the in-group dynamic whether it is in the form of family or company, as opposed to those belonging to the out-group. Moreover, it is understood that there is a strong need for cooperation, as opposed to competition, in dealings with others. Maintaining the social norm of harmony within the in-group of the collectivist cultures is a guiding factor in obedient behavior. In essence the group's goals, values, and beliefs take precedence over the individual's goals and needs. The founder of Armco Steel Corporation, George M. Verity captures the collectivist culture in his quote about co-operation, "Co-operation is spelled with two letters—WE."

Understanding the distinction between the individualistic and collectivist cultures can help a speaker when making persuasive appeals to a given audience. For example, if you were speaking to a group representing a collectivist culture you would stress the importance to the value of the in-group, and how your message will benefit the family, company, or group membership as opposed to how it would benefit the individual. Moreover, your purpose will push towards the betterment of the group, respecting the social hierarchy, and cooperation instead of the betterment of the individual.

Power Distance

Another key finding of Hofstede's research is the relationship of power and its allocation within organizations. There are two kinds of power distances, high-power distances, and low-power distances. **High-power distances** would represent those who hold high power and the wide separation between the decision makers and those implementing the decisions. On the other hand, **low-power distance** is the narrow distance between those in power and those implementing the decisions.

Countries that would fall in the high-power distance category would be Venezuela, Brazil, Mexico, and India, to name a few. In these cultures, it is understood that people are not created equal and have a specific status in the hierarchy. The distribution of power is also seen in family dynamics where the grandparents carry a tremendous influence over the entire family and each member of the family knows their traditional roles. For example, Kevin, a salesman, went door to door selling cable packages to a predominantly collectivist culture neighborhood. As Kevin entered the house there were three generations of family members sitting in the living room anxiously ready to listen to his sales presentation. Kevin's worldview told him to tailor his message toward the middle generation and the children of the middle generation. Yet because he understood the dynamic of the individualistic and collectivist culture and the distribution of influence in power distance, Kevin focused his persuasive message on the grandparents and how the package would improve the quality of life for the entire family. He made it a point not to ignore or disrespect any member of the family, but demonstrated strong respect to the grandparents. Sure the kids were the ones who were going to enjoy the expanded cable and Internet package, but the grandparents wielded the decision making power. Understanding the principles of power distance and individualistic and collectivist cultures helped Kevin make the sale—launching a subsequent successful sales career.

Other nuances of how the high-power distance operates are how one would address those in power positions. Since there is a large gap between the decision makers and those implementing those decisions, more formality is shown in how one would address another person in a company, organization, or family. For example, in a high-power distance culture, instead of calling your boss Mike, you would address your boss as Mr. Johnson or by the formal title in the given company, organization, or family.

The low-power distance philosophy believes that the disproportion of distance should be minimized as much as possible. Countries that would fall under the low-power distance category would be New Zealand, Austria, Finland, and Denmark, just to name a few. The philosophy in the workplace in these countries says that subordinates consider superiors to be on the same level in their interactions and status of importance to the organization or group. For example in an educational setting, calling a teacher or superior by their first name would be appropriate behavior as opposed to using a formal title like Dr. or Professor Johnson. Those in power create a culture of equality with those who are not in power.

Masculinity and Femininity

Hofstede's research study yielded findings in the area of masculinity and femininity. It must be said that Hofstede did not use the words masculinity and femininity to refer to men and women per se; instead he used the words to refer to characteristic traits that are masculine or feminine. **Masculinity** refers to the values and beliefs of a country's society in the areas of achievement, attainment of money, and accepted male-oriented roles. Countries that embody masculine worldviews would be South Africa, Japan, Italy, Mexico, and the Philippines. Masculine societies teach men that they are the central dominant figures, and women are expected to be encouraging and supportive of men. Understanding the masculine/feminine roles allows for a clear division of labor in a household.

Cultures that embrace **femininity** value more caring and nurturing behaviors. It is validated that men do not need to be assertive, and can accept caring and nurturing roles in society. Countries that embody the femininity values would be Finland, Sweden, the Netherlands, and Norway.

Uncertainty Avoidance

At the core of studying uncertainty avoidance is the relationship between the future and the unknown. The direction of Hofstede's ideas about uncertainty avoidance is how a particular culture feels about uncertain and ambiguous situations. **High-uncertainty-avoidance** cultures work at avoiding uncertainty by utilizing written rules, regulations, and a strong structure in their daily lives. Countries that fall under the high-uncertainty-avoidance category would be Japan, Belgium, Portugal, and Greece. High-uncertainty-avoidance groups move at a slower pace and spend more time in the planning and detailing phase when making decisions.

On the flip side the **low-uncertainty-avoidance** cultures accept the uncertainty in life. Low-uncertainty-avoidance cultures are willing to take risks, are not in favor of rigid protocols, and are comfortable with the unusual. Low-uncertainty-avoidance cultures run at a faster pace and make decisions more quickly. Countries that are considered low-uncertainty-avoidance cultures are the United States, Netherlands, Ireland, Singapore, and Sweden, just to name a few.

High-Context and Low-Context Communication

Another valuable area of intercultural communication that will give you tools to apply in the public speaking context is from the work of anthropologist Edward T. Hall. Hall used the terms high-context and low-context communication in grasping whether communication can be understood by the context or setting of the message or by the actual verbal messages being exchanged. Hall defined "context" in his book *Understanding Cultural Differences: Germans, French and Americans* (Yarmouth, ME: Intercultural Press, 1990) as "the information that surrounds an event; it is inextricably bound up with the meaning of the event."

In **high-context** cultures tradition and history are consistent over time. In the high-context culture the message is communicated through nonverbal gestures, proximity, and silence. In addition, the high-context cultures demonstrate a stronger awareness of the overall background of the environment of the communication, as opposed to words alone. Moreover, one's position in a hierarchy—such as one's age, rank in the family or organization, and education level—also influences the meaning of high-context communication. In short, more nonverbal communication is valued in the high-context cultures. High-context cultures would include Japan, China, Korean, Native American tribes, and Latin America.

High and Low Context Communication	
High Context Information is carried within the scope of the environment (time, place, social rank, age, and relationship). The message is not dependent on the verbal message, the nonverbal message is closely observed. Relational agreement is prized and maintained by hinted expressions of opinions. Communicators refrain from saying "no" directly. Vagueness and silence are common.	**Low Context** Information is communicated in clear verbal messages, with the situational context carrying less significance. Communicators articulate opinions and feelings directly. Oral confidence is valued and considered admirable.

In **low-context** cultures the verbal message is the driver of the message and little "context" is incorporated into the meaning of the message. Low-context cultures would include America, Germany, and Switzerland. Communication tends to be direct and unambiguous, so the message is clearly stated with little "context."

Summary: Embrace Your Multicultural Audience

On your pathway to success you will learn that the world is getting smaller and smaller and your ability to effectively interact with people from around the world is essential to your success. Taking steps to understand your worldview and the worldview of your audience will provide insights as to how to appropriately communicate your message to effectively meet the needs of a multicultural audience. In stark contrast to analyzing one's worldview is the idea of ethnocentrism. Ethnocentrism may be defined as "when one holds the mindset that one's own culture is superior to others." Someone who is ethnocentric believes that anyone who does not belong to his or her in-group is in the wrong, and inferior. When ethnocentrism is taken to an intense fanatical level, it may create an adversarial relationship between the speaker and the audience. Public speaking is an audience-focused activity.

Stereotyping classifies individuals according to a set of behaviors believed to belong to all members of a distinct group. One strategy to avoid stereotyping as a speaker or as an audience member is through the process of decategorization. Decategorization is the practice of regarding the person as an individual, instead of clumping people into groups and presuming that every person in the group holds matching traits. The goal for understanding your audience or the public speaker is accuracy of information.

Learning about the work of Dutch researcher Geert Hofstede will provide insight to the multicultural society we live in, which is applicable to the public speaking dynamic and the relationship between the speaker and the audience. Hofstede's work can be studied in greater detail in his book, *Culture's Consequences: International Differences in Work-Related Values,* (Beverly Hills: Sage 1980), which yielded four distinct themes: Individualism vs. Collectivism, Power Distance, Masculinity, and Uncertainty Avoidance.

Another valuable area of intercultural communication research that is applicable toward your public speaking development is the work of anthropologist Edward T. Hall. Hall used the terms high-context and low-context communication in understanding if communication could be comprehended by the context or setting of the message or by the actual verbal message being exchanged. In understanding the context of the culture you are speaking to will give you insight as to how to use language and non-verbal communication in your presentation for maximum impact.

On your pathway to success it will be imperative that you widen your communication repertoire to meet the demands of our multicultural business climate. By understanding basic theories of intercultural communication you will put yourself in a position to excel and separate yourself from the pack and distinguish yourself as a world wide leader in your given field. The perspective of the workplace is now global requiring you to think big while on your pathway to success, American author Marianne Williamson has this to say about maximizing your potential, "Your playing small doesn't serve the world. There's nothing enlightened about shrinking so that other people won't feel insecure around you. We are all meant to shine as children do." Understanding multicultural communication dynamics will strengthen your ability to manage your messages and shine before a global audience.

Name: _____

True-False

1. (T) F   Studying your worldview will allow you to see how you perceive the world and how that impacts the communication you may have with others.

2. T (F)   When addressing a multicultural audience it is not necessary to assess your worldview in your speech preparation.

3. T (F)   Ethnocentrism may be defined as the tendency to perceive, understand and interpret the world in terms of the self.

4. T (F)   Decategorization is classifying individuals according to a set of characteristics assumed to belong to al members of a group.

5. (T) F   High-power distance represents those who hold high power and the wide separation between the decision makers and those implementing the decisions.

Multiple Choice

6. Which of the following types of cultures emphasize individual goals over group goals?

   (a.) Individualistic cultures
   b. High power distance cultures
   c. Low power distance cultures
   d. High context cultures

7. Which of the following countries is the most collectivistic?

   a. The United States
   (b.) Japan
   c. Russia
   d. Brazil

8. Which of the following statements best describes a low context culture?

   a. People communicate using a restricted code.
   b. Nonverbal code is the primary source of information.
   (c.) Verbal code is primary source of information.
   d. Heavy reliance of the contextual elements of the communication setting.

9. Which of the following statements best describes a high power distance culture?

   (a.) Inequalities among people are expected and desired.
   b. Inequalities among people should be minimized.
   c. People communicate using "powerful" messages (e.g., direct, assertive).
   d. People communicate using "powerless" messages (e.g., indirect, hesitant).

10. Which of the following statements best describes a low power distance culture?

   a. Inequalities among people are expected and desired.
   (b.) Inequalities among people should be minimized.
   c. People communicate using "powerful" messages (e.g., direct, assertive).
   d. People communicate using "powerless" messages (e.g., indirect, hesitant).

11. Which of the following statements best describes a strong uncertainty avoidant culture?

    a. Uncertainty is seen as a normal part of life.
    b. Uncertainty is seen as a continuous threat.
    c. Most of the population experiences communication apprehension.
    d. Few people experience communication apprehension.

12. Which of the following is associated with increased uncertainty?

    a. minimum tolerance
    b. maximum tolerance
    c. increased anxiety
    d. decreased anxiety

13. Which of the following is not a theme with the work of Geert Hofstede

    a. Individualism versus Collectivism
    b. Femininity
    c. Power Distance
    d. Masculinity
    e. Uncertainty Avoidance

Essay

14. Explain how your worldview shapes your public speaking message to an audience.

15. When persuading an audience how will understanding individualism and collectivism help you prepare for your speech.

Pillar 2

Speech Preparation: The Foundation to Success

Chapter 4

Know Your Purpose and Select a Topic

"Efforts and courage are not enough without purpose and direction."
— JOHN FITZGERALD KENNEDY, 35TH PRESIDENT OF THE UNITED STATES

Welcome to the starting point on your pathway to success in your speech preparation pillar. In this chapter you will learn how to select a topic, determine your general purpose, craft a specific purpose, and compose a central idea. As you can see we are going from a very broad perspective in your topic selection to a specific viewpoint of the main points of your speech. In the figure below, we can visualize how we will be navigating from the topic selection process all the way down to the main points of your speech as they are stated in the central idea.

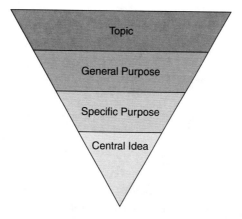

We will be kicking around speech topics throughout the chapter, but here are some examples and food for thought for potential speech themes.

Adoption	Animal Rights
Affirmative Action Laws	Are There Angels among Us?
Aids Choices for Life	Assisted Suicide
Air Bags	Bigamy

Euthanasia	Human Cloning
Feminism	Prayer in Schools
Food Stamps	Privacy Rights for Celebrities
Foreign Policy	Right to Own Pit Bulls
Should American Companies Go Overseas	Smoking in Public Places
for Workers?	Space Program
Gay Marriage	Steroids
Genetic Testing	Tax Laws
Genetic Engineering	Terrorism
Global Warming: Fact or Fiction?	Tobacco
Government Regulation of Utilities	Unemployment Compensation
Gun Laws	Women in the Military
Gun Control	

SELECTING A TOPIC

Selecting a topic may be the hardest step in the speech communication process. Anytime you start anything new, most of your energy is utilized at the beginning. Think of an airplane that takes off and finally reaches its cruising altitude. Most of its energy and force is used in the take-off but once it hits its cruising altitude less energy is needed to sustain the plane's pace. One of the biggest tips for a public speaker is *not* to procrastinate at this phase of the process of building a speech.

Norman Vincent Peale said it best, "Action is a great restorer and builder of confidence. Inaction is not only the result, but the cause, of fear. Perhaps the action you take will be successful; perhaps different action or adjustments will have to follow. But any action is better than no action at all." By postponing the start of your speech development process you are shrinking the window of time for developing an effective speech. In addition, by delaying the first step, you are minimizing the time available to adequately research, organize, and practice your speech before getting up in front of your classmates to delivering your presentation. There is nothing more embarrassing than standing before your classmates delivering a speech that you are not adequately prepared to deliver. Spare the embarrassment and get started early by selecting a topic.

Start thinking about your topic as soon as you receive your assignment. More often than not, speech topics are determined by the occasion, the audience, and the speaker's qualifications. More than likely in your speech class you will have the flexibility to select a topic of your choice as long as it falls under the assigned general purpose. If this is the case, it is helpful to read the chapter that corresponds to your assignment. For example, if your teacher has you doing an informative speech, go read the chapter for informative speeches. By reading the chapter you will also generate topic ideas, and have a wider perspective on what is expected for your assignment.

Another strategy for helping you decide on a topic is to keep a page in your notebook titled "Potential Speech Topics." As you go through your speech class, many in-class discussions may occur that are potential speech topics, so you can jot those down in your log. In addition, staying current with the recent happenings in the news usually generates potentially rich speech topics for your class. By getting started early you will allow yourself more time to prepare for your speech leading to a more well-thought address for your audience. What follows is a further examination of plans to help you select your speech topic so that you can start off on the right foot.

THE PROCESS OF SELF-EVALUATION

The process of self-evaluation has you explore topics that you know a lot about, and topics you would like to know more about. Begin by asking yourself some of the following questions to get a sense as to what you know a lot about:

What are my interests?

Where have I traveled?

What jobs have I held?

What is my major?

What is my cultural background?

Where are the different parts of the world, country, state, or city I have lived?

What do I do in my free time?

You want to ask these questions to learn about your knowledge base or possibly discover an area of expertise you have developed so far in your life.

Another direction we can go in the self-evaluation process is to reflect on topics you would like to know more about. Your public speaking class is an excellent opportunity for you to learn about something you have always wanted to explore. For example if you have always wanted to visit Italy, but do not know much about the history, culture, or language, you may want to consider this a topic for your informative speech. Your speech class can give you outstanding opportunities to learn something new. Another example of selecting a topic that you want to know more about may be if you are having trouble sleeping and cannot figure out why you are having this trouble. A speech about insomnia may help you understand your sleeping troubles and complete an assignment at the same time. Let us hope that the pressure of delivering your speech is not the cause of your insomnia.

So you may want to ask yourself whether there are topics you would like to know more about, and hopefully these prompts will help you answer that question:

If I could go anywhere in the world that I have not visited, where would I go?

What are some other professions I may consider looking at that I do not know much about?

I keep hearing this person's name in the news, but I do not know really who this person is.

Are there any religions or spiritual philosophies I have considered learning more about?

Are there ballot initiatives that I need to be informed about so I can make an educated vote at the upcoming election?

Boy, was I grateful that Steve knew how to change the car tire when the tire blew out on the way to the party. Would I have been able to do that if I were alone?

So if you had any interest in learning something new but for whatever reason do not have the time to learn about the topic, your speech class may offer you a good avenue to expand your horizons and learn something new. Selecting topics that you know a lot about or a topic you want to know more about will give you added confidence in your presentation, as you learn the specific techniques of public speaking on your pathway to success.

BRAINSTORMING FOR TOPICS

When brainstorming for potential topics you may need some prompts to get the ball rolling in your topic selection process. Your prompts will range from personal interests, grouping, and reference searches to an Internet search. The goal of brainstorming is to try to think of as many topics as you can in a brief amount of time. During this phase of the creative process, judging and criticizing your ideas is not appropriate.

Personal Interests

Think about your life experiences, interests, hobbies, skills, attitudes, values, beliefs, and write those down. Do not let your pen stop; just keep writing and be creative in your thoughts regardless of how ridiculous some of your thoughts may be, just keep writing.

Grouping

If your personal interests list did not produce just the right idea, do not be discouraged, and try the grouping strategy for selecting a topic. Take a sheet of paper, pencil-in six columns and label those columns with these headings: people, places, things, events, processes, and concepts. From there fill in the blanks. Again be free with your ideas and jot down what comes to mind, and do the evaluation of the generated ideas later in the process. Here are some random examples:

People	Places	Things
Beyoncé	Hawaii	Computers
Lindsay Lohan	China	Cell phones
George W. Bush	San Francisco	Mp3 players
Oprah Winfrey	New York	Books
Arnold Schwarzenegger	Las Vegas	Planes/Trains/Automobiles
John Lennon	Disneyland	Rocks
Dalai Lama	Dodger Stadium	Trees
Martin Luther King, Jr.	The Alamo	Plastic
Barack Obama	Australia	Metal
Jack Welch	Italy	Concrete
Bill Gates	Graceland	Wood
Warren Buffett	India	Lamps
Sandra Day O'Connor	South Africa	Thumb tacks
Richard Branson	London	Newspapers

Events	Processes	Concepts/Philosophies
Mardi Gras	Changing a car tire	Buddhism
World Cup	Fixing a leaky faucet	Afro-centrism
Super Bowl	Cooking an Italian dish	Judaism
Presidential Elections	Building your own computer	Catholicism
Christmas	CPR	Philosophy of education
Chinese New Year	Purchasing a car	Confucianism
4th of July	How to make a documentary	Capitalism
Thanksgiving	How to raise a puppy	Communism
World Series	Weight loss	Marxism
Academy Awards		

As you can see, grouping ideas into categories gives you a good prompt to come up with potential topics for your upcoming speech assignment.

Reference Search

Another technique is to use the reference area in your library and look through an encyclopedia, a periodical database or some other reference work until you find a good speech topic.

Internet Search

One of the easier ways to find a speech topic is to hop on the Internet and conduct a web directory search on either Google or Yahoo!. Go to either the Yahoo! or Google home page and type in "Web Directory Search" and these pages should come up.

As you can see, they provide a wide range of topics, and when you select a topic that interests you, you will be shown more specific topic ideas of the broader theme you selected. This strategy also gives you insight as to the amount of information that is available to you if you decide to select this topic. Nothing is more frustrating than when you select a topic and come to find out that there is very little information about your topic.

Moreover, another strategy using the Internet would be to just type in the idea you had in mind in the search box and see what comes up. From that initial inquiry you can usually narrow your topic down to something you can adequately present in the given time allocated by your teacher. Furthermore, you can simply type in "speech topics" in the search box. In addition, as you research your topics do not be afraid to sign up for email alerts regarding your topic so you can be sure that you have the latest and most accurate information to use in your speech research process. Additional information regarding the researching of your speech is in Chapter 6.

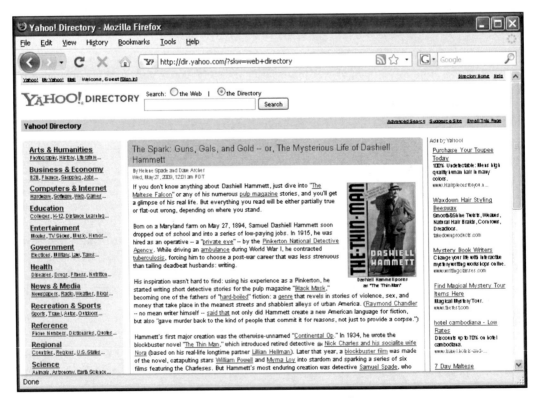

http://www.google.com/dirhp

http://dir.yahoo.com/?skw=web+directory

DETERMINING THE GENERAL PURPOSE

When starting the speech preparation process you need to know your purpose. Understanding your purpose gives you insight into "why" you are delivering your speech. Once you have a purpose, you will then have focus, something your audience will appreciate as they listen to your presentation. The general purpose may be defined as the broad goal of your speech, and there are three kinds of general purposes in public speaking:

1. To entertain

2. To inform

3. To persuade

The Special Occasion Speech (To Entertain)

The formal general purpose for the special occasion speech is *to entertain*. This does not mean that your speech requires you to conduct a Broadway song and dance routine for your audience or that you need to be funny. The **special occasion speech** is a speech that concentrates on a special event. The special occasion speech is a common occurrence as you go through life, but it is distinct from the speech to inform or the speech to persuade. Special occasion speeches include presentations that have their purpose to introduce the main speaker; present an award or public recognition; accept an award; commemorate by paying tribute to a person, group institution, or an idea; and give an after dinner speech. Other common special occasion speeches are made at weddings when presenting the bride and groom a toast. They also happen at retirement parties, when a company representative bids farewell to the loyal employee. We see the speech to entertain during award shows when our favorite entertainers accept an Oscar, Emmy, or MTV Award for their work. Special occasion speeches are also prominent at funerals when one delivers the eulogy for the deceased. On a happier note, a special occasion speech occurs when you salute and toast an important person in your life at his or her birthday party.

As you can see these speeches are delivered in a more "social" setting, but the speeches you deliver in this setting are noticed by all who are in attendance. Those in attendance may be your boss, a prospective funding source for the business start-up you want to launch, a potential mentor, or a key admissions officer at the graduate school of your first choice. My point is, yes the environment is more social, but be aware of who is listening to your speech, because your conduct and skills are being noted.

Life is a contact sport, meaning it is your contacts that help you get a position, or introduce you to an influential person for your future, so do not take these "special occasion" speeches lightly.

Examples of a special occasion speech would be:

- To entertain my audience and present Jack Nicholson the Academy Awards Lifetime Achievement Award.

- To entertain my audience and pay tribute to the fallen New York City police and fire officials after the 9/11 attacks.

- To entertain my audience and accept my gold watch after thirty years of service at the Acme Trading Company.

- To entertain my audience and commemorate Tim and Jill on their 50th wedding anniversary.

The special occasion speech will be discussed at greater length and depth in Chapter 14, Speaking on Special Occasions.

Speech to Inform

When your general purpose is to inform, your objective is to enhance the audience's awareness, understanding, or knowledge about a topic. You do this by communicating the information clearly, correctly, and interestingly. While delivering a **speech to inform**, you may sound like a teacher or a lecturer. In a speech to inform, you do not try to persuade your audience to do or believe something as a result of your speech. You are there just to convey new information or show how existing information can be applied in new ways.

Some examples of a speech to inform would be:

- To inform my audience about how to change the oil in their own cars.
- To inform my audience about how to purchase a home using first time buyers programs.
- To inform my audience about the basic principles of Zen Buddhism.
- To inform my audience of the festivities at the Mardi Gras celebration in New Orleans.

Further discussion about the speech to inform is in Chapter 14.

Speech to Persuade

The **speech to persuade** needs to influence, strengthen, or change the audience members' attitudes, values, beliefs, or behaviors. The persuasive speaker attempts to modify how the audience feels about what they know and in the end how they behave. The persuasive speaker serves as a promoter and is biased to a given argument.

Some examples of a speech to persuade would be:

- To persuade my audience that same-sex marriage should be legalized.
- To persuade my audience that their next new car purchase must be a hybrid car.
- To persuade my audience that they should attend a state university as opposed to a private university.
- To persuade my audience to vote no on the "banning alcohol on campus" campaign.

Your assignments given by your teacher will more than likely have one of the three types of general purposes identified for you. However, when you head out onto your pathways to success keep these three purposes in mind to help you achieve your goals in any given situation. Our next step is to establish our specific purpose.

THE SPECIFIC PURPOSE

Ralph C. Smedley, the founder of Toastmasters, had this to say about the specific purpose, "A speech without a specific purpose is like a journey without a destination."

The **specific purpose** is a single sentence that specifically states what the speaker hopes to accomplish in his or her speech. The point here is that you need to spend time thinking about what you want the end results of your speech to be. With this clarity, the specific purpose will serve as your compass as you navigate through the speech preparation process. During the speech preparation process it is easy to get sidetracked and distracted, but establishing your specific purpose will keep you anchored and on track.

When wording your specific purpose it is paramount that you mention the audience. Public speaking is an audience-focused activity, so do not forget the audience. When crafting your specific purpose statement, think of it as a three-step process. The first step is to state your general purpose. You have three options here; it is to entertain, to inform, or to persuade. The second part of the sentence is *always* "my audience," regardless of what kind of speech you are delivering. You must think of the audience at every step of the speech preparation process. The third part of your specific purpose statement is the piece where you express what you hope to accomplish. The specific purpose statement includes your general purpose, your intended audience, and your specific goal. Here are some examples of the specific purpose statement.

- To entertain my audience and present Ralph Adams the Anderson Accountants Company Employee of the Year Award.

  (General Purpose) To entertain (my audience) my audience (specific goal to be accomplished) present Ralph Adams the Anderson Accountants Company Employee of the Year Award.

- To inform my audience so that they will be able to distinguish between legal and illegal street-car racing.

  (General Purpose) To inform (my audience) my audience (specific goal to be accomplished) so that they will be able to distinguish between legal and illegal street-car racing.

- To persuade my audience to vote no on the "banning alcohol on campus" campaign.

  (General Purpose) To persuade (my audience) my audience (specific goal to be accomplished) to vote no on the "banning alcohol on campus" campaign.

Writing your specific purpose comes with four rules that must be observed.

Write your specific purpose statement NOT as a fragment but as a complete sentence.

Poor Specific Purpose: Watches

Appropriate: To inform my audience of the declining demand for wristwatches due to the popularity of cell phones.

By just stating "watches" there is not a clear idea as to what the speaker hopes to accomplish in his or her speech. Moreover, with this ineffective specific purpose, there is no mention of the audience. Public speaking is an audience-focused activity.

Write your specific purpose statement as a statement NOT as a question.

Poor Specific Purpose: Are the Boston Celtics the best NBA franchise?

Acceptable: To persuade my audience that the Boston Celtics are the greatest NBA franchise in history.

Writing your specific purpose in the form of a question does not answer the question of what you hope to accomplish in your presentation. Moreover, there was no mention of the audience or the general purpose.

Avoid using figurative language in your specific purpose.

> **Weak Specific Purpose:** To inform my audience that bicycle riding is trendy due to the high price of gasoline.

> **Acceptable:** To inform my audience of the cost effectiveness of bicycle riding.

The specific purpose needs to be clear and concise as to what the speaker hopes to accomplish in his or her presentation. Using imagery, analogies, and metaphors are strong strategies to visualize your points, but those strategies are appropriate in the body of the speech and not in the formation of the specific purpose.

Keep your specific purposed focused on ONE clear-cut idea

> **Confusing Specific Purpose:** To persuade my audience to exercise three times a week and pursue a college degree.

This specific purpose is communicating two distinct directions that the speaker wants to take us. The specific purpose must avoid two isolated ideas, in which either of the ideas can be developed into a speech in its own right. Unfortunately for the speaker we can only go in one direction. Let us see how we can take this multi-purpose statement and clarify a clear direction for this speech.

> **Acceptable:** To persuade my audience that they must exercise three times a week for a healthy lifestyle.

or

> **Acceptable:** To persuade my audience to complete their college education to maximize their future incomes.

Again the specific purpose is a single sentence that specifically states what the speaker hopes to accomplish in his or her speech. Additional guidelines for the specific purpose are: the purpose statement must *not* be a fragment, must *not* be in the form of a question, must avoid using figurative language, and must present *one* clear-cut idea. Once the specific purpose has been established you can now move on to begin crafting your central idea.

THE CENTRAL IDEA

The specific purpose is your compass, the direction you are taking your speech, and the end destination of what you hope to achieve. The central idea is your road map, as to *how* you will get to your end destination. The central idea may be defined as a one-sentence statement that sums up the main ideas of your speech. The **central idea** may also be known as a subject sentence, a thesis statement, or a major thought. Like the specific purpose the central idea has the following guidelines that need to be met. The central idea needs to be expressed in a full sentence, should not be in the form of a question, should avoid using figurative language, and should not be overly general or vague.

Using the term residual message is another way of conceptualizing the purpose of your central idea in your speech preparation. The **residual message** is what a speaker wants the audience to remember after it has forgotten everything else in the speech. So ask yourself "what is the core theme I want my audience to remember as a result of my speech?"

When developing your central idea statement, it is easier to craft the statement after doing your research and your main themes of your speech have been established. It is hard to commit to main points of your presentation if while doing the research you realize there is little support for those preconceived main points. The central idea serves as a check and balance with the main points of your presentation. By reading your central idea, one should be able to accurately identify the main points of your speech.

Here are some examples that show how the topic selection, general purpose, specific purpose, and central idea all come together.

Topic: Computers

General Purpose: To inform

Specific Purpose: To inform my audience of the key criteria to consider when buying a laptop computer.

Central Idea: When purchasing a laptop computer pay attention to the cost, speed and storage space, screen resolution, and the manufacturer's warranty.

By studying this breakdown of this speech, you can tell what the speaker hopes to accomplish and by reading the central idea you know how the speaker will achieve the goal. Moreover, you can tell by reading the central idea that the speaker will have four main points in his or her presentation.

Topic: Entrepreneurship

General Purpose: To persuade

Specific Purpose: To persuade my audience that they should start their own business.

Central Idea: Starting a business will help your tap into your creativity, build wealth, and allow you flexibility in your schedule.

The goal of this speech is to have the audience start their own business. The speaker plans to persuade his or her audience by focusing on three main points, tapping into your credibility, building wealth, and the flexibility in one's schedule. So, as you can see, the speech will develop from a very broad perspective to very specific points.

Summary: If you know where you are going, your audience will surely follow you, so understand your purpose and take your audience there

The first step in the speech preparation, your starting point to success, is selecting a topic. There are strategies that are helpful in choosing your topic for your presentation. First is the process of self-evaluation where you examine topics you know a lot about, and topics you want to learn more about. Next is brainstorming, and the goal of brainstorming is to try to think of as many topics as you can in a limited amount of time. During this phase of the creative process, judging and criticizing your thoughts is not appropriate. Also, in this phase you can examine your personal interests. A further aid is the idea of grouping where you take a sheet of paper, draw columns, and label them with these headings: people, places, things, events, processes, and concepts. Following brainstorming is the reference search at the library, and finally comes the Internet search using the "Web Directory Search" on Yahoo! or Google.

Once you have chosen your topic the next phase in the speech preparation process is to select your general purpose. The general purpose may be defined as the broad goal of your speech, and there are three kinds of general purposes in public speaking:

1. To entertain

2. To inform

3. To persuade

The special occasion speech is a speech that concentrates on a special event.

When your general purpose is to inform, your objective is to enhance the audience's awareness, understanding, or knowledge about a topic. This is done by communicating the information clearly, correctly, and interestingly. While delivering a speech to inform, you may sound like a teacher or a lecturer.

The persuasive speaker attempts to modify how the audience feels about what they know and in the end how they behave. The speech to persuade needs to sway, strengthen, or change the audience members' attitudes, values, beliefs, or behaviors. Now that you have determined your speech topic, and your general purpose, you are off to the specific purpose.

The specific purpose is a single sentence that specifically states what the speaker hopes to accomplish in his or her speech. When crafting your specific purpose statement, think of it as a three-step process. The specific purpose statement includes your general purpose, your intended audience, and your specific goal of what you hope to accomplish. Here is an example of the specific purpose statement.

(General Purpose) To entertain (my audience) my audience and (specific goal to be accomplished) present Jack Nicholson the Academy Awards Lifetime Achievement Award.

The final step in this process is creating the central idea. The central idea may be defined as a one-sentence statement that sums up the main ideas of your speech. The central idea may also be known as a subject sentence, a thesis statement, or a major thought.

Both the central idea and the specific purpose have the following guidelines that need to be met. The specific purpose and the central idea need to be expressed in a full sentence, should not be in the form of a question, should avoid using figurative language, and should not be overly general or vague. By having a clear purpose and a specific goal to accomplish with your speech you will be on your pathway to success.

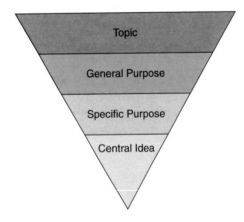

Name: _____

True-False

1. T F "How can the city reduce crime?" is an example of a well-worded specific purpose statement for a speech.

2. T F After choosing a topic, the next step in speech preparation is determining your general purpose.

3. T F When your general purpose is to inform, you act as an advocate or an opponent.

4. T F The specific purpose statement should avoid being a complete sentence.

5. T F The specific purpose discloses more about the content of a speech than does the central idea.

6. T F "My audience" must be included in the specific purpose.

Multiple Choice

7. "The four areas to tour the San Francisco Bay Area are the North Bay, South Bay, East Bay and the Peninsula," is an example of a

   a. specific purpose.
   b. transition.
   c. general purpose.
   d. signpost.
   e. central idea.

8. The text states that the brainstorming strategy is particularly useful when you are having trouble

   a. choosing a speech topic.
   b. determining the general purpose.
   c. determining the specific purpose.
   d. phrasing the central idea.
   e. analyzing the audience.

9. Using Yahoo or Google of the subject-based search engines on the Internet is recommended in your textbook as one method of for _____ a speech topic.

   a. filtering
   b. consulting
   c. brainstorming
   d. deliberating
   e. learning

10. The central idea of a speech should be

    a. written as a complete sentence.
    b. articulated as a statement, not a question.
    c. not having figurative language.
    d. all of the above.
    e. a and b only.

11. "To inform my audience how corporate headquarters let the cat out of the bag on the proposal of layoffs" is a inadequately expressed specific purpose statement for a speech because it

    a. includes a reference to the audience.
    b. is written as a declarative sentence rather than a question.
    c. is expressed in figurative language.
    d. all of the above.
    e. a and b only.

Essay

12. Your textbook discusses four approaches of brainstorming for a speech topic. In a brief essay, identify and explain three of those methods.

13. Clarify the distinguishing factors between informing and persuading as general speech purposes.

14. What is the primary function of the specific purpose in the process of preparing a speech?

Chapter 5

Public Speaking is an Audience-Focused Activity, so who is your Audience?

THE MINDSET OF THE AUDIENCE

Why does this speech matter to me? That is a common thought of an audience member listening to a speech, and is also a public speaker's biggest challenge. Public speaking is an audience-focused activity, so as you prepare for your speeches, your audience must be first and foremost in your mind and in your preparation. Keep some of these questions in mind during your preparation process:

- To whom am I speaking?

- What do I need my audience to know, to do, or to believe as a result of my speech?

- How can I best put together my speech to meet the needs of my given audience?

Public speaking is not a forum for you to get up to the podium and show off to the world how much you know, or how fantastic you are. The successful public speaker is focused on delivering and adapting a message to the audience. Your audience—whether it is your classmates or the Board of Directors of your company—deserves your absolute best effort to communicate your point of view and/or beliefs.

The importance of knowing who you are presenting your message to is highlighted by United States Supreme Court Associate Justice Antonin Scalia in his book called *Making Your Case: The Art of Persuading Judges*. The book provides guidance to lawyers presenting oral arguments, and Scalia says "learn as much as you can about the judge's background." This sounds similar to the advice given in this textbook in relation to learning about your audience. Scalia goes on to suggest that it is helpful to talk to a real person because it humanizes the judge instead of just addressing a black robe and builds rapport and confidence with the presenting attorney. Moreover, it is commonly known that law firms keep "books" on judges that lists their characteristics and past cases, giving presenting lawyers an edge. If powerful law firms around the nation can do this and succeed, this practice of understanding your audience will also help you with your speech preparation.

Egocentrism may be defined as the tendency of people to be concerned above all with their own values, beliefs, and well-being. So when presenting your speech, the odds are the audience is thinking, "how does this speech apply to me?" or "how will I benefit from this speech?" The audience does not process a speaker's message exactly as the speaker intends. The auditory perception is always selective; so if the information presented is significant to the listener then that information will stick, while other valuable information would slip by the wayside. When presenting your speech realize that your speech will contain two messages. First will be the information transmitted by you, followed by how the audience receives and interprets the message you sent. A real challenge in public speaking and in communication in general is to have your message received and interpreted accurately, that is, as you intended it to be received.

Keep in mind that your listeners will hear and judge what you say based on what they know and already believe. As a responsible public speaker you need to be proactive in learning about what your audience already knows about your topic and their level of involvement with your topic. This will allow you to prepare and deliver a speech that is pertinent and enriching to the audience.

DEMOGRAPHICS

Demographics are an important aspect of the daily life of the billions of people who live in the world today. You see the results of demographics when you watch television, and how those commercials you watch carry the same vibe as the actual program you are watching. Think about the magazines and websites you frequent, is it not interesting that advertisers place their products and services in the publications that would reach their desired market? In short, studying the dynamics of demographics is a billion dollar industry in our world economy.

Webster's defines **demographics** as: "the statistical characteristics of human populations (as age or income) used especially to identify markets; or a market or segment of the population identified by demographics." So why does this matter to you? Well, when delivering a speech you need to know who you are speaking to, and not just guess who will be out in the crowd. A demographic study of your audience provides you with clues for how present your message successfully. Here are the different categories that make up demographics, so as you prepare for your next speech you can understand how demographics can shape your message to engage your audience.

Age

By grasping the collective age groups of your audience it is easier to speculate on the range of life experiences they may have had. For example, a speech to persuade presented in a senior-level high school class urging the class to write to their congressman regarding out-of-pocket costs and affordability of Medicare probably would not generate much interest. It is not to say that the Medicare topic is unimportant, but in reality the audience is not at that particular life stage where Medicare is a high priority. Conversely, this speech would be a hit at the local senior center. However, if the speaker changed his topic to fight proposed federal cuts to student loans for higher education he would likely gain the high schoolers' attention and support, assuming the class members will be attending college the following year.

Gender

When selecting a topic for your speech, take some time to consider how the gender make-up of your audience may affect how the members perceive your topic. Some topics may be geared to either men or women. For example, consider the speech: To persuade my audience that the muscle cars of the 1960's are far superior to the muscle cars of the 2000's. If your audience is predominately women, you may have your work cut out for you to build a connection between the topic and the audience (unless this topic is delivered to the local chapter of the muscle car association and the audience is fully engaged with the topic). If this is not the case you must make a special effort to link your topic to the other gender so they do not feel left out or even alienated. A speaker who ignores the gender of his or her listeners is almost certain to put-off some members of the audience.

When thinking about gender relations, it is easy to come up with stereotypes and assumptions. However, in speechmaking you need to take your thinking a step further and question those assumptions and find them to be correct before presenting them.

The social roles of men and women have been fading away for many years. For example, it was common that women stay home and tend to the children and cook dinner for their families. Now it is socially acceptable for men to be in the kitchen, just take a look at our male celebrity chefs such as Emeril, Wolfgang Puck, and Bobby Flay. Today, we see many male nurses, kindergarten teachers, hairstylists, and secretaries. Moreover, the presence of women is becoming more and more prominent in traditionally male dominated fields such as plumbing, car mechanics, CEO's of companies, and high-level politics.

A perceptive public speaker will be equally attuned to both the differences and the similarities between the sexes. With that said, a well-prepared public speaker will be sure to avoid using sexist language. Almost any audience you address will contain both men and women who will take offense at words and phrases that suggest gender stereotypes or put down people on the basis of their gender.

Race/Ethnicity

Our world is getting smaller and smaller every day with the developments of technology and our global economy. Therefore understanding the cultural dynamic of your audience is becoming more and more prominent. Realize that some of your audience members have racial, ethnic, or cultural worldviews that will affect their approach toward your speech topic. During your preparation phase, try to determine what those perspectives are and how they are likely to affect the audience's response to your message. Public speakers who have honorable intentions can inadvertently use figures of speech, metaphors, language, or examples that members of your audience may find offensive. When in doubt, run your speech by someone who can give you an accurate account of your presentation before delivering your speech to the class.

Educational Level

One's highest educational degree is often related to his or her socio-economic status and profession. A person's educational status may tell you very little about his or her intelligence, self-motivation, or personal refinement. However, people with more formal education tend to read more, are more familiar with current events, have probably traveled extensively, and are likely to have higher incomes.

With this in mind, how does this influence the way you approach your topic to meet the needs of your audience?

Readers are more likely to have a wider range of vocabulary, so you may have more options in your word choice. However, if your audience is not knowledgeable about your given topic, this is a reminder to use elementary terminology to best meet the needs of the audience. You never want to talk down to your audience but realize that they do not have the same expertise on the topic as you do.

Religion

When you speak on a topic with religious overtones, be sure to consider the religious affiliations of the audience. By considering their affiliations you will avoid a potentially awkward relationship with your audience; in some cases, it may make the difference between an unsuccessful speech and a successful one.

Speaking about religious matters can be a sensitive issue, so apprehensive public speakers may consider speaking about another topic so they will not offend anyone. Keep in mind when discussing religious issues that you must respect the diverse religious beliefs of your audience. Again the key word here is respect, it is okay to disagree, but you must communicate respect for the dignity of the diversity of your audience members' religious beliefs.

Knowing the religious affiliations of your audience can give you some good clues about their values, beliefs, and attitudes. However, you cannot assume that all members of a religious group follow the organization's official doctrines and declarations. For example, a denomination's leadership may stand for a particular position, but the majority of the members of that denomination may not agree with their leader's view. So do your homework.

Group Membership

Think about the numerous groups you may belong to, such as the Associated Students (student government), your school's athletic team, the photography club, or a fraternity or sorority. Professionally, you may belong to the American Medical Association, the Young Entrepreneurs Society, National Education Association, Sierra Club, or the National Rifle Association.

For speeches in the classroom as well as for those outside the classroom, the group affiliations of your audience may provide excellent clues about listener's interests and attitudes. Ask yourself what are the characteristics of the members of the group. This can give you incredible insight as to what makes this group membership tick. Getting into the minds of the group's philosophy will help you customize your message to the particular group. There are a variety ways to gain information about the group's core values, such as their websites, interviews with the group's leadership, and perhaps profiles of prominent members in newspapers, magazines, radio, television, and Internet channels.

In addition to age, gender, race/ethnicity, educational level, religion, and group membership, a wider scope of demographics would include: intelligence, geography of where one lives, and socioeconomic status. Furthermore, when analyzing demographics in a classroom setting consider examining your audience's academic majors, their highest educational standing (freshmen, sophomore, junior, senior, earned Bachelor's, Master's, PhD, etc), hobbies, potential career aspirations, and living arrangements.

As a student in a public speaking class you are lucky, because you can informally scope out this information while in class. That is a huge advantage as a public speaker who is attempting to understand the demographic make-up of your audience. However, as you leave your public speaking class and are on your pathway to success, you will need to find this information about your audience through audience surveys and interviews. Your audience will thank you.

Gathering Audience Intelligence

Gathering audience information is incredibly important because it takes the unknowns to knowns, and makes the invisible visible. Many untrained public speakers are frightened of public speaking because they are afraid of the audience's reaction to their message. In general, the higher the level of uncertainty that exists in a given situation, the higher the level of anxiety. They are not sure that they will be accepted, or that their thoughts will be supported or opposed. In short, public speakers are afraid of rejection and gathering audience information takes the guesswork out of what will or what may not work.

To illustrate this point in an everyday life situation, let us imagine that you see that special someone across the room at a party. You would really like to go up to that person and introduce yourself, but because you do not know how this person would react to your advances you stay on the sidelines. Now imagine seeing this same person across the room and knowing that this person is interested in you and that all you have to do is walk up to that person and introduce yourself. Knowing the audience makes a big difference in your confidence which translates to success. That is what gathering audience intelligence does, it leads you down that pathway to success in the face of uncertainty. Two ways to collect valuable information about your audience is through audience surveys and interviewing audience members.

The Audience Survey

An **audience survey** is outstanding way to gain information about your audience. The survey helps you know, the level of knowledge the audience members may have about your topic, the level of interest in your topic, and their attitude towards your topic. For example imagine presenting an informative speech about the basic principles of playing ice hockey and failing to realize that the audience is mostly composed of your college's hockey team. This speech would fail because of the knowledge and level of engagement the audience has about the topic. At first the audience may be engaged because of your topic selection, but when basic rules of icing and off-sides are discussed the audience would want to put the speaker in the penalty box for two minutes for boredom. In order for this speech to be a success the speaker needs to able talk about more advanced information regarding the sport of ice hockey. Now if the same speech were presented to an audience who has limited knowledge and minimal involvement with ice hockey and is interested in learning more about the topic, the presentation would go over much better, so know your audience.

The keys with the audience survey are to be brief and to the point and to make replying to the survey user-friendly for the responders. There are three types of questions you want to ask when assembling an audience survey: the fixed-alternative question, the scale-question, and the open-ended question.

The **fixed-alternative question** offers a fixed choice between two more alternatives. The purpose for asking the fixed-alternative question is to establish the listener's knowledge base and their amount of involvement with the topic. By asking the fixed-alternative you are limiting their responses to produce clear-cut answers.

1. Are you a:

   Male ————————————————————

   Female ——————————————————

2. Do you have diabetes?

   Yes ————————————————————

   No —————————————————————

3. Do you know of anyone who does have diabetes?

   Yes ————————————————————

   No —————————————————————

4. If yes is that person related to you?

   Yes ————————————————————

   No —————————————————————

5. Is diabetes the sixth leading cause of death in the United States?

   Yes ————————————————————

   No —————————————————————

6. Do you agree or disagree with this statement: Diabetes can cause serious health complications including heart disease, blindness, kidney failure, and lower-extremity amputations?

Strongly agree	Somewhat agree	Undecided	Somewhat disagree	Strongly disagree

7. Can diabetes be prevented?

Strongly agree	Somewhat agree	Undecided	Somewhat disagree	Strongly disagree

8. How many different types of diabetes exist?

1	2	3	4	5

9. Which cultural group best describes you?

African American	Asian	Hispanic	Native American	White	White, Non Hispanic	Pacific Islander	Decline to State

10. How would you define diabetes?

11. What are the symptoms of diabetes?

12. How do diabetics treat their disease?

Figure 5.1   A Sample of an Audience Survey on the Topic of Diabetes

Examples of a fixed-alternative question look like this:

Which ethnicity group do you affiliate yourself with?

African American ___ Asian ___ Hispanic ___ Native American ___ White ___

White, Non Hispanic ___ Pacific Islander ___ Decline to State ___

Do you smoke at least one cigarette a day?

Yes ___ No ___

Did you vote in the last presidential election?

Yes ___ No ___ Not sure? ___

Do you spend more than $50 a week on gasoline for your car?

Yes ___ No ___ Not sure? ___

Should public elementary schools not offer physical education courses?

Yes ___ No ___

Scale questions are used to gain more accurate information about the audience members to gain an understanding of how they fit in a range of possible responses to a question. The range of possible responses is usually made into fixed intervals along a scale. The scale questions are similar to the fixed-alternative questions, but provide the respondent more options. Scale questions offer a glimpse into the attitudes of listeners towards a particular topic.

Examples of a scale question look like this:

How many hours do you work while attending college?

40+ ___ 30–40 ___ 20–30 ___ 10–20 ___ 1–10 ___ Do not work ___

Specify to the degree to which you agree or disagree with the following statement:

The federal government should mandate a $250 annual tax that will be exclusively used to pay off the national debt.

Strongly agree ___ Somewhat agree ___ Not sure ___ Somewhat disagree ___ Strongly disagree ___

The legal drinking age should be raised to 25 years old.

Strongly agree ___ Somewhat agree ___ Not sure ___ Somewhat disagree ___ Strongly disagree ___

How often do you exercise per week?

7 days ___ 5–6 days ___ 3–4 days ___ 1–2 days ___ I'm the person in the "After" photo ___

The **open-ended question** allows the respondent to answer freely. Because you are giving the respondent the keys to the car, they may take you places you do not want to go, or provide information that is irrelevant to the purpose of your speech. On the flip side you may find that the respondent answered your questions and illustrated a new way of thinking about your topic, or an area of expertise you did not expect an audience member would have. Open-ended questions are tricky because they are more difficult to tabulate findings, whereas the fixed-alternative and scale questions make things easier for tabulating statistics about your audience.

Here are some examples of an open-ended question:

How do you feel about the proposal to ban alcohol on campus?

Why do you think America is facing such an obesity problem?

Do you feel video games contribute to the high absenteeism in our Speech class?

Now that you have this information about your audience, make sure to implement the findings from your survey into the presentation. Using these findings shows the audience that you took the time to get to know them and that you tailored your message to meet their pressing needs. By this simple act you establish goodwill and gain the respect of your audience.

Interviewing Audience Members

Interviewing your classmates on a one-on-one basis is the most thorough way to learn about each of your audience members. Interviewing your audience requires you to be very organized in devising your questions and coordinating the time to meet the individual audience members. The interviewing practice is by far the most meticulous, but is the least practical to implement. A more efficient approach to gather intelligence about your audience is to use the audience survey.

However, if you decide to interview audience members here are some tips to help you through the process. First you need to define the purpose of your interview. Ask yourself, "what do I hope to accomplish with this interview?" By answering this question, you will be on your way. Next, you need to know whom to interview. Ask yourself, "will this person provide me the information to fulfill my purpose?" The most important task when preparing for an interview is formulating your interview questions. Write those

Interviewing audience members is a thorough way to learn what makes your particular audience distinct.
Source: Shutterstock © Andresr

questions out and spend time wording those questions appropriately so you sound credible. If the person you are interviewing sees that you are fumbling with papers and trying to think of a question to ask, your credibility and trustworthiness as an interviewer will go down the tube. In addition, the interviewee will begin to see the interview as a waste of time.

During the interview be sure to be on time for your appointment. By being prompt you are communicating to the interviewee that you are taking this interview seriously. In addition being on time expresses the message of respect, and your interviewee will appreciate that gesture. When arriving for the interview, introduce yourself, restate the purpose of the interview, and start asking your questions. The best interviewers are usually the best listeners, so listen up, and feel free to ask probing questions. Remember your purpose for the interview, because it is easy to go off track in many different directions so stay focused to get the information you need for your speech. Once you have gathered the information you need to adequately move forward in your research, end the interview and thank the interviewee for his or her time. Do not outstay your welcome, because you do not want to be remembered as "the thing that never leaves."

Just because the formal interview is done, does not mean that you are done with your work. Immediately after the interview review your notes while the dialogue is still prominently in your mind. Write-out those notes clearly so you can implement the interview in your presentation. Other tips: make sure that you have written the person's name, title, and organization accurately. Nothing hurts your credibility more than calling someone by the wrong name. Finally, send a thank you note to the person you interviewed. This person took the time out of his or her busy schedule to help you with your presentation, give them the common courtesy to say thank you. The interviewee will remember your thoughtfulness and will be more willing to be a resource at a future date.

ANALYSIS AND AUDIENCE EXPECTATIONS OF THE SITUATION

There are five factors to consider when examining the audience's expectations of the situation of the speech.

Size of the Audience

The size of the audience is something to consider because the number of listeners may determine your level of formality, the amount of interaction you have with the audience, the use of a microphone, and your need to make adjustments to your visual aids. A larger audience requires more of the speaker by using an appropriate tone of voice and correct use of language, small intricacies that make a big difference. Smaller audiences allow for a more casual approach, a less formal tone, and informal language. However, speaking to a smaller audience does not mean you can conduct yourself in an overly familiar way. Speaking to a large audience reduces the speaker's capability to observe and respond to facial expressions, posture, and other nonverbal messages sent by the audience. In larger settings the audience's role becomes more passive than that of smaller, more intimate settings. Moreover, when using a microphone be mindful that the acoustics will be different than not using a microphone and alter your rate of speech accordingly. You do not want to sound like you are going through the drive-through at your favorite fast food restaurant.

The Environment

Where you deliver your speech may be less than desirable, but the show must go on. Interesting décor may be large pillars blocking the view between the speaker and the audience, light bulbs that are out, the heater that is permanently on during the hot humid summer months, or no podium on which to place your notes. Another shortfall that will make a speaker's day is if the audio and visual equipment is not working. With all of this stuff that can go wrong it is your responsibility to build contingency plans so you are not caught off-guard in case something goes awry.

There will be times when your room will be less than optimal. This is *not* your time to announce to your audience that the room is small, or hot, or uncomfortable. By doing this, you have planted the seeds of uneasiness in your audience. From there on in, your audience will be thinking about what the room lacks instead of your message. When the room you are speaking in is not the best, it is at that time you must focus on being at your best, and channel your energy into delivering your message to this particular audience.

At the very least you will want to inquire in advance about the room in which you are to speak. As a guest speaker you need to take the lead to learn about the room in which you will be speaking. Visiting the room will help you get the look and feel of where you will be presenting, in addition, going the extra mile here will allow you to visualize your success in the preparation of your speech.

One advantage you have in your public speaking class is that you will be familiar with the room in which you will be delivering your speech to your classmates. By minimizing much of the uncertainty as to where you will be presenting, you will be lowering your anxiety about delivering your speech, thereby allowing you to focus on delivering your message and meeting the needs of your audience. By spending your class time in your classroom you will be familiar with the layout of the room, the podium, the audio visuals, the acoustics, lighting, and the temperature.

By checking out the physical location of your
upcoming speech can help you visualize your speech,
thereby minimizing unneeded uncertainty.
Source: Shutterstock © fotoadamczyk

The Occasion

Your disposition and demeanor need to match the mood of the occasion. With the numerous occasions and interactions we have, there is an unwritten expectation of acceptable behavior. For example a speaker needs to communicate joy and hope with a smile at a wedding celebration while being solemn and heartfelt as the appropriate mood at a funeral. During your classroom assignment you are expected to follow the rules that your professor has set, keep to the time limit, and respect your classmates. For the different environments you will be speaking, think ahead and make sure that the emotional tone of your speech matches the mood of the occasion.

Time

The occasion that you will be speaking at will dictate the appropriate time of your speech. For example if you were to win an Academy Award you would have approximately two minutes to say your thank you's before the music starts to play and the show goes to a commercial. On the other hand when the president of the United States delivers his State of the Union address the speech will usually last between forty-five minutes to an hour. Now I am sure many actors accepting awards would love to have forty-five minutes to thank everyone from their parents to a special caterpillar in the Brazilian rainforests, but that would not be appropriate for the occasion. In contrast, if our president delivered a State of the Union speech in under two minutes, that speech would fall short of the world's expectation of the occasion.

Importance

The last factor to consider when assessing the situation is the importance of the occasion, and the significance that is attached to the circumstances. The importance of the occasion will lead to the speaker's content and approach. A speaker must carefully determine the importance of an event so that the audience is not offended by his or her thoughtless treatment of what the audience regards as serious business.

ADJUSTING TO THE AUDIENCE'S SIGNALS

Adjusting to your Audience Before Your Speech

Public speaking is an audience-focused activity and you must keep them in mind during all phases of your speech preparation. As part of your preparation you need to predict how your audience will respond to your message, and make adjustments to your message so the audience finds your speech clear, appropriate, and convincing. The findings from your audience survey will help you anticipate how your audience will react to your message.

During your preparation phase much-needed thought must be devoted to examining your topic and your goals through the eyes of your audience members. This is challenging because we are so engaged in our own ideas and concerns that we have trouble seeing things from other people's perspectives, especially if their perspective is different from ours. For example, if you have spent your life around pianos and piano playing, it may be difficult for you to inform the audience about the basic principles of the piano to a group of non-musicians. What seems like common sense to you may be a completely new paradigm of thinking for your audience and needs to be communicated that way. Stepping out of your frame of reference and into the perspective of the audience is a big step towards being an effective public speaker and on your pathway to success.

Audience Adaptation During the Speech

While delivering your speech, be on the lookout as to how your audience is receiving your message through their feedback. If your listeners are leaning forward in their chairs, looking at you fully engaged in your speech, and nodding their heads in approval, it is safe to assume you are on the right track. On the other hand if you find your audience disinterested, slouching in their chairs, or giving you quizzical looks, you need to make some adjustments to your presentation on the fly. You may want to adjust your rate of speech (either faster or slower), alter the volume of your speech, restate some of your points, or implement a well-timed dramatic pause as a way to get your audience's attention.

Adapting to your audience before and particularly during a speech takes time, practice, and experience to be able to achieve seamlessly. These skills, though, will distinguish you as a proficient public speaker and will propel you to new heights of success in your given field.

In closing, understanding your audience is paramount to your public speaking success. Author Steven Covey said it best, "you need to understand and then be understood." By learning about the psychology of the audience, their demographics, conducting an audience survey, and making adaptations during your speech, you will understand your audience better and make better speeches, which will lead you to your pathway to success.

Summary: Tips for taking the guesswork out of who you are speaking to when preparing your speech

Public speaking is an audience-focused activity. The listeners to your message will be listening to your presentation and thinking, "what is in it for me?" Egocentrism may be defined as the tendency of people to be concerned above all with their own values, beliefs, and well-being. So when presenting your speech, the odds are the audience is thinking, "how does this speech apply to me?" or "how will I benefit from this speech?" Your job as a speaker is to solve that mystery for the listener. There are a variety of strategies to help you achieve that goal.

One strategy is to make the unkown into a known. So study the demographics of your audience. Demographics look at gathering information based on age, gender, race/ethnicity, educational level, religion, and group membership.

The next strategy is to conduct an audience survey where you would ask three different types of questions, the fixed-alternative question, the scale question, and the open-ended question. The goal here is to gauge the audience's interest, knowledge, and attitudes towards your speech topic.

Moreover, understanding the audience's expectations about your speech gives good insight as to what the audience wants. Elements to consider during your preparation are the size of the audience, the environment in which you will be speaking, the occasion, the accepted amount of time allotted to the speech, and the importance of the speech.

Finally, by making adjustments before and during your speech, you will be able to make your message more compelling and substantial for your audience. Conducting your demographic study and your audience survey are strategies to be used before presenting your message, while observing the nonverbal reactions of your audience during your speech will offer valuable insights for you to make the necessary delivery adjustments as you talk. By understanding your audience and customizing your message to your listeners, you will put yourself onto the pathway to success.

Name: _____

True-False

1. (T) F   Egocentrism means that audiences typically approach speeches by asking "Why is this important for me?"

2. T (F)   Gender, sexual orientation, age, race, ethnicity, and group membership are all factors to consider when conducting a demographic audience analysis.

3. (T) F   Unlike beginning speakers, experienced speakers have little need for audience analysis.

4. (T) F   When you create an audience-analysis questionnaire, open-ended questions are valuable because they usually produce clear, unambiguous answers.

5. (T) F   Even though most of the process of audience adaptation happens as part of preparing a speech, a speaker may still need to adapt her or his comments to the audience during the presentation of the speech.

6. T (F)   The *least* important task when preparing for an interview is formulating your interview questions.

Multiple Choice

7. The key benefit of using fixed-alternative questions in an audience analysis questionnaire is that they
   a. strengthen the ethos of the questionnaire.
   b. dig deeper into the respondents' beliefs.
   c. produce clear, unambiguous answers.
   d. give respondents maximum flexibility in answering.
   e. request that respondents give honest answers.

8. If you were constructing an audience-analysis questionnaire and wanted to learn the strength of your listeners' attitudes for or against stem cell research, which of the following would be the best kind of question to ask?
   a. demographic question
   b. open-ended question
   c. leading question
   d. scale question
   e. fixed-alternative question

9. Audience adaptation is an important factor in which of the following?
   a. choosing the speech topic
   b. preparing the speech
   c. presenting the speech
   d. all of the above

10. To say that people usually want to hear about things that are meaningful to them is to say that people are
    a. empathic.
    b. entitled.
    c. ethnocentric.
    d. exaggerated.
    e. egocentric.

11. Which of the following is a demographic characteristic of a speech audience?

    a. interest
    b. attitude
    c. size
    d. age
    e. knowledge

12. If you were giving a persuasive speech on academic standards in college athletics to members of the college coaches association, the most important factor to consider in audience analysis would probably be the

    a. knowledge of your audience.
    b. group membership of your audience.
    c. socio-economic status of your audience.
    d. educational level of your audience.
    e. size of your audience.

Essay

13. What are the three types of questions for audience analysis questionnaires? Give an example of each type and explain the advantages and disadvantages of each.

14. Describe how the size of the audience influences the formality of your presentation.

15. Clarify why each of the following is an important aspect in demographic audience analysis: age, gender, religion, group membership, racial, ethnic, educational level, or cultural background.

Chapter 6

Researching Your Sources for the Ultimate Credibility

GATHERING YOUR MATERIALS

On your pathway to success the quality of support you use in your speech is essential. Due to the vast array of informational sources we have at our convenience, making the appropriate choices in sources can make or break your speech. By accessing information from your college or university library, you will put yourself in a stronger position to be more informative and persuasive. Using your college or university library and all of its resources will help establish your credibility, competence, and confidence as a public speaker. This chapter will help you organize your research process, which includes determining what kind of information you will need to gather, where you mπay find that information, and judging the strengths and weaknesses of the information you acquire. The three primary areas where your information for your speech will be coming from are: library research, Internet research, and field research.

ORGANIZING YOUR DATA GATHERING PROJECT

As you go through the research process you will need to have an organizational system to hold all of the materials that will be coming your way. Here are some tips that will help you keep all of your sources organized and easily accessible as you research materials for your speech.

Consider using file folders representing each of your potential main points as a place to hold your printed materials. For each of your printouts or photocopies be sure to have all bibliography information clearly written so you can track down the original source if necessary. In addition, when you document your bibliography on your outline, all of the needed information will be readily available. The formal method of using the MLA or APA style guide of documenting your sources will be discussed later in the chapter.

Another strategy that may be helpful is using note cards for key ideas. For each of your note cards a heading is needed, with the author's name, page number of the work that the information came from, and a summary of the line of reasoning you want to remember. Be careful not to put so much information on a single card that it becomes cluttered and difficult to read through. Quotes and catchy phrases used by the author would be good notes to put on your card. From there you can stack the cards into common themes representing each of your main points.

Another strategy to note when gathering your information is to evaluate whether the information is from primary or secondary sources. **Primary sources** are first-hand accounts, much like your class audience survey, and your one-on-one individual interviews. **Secondary sources** are information coming from books, magazines, databases, and newspapers.

FINDING YOUR MATERIALS

"No university in the world has ever risen to greatness without a correspondingly great library . . . When this is no longer true, then will our civilization have come to an end."
—LAWRENCE CLARK POWELL (AMERICAN LIBRARIAN, WRITER, AND CRITIC)

Visiting your college or university library may be a daunting experience especially if you do not know what you are looking for, or are not familiar with the terrain. Before heading into the library to research your speech, you must know your specific purpose, that is, what you hope to accomplish with your speech. Once you have this understanding as to what you hope to accomplish, write your statement down on a 3 × 5 card, and carry that card with you while researching. That 3 × 5 card with your specific purpose will serve as your anchor when you get hit with information overload. Understanding the purpose of your speech will make your decision process easier as to whether the information you access will work or not work for your speech. Understanding your purpose clarifies the data gathering decision making process.

With your specific purpose in hand, you now need a plan to navigate through the thousands of sources you will be exposed to in your search for supporting materials for your speech presentation. It is to your advantage to *start early* in researching for your speech. The later you start the researching phase of the speech preparation process, the less time you are giving yourself to succeed once you stand behind the podium. It is best to develop a timeline to schedule where you want to be and when, and stick to the schedule. Other things to consider when putting together your plan is scheduling expert interviews, meeting with librarians, conducting surveys, and even deciding which libraries you will visit. If you wait too long, these valuable resources may not be available to you, so *start early*.

When using the many electronic databases at the library, it is to your advantage to use the database's built-in bibliography feature and create the bibliography as you go. For non-database sources, document those sources in either the MLA or APA format on 3 × 5 cards. By documenting those sources while you come across them in the first place, you will save time from backtracking and trying to relocate those sources.

LIBRARY RESEARCH

"It was from my own early experience that I decided there was no use to which money could be applied so productive of good to boys and girls who have good within them and ability and ambition to develop it, as the founding of a public library"
—ANDREW CARNEGIE (SCOTTISH-BORN AMERICAN INDUSTRIALIST AND PHILANTHROPIST, 1835–1919)

Your college library is your strongest asset in gathering high quality materials for your speech. Your college or university invests a lot of money for paid subscriptions that are of higher caliber quality than an ordinary Internet search. In addition, you will have the opportunity to have highly qualified and devoted librarians help you gather your materials for your speech. Your librarians are a truly valuable asset to any college or university community, and are happy to assist you in your researching goals.

Other alternatives you may have besides your college or university library are your local public library, or dedicated libraries operated by historical societies, museums, professional associations, or corporations.

Your Librarian is Your Friend

Entering into your college or university library may be an intimidating experience, especially if you are trying to navigate through the numerous book stacks, computer databases, newspapers, magazines, and reference materials. The best advice is to utilize the library's orientation workshops that will walk you through how to utilize all of the valuable information available at your fingertips. By participating in the workshop orientations you will learn the finer points of how to gather materials, saving you hours of time and needless frustration. Moreover, by participating in the workshop orientation, you will have the opportunity to meet the library staff, and build a relationship with the librarians that will help you in your researching needs during the duration of your college experience. In summary, your librarians are your friends, and they are a potential asset to your success development.

Approaching your reference librarian is a smart start to the research process because it can save you time, energy, and the task of having to hack through unwanted material. The reference librarian has specific training and skills to find information to best meet the needs of his or her patrons. A tip that should be abided by before talking to the librarian is to have your specific purpose clearly stated, along with any specific directions for the particular assignment, so the librarian can get the appropriate context of the assignment to better serve you. In short, you want to respect the time and effort of your librarian so be prepared ahead of time.

Books

"I must say I find television very educational. The minute somebody turns it on, I go to the library and read a good book."

—Groucho Marx (American Comedian, Actor, and Singer, 1890–1977)

Building a relationship with your reference librarian will make the researching process more efficient in your data gathering.
Source: Shutterstock © Dmitriy Shironosov

In locating a specific book in your library, you will have to access your library's catalog, which allows you to compose a quick search using at least three categories, the author's name, the title, or the subject. Locating the call number of the book will inform you where this book is located in the library's stacks so that you can find the book in an organized and systematic fashion. Moreover, if you are using a computerized catalog, the computer may tell you whether the book is checked out, or on hold, maximizing your time as opposed to looking for a book that is already checked out. When looking at the option of using books in support of your ideas for your speech, keep an eye out for the book's publication date to check for relevance. For example if you see an interesting and potentially useful book about computer networking that is dated 2001, you can bet there have been developments in the field of computers that have not been captured in the 2001 book. So you may want to find a book that is more relevant and timely.

Articles

Articles that support your ideas may come in three different forms of periodicals at the library: newspapers, magazines, and academic journals. Usually, articles in these three formats may come in either an electronic form or in a paper form. Due to space issues, the print form for many of these periodicals may be held for approximately one year, but consult with your librarian about their policies.

When accessing articles via electronic databases, the data are commonly provided in three different forms. First is the citation, in the simple bibliographical reference that includes the title of the article, the name(s) of the author(s), the name of the publication, publication date, and page numbers. Next is the abstract form, where a brief summary of an article is shown for you to decide whether the information presented is what you were looking for in your source. The abstract provides just enough information for you gauge whether you want to see the article in its entirety. Lastly, some databases offer a full-text view of the article you have retrieved.

When searching for sources using an electronic database using Boolean operators can save you time by accessing the information you need using a couple of simple tips. Boolean operators use words to create definite phrases that expand or constricted your search. The most frequently used words in a Boolean search are: *and*, *not*, and *or*. *And* and *not* will restrict your search and limit the number of results you will receive; *or* will expand your search and thus the number of hits.

When searching your library's electronic resources for articles you will be exposed to all or some of these electronic databases.

InfoTrac offers over 20 million full-text articles from nearly 6,000 scholarly and popular periodicals. Articles cover a broad spectrum of disciplines and topics.

Academic Search offers full texts of popular and scholarly periodicals.

LexisNexis Academic Universe offers: full text from 350 newspapers and more than 300 magazines and journals from the United States and around the world; broadcast transcripts; non-English-language news sources available in Spanish, French, German, Italian, and Dutch, including both newspapers and magazines.

Educational Resources Information Center (ERIC) supplies unlimited access to more than 1.2 million bibliographic records of journal articles and other education-related materials, with new records added frequently. Within the ERIC Collection, you will find records for: journal articles, books, policy papers, and other education-related materials.

ProQuest Research Library database includes more than 3,950 titles, over 2,700 in full text, from 1971 forward. It features a highly respected, diversified mix of scholarly journals, trade publications, magazines, and newspapers.

Newspapers

"It's amazing that the amount of news that happens in the world every day always just exactly fits the newspaper."

—JERRY SEINFELD (AMERICAN COMEDIAN AND ACTOR)

Newspapers are a useful source of information that can add value to your research for your speech. When researching newspapers to support your ideas the common papers to look for are prominent papers like: *The New York Times, The Los Angeles Times, The Chicago Tribune, The Washington Post, The Wall Street Journal,* and *USA Today.* However, the real hidden gem is the local coverage of an event. The local paper will have more reporters covering more angles and have more dedicated space for their "big" event. Conversely, the bigger papers will devote only a small portion of their space to a "big" happening in other parts of the country. So spend time reading the local papers when preparing for a presentation.

Reference Works

When you are looking for factual information to implement in your speech, utilizing the reference area of your library is a good bet. Reference works contain useful facts and information that will provide you the data you need in a timely and efficient manner. The reference area is composed of encyclopedias, dictionaries, yearbooks, quote books, and maps. These resources are carefully researched and verified for accuracy. Reference materials come in three different forms: print, CD-ROM, and the Internet. Other advantages to using reference works are that they can provide a synopsis of your topic, verify information gathered from other sources, or find a person's credentials.

The reference source *The Statistical Abstract of the United States* is a valuable source when gathering information. *The Statistical Abstract of the United States* is a standard summary of statistics on the social, political, and economic organization of the United States. *The Statistical Abstract of the United States* may also be accessed through the Internet at http://www.census.gov/compendia/statab/.

DOCUMENTATION OF YOUR SOURCES FOR YOUR BIBLIOGRAPHY

There are two major style guidelines that are used to document your sources for the bibliography of your speech. The first is the Modern Language Association style guide also referred to as "MLA" or the American Psychological Association style guide also referred to as "APA." Ask your instructor what his or her preference is when documenting sources for your speeches.

In your works cited or bibliography page, each of your citations will be listed in alphabetical order, according to the last name of the author. If there is no author listed, then alphabetize by the first word in the title (disregard "A," "An," or "The" at the start of a title).

Here are some examples as to how to document your sources using the style guides for both MLA and APA.

MLA

Book with More than One Author
Angelo, Thomas A., and Patricia K. Cross. *Classroom Assessment Techniques*. 2nd ed. San Francisco, CA: Jossey-Bass, 1988. 65–72.

Field Research/Raw Data
Desert, James. Speech 100 LA In-Class Survey. Raw data. 6 Nov. 2008.

Magazine
Foley, Kathleen. "High Tech in Nevada." *Nevada Business Journal* Mar. 2008: 20–25.

Academic Journal
Guerrero, Laura K., and Susanne M. Jones. "Differences in One's Own and One's Partner's Perceptions of Social Skill as a Function of Attachment Style." *Communication Quarterly 51* (2003): 277–295.

Web Page
Orman, Suze. "Dusting Off the Rules of Financial Responsibility." *Yahoo! Finance*. 18 Sept. 2008. Yahoo! 6 Oct. 2008 <http://finance.yahoo.com/expert/article/moneymatters/108818>.

Book with One Author
Peale, Norman V. *The Power of Positive Thinking*. New York: Fawcett, 1996.

Newspaper
Ratto, Ray. "Tough to Win Games without Having the Ball." *San Francisco Chronicle* 6 Oct. 2008: C1.

APA

Book with More than One Author
Angelo, T., Cross, P. (1988) *Classroom Assessment Techniques*. (2nd ed.). San Francisco: Jossey-Bass.

Field Research/Raw Data
Desert, J. (2008, November 6). Speech 100 LA In-Class Survey. San Bruno, CA: Skyline College.

Magazine
Foley, K. (2008, March). High Tech in Nevada. *Nevada Business Journal,* 20–25.

Academic Journal Article
Guerrero, L., Jones, S. (2003). Differences in One's Own and One's Partner's Perceptions of Social Skill as a Function of Attachment Style. *Communication Quarterly,* 51, 277–295.

Web Page
Orman, S. (2008, September 18). *Dusting Off the Rules of Financial Responsibility*. Retrieved October 6, 2008, from *Yahoo! Finance Web site:* http://finance.yahoo.com/expert/article/moneymatters/108818

Book with One Author
Peale, N. (1996). *The Power of Positive Thinking*. New York: Fawcett.

Newspaper
Ratto, R. (2008, October 6) Tough to Win Games without Having the Ball. *San Francisco Chronicle,* C1.

*For situations that are not covered in this text refer directly to the MLA or APA style guides.

In addition to properly citing your sources on your outline, the appropriate oral citing of your sources is needed during your speech. Your audience does not have the luxury of reading your speech while you are delivering your message so it is essential to mention your sources during your speech. During the oral citation, the speaker shares with the audience what the source is, a date reference for the information presented, and the source's credentials. Here are some hypothetical examples as to how you would orally cite your sources in your speech.

According to the March 29th 2009 issue of Sports Illustrated, Pablo Torre explains how many professional athletes lose all of their money due to poor investment choices.

Author Harold Kushner in his book, Living a Life that Matters, says "Every life touches many other lives, and rare is the person who knows how much of a difference he or she has made."

"In a 2008 research study in the *Relationships Journal* conducted by Dr. Louis Stern, he found that marriages go through seven stages of development before hitting maturity."

"On the American Cancer Society's Web site, it states that well over 500,000 people will die of cancer during 2008."

When orally citing a Web site, it is not customary to say the address during your presentation unless you specifically want your audience to visit the site.

In short, by orally citing reputable sources in your speech, you will meet your responsibility and drive home the point to your audience that you did your research. Moreover, orally citing sources demonstrates a high regard for your audience, because you are providing the best possible information for their listening experience.

INTERNET RESEARCH

There are many terms that are used to describe using the Web for research or browsing. In this section we will look at notable terms for using the Internet, and how to successfully use the Internet to support you in your research needs. The Internet is an immense network of networks, linking computers throughout the world. While the World Wide Web may be portrayed as a global Internet scheme for presenting and displaying documents that may include text, video, sound, and images. A Web site is simply a place on the World Wide Web, and each Web site contains webpages, which are files you see on the screen when visiting a Web site. A hyperlink may be defined as a highlighted word, phrase, or picture that when clicked takes you to another place within a document or to another Web site.

A search engine is a service that lets you search for information using keywords that may appear on webpages. When performing a subject search, be mindful that you will accumulate thousands of sites that will not serve your purpose. An alterative to using a search engine is to use a virtual library, which presents links to Web sites that have been evaluated for importance and functionality.

> "When I took office, only high energy physicists had ever heard of what is called the World Wide Web. . . . Now even my cat has its own page."
> —BILL CLINTON (FORMER PRESIDENT OF THE UNITED STATES)

It is recommended that the use of the Internet for gathering research materials should be a supplement to the library-based research avenue. An area of concern for the researcher who uses the Internet is how easy it is to post information on the Web regardless of its legitimacy. The Internet is not regulated and consequently anything goes for the medium. Therefore the information may be very biased and erroneous, because no one is monitoring the content. Web sites need to be incessantly updated and regrettably many are not regularly updated and maintained. As you gather information for your presentation, you will be looking for sound reasoning and evidence, and on the lookout for biases and opinions without much support. In addition, many sites look professional, so in a lot of viewer's minds the material must be timely, and accurate. Thinking critically about the Web sites you visit is important when evaluating information from even the most credible sites. For example on cnn.com there is a movement towards citizen journalism, and a site called iReport that is on the cnn.com site. A report was published on the site that the CEO of Apple Steve Jobs suffered a heart attack. Because the Internet is not regulated, and did not go through an editorial process where facts are checked, the erroneous story was posted on the cnn.com site. Apple's stock dropped 10% in 10 minutes based on this false story. Again, when browsing for information on the Internet, take the time to verify your information with other reliable sources as a cross reference in the reference works section of your library.

The Internet does have its benefits. First the Internet is easily accessible to almost everyone. If for whatever reason you do not have access at home, just head over to your local public library and/or school library where there is Internet access. Next the Internet provides numerous multimedia files for you to download, like videos, audio, pictures, and the like from reputable sites, that can add value to your material gathering for your speech.

In addition, the Internet allows you to quickly find information for your topic selection or general interests. One of the more efficient ways to research a topic or gather information about your speech is

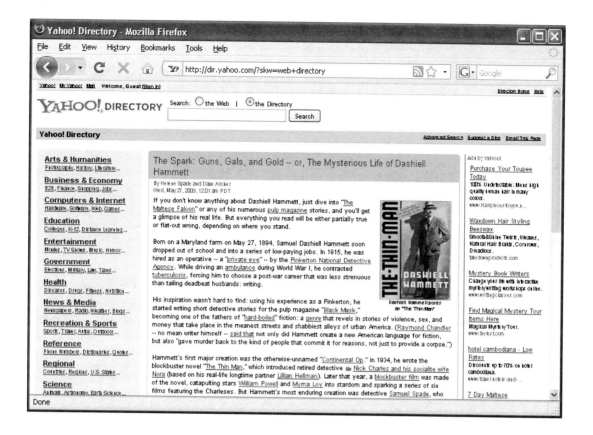

using the Internet subject directory search. The subject directory from Yahoo! Directory or Google Directory shows the viewer a broad range of categories such as news, business, sports, and entertainment. From there it is up to you to narrow your topic of research down into smaller categories using the directory. Using the subject directory allows you to access hard to navigate information cleanly.

Another advantage of the Internet is the use of Really Simple Syndication (RSS). You can subscribe to an RSS feed, which allows you to receive and save up-to-date information from the participating site. So, instead of having to repeatedly access the page to see if any updates have happened, you will be notified of any updates.

Evaluating Information from the Internet

When evaluating a Web site for your speeches there are numerous criteria you need to look at before using the gathered information in your speech. The first thing you want to look at is the site's extension on its URL.

The dependability of information needs to be explored and one way of doing that is looking at the site's extension. For example, if the site is a .com, the site may have a financial angle that it is trying to communicate with their information presented on their site. An .org extension indicates a non-for-profit site, so explore the site's mission and purpose, by doing this you can see the motivation for information presented on the site. An .edu extension is an educational institution. A .gov site is a government-sponsored site. Questions you need to ask yourself when evaluating Internet sites is, "do the Web site

Service Extensions	
Extension	Description
.com	Principally used in commercial or for-profit Web sites
.net	Usually public sites for an Internet service provider
.org	Commonly used for not-for-profit organizations
.gov	Government Web sites
.edu	Extensions for college/university Web sites

sponsors have a bias in regards to how they present their information?" You can learn about the site's sponsors by simply accessing the "About Us" link. Here you will find out about the origins and purpose of the site, as well as the site's founders.

After exploring the reliability and credibility of the sponsors of the site, you need to explore the timeliness of the site and information presented in the site. Look for the date that the Web site and/or article you are accessing has been updated. Because of the fast moving world we live in, information becomes obsolete much more quickly; therefore a site that continually updates itself to meet those challenges can be a worthwhile site to use in your data gathering process.

After looking at the timeliness of the information you have gathered, ask yourself if the information presented is verifiable with other library-based sources such as those found in reference materials. Another area that is worth looking into when evaluating a webpage is if the supporting material is complete. Look for the qualifications of the people writing the material, does this person have the appropriate credentials to talk about the given topic? Also examine the relationship between the organization sponsoring the site and the article, from there you can examine any hidden agendas or biases in the information presented.

Having the ability and the skill to evaluate Web sites will enable you to be more efficient with your time and resources. In addition, when presenting your speech, your audience will be impressed with the quality of your sources and the ability to distinguish between strong sources and poor sources. Again the caliber of your support can make or break a speech.

Access to Government Publications

One of the strengths of using the Internet is for its access to government documents. *FirstGov* is a good site that serves as a portal to government documents (federal, state, local, and tribal government levels) FirstGov is located at http://www.usa.gov/.

On the state and local level there is a Web site called *State and Local Government on the Net* which offers a practical "one-stop" to the Web sites of thousands of state agencies and city and county governments. State and Local Government on the Net is located at www.statelocalgov.net/.

SearchGov is a search engine that provides access to federal, state, and local government Web sites. In addition, the site has the ability to search military Web sites. SearchGov may be accessed at www.searchgov.com.

The CIA World Factbook offers detailed information about every country in the world that is timely, relevant, and credible. Information provided in the CIA World Factbook contains geographical, economic, life expectancy, diseases, and the like specifically for each country of the world. The CIA World Factbook may be accessed at https://www.cia.gov/library/publications/the-world-factbook/.

Internet Communities

"The Internet is becoming the town square for the global village of tomorrow."
—Bill Gates (Founder of Microsoft)

The Internet offers like minded users of topics to form message boards, discussion forums, blogs, vlogs, and podcasts as options for you to gather information for your speech.

Blogs are common on the Internet and the term "blog" is short for the term Web log. Good blogs are updated fairly regularly, and usually appear with the most recent entry shown first. In addition to text, a blog may contain images and videos. If its content is primarily in video format, it is sometimes called a vlog (video blog). Again when assessing the validity of blogs, vlogs, and podcasts, check the credentials of the people driving the content.

FIELD RESEARCH

"Academic success depends on research and publications."
—Philip Zimbardo (Psychologist, Professor Emeritus Stanford University)

Field research is the process of gathering information first-hand by observing, surveying, interviewing, or being part of some activity. Under the field research arm of data gathering, interviewing experts or people who have first-hand experience (peer testimony) with your topic would fall under this category. The nuances of interviewing subjects were covered in depth in the Supporting Your Ideas chapter.

In addition to individual interviews, your audience analysis surveys would fall under the field research category. The details of implementing your audience analysis survey are covered earlier in the text in the Audience-Focused Activity chapter. When analyzing surveys for your speech study the reliability of the sources, the breadth of the sample of people surveyed, the representativeness of the people sampled in the survey, who conducted the survey, and why the survey was conducted in the first place. Studying all of these factors will allow you to have the appropriate context around the survey and its findings.

Summary: Tips for researching your sources for the ultimate credibility

On your pathway to success developing and mastering the skills for finding, evaluating, and properly using data will serve you well. Competence in data gathering is in demand by employers and will lead you down the path for lifelong learning and productivity in your chosen career.

The data gathering process has three areas from which to gather your materials for your speech: the library, the Internet, and through field research. In addition, how you organize your research efforts is an important course of action in the data gathering process. The first step is to be absolutely clear about your specific purpose, the "what you hope to accomplish in your speech." It is a good idea to have your specific purpose documented on a 3 × 5 card and use that as a reference as you scour the thousands of sources that will come your way. If you are new to your respective college/university library, consider participating in an orientation or workshop provided by the trusted library staff to maximize your time, and minimize your anxiety about using all of the wonderful sources that the library has to offer.

As you go through the research process, you need to have a system to keep and organize all of the sources that you will be gathering. Consider using 3×5 cards for brief notes and/or file folders as a holding place for all of the information that you will accumulate. Each folder will represent a potential main point, and be sure to document the bibliographical information on those 3×5 cards so you do not need to backtrack to find valuable sources. In addition, when accessing the electronic databases simply use the bibliography feature and place that information in your file folders to maximize your efforts.

Your college or university library is a gold mine for resources to help you gather materials for your speech. At your fingertips are numerous paid subscriptions to prestigious databases and reference materials, in addition to the trained librarian staff there to help you succeed in your academic pursuits.

The Internet provides quick accessible information. Areas to closely scrutinize are the quality and validity of the information presented on the Web. Since there is no regulation as to what can be posted there is a lot of inaccurate information that is read by millions of Web surfers. So evaluate those sources, by scrutinizing the sponsor of the site, the credentials of the author, and the last time the information on the site was updated.

Field research is the process of gathering information first-hand by watching, interviewing, or surveying. The in-class audience survey that you performed with your classmates would be considered an example of a field research project.

After gathering information through the library, the Internet, and field research, you now must properly document those materials on your bibliography. The two chief style guidelines used to document your sources for the bibliography are the Modern Language Association (MLA) and the American Psychological Association (APA) formats. Consult with your instructor as to what style guide they prefer you use.

On your pathway to success, you will be judged by the quality of information you present to others, whether they are your teachers, classmates, professional colleagues, or other people you may come across that will help you get to where you want to go. By accessing and using the resources of the library, the Internet, and field research, you will be on your pathway to success.

Name: _____

True-False

1. (T) F   You can find a great deal of information on the Internet, but you cannot always find the same depth of research materials as in a good library.

2. (T) F   The *Statistical Abstract of the United States* is the standard reference source for numerical information on the social, political, and economic aspects of American life.

3. T (F)   Field research entails gathering second hand information.

4. T (F)   As your textbook explains, when you locate an abstract of a magazine article using a computerized periodical database, you should feel free to cite the article in your speech on the basis of the abstract alone.

5. T (F)   Like magazine and journal articles, most documents posted on the Internet have been subjected to close editorial review.

Multiple Choice

6. The library's catalogue allows you to search for books by
   a. author.
   b. title.
   c. keyword.
   d. all of the above.
   e. a and b only.

7. The two major formats mentioned in your textbook for citing works in a speech bibliography are from the
   a. American Library Association (ALA) and National Bibliography Center (NBC).
   b. Educational Testing Service (ETS) and American Style Manual (ASM).
   c. International Citation Index (ICI) and American Communication Association (ACA).
   d. Social Science Manual (SSM) and Humanities Bibliography Guide (HBG).
   e. Modern Language Association (MLA) and American Psychological Association (APA).

8. During the oral citation of your sources in a speech you should state the following *except*:
   a. The source
   b. The reference date
   c. The rational behind the source
   d. The sources credentials
   e. none of the above

9. Secondary sources of research does not come in the from of
   a. Magazines
   b. Audience Surveys
   c. Books
   d. Newspapers
   e. Internet

10. What piece of information *should not be included* on a note card when gathering data
    a. Page number of the work
    b. Author's name
    c. A description of the author's credentials
    d. Heading
    e. Summary of information from material

Essay Question

11. Describe the distinct characteristics of the three areas of where your research will come from.

12. Explain the advantages of using a local newspaper for your research efforts.

Chapter 7
Supporting Your Ideas

Public speakers have a responsibility to themselves and their audience to use the most accurate information possible to support their ideas. Throughout your formal educational experience you have probably heard your teachers tell you that you need to "add more development" or "your ideas need to be more concrete" with your assignments. What they are trying to tell you is that you need to add more examples, statistics, and testimony to support your ideas. In other words, take your abstract ideas and make them more tangible. The practiced art of supporting your ideas can make the difference between a poor speech and an outstanding speech.

As you learned in the analyzing your audience chapter, your examples, statistics, and testimony must be relevant and applicable to your audience. So as you go through the vast array of research to support your ideas, make sure that the support you choose significantly adds value to your speech and enhances the learning experience of your audience. Moreover, your critical thinking skills need to be sharpened so that the materials used in your speech really do back up your ideas.

As you assemble the materials for your speech, extra care is needed in assessing that your supporting materials are precise, applicable, and dependable. Questions that you should be asking yourself are, "Am I quoting highly regarded, authorized sources?" "Am I using statistical measures properly?" "Are my examples typical?" In addition to asking these critical questions of yourself while preparing your speech, those same questions can be asked when listening to your classmates' speeches.

In this chapter we will be focusing on the customary forms of supporting materials: examples, statistics, and testimony. As a result of drawing on the tips in this chapter you will be able to use these three fundamental strategies to support your ideas for your future speeches and on your pathway to success.

EXAMPLES

It is commonly known that clear, tangible examples have a lasting impression on listeners' attitudes and actions. A speech without examples may lead your audience to think that your thoughts are abstract, impersonal, and not real. Conversely, a speech filled with useful examples will help your audience interpret your ideas as specific, personal, lively, and believable. We will be examining various types of examples for you to implement in your upcoming speeches—making your pathway to success vibrant and memorable for your audience.

Brief Examples

A **brief example** is often noted as being a specific instance, and may be referred to in passing, to illustrate a point. A brief example that is verifiable means that the example can be supported by a source that the audience can check. Verifiable examples are a strong way to support your ideas, and audiences find examples that are realistic to be more credible. Consider the following brief examples from student speeches.

In Dave's speech regarding the dangers of obesity he uses to the following brief example, "obesity can not only increase the danger of psychological problems in kids, like eating disorders, depression, and anxiety problems, but it also can put them at risk of physiological problems including diabetes, high blood pressure, and heart disease.

In Ron's speech persuading his audience about the possible dangers of working yourself to death he uses, this brief example to illustrate his point: "workplace stresses can double the rate of death from heart disease, according to a 2002 study of 812 healthy employees."

Both Dave and Ron used brief examples to illustrate and clarify what they meant regarding obesity and workplace stress. Their examples are verifiable and realistic, thus establishing a strong credibility with their audience.

Narratives

Narratives are also called anecdotes, illustrations, and extended examples. The narrative is longer and more detailed than the brief example. Narratives are an attractive option for you to develop your ideas and draw your audience into your speech. Another place to use a narrative is to draw your audience in by telling a good anecdote in the introduction of your speech. Using a story in the introduction will allow you to connect with your audience through a good story. Stories are often easier to remember and this allows you to maintain good eye contact, because you are not constantly referring to your notes. In addition, because stories are easier to remember, a story helps you build good momentum. The beginning of a speech is like a runner at the starting blocks, and telling stories gives you an edge, like getting a running start in a race. However, make sure that your narrative directly relates to your speech topic and the specific point you are trying to make. It is easy to get off on an unrelated tangent.

A student in a public speaking class decided to use this narrative example in her introduction to a persuasive speech:

> "When I started college two years ago, I was new to handling my money. On my first day of college, I was attracted to the tables set out on the quad with the cool blankets with our school's logo on them, and they were giving them away for free if I signed up for a credit card. I figured, how can this hurt? I won't get into trouble, I know my financial limit and not only that, the blanket would be great to have during the upcoming football season. Two years later I have collected five more credit cards and found myself owing these credit card companies more than $27,000. I didn't realize that I was paying 19.5% in interest and I only made the minimum payments because my boss cut my hours due to slowing business. I was in real trouble and did not know what to do. I'm here to persuade you to cut up your credit cards and if you are in debt, I will show you strategies to become debt free. It may take a while but it is best for your financial well-being."

This narrative example discusses the dangers of getting into credit card debt and the speaker uses herself as an example to personalize her idea. The narrative example above is effective because most of her classmates have been exposed to those tables with the fun "free" gifts for signing up for a credit card.

Moreover, she gathered information about her classmates regarding this topic in her audience survey which will be discussed at length in the Audience-focused activity chapter.

Hypothetical Example

A **hypothetical example** is speculative, imaginative, and fictional. The hypothetical example cannot be verified for its legitimacy, and can be either in the brief or narrative format. A speaker using the hypothetical example is painting a picture for the audience using an imaginary circumstance. A speaker would use this strategy simply to support a general theory. A public speaking student used this hypothetical example in his speech introduction about the onsets of panic attacks.

"Imagine that you are on an isolated island—trees sway in the light wind, the hot sun is on your face, and the scent of tropical vegetation is in the air. Suddenly, the sound of distant crash breaks your joy. What do you do—panic? What would you do if you found yourself in such a situation? I'm here to inform you about the causes and effects of panic attacks."

Why Examples are a Viable Option to Reinforce Your Message

Examples are an excellent way to clarify unfamiliar or difficult ideas. That is why so many teachers use examples in the classroom. Examples put theoretical ideas into tangible terms and build inclusivity and credibility with your audience. Be careful to use examples that are representative, and do not deal with uncommon or extraordinary cases. Your listeners are likely to feel deceived if they believe you have chosen an uncharacteristic example to prove a general point.

People are fascinated with people. Whenever you talk to a general audience you can include examples that add human interest to your speech. The abstract idea becomes more meaningful when applied to a person. Which of the following would you likely respond to?

Many college students are struggling to pay for their college education, and many of you are currently are working part-time jobs just to make ends meet.

Or

Our classmate Vince is currently working 30 hours a week at the local grocery store, and has earned $3,000 annually in scholarships from the Bell Family Educational Foundation here in town just to cover his costs of attending college.

As you can see, the second example has been worded in humanizing terms to illustrate the speaker's point of how to pay for their college education. Since the speaker's classmates see Vince every day in class they are able to connect the subject matter to the person behind the example, making it a real experience for them. The more concrete your description is the more likely your audience will be engaged in your message.

STATISTICS

Statistics are used to quantify the speaker's idea, and are mentioned in passing to simplify or bolster a speaker's points. The use of statistics makes the speaker's claim credible and clear. One pitfall many public speakers fall into is to clutter their speech with statistics. Using a large amount of numbers in a short span of time in your speech is a sure way to confuse, and lose, your audience. So use statistics in moderation, and make them easy for your audience to grasp. When using statistics for your speeches, be sure to evaluate them using the following benchmarks: Are the statistics used representative? Are the statistics measured correctly? And are the statistics from a reliable source?

Are Your Statistics Representative

Let us say that you took a random poll in your public speaking class and found out that 50% of your classmates are part of a social networking site. After class you head on over to your college's newspaper and talk to the editor stating that 50% of the students attending the college are a part of a social networking site, and that an article in the college paper needs to be written on this theme. Would this discussion with the college's newspaper editor be accurate?

Members of one public speaking class would not be a large enough survey sample to accurately represent an entire college or university. Other points that need to be addressed with your sample are how many men or women were surveyed, what majors were represented in the sample, and what was the age range of the sample? When surveying a cluster of subjects, remember to have your sample collection represent the population as much as possible.

The Mean, The Median, and The Mode

The mean, median, and mode are three kinds of "averages." The **mean** can be defined as the average value of a group of numbers. The mean of a group of numbers is found by adding the numbers and dividing that number by the number of numbers. For instance if we were to add $8 + 4 + 7 + 2 + 6$ that would total 27. So we would take 27 and divide that number by 5 (the number of numbers) and the mean would be 5.4.

The **median** may be defined as the "middle number" in a group of numbers arranged from highest to lowest. So using the set of numbers in the above example we would reorder the list of numbers from highest to lowest (8, 7, 6, 4, 2) and the median would 6.

The **mode** is defined as the value that occurs most frequently in a group of numbers. If no number is repeated, then there is no mode for the list. So continuing with the previous examples of the numbers (8, 7, 6, 4, 2), there would be no mode considering none of the numbers is repeated. However, if we changed the numbers to 8, 8, 4, 3, 2, and 0, the mode would be 8.

Are Your Statistics From a Reliable Source?

As a public speaker researching for your speech, you must be aware of the possibility of favoritism in the use of numbers. Since statistics can be interpreted and manipulated in so many ways, you should look for figures that are gathered by neutral, nonpartisan sources. When looking at statistical information, take the time to examine who collected the statistics, why the statistics were compiled, when they were compiled, where the subjects were surveyed, and who comprised the pool of people surveyed. In short, you need to understand the motives behind the survey's statistics to understand the context of the numbers more precisely.

Say for example that there was a new wonder drug that was put on the market that guarantees that if your take this pill you would be able to lose one to two pounds a day. How would this pill be received if the message was delivered by a pharmaceutical company or by the U.S. Food and Drug Administration (FDA)? One question to ask yourself is, who can profit from this pill being sold? Obviously the FDA would not have an interest, since there would be no gain to the FDA if this pill were to sell millions of units of products. It is a different situation if the same product were offered by a private pharmaceutical company offering statistics that the pill will quicken your metabolism by 15 percent and kill off fat cells. If you get suspicious about the statistical claims, then verify your concerns and start asking the tough questions regarding the validity of the company's claims.

Your critical thinking skills will be given a workout when competing statistics are offered by groups who are for and against controversial topics like budget deficit reforms or health care reform. When examining divisive issues where the solutions are not clear-cut take the time to look at each of the group's motives. As a speaker, you must be aware that numbers are not cut and dried, they offer numerous possibilities of interpretation. When in doubt try finding statistics that are compiled by impartial independent sources.

The Implementation of Your Statistics

When using your statistics in a speech there is a three-point process to implement those statistics effectively.

1. Identify the Source of your Statistic

2. State Your Statistic

3. Explain Your Statistic

The audience needs to know where these statistics you are using came from. Citing your source for the statistic will often build or crash your credibility. By stating a reputable source when introducing your statistic, you can tip the audience that an important statistic will be delivered so your audience will pay closer attention to your point. After stating the source of your statistic, remember to actually state the statistic you are citing. Finally, relate your statistic to your audience, because statistics alone do not clarify themselves. Statistics need to be interpreted and related to your audience so they can make sense of them. This is almost certainly the single most vital step you can take to make statistics successful in your speeches.

One suggestion for using statistics in your speech is to illustrate them on a PowerPoint slide. The visual of the statistic will help your audience make sense of the numbers being presented. Here is an example of how a public speaker might use a statistic and visual to meet the needs of the audience.

According to my in-class survey, 70% of the class was born in 1990. According to a survey conducted by the U.S. National Center for Health Statistics, those born in 1990 have a life expectancy of 75.4 years. Due to advances in medicine and general health care we can expect to have longer life expectancies than those born in 1970, where on average, they are expected to live only about 70.8 years. Furthermore, because our class comprises 75% women, our class will fare better as a whole. As you can see on the chart, the women in the class have a life expectancy of 78.8 years, as opposed to the 71.8-year life expectancy for the men.

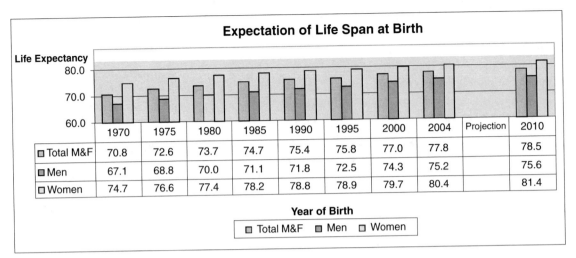

Expectation of Life Span at Birth

	1970	1975	1980	1985	1990	1995	2000	2004	Projection	2010
Total M&F	70.8	72.6	73.7	74.7	75.4	75.8	77.0	77.8		78.5
Men	67.1	68.8	70.0	71.1	71.8	72.5	74.3	75.2		75.6
Women	74.7	76.6	77.4	78.2	78.8	78.9	79.7	80.4		81.4

Year of Birth

Total M&F   Men   Women

Source: US National Center for Health Statistics.

The speaker used a visual to help explain her statistics regarding the life expectancy of her classmates. First she identified the sources of her statistics, then she stated the statistics, and finally she made them real for her classmates in the room. More about using visual aides in your speech will be covered in Chapter 12.

A challenge in the research area is finding accurate and appropriate statistics located in books, magazines, newspapers, academic journals, government publications, and business reports. In addition to these helpful sources, there are books that are wholly dedicated to statistics, such as *The World Almanac and Book of Facts* and the *United Nations' Statistical Yearbook*. These books hold statistics on everything from world population to the U.S. economy.

Aside from using physical books, using the Internet is a cut-above method to find more well-timed statistics to support your speech. When using the Internet take the time to evaluate the quality of the sources you are using. A first-rate source to be familiar with is the *Statistical Abstract of the United States* Web site (www.census.gov/statab/www). The *Statistical Abstract of the United States* provides statistics on many social and economic issues that affect everyday life in the United States.

TESTIMONY

A common conversation that happens at colleges and universities around the country revolves around, "who should I take for my speech class?" Depending on your friends they may recommend one teacher over another for a variety of reasons such as "little homework assigned throughout the term," a teacher's sense of humor, or maybe even that the teacher is an easy "A." Also consider the choice of what movies you will watch, or which restaurant you will eat at after the show. Many of these decisions are derived from the opinions of other people in which you trust their judgment. Your friends' influences and insights are very persuasive in the decisions you make.

These examples illustrate the influence that the testimony of others has on us in our everyday decisions. Just as you are likely to be swayed by your friend's recommendation about which class to take, audience members tend to respect the opinions of people who have special knowledge or experience on the speech topic being delivered. By quoting or paraphrasing such people, you can give your ideas greater strength and impact. There are two kinds of testimony, expert testimony and peer testimony.

Expert Testimony

In most speeches you will probably rely on **expert testimony**, testimony from people who are recognized authorities in their field. Expert testimony is especially helpful for student speakers because citing the views of people who are experts is a good way to lend credibility to your speeches. It shows that you are not just sharing your own unproven opinions, but established experts knowledgeable about your speech topic support your position. Your listeners should perceive the person quoted to be an actual authority. For example the Pope would be an accepted authority by a Roman Catholic audience, but not if he were speaking to a Baptist or Buddhist listener base. The best testimony comes from subject-matter experts whose qualifications your audience will recognize.

In an informative speech discussing the impact of negative ads with undecided voters a student public speaker used testimony from a recognized expert in the field in her speech:

"Psychologist Dr. Drew Westen, who wrote *The Political Brain*, said fear-based attack ads are effective because they tap into a voter's subconscious."

In another quote using expert testimony the speaker says,

"Those kinds of gut-level reactions tell us things like, 'I don't feel like this person is telling us the truth,'" Westen said. "Unless someone is a really good con man, those reactions are extremely helpful. The conscious brain processes only a tiny percent of information."

Quoting an expert in the field of studying psychological impacts of negative ads, lent credibility to the speaker's topic as well as to herself as a public speaker. Remember, however, when quoting an expert, to make sure that the person's name, organization, and title are correct. Having incorrect information about the "expert" will hurt your credibility as a public speaker.

Peer Testimony

Another type of testimony often used in speeches is **peer testimony**, the opinions of ordinary people who have first-hand experience on the topic. This kind of testimony is especially valuable because it gives a more personal viewpoint on issues than can be gained from expert testimony. It conveys the feelings, the knowledge, and the insight of people who speak with the voice of genuine experience. For example, a student public speaker delivered a speech regarding the foreclosure process and the psychological effects of losing one's home. The speaker shared a story from Sandy Anderson who lost her home shortly after moving to Florida to personalize the pain of losing one's home.

"My new job didn't provide health insurance. I'd thought that wouldn't be a big deal. I was wrong. Judy's (Sandy's daughter) medications had always been covered by my employer's health insurance plan. Now they were coming out of my pocket at $1,500 a month. Our mortgage was $1,300 a month and I was grossing $3,500 a month. Negative financing is okay for the federal government, but for everyday people, deficits are not permissible. I simply could not do it all. I needed to make a choice—Judy's health or the house."

This testimony is powerful because it puts a face and a name to the loss of someone's home. In addition, it allows us a glimpse into the different aspects of life and finances that play a prominent role in the housing foreclosure. No expert testimony can capture the pain that was endured by Sandy Anderson.

Quoting versus Paraphrasing

Testimony may be communicated by either quoting or paraphrasing. A direct **quotation** may be defined as a testimony that is presented word for word. In contrast, **paraphrasing** may be defined as restating or summarizing a source's ideas in one's own words.

The general guideline is that quotations are most successful when they are brief, when they convey your meaning better than you can, and when they are particularly convincing. If you find a quotation that meets these standards, then deliver the quotation word for word.

Paraphrasing surpasses a direct quotation in two situations: (1) when the wording of a quotation is confusing or awkward, as is often found with government documents; (2) when a quotation is longer than two or three sentences. Audiences will tune out through a lengthy quotation. The audience wants to hear your thoughts and ideas as opposed to reciting someone else's points.

When using testimony in your speech accuracy is needed with the quote and paraphrase. This means making sure that you do not misquote someone, do not violate the meaning of statements you are paraphrasing, and that you do not quote out of context. Also, verification is needed that the person you are quoting is qualified on the subject matter of your speech. Would it make any sense to quote the surgeon general about the state of the world economy? I hope not, but if you were asking the surgeon general about a health issue, you are in the money. Moreover, when quoting or paraphrasing, state the person's name before presenting the testimony. For instance, "Larry Kingsley, the President of the National Bottled Water Association, says that water sales will increase by 30% in the next three years." Using testimony is a value-added method of supporting your ideas on your pathway to success.

Summary: Supporting your ideas

Three good ways to support your ideas are examples, statistics, and testimony. If you read any newspaper or magazine article you will see how examples, statistics, and testimony add support to the author's ideas. The same can be said for speeches. When using examples you have three different options to support your speeches: the brief, the narrative, and the hypothetical example.

A brief example is often noted as being a specific instance and may be referred to in passing, to illustrate a point. A brief example that is verifiable means that the example can be supported by a source that the audience can check. A narrative example is also known as anecdotes, illustrations, and extended examples. The narrative is longer and more detailed than the brief example—much like a story. A hypothetical example is speculative, imaginative, and fictional. The hypothetical example cannot be verified for its validity, and can be either in the brief or narrative format but it is used to illustrate a general point.

The next way to support your ideas is to use statistics. Statistics quantify the speaker's ideas. An error that many speakers fall into is to clutter their speeches with numbers to impress their audience members. So use statistics in moderation, and make them easy for your audience to grasp. When using statistics for your speeches, be sure to evaluate them using the following springboards: Are the statistics representative? Are the statistics measured correctly? Are the statistics from a reliable source? When implementing your statistics in a speech there is a three-step process to weave those statistics effectively.

1. Identify the Source of your Statistic

2. State Your Statistic

3. Explain Your Statistic

The final way to support your ideas is to use testimony in your speech. There are two types of testimony to choose from, expert and peer testimony. Peer testimony may be defined as stating the opinions of ordinary people who have first-hand experience on the topic. This kind of testimony is especially valuable because it gives a more personal viewpoint on issues than cannot be gained from expert testimony. Peer testimony conveys the feelings, the knowledge, and the insight of people who speak from genuine first-hand experience.

Another option you may have is using expert testimony. Expert testimony may be defined as using quotes or paraphrases from people who are acknowledged authorities in their field. Testimony may be communicated by either quoting or paraphrasing. A direct quotation is testimony that is presented word for word. In contrast, paraphrasing restates or summarizes a source's ideas in one's own words.

In writing your speech you have three avenues to choose from to support your ideas: examples, statistics, and testimony. Using these three strategies will bring a vibrancy to your message and a relevant learning experience for your audience on your pathway to success.

Name: _____

True-False

1. T **F**   As a speaker, you should usually avoid examples when explaining complex or unfamiliar ideas.

2. T **F**   The median is established by summing all the items in a group and dividing by the number of items.

3. **T** F   Peer testimony is derived from the opinions from ordinary people with firsthand experience or insight on a topic.

4. **T** F   An advantage of using examples in a speech is that they put abstract ideas into concrete terms that listeners can easily understand.

5. **T** F   Unlike testimony, which can easily be quoted out of context, statistics are difficult to manipulate for biased purposes.

Multiple Choice

6. The more _____ your examples, the greater impact they are likely to have.

   a. hypothetical
   b. intricate
   c. rare
   d. authoritative
   e. clear

7. An imaginary story that makes a general point is called a(n)

   a. fictitious example.
   b. insincere example.
   c. actual example.
   d. hypothetical example.
   e. man-made example.

8. To say that the *median* house value in San Francisco is $800,000 is to say that

   a. more houses are valued at $800,000 than other houses.
   b. when you average all the values of houses in San Francisco, the result is $800,000.
   c. when you list all the houses in order, $800,000 is the middle value.
   d. no house in San Francisco is valued less than $800,000.
   e. none of the above.

9. When using statistics in a speech, you should usually

   a. alter the statistics to make your point.
   b. cite precisely the exact numbers and NOT round off.
   c. quicken your rate of speech when providing statistics.
   d. avoid cluttering your speech with too many statistics.
   e. do not reveal the source of the statistics.

10. If you quoted Stanford business professor Lance Cash on the current trends of American business schools, you would be using _____ testimony.

    a. authoritative.
    b. professional.
    c. expert.
    d. amateur.
    e. peer.

Essay

11. Explain the differences among the mean, the median, and the mode as statistical measures.

12. Explain the differences among the three types of examples discussed in the textbook. How can each be used effectively to support a speaker's ideas?

Pillar 3

Speech Preparation: Organizing and Outlining your way to Communicating a Successful Message

Chapter 8

Organizing and Outlining Your Speech

"In order to be the winner you were born to be, you must plan to win and prepare to win. Then and only then, can you legitimately expect to win."
—ZIG ZIGLAR (AMERICAN AUTHOR, SALESPERSON, AND MOTIVATIONAL SPEAKER)

Succeeding in public speaking requires a great deal of planning and organizing. Public speaking gets a bad rap for being one of the more frightening events someone may have to do. The bulk of your success as a public speaker happens during the planning and organizing phases in your speech preparation process and not during that brief time at the podium. Those who are terrified to be at the podium are more than likely the same people who did not plan for that event. Mark Twain said it best, "it usually takes more than three weeks to prepare a good impromptu speech." Do you honestly think that the people who are terrified of public speaking spent any time planning for their moment at the podium?

The process of organizing and outlining your speech will take much of the nervousness out of the public speaking experience, because planning and organizing your speech is an empowering process. Being organized is a quality trait that will make your life more manageable. Organization allows you to be more efficient with your time, it allows you to have mental clarity, and you will feel more like the windshield and not the bug. Organizing your thoughts will build your confidence as a public speaker, and in return, your audience will find you more truthful and proficient.

In the public speaking realm organizing your thoughts allows you to communicate the most important points of your speech, and serve your audience's need more effectively. Having understandable and reasoned thoughts will send the message to your audience that you have taken the time to think through your message, and your audience will respond positively to your message and to you as a public speaker. On the other hand a disorganized speech makes it very difficult for the audience to follow along with your message, therefore the probability of your audience daydreaming and thinking of everything else besides your presentation is highly likely. One goal to have is to organize and outline your speech in a way that will engage the listener and make a strong impact on your audience.

By placing yourself in the audience's position you will realize that members of your audience demand a logical presentation as opposed to listening to someone aimlessly rambling from one unrelated issue to another. Your listeners do not have the luxury of rereading a particular part of your speech; they need to hear your message the first time around. Think of your speeches as being like your favorite television programs with a clear beginning, middle, and end. As a speaker you need to clearly and seamlessly lead your audience through the beginning, middle, and end of your presentation.

By having a strong grasp of the three parts of a speech, the introduction, the body, and the conclusion, you will be able to navigate your audience so they can capture your core message. The heart of a speech is the body, which is the longest component of your speech, and that contains all of your examples, statistics, and testimony supporting your main points. So once the main points in your body are clearly established, supported, and written, from there it is much easier to write the introduction and conclusion. The process of organizing the body of the speech starts when you determine the main points.

MAIN POINTS

The main points in your presentation are the focal points of your message. Having your main points established clarifies your intended residual message that you want your audience to grasp. Meticulous selection and order of your main points will distinguish a fruitless speech from a flourishing speech. So how do you select the main points of your speech? Often the main points will emerge as you research the topic of your speech followed by evaluating the soundness of your supporting materials. Researching for your speech is an interesting process that will be covered in chapter six: researching your sources for the ultimate credibility. When you embark on your research journey, you may have preconceived notions as to the desired main points, but there are times that those themes do not emerge when gathering materials to support your topic. One way to illustrate this idea is to think about your food cravings. Let's say that you are going home and you want to have Chinese food, but when looking in the refrigerator, all you have are the ingredients to make Mexican food. As much as you want Chinese food, it looks like it's going to be Mexican food. By going with the research flow, your main points will materialize, and once those main points have been established, it is much easier to accurately write your central idea.

Number of Points

A common question that is asked by college-level public speakers is "how many main points should my speech have?" The usual rule of thumb is your speech should have between two and five main points. One factor to consider is how much time you have to present your speech. Some assignments may be for you to speak for two minutes or even forty-five minutes. It would be very difficult to adequately discuss three main points in two-minute speech or two main points in a forty-five minute speech. Another factor to consider is that as you research, several important themes may surface and it would be your job to present those themes. By limiting the number of main points to between two and five your audience will have an easier time remembering your main points. In contrast, if you have too many main points in the body of your speech, your audience will have a difficult time remembering your main points. The purpose of limiting the number of your main points is so that they stand out and are remembered by your audience.

ORGANIZATIONAL STRATEGIES FOR YOUR MAIN POINTS

Once your main points have been established you can now think about where in the body of your speech they will go. Much like a puzzle you can see how the different parts (each of your main points) fit together and how you can best organize them. Clear organization is vital to effective public speaking.

Your audience must be able to grasp the advancement of your ideas in your presentation from your introduction through the conclusion. The effectiveness of organizing the main points of the body will fortify the clarity and persuasiveness of your ideas. Understanding your topic, your purpose, and your audience will help you decide the most effective organizational strategy for your speech.

Chronological Order

Speeches arranged in the **chronological order** follow a time pattern. The main points used in the chronological order may describe a series of events in the order in which they occurred. For example:

Specific Purpose: To inform my audience of the professional achievements of Arnold Schwarzenegger.

Central Idea: Arnold Schwarzenegger's professional achievements range from the time he was the Mr. Olympia bodybuilding champion, a professional businessman, and an action movie star, to the governor of California.

Main Points:

I. Arnold Schwarzenegger reached the pinnacle of the body building world by winning the Mr. Olympia title seven times during the 1970's through 1980.

II. While Schwarzenegger was active in professional bodybuilding, he parlayed his popularity into numerous successful business ventures making him a millionaire by the time he was 30 years old.

III. In the early 1980's after retiring from the world of bodybuilding Arnold Schwarzenegger began a successful movie career, becoming a worldwide celebrity.

IV. Schwarzenegger was engaged in public service roles while acting, and later became the governor of California in 2003.

The chronological order is also used in speeches explaining a process or demonstrating how to do something. For example:

Specific Purpose: To inform my audience how to treat a sprained ankle.

Central Idea: To properly treat a sprained ankle requires you to stay off your injured ankle and rest, ice your ankle, compress the sprained ankle, elevate your ankle, and gradually put weight on your ankle.

Main Points:

I. When treating a sprained your ankle you must keep your weight off your ankle and rest.

II. Ice needs to be immediately applied for about 20 minutes every hour until the swelling goes down.

III. Your ankle needs to be compressed with an elastic bandage to help reduce the swelling.

IV. Elevate your ankle above your heart for two to three hours a day to reduce swelling.

V. Once you can put some weight on your ankle, light stretching and walking will help strengthen your ankle and bring it back to health.

The chronological order is especially useful for informative speeches.

Spatial Order

Speeches using the **spatial order** follow a directional pattern. Main points continue from top to bottom, left to right, east to west, front to back, inside to outside, or some other route. For example:

Specific Purpose: To inform my audience of the key visitors' attractions around the San Francisco Bay area.

Central Idea: The San Francisco Bay area has vibrant visitors' attractions in the North Bay, East Bay, South Bay, and finally along the peninsula.

Main Points:

 I. In the North Bay a prominent visitors' attraction is Muir Woods National Monument.

 II. Located in the East Bay, a fun-filled day can be had at Jack London Square in Oakland.

 III. The South Bay is often referred to as the "Silicon Valley," the home of technology, so why not a trip to the Tech Museum of Innovation in downtown San Jose?

 IV. Along the peninsula you can visit one of the most famous bridges in the world, the Golden Gate Bridge, spanning from San Francisco to Marin County.

When preparing an informative speech, the spatial order might be an appropriate organizational choice.

Causal Order

The **causal order** strategy is used to underline the cause-effect relationship. The causal order regularly contains two main points, one addressing the causes of an event, the other concentrating on the effects. Depending on your topic you can either dedicate your first main point to the causes and the second to the effects, or you can tackle the effects first followed by the causes.

Specific Purpose: To inform my audience of the causes of rising gas prices and their effects on our lifestyles.

Central Idea: Higher demand for oil in China and India has led to higher gasoline prices in the United States, affecting our daily lifestyles.

Main Points:

 I. Growing demand for oil in countries like China and India has lowered the supply of oil, therefore causing higher prices at the pump here in the United States.

 II. Higher gas prices have made our food cost more, thus we have less money in our wallets, which shrinks our lifestyle choices.

Because of its adaptability the causal order can be used for both informative and persuasive speeches.

Problem-Solution Order

Main points structured in the **problem-solution order** are divided into two key parts. The first explains the existence and seriousness of a problem. The second reveals a realistic solution to the problem. For example:

Specific Purpose: To persuade my audience that they should donate their organs because of the dire need for organs for transplantation.

Central Idea: Approximately 77 people receive organ transplants every day, but roughly 18 people die each day waiting for transplants that cannot take place because of the shortage of donated organs.

Main Points:

    I. Thousands of American lives are lost every year because a lifesaving organ donation did not become available for a patient in need.

    II. You can save lives by donating your organs after you die, so become a donor by registering with the National Organ and Tissue Donor Registry.

The problem-solution order is most appropriate for persuasive speeches.

Topical Order

Speeches that are *not* chronological, spatial, causal, or problem-solution order usually fall into topical order. The **topical order** is derived when you divide the speech topics into subtopics, each of which becomes a main point in the speech. The main points are not part of a chronological, spatial, causal, or problem-solution sequence, but are simply parts of the whole.

    Specific Purpose: To inform my audience of the five kinds of environmentally friendly cars.

    Central Idea: The following five types of automobile are considered to be environmentally friendly cars: Hydrogen-powered, hybrids, bio-diesel, bio-ethanol, and liquefied petroleum gas (LPG).

Main Points:

    I. The first type of environmentally friendly car is the hydrogen-powered vehicle that only releases water.

    II. Hybrid vehicles commonly use two types of power sources gasoline and an on-board rechargeable energy storage system.

    III. Bio-diesel vehicles use a clean burning alternative fuel, produced from domestic, renewable resources that contain no petroleum.

    IV. Bio-ethanol fuel is mainly produced by the sugar fermentation process.

    V. Vehicles powered by liquefied petroleum gas (LPG) use a mixture of hydrocarbon gases, replacing chlorofluorocarbons to reduce damage to the ozone layer.

The topical order is an effective organizational strategy for both informative and persuasive speeches. In a persuasive speech, each of your topical subdivisions are the reasons/arguments why a speaker has chosen to advocate for a certain point of view.

The topical order is the most commonly used organizational strategy in public speaking because it is applicable to almost any subject and any kind of speech.

How Much Time Should I Allocate for Each of My Main Points?

The main points of your speech are the driver of your message. Each of your main points needs to be an independent idea from the other main points in your speech. Yet each point should be connected to the other points as well. Since you have boiled your topic down to a few main themes, now consider how much time you will spend developing each of those points for your presentation. The greater the importance of your main points the more time you will spend discussing that main point. Furthermore, the amount of time spent on each main point depends on the quantity and complexity of the supporting materials for each theme.

The average American speaks at approximately 125 to 150 words per minute. Use this numerical gauge a guide as to how many words you should have in your speech. For example if you are delivering a five-minute presentation, you should have between 625 and 750 words in your entire presentation. Keep this in mind, when you are at the podium your rate of speech will be a lot faster due to adrenaline, so plan accordingly.

SUPPORTING MATERIALS

Your supporting materials will come in the way of examples, statistics, and testimony. There are three types of examples to support your main points, brief examples, narrative examples, and hypothetical examples. Statistics quantify the speaker's ideas and should be used in moderation so they stand out more and become more memorable to your audience. If too many statistics are used in a compacted place in your speech, that is a sure way to confuse and lose your audience. Testimony is the third way to support your main points. There are two types of testimony a public speaker can use to strengthen his or her main points, peer testimony and expert testimony. Peer testimony is the opinions of ordinary people who have first-hand experience on the topic. This kind of testimony is especially valuable because it gives a more personal viewpoint on issues than can be gained from expert testimony. In most speeches you will probably rely on expert testimony, and that is testimony from people who are acknowledged authorities in their fields. Citing the views of those who are experts is a good way to lend credibility to your speeches. Further discussion about supporting your ideas for your presentation is discussed in more detail in Chapter 7.

CONNECTIVES

Connectives are an important component to a successfully assembled speech. The concept of connectives is much like driving a stick shift car. Each gear represents one of your main points and your clutch work represents the connectives and the smooth ride of driving a stick shift car. Think about how when you first learned how to drive a stick shift and you were still trying to figure out the balance between the clutch and the gas. Often times at the beginning stages of learning how to drive a stick the ride was clunky and you may have even stalled the car a time or two. The same goes for constructing a speech with outstanding main points but without the connectives to pull the message together for an orderly speech.

Connectives are words or phrases that join one thought to another and reveal the relationship between them—much like going from first gear to second gear efficiently. There are four types of connectives that would be appropriate for a speech: transitions, internal previews, internal summaries, and signposts. Connectives are like the fluid gear shifts that make the ride smooth for your passengers or, in our context, our audience.

Transitions

Transitions are words or phrases that reveal when a speaker has just finished one thought, and is moving on to another. In theory, the transitions state both the idea the speaker is leaving and the idea she or he is coming up to. Here is an example from the donating your organs speech.

"We have just heard how so many lives are lost because there are not enough organ donors, let's see what you can do to solve this tragic problem by becoming an organ donor."

Another example for transitions would be following up on our travel destinations in the San Francisco Bay area example.

"Now that you have spent an exciting day at Oakland's Jack London Square, let's head south to the Silicon Valley's Tech Museum of Innovation."

Internal Previews

Internal previews give the audience a "heads up" so they know what the speaker will discuss next; however, internal previews are more detailed than transitions. An internal preview works like the preview statement in a speech introduction, but it happens in the body of the speech, as the speaker is starting to discuss a main point. For example:

"My next point will discuss the importance of applying ice for at least 20 minutes per hour to your sprained ankle for a speedy recovery."

"I will now explain how driving a hybrid vehicle will save you money and the environment."

You will hardly ever need an internal preview for each of your main points, but if you think it will help the listeners stay on track with your message, then go ahead and use an internal preview.

Internal Summaries

Internal summaries remind the audience of what was just stated. A speaker may have just completed a point that was particularly complex or complicated and the internal summary reviews what the speaker just talked about in a concise way. So the next time you have a challenging or convoluted main point to discuss, consider taking the time to summarize your point before moving to the next main point. For example:

"In short we have seen how Arnold Schwarzenegger used his business acumen to start a bricklaying business and a mail order business, and then used his profits to invest in real estate in Santa Monica, California, eventually became an owner of a shopping mall in Columbus, Ohio. Schwarzenegger's tenacity in business made him a millionaire by the time he was 30 years old—even before his movie career took off."

Signposts

Signposts are concise statements that show the audience where you are in the speech. This approach is particularly effective because it keeps the audience in the loop as to where the speech is going. A common signpost strategy is to use numbers as a way of letting your audience know where you are in your speech. Here is an example that uses a basic numbering scheme to tell the audience which main point the speaker is on regarding the causes of high gasoline prices:

The first reason for higher gas prices is the higher demand for oil in growing countries like China and India.

The second reason for higher gas prices is the war in the Middle East.

The third reason for higher gas prices is that there are too few refineries in the United States.

The fourth reason for higher gas prices is that the fuel economy in our cars and trucks are too low, which drains the oil supply.

Signposting is a simple yet effective connective strategy that keeps your audience briefed as to where the speaker is in the presentation.

In short, accurately applied connectives can make your speech much more unified and coherent for your audience to comprehend.

OUTLINING THE SPEECH

Henry Ford once said "Thinking is the hardest work there is, which is probably the reason why so few engage in it." Critical thinking is an important facet of the planning, organizing, and outlining of a successful speech. Your **speech outline** is your game plan during the preparation phase of your speech development and requires a good amount of thinking. By outlining your speech you are laying the foundation of the direction of your speech and examining how the pieces of the puzzle come together. Putting together your outline allows you to see your speech in both a big picture view and a more detailed view. The process of outlining requires you to consider if each part (introduction, body, and conclusion) of the speech is fully cultivated, if the supporting materials for your main points are appropriate, and if the main points are properly composed. An outline assures you that your core ideas connect, and there is a logical flow from one point to another.

There are two kinds of outlines you will use in preparing for a speech. First is the **preparation outline** that is a detailed roadmap of your speech. The second type of outline is the **speaker's outline** which is less detailed, but offers valuable delivery cues while you are at the podium. The preparation outline forces you to make a firm decision as to what you will say in your speech, and the supporting materials you will use in your speech.

Your preparation outline includes the labeling of the parts of the speech (introduction, body, conclusion, and bibliography), which can be broken down into the specific purpose, central idea, introduction, main points, subpoints, sub-subpoints, sub-sub subpoints, connectives, conclusion, and the bibliography.

As you can see in the example of a preparation outline, your specific purpose and central idea are documented at the top of the page, above the introduction. A title would go on top of the specific purpose and central idea, but that is optional for a speech, so ask your teacher if a title is needed with your preparation outline. Including your specific purpose with the outline makes it easier to assess how well you have constructed the speech to accomplish your purpose. Moreover, placing your central idea below your specific purpose will allow you to see if your central idea sums up the main points of your presentation.

Your speech will have three parts, the introduction, the body, and the conclusion. Each of these parts needs to be labeled and is usually centered on the page on your preparation outline. The labels distinguish the different parts of a speech and are *not* included in the procedure of symbolization used to classify main points and supporting materials.

A challenging aspect in the outlining process is using a harmonious pattern of symbolization and indentation, also know as your **visual framework**. Main points are identified by Roman numerals and are on the left margin down the page. Your subpoints (components of the main point) are identified by capital letters and are indented to the right equally so as to be lined up with each other. Continuing the visual framework are your sub-subpoints and your sub-sub subpoints, which are also aligned with each other and indented to the right. Here is how they would look on a page.

I. Main point

    A. Subpoint

        1. Sub-subpoint

        2. Sub-subpoint

           a. Sub-sub subpoint

           b. Sub-sub subpoint

II. Main Point

    A. Subpoint

        1. Sub-subpoint

        2. Sub-subpoint

    B. Subpoint

The visual framework of this outline helps you visualize the relationships among the ideas of the speech. Remember that all points at the same level should immediately support the point that is just above and one level to the left in your outline. Here is a sample organizational structure, for a college administration.

I. College President

    A. Vice President of Instruction

        1. Dean of Business

           a. Professors

           b. Adjunct Professors

           c. Staff Assistants

        2. Dean of Language and Creative Arts

           a. Professors

           b. Adjunct Professors

           c. Staff Assistants

        3. Dean of Physical Education

           a. Professors

           b. Adjunct Professors

           c. Staff Assistants

        4. Dean of Science Math and Technology

           a. Professors

           b. Adjunct Professors

           c. Staff Assistants

    B. Vice President of Student Affairs

      1. Dean of Counseling

        a. Counselors

        b. Administrative Staff

      2. Dean of Financial Aid

        a. Financial Aid Clerks

      3. Dean of Admissions

        a. Admissions Staff

        b. Outreach Coordinator

        c. Staff Coordinator

        d. Administrative Staff

Every school employee on this outline is accountable to the employee who is above and one indentation to the left, except for the college president, who is the main point. As you can see, the points all interconnect with each other. Much like a puzzle, just by looking at your outline you can see how your supporting materials fit with the framework of your main points, and how the parts of the speech relate to the speech as a whole.

For example purposes, we used only one or two words to the corresponding point, but your preparation outline *must be in complete sentences*. Giving only vague points rather than detailed ideas does not reveal whether the speaker has thought out his or her ideas. It is really important to get your thoughts out on paper, and to really think out your points in their entirety. Unfortunately beginning public speakers believe they can just go up to the podium and "wing it." But they do not realize that they have not thought through their ideas. By working on your preparation outline, you can spend time writing your sentences, and then rewriting your sentences to capture the thoughts and emotions you want to deliver to your audience for maximum impact. Moreover, by spending time writing your thoughts out as complete sentences you are learning your material and becoming more familiar with how you want to say what you want to say.

In short, if you shortchange yourself during the preparation outline phase in planning for a speech, your efforts will create little value or success when delivering your speech. By stating the contents of your speech (introduction, body, and conclusion) in complete sentences you will ensure that you develop your ideas fully.

Finally, the preparation outline needs to include a bibliography attached at the end of your speech. The bibliography will confirm all the books, magazines, newspapers, and Internet sources you referred to, as well as any interviews or field research you performed.

The two chief bibliographic formats are the Modern Language Association (MLA) and the American Psychological Association (APA). These bibliographic formats are commonly used in your college courses, so ask your teacher his or her preference when documenting your consulted sources. Details of how to document your sources are explained in Chapter 6 on researching your sources.

Sample Special Occasion Speech–Preparation Outline (Complete Sentence Format)
The Acceptance of the Commerce Association's Business Person of the Year Award

Specific Purpose: To entertain my audience and accept the Commerce Association's Business Person of the Year Award.

Central Idea: Three key business mentors have shaped my personal and professional life as I accept the Commerce Association's Business Person of the Year.

Introduction

I. Wow, I would like to thank the selection board at the Commerce Association for honoring me with this prestigious Business Person of the Year award.

    A. I would have never thought in a million years, that out of the many deserving members, I would have been selected to represent the Commerce Association as the Business Person of the Year.

    B. One of Rome's greatest orators Cicero once said, "gratitude is not only the greatest of virtues, but the parent of all others."

(Transition: The valuable members of the Commerce Association have served as outstanding mentors and in some cases surrogate parents for me in my business success and I want to express my gratitude.)

Body

I. First and foremost I need to thank my mentor, my friend, and my father figure, Jim Newell, the guy who graciously nominated me for this award.

    A. When we first met I was an employee in his business and I was simply happy to have a job, and hoped to stay there for the next thirty years of my life.

        1. However, Jim, you saw something in me, and Jim told me something interesting, "profits are better than wages," and that stuck with me.

        2. I then started my hardware store and connected to my community.

        3. Jim would come in and visit me just to touch base, and I appreciate that.

    B. Because of Jim I have a successful business and I spend a lot of time serving my community through the store, and talking to school-age kids about entrepreneurship.

        1. Jim, thank you so very much for your guidance and leadership.

II. Next I would like to thank Isabella Stapleton, the owner of our all-news radio station here in town.

    A. When I first met you I was a caterpillar, very introverted.

        1. With Jim's help you also took me under your wing and pushed me out of the nest so to speak.

        2. Your core message to me was to go socialize, because success is something you can't do by yourself.

        3. I took that advice, and I became a better person because of that wisdom.

B. We will forget about the time you had me as a guest on your radio show and I did not realize my microphone was on.

    1. I was going on and on about how nervous I was, and how I wasn't sure if I could take a big step like this.

    2. After 35 interviews I think I got the hang of the radio thing. I now feel more comfortable talking and connecting with others because, Isabella, you showed me the way.

C. Now I believe I'm a butterfly.

    1. Because of your support, I now will leave a legacy for my two beautiful children.

    2. My business has allowed me to leave my future grandchildren the opportunity to be educated, and to be contributors to our community.

    3. If it weren't for Isabella, I would be living a life that would be "good enough," but not living a life of abundance.

    4. Because of your imprints on me, my relationships with my wife, children, my business associates, and my friends have been richer, so I say thank you for your graciousness and support.

III. Finally, I want to thank my dear friend Max Barker who always encouraged me to take the big picture approach to life.

A. I will always cherish our walks and the discussions about why we do what we do.

    1. In a way you were my workout buddy, because every time we talked, you made me put my sneakers on and we hit the pavement.

B. Being in the hardware business is not the sexiest business to be in, but Max helps me understand that this venture is for my family and for a better quality of life with my loved ones.

    1. So, Max, thanks for the continue support.

(Transition: I have so many more people to thank, but I think I hear the music to wrap things up.)

Conclusion

I. In closing I want to thank the Commerce Association for embracing me as a member and naming me the Business Person of the Year.

A. I know I'm forgetting other valuable people in my development so I'll quote baseball great Yogi Berra who said it best, "I want to thank everybody who made this day necessary."

The Speaking Outline

In public speaking it is not only what you say, but also how you say it that matters and that leads us to understanding the nuances of the speaker's outline. The speaker's outline is used while you are delivering your extemporaneous speech in front of your classmates. The purpose of the speaking outline is to serve as a memory aid while at the podium. It is a more compact translation of your preparation outline that limits itself to key words or phrases so you can remember what you want to say. It is up to you the degree of detail you would like on your speaker's outline. Additional information that should be included in your speaker's outline would be your very important statistics and quotations so you do not forget to tell them to your audience.

Other guiding principles to follow for your speaker's outline are to go along with the framework used in your preparation outline, using the same symbols, and the same indentation pattern. Doing this will make it easier for you to see instantly where you are in the speech at any given moment while you are speaking. You will find this as a great advantage. As you speak you will look down at your outline periodically to make sure you are covering the right ideas in the right order. It will be of little help if you have to hunt around to find where you are every time you look down. Try finding your place if your notes consist of text—much like in an essay format. This could become problematic and can hurt your confidence if you trying to find your place in front of your audience.

A key distinction between the preparation outline and the speaker's outline is that the speaker's outline provides delivery cues for you to follow while delivering your speech. As you progress in your public speaking development you will create your own shorthand for your memory aids on your outline, but for now these guidelines will provide you the tools on your pathway to success.

Sample Special Occasion Speech Essay Format
The Acceptance of the Commerce Association's Business Person of the Year Award

Wow, I would like to thank the selection board at the Commerce Association for honoring me with this prestigious Business Person of the Year award. I would have never thought in a million years, that out of the many deserving members, I would have been selected to represent the Commerce Association as the Business Person of the Year. One of Rome's greatest orators Cicero once said, "gratitude is not only the greatest of virtues, but the parent of all others" The valuable members of the Commerce Association have served as outstanding mentors and in some cases surrogate parents for me in my business success and I want to express my gratitude.

First and foremost I need to thank my mentor, my friend, and my father figure, Jim Newell, the guy who graciously nominated me for this award. When we first met I was an employee in his business and I was simply happy to have a job, and hoped to stay there for the next thirty years of my life. However, Jim, you saw something in me, and you told me something interesting, "profits are better than wages," and that stuck with me. I then started my hardware store and connected to my community. Jim would come in and visit me just to touch base, and I appreciate that. Because of Jim I have a successful business and I spend a lot of time serving my community through the store, and talking to school-age kids about entrepreneurship. Jim, thank you so very much for your guidance and leadership.

Next I would like to thank Isabella Stapleton, the owner of our all-news radio station here in town. When I first met you I was a caterpillar, very introverted. With Jim's help you also took me under your wing and pushed me out of the nest so to speak. Your core message to me was to go socialize, because success is something you can't do by yourself. I took that advice, and I became a better person because of that wisdom. We will forget about the time you had me as a guest on your radio show and I did not realize my microphone was on. I was going on and on about how nervous I was, and how I wasn't sure if I could take a big step like this. After 35 interviews I think I got the hang of the radio thing. I now feel more comfortable talking and connecting with others because, Isabella—you showed me the way. Now I believe I'm a butterfly. Because of your support, I now will leave a legacy for my two beautiful children. My business has allowed me to leave my future grandchildren the opportunity to be educated, and to be contributors to our community. If it weren't for Isabella, I would be living a life that would be "good enough," but not living a life of abundance. Because of your imprints on me, my relationships with my wife, children, my business associates, and my friends have been richer, so I say thank you for your graciousness and support.

Finally, I want to thank my dear friend Max Barker who always encouraged me to take the big picture approach to life. I will always cherish our walks and the discussions about why we do what we do. In a way you were my workout buddy, because every time we talked, you made me put my sneakers on and we hit the pavement. Being in the hardware business is not the sexiest business to be in, but Max helps me understand that this venture is for my family, and a better quality of life with my loved ones. So Max, thanks for the continued support.

I have so many more people to thank, but I think I hear the music to wrap things up. In closing I want to thank the Commerce Association for embracing me as a member and naming me the Business Person of the Year. I know I'm forgetting other valuable people in my development so I'll quote baseball great Yogi Berra who said it best, "I want to thank everybody who made this day necessary."

One tip that may seem like commonsense but often goes overlooked is to make sure your speaking outline is easy to read. If you are delivering a speech for class it is strongly recommended that you type your speaker's outline out so that it is legible. Moreover, utilize the advances in technology by using a larger font, extra space between lines, ample margins, and different colors to bring particular points you are trying to make to your attention. Finally, use only one side of the paper for clarity. If you are using more than one sheet of paper, be sure to number those pages in the 1 of 3, 2 of 3, and 3 of 3 format. Some may recommend using 3 × 5 cards, but that is not advisable. The reason for not using 3 × 5 cards is that you cannot put much information on a card, cards may become shuffled in the wrong order, and you would need to hold those cards, limiting your hand gestures when speaking. In short they can become very distracting to an audience, and let us hope you do not drop those cards while presenting to a full room.

Another aspect of the speaker's outline is to give yourself delivery cues as they relate to particular parts of your speech. You may want to write down delivery cues like, pause here, more eye contact here, speak slower hear, raise my volume here, and so on.

Sample Special Occasion Speech–Speaker's Outline (Complete Sentence Format) The Acceptance of the Commerce Association's Business Person of the Year Award

Specific Purpose: To entertain my audience and accept the Commerce Association's Business Person of the Year Award.

Central Idea: Three key business mentors have shaped my personal and professional life as I accept the Commerce Association's Business Person of the Year.

Introduction

I. Wow, I would like to thank the selection board at the Commerce Association for honoring me with this prestigious Business Person of the Year award.

MAKE EYE CONTACT HERE

A. I would have never thought in a million years, that out of the many deserving members, I would have been selected to represent the Commerce Association as the Business Person of the Year.

B. One of Rome's greatest orators Cicero once said, "gratitude is not only the greatest of virtues, but the parent of all others"

PAUSE HERE

(Transition: The valuable members of the Commerce Association have served as outstanding mentors and in some cases surrogate parents for me in my business success and I want to express my gratitude.)

Body

FIND JIM IN THE AUDIENCE AND TALK TO HIM

I. First and foremost I need to thank my mentor, my friend, and my father figure, Jim Newell, the guy who graciously nominated me for this award.

A. When we first met I was an employee in his business and I was simply happy to have a job, and hoped to stay there for the next thirty years of my life.

SCAN ENTIRE ROOM HERE AND PAUSE

1. However, Jim, you saw something in me, and you told me something interesting, "profits are better than wages," and that stuck with me.

2. I then started my hardware store and connected to my community.

3. Jim would come in and visit me just to touch base, and I appreciate that.

B. Because of Jim I have a successful business and I spend a lot of time serving my community through the store, and talking to school-age kids about entrepreneurship.

1. Jim, thank you so very much for your guidance and leadership.

II. Next I would like to thank Isabella Stapleton, the owner of our all-news radio station here in town.

A. When I first met you I was a caterpillar, very introverted.

1. With Jim's help you also took me under your wing and pushed me out of the nest so to speak.

RAISE VOLUME FOR THIS NEXT POINT

2. Your core message to me was to go socialize, because success is something you can't do by yourself.

3. I took that advice, and I became a better person because of that wisdom.

B. We will forget about the time you had me as a guest on your radio show and I did not realize my microphone was on.

   1. I was going on and on about how nervous I was, and how I wasn't sure if I could take a big step like this.

   2. After 35 interviews I think I got the hang of the radio thing. I now feel more comfortable talking and connecting with others because, Isabella—you showed me the way.

SLOW RATE OF SPEECH HERE FOR THIS POINT

C. Now I believe I'm a butterfly.

   1. Because of your support, I now will leave a legacy for my two beautiful children.

   2. My business has allowed me to leave my future grandchildren the opportunity to be educated, and to be contributors to our community.

   3. If it weren't for Isabella, I would be living a life that would be "good enough," but not living a life of abundance.

   4. Because of your imprints on me, my relationships with my wife, children, my business associates, and my friends have been richer, so I say thank you for your graciousness and support.

III. Finally, I want to thank my dear friend Max Barker who always encouraged me to take the big picture approach to life.

PICK UP RATE OF SPEECH

A. I will always cherish our walks and the discussions about why we do what we do.

   1. In a way you were my workout buddy, because every time we talked, you made me put my sneakers on and we hit the pavement.

B. Being in the hardware business is not the sexiest business to be in, but Max helps me understand that this venture is for my family, and a better quality of life with my loved ones.

   1. So Max, thanks for the continue support.

(Transition: I have so many more people to thank, but I think I hear the music to wrap things up.)

Conclusion

I. In closing I want to thank the Commerce Association for embracing me as a member and awarding me the Business Person of the Year.

A. I know I'm forgetting other valuable people in my development so I'll quote baseball great Yogi Berra who said it best, "I want to thank everybody who made this day necessary."

BE SURE TO PAUSE AND WAVE TO THE AUDIENCE

Preparation Outline Checklist

❏ Is the specific purpose and the central idea at the top of the page?

   ○ **Specific Purpose:** To inform my audience . . .

   ○ **Central Idea:** _____

❏ Does your central idea specifically reflect the main points of your speech?

❏ Did you label and center the three parts of the speech?

Introduction

Body

Conclusion

Bibliography (when necessary)

❏ Does the first sentence in each of your parts (Introduction, Body, Conclusion) start off with a Roman numeral I?

❏ Do each of your points only have one sentence? Remember only one sentence per point!

❏ Are each of your points in a complete sentence?

❏ There must be <u>No</u> bullets, or *i, ii, iii,* documented on your outlines.

❏ Do you have between 2 and 5 main points in the body?

❏ Do you have a transition between the introduction and the body and the body and the conclusion? (Transition: _____.)

❏ Did you outline your introduction and conclusion?

❏ Did you appropriately document your oral citations throughout your speech?

❏ Please check for proper punctuation, spelling, and grammar.

❏ Are the pattern of symbolization and indentation in your speech appropriate? Here is a sample of the visual framework.

  I. Main Point

    A. Sub-Point

      1. Sub-sub point

        a. sub-sub sub-point

Summary: Tips for organizing and outline your speech for maximum impact

"An intelligent plan is the first step to success. The man who plans knows where he is going, knows what progress he is making and has a pretty good idea when he will arrive." Planning is the open road to your destination "If you don't know where you are going. How can you expect to get there?"
—BASIL S. WALSH, AUTHOR

Our chapter discusses both organizing your thoughts and outlining your ideas; these themes are key foundations in becoming a sound public speaker. Organization and planning are essential tools for becoming a successful public speaker. By learning the dynamics of organizing your speech and outlining your thoughts you will be on your way to presenting a well thought-out address that your audience will appreciate and learn from. Proficient outlining and outlining skills will serve as your game plan for your presentation.

The main points of your speech are the driver of your message. Speeches usually have between two and five main points. If you have too many points your audience will likely not remember your main points. It is better to limit your main points, so they stand out and are remembered. In addition, remember to allocate an appropriate amount of time in your presentation in proportion to the level of importance of each of your main points.

There are a variety of organizational strategies that will help you package your thoughts in a logical way to effectively communicate with your audience. The chronological order follows a time sequence and is usually used in informative speeches. Next is the spatial order that follows a directional pattern such as going from left to right, north to south, or inside to outside and is usually used in an informative speech. The causal order reflects the cause and effect relationship. Because of its adaptability the causal order can be used for both informative and persuasive speeches. The problem-solution order is divided into two key parts, the first explains the existence and the second describes the solution to a problem. The problem-solution strategy is usually used in a persuasive speech. Speeches that are *not* chronological, spatial, causal, or problem-solution order usually fall into topical order. The topical order is derived when you divide the speech topics into subtopics, each of which becomes a main point in the speech. The main points are not part of a chronological, spatial, causal, or problem-solution sequence, but are simply parts of the whole. The topical order is an effective organizational strategy for both informative and persuasive speeches. When delivering a persuasive speech, each of your topical subdivisions are the reasons/arguments why a speaker has chosen to advocate for a certain point of view. The topical order is the most commonly used organizational strategy in public speaking because it is applicable to almost any subject and any kind of speech.

Supporting materials add the bulk to your main points and the quality of your supporting materials can distinguish a poor speech from an outstanding speech. A public speaker would support the main points by using examples, statistics, and testimony.

Connectives are words or phrases that join one thought to another and reveal the relationship between them much like going from first gear to second gear efficiently. There are four types of connectives that would be appropriate for a speech: transitions, internal previews, internal summaries, and signposts. Transitions are words or phrases that reveal when a speaker has just finished one thought, and is moving on to another. Internal previews give the audience a "heads up" so they know what the speaker will discuss next; however, internal previews are more detailed than transitions. Internal summaries remind the audience of what was just stated. A speaker may have just completed a point that was particularly complex or complicated and the internal summary reviews what the speaker just talked about in a concise way. Signposts are concise statements that show the audience where you are in the speech.

The process of outlining requires you to consider if each part (introduction, body, and conclusion) of the speech is fully cultivated, or if the supporting materials for your main points are appropriate, and if the main points are properly composed. An outline assures you that your core ideas connect, and that there is a logical flow from one point to another.

There are two kinds of outlines you will use in preparing for a speech. First is the preparation outline, which is a detailed roadmap of your speech. The second type of outline is the speaker's outline which is less detailed, but offers valuable delivery cues while you are at the podium.

Your preparation outline includes the labeling of the parts of the speech (introduction, body, conclusion, and bibliography), which is further divided into specific purpose, central idea, introduction, main points, subpoints, sub-subpoints, sub-sub subpoints, connectives, conclusion, and bibliography. Each of your points will be only one sentence long; hence another name for this type of outline is the complete sentence outline.

The visual framework of a preparation outline would look something like this:

I. Main point

    A. Subpoint

        1. Sub-subpoint

        2. Sub-subpoint

           a. Sub-sub subpoint

           b. Sub-sub subpoint

In public speaking it is not only what you say, but also how you say it that matters, and that leads us to understanding the nuances of the speaker's outline. The speaker's outline is used while you are delivering your extemporaneous speech in front of your classmates. A key distinction between the preparation outline and the speaker's outline is that the latter provides delivery cues for you to follow while giving your speech. As you progress in your public speaking development you will create your own shorthand for your memory aids on your outline, but for now these guidelines will provide you the tools on your pathway to success.

True-False

1. T F   Most speeches should contain from two to five main points.

2. T F   Speeches arranged in problem-solution order are divided into four main parts.

3. T F   In topical order the main points proceed from top to bottom, left to right, front to back, east to west, or some similar route.

4. T F   Chronological organization is used primarily for informative speeches.

5. T F   In a preparation outline, the specific purpose and central idea are identified by Roman numerals.

6. T F   According to your textbook, transitions and other connectives should be identified with Roman numerals on a speech preparation outline.

7. T F   Delivery cues should be included on both the preparation and speaking outlines.

8. T F   A preparation outline should include your final bibliography.

Multiple Choice

9. According to your textbook, what is the *most* important reason for limiting the number of main points in a speech?

   a. It is hard to maintain parallel wording if there are too many main points.
   b. It is hard to phrase the central idea if a speech has too many main points.
   c. It is hard to organize supporting materials if there are too many main points.
   d. It is hard to deliver a speech extemporaneously if it has too many main points.
   e. It is hard for the audience to keep track of too many main points.

10. When main ideas follow a directional pattern, they are organized in

   a. geographical order.
   b. topical order.
   c. spatial order.
   d. causal order.
   e. chronological order.

11. Which of the following organizational patterns is used more than any other method of speech organization because of its applicability to almost any subject?

   a. chronological
   b. spatial
   c. problem-solution
   d. topical
   e. causal

12. Problem-solution order is most appropriate for organizing _____ speeches.

   a. acceptance
   b. persuasive
   c. after-dinner
   d. commemorative
   e. informative

13. Two types of speech outlines discussed in your textbook are the

    a. preparation outline and the delivery outline.
    b. rough draft outline and the polished outline.
    c. preparation outline and the speaking outline.
    d. speaking outline and the audience outline.
    e. audience outline and the preparation outline.

14. A preparation outline

    a. should be as brief as possible.
    b. states main points and subpoints in full sentences.
    c. contains the speaker's preliminary bibliography.
    d. all of the above.
    e. b and c only.

15. The main points in a preparation outline are

    a. identified by Roman numerals.
    b. identified by capital letters.
    c. located farther to the right than subpoints.
    d. identified by Arabic numbers.
    e. written in phrases, not full sentences.

16. Subpoints in a preparation outline are indicated

    a. by Roman numerals.
    b. by Arabic numbers.
    c. by capital letters.
    d. in the same manner as sub-subpoints.
    e. in the same manner as main points.

17. According to your textbook, a speaking outline

    a. includes the final bibliography.
    b. states the specific purpose at the start of the outline.
    c. contains delivery cues for the speaker.
    d. all of the above.
    e. a and b only.

18. Words or phrases that indicate when a speaker has completed one thought and is moving on to another are called

    a. transfers.
    b. internal summaries.
    c. speech bridges.
    d. transitions.
    e. signposts.

Essay

19. In a well-developed essay, explain the similarities and differences between a preparation outline and a speaking outline. Be sure to consider what a preparation outline includes that is not part of a speaking outline.

20. Write an essay in which you (a) identify the four kinds of speech connectives explained in your textbook, (b) give an example of each, and (c) discuss the role of each in a speech.

Chapter 9

Introductions and Conclusions

First impressions have a powerful impact on how others perceive you. Think about when you first met your best friend, your roommate, or even your teacher. Ask yourself, what was your first impression of those people? Moreover, to take this a step further, what was the first impression you left on others when they first met you? Another point to consider is, how did your first impressions shape your relationship with the other person? In short, you are developing a relationship with your audience, so what first impression do you want to leave with your audience? There is no difference between these other first impressions and the first impression your audience will have of you when you deliver your presentation. On your pathway to success developing a strong introduction will leave a good impression on your audience.

In our everyday first impressions there are standard strategies that will lead to you making a more favorable first impression, such as: being properly groomed, smiling, eye contact, a friendly handshake, and a hearty how-do-ya-do. Some of the same principles apply with the introduction when establishing a rapport with your audience. An effective introduction should be structured so the speaker will: get the listeners' attention, express that the topic is something that will relate to the audience, set themselves up as trustworthy to speak on the topic, clarify their purpose, and preview the main points of the speech. So as you strategize, ask yourself how you will word your introduction so that the audience feels that the presentation is a speech that they want to hear.

In an introduction your speech must have the following four goals. First, you need to get the attention and interest of your audience. Next, you need to reveal the topic of your speech. Third, establish your credibility and goodwill towards your audience, and finally preview the body of speech.

GET THE ATTENTION AND INTEREST OF YOUR AUDIENCE

Once you walk up to the podium you will have the initial attention of your audience even before starting your speech. The real challenge is keeping that attention on you and your message throughout your speech. Your audience will be asking themselves, "why is this topic relevant to me?" and it is your job to figure that question out before heading to the podium. So during the introduction of your speech, spend some time building bridges by connecting your topic to the audience. The following attention-getting strategies will help you capture and maintain the audience's interest level.

Relate the Topic to the Audience

Your audience will listen to your speech as long as your content has something that directly relates to their interest. One strategy that will work in achieving this specific goal is to utilize your audience survey. Before presenting a speech, it is to your advantage to conduct an audience survey. You can read more about the details about how to craft a survey in the audience analysis chapter. After compiling your findings from your audience survey, you will really begin to learn how your audience thinks, feels, and believes about your subject matter. So in your preparation phase compile those findings and state those findings in your introduction. One strong advantage you will have is your audience will have a vested interest in your speech because they spent the time filling out your survey. For example you may say something like, "according to my in class survey 73% of you have downloaded music illegally." In short, your audience will be curious to see how they fit in with your findings. So as you deliver your introduction refer to your audience survey and that will definitely hook your audience, because those findings directly relate to the audience. Do not be surprised if your audience members look around trying to figure out how their classmates fit in the range of your survey findings. Remember public speaking is an audience-focused activity.

Startle the Audience

One strategy to get the attention of your audience is to startle your audience with an astonishing or captivating statement. This strategy is easy to implement but you need to remember that the statement needs to directly relate to the audience. For example, here is a sample from a speaker who startles his audience regarding genital herpes.

"Let's take a look around the room at our classmates and you will notice that 35 people have been in our public speaking class this semester. Statistically speaking, at least seven of us in this room will contract genital herpes in our lifetime. According to a report from the Centers for Disease Control and Prevention published in 2006, 'In the United States at least 45 million people ages 12 and older, or one out of five adolescents and adults, have had genital HSV infection.'

This particular statement did get the attention of the audience, because it directly related to them. If for whatever reason you decide to make a shocking statement and proceed with your speech and your message does not relate to your statement, your audience will be confused and that will discredit your authenticity.

Stir-Up the Curiosity of the Audience

One way to lure the audience into your speech is with a succession of statements that increasingly awakens the interest about the subject for the audience. For example this student delivered a speech about the major oil suppliers to the United States.

"As we look ahead to the weekend and get ready for that road trip across state, I'm sure you will need to fill up your car with gas. As you look at how much it cost to fill up your tank, you realize that filling up takes a lot out of your wallet leaving you less money for food and entertainment. You then begin to remember the numerous discussions about how the United States needs to rely less on foreign oil. So you begin to think about countries like Saudi Arabia, Venezuela, Nicaragua, Iraq, Iran, and Mexico that must be profiting from you filling up your gas tank. If you think that those are the countries that are the largest suppliers of oil to the United States, you are incorrect. According to an April 2008 report from the Energy Information Administration (EIA), the largest supplier of oil to the United States is our neighbor to the north—Canada."

Stirring-up the curiosity of the audience is a strong tactic to capture and hold the audience members' attention and interest.

Begin with a Quotation

Using a quote may be an outstanding alternative for you to capture the attention and interest of your audience. There are numerous resources in selecting a quotation, and they are often categorized by subject matter, theme, or by author. When using a quote make sure it is brief and catchy. If the quote is too long, your audience will lose its attention and begin to wonder when they get to listen to the speaker's ideas as opposed to someone else's ideas.

Tell a Story

Telling a story is a powerful way to get the attention and illustrate the point you are trying to make. In order for a story to work in an introduction the story needs to be clearly relevant to the specific purpose of your speech. Stories can serve a couple of purposes; they can stir the interest of the audience and they can move the listeners emotionally to become involved in the subject of the speech.

When telling a story not only is the content important, but also your delivery can make or break the success of the story. Extra time and care is needed in working with the delivery aspect to capture the true essence of your story.

Humor

Using humor in your introduction requires you to use some caution and have a good sense as to what makes your audience tick. Remember that your stories and jokes need to illustrate a point that is reflective of your specific purpose and central idea. A joke that falls short of the audience's expectations can start your speech off on the wrong foot, and if you happen to offend an audience, the probability of your audience listening to the rest of your message will be small.

Ask a Question

Asking a question is a useful way to get the attention of the audience; however, there are some pitfalls to avoid. Let us say you ask a thought-provoking question and pause after asking the question. Ask yourself, will my audience be listening to me or will they still be reflecting on what was just said? Conversely, what if the question you asked is really weak, bordering on silly. Your audience may consider your topic, and you the speaker, as insignificant and questionable, and you will lose credibility with your audience. So think long and hard about the questions you ask at the beginning of your speech. However, closing your speech with a question can really shape a lasting impression of your speech.

In some situations you may want to consider asking a series of questions to draw the audience to take a deeper interest in your subject. When using this strategy, your delivery will impact how your questions will be received. Consider implementing a dramatic pause after each question, so your audience can have time to contemplate each of your questions.

Other strategies that may be used to get the attention and interest of your audience include audio equipment, visual aids, and relating to a previous speaker. For any given speech, think about which method will best suit your topic, the audience, and the occasion.

REVEAL THE TOPIC

In the process of crafting a strong introduction, you must reveal the topic of your speech to your audience. If you do not reveal your topic, your audience will not grasp what you are trying to accomplish and will likely be confused. Once your audience becomes confused, you can be sure that your audience will check-out and start thinking about things that do not pertain to your message. As a public speaker you want your audience to listen to you, so do not confuse your audience or you will lose your audience.

In a speech delivered by a student, the student made the fatal flaw of not revealing her topic in her introduction, and throughout her entire speech. Her speech was to persuade her audience to visit her country for their next vacation.

"I came to the United States five years ago from my country. My country is located in Central America near Honduras and Costa Rica. You should visit my country on your next vacation because it is a very beautiful country with so many things to see and do. When visiting my country you need to explore the cultural events, enjoy the weather, and taste the food that makes my country the best place to visit."

The speaker did not mention which country she came from, and after seven minutes she still never revealed her topic. The student painted a beautiful picture of the wonderful landmarks, food, weather, and the kindness of the people of her country. The speech really captured her audience, and many wanted to consider her country as a vacation destination. So when she sat down, there was an awkward silence in the room, which left the class puzzled. So a classmate asked, "which country are you from and that you just described in your speech?" She replied, "Nicaragua!" as if her classmate had a screw loose. Obviously, if the student had revealed "Nicaragua" in the introduction to her speech, she would have had stronger impact on the audience.

If do not clearly reveal the topic of your speech in your introduction you may lose listeners. Even when the audience knows your topic, it is a good idea to restate your topic clearly in your introduction.

ESTABLISHING YOUR CREDIBILITY

If you are delivering a speech in which you have experience that would enhance your status relating to your speech topic, make sure to disclose this information to your audience. Your introduction is a critical time to establish yourself as a person who can talk about this topic so it makes sense to your audience. Another objective in establishing your credibility is to be perceived as qualified by your listeners. As you grow in your professional and public speaking experience this becomes a less difficult challenge. For example, let us say that you are delivering a speech on how to change the oil in your car. If you happen to work at the local oil change company, it is to your advantage to mention that fact, since it adds to your believability.

Confirming your credibility in your introduction can either come from first-hand experience with your subject matter, or through studying applicable documentation about your topic, interviewing authorized people in the field, or taking a class relating to your speech topic. For information that does not come from personal experience, it is important to cite top-quality sources. For example, if you were delivering a speech regarding a medical topic, you could add credibility to your speech by citing sources like the *JAMA: The Journal of the American Medical Association* or *The New England Journal of Medicine*.

Establishing your goodwill is another challenge you will face in your introduction. In a classroom setting establishing your goodwill is more manageable than in more professional settings where your reputation follows you. When your reputation follows you, a more mindful effort will be needed to establish your goodwill in hostile environments. Occasionally you may have to go a little further in establishing your goodwill because your audience may not be in support of your presentation. Of course you would learn about the audience's position from your audience survey. If you are facing a hostile environment you must make special efforts to consider the opposing views, which builds goodwill.

PREVIEW THE BODY OF THE SPEECH

The last step of the introduction before moving to the body of the speech is to preview the body of the speech. The preview introduces your main ideas, so that your audience can follow you along the main points of your presentation. The preview statement is a signal that the speaker is transitioning from the introduction into the body of the speech. You can also use your introduction to give specialized information such as definitions or background information that your audience will need so they can have a stronger concept of your overall message.

OTHER TIPS FOR THE INTRODUCTION TO YOUR SPEECH

The length of the introduction varies from speech to speech, but should be relatively brief. When preparing for your speech it is easier to develop your introduction only after the main points have been identified and developed. Once those main points are established you will have stronger leverage to introduce them more effectively.

Another common error made by beginning public speakers is to apologize for one reason or another. There is nothing like having a speaker come up to the podium and say, "I'm so nervous, I'm not used to having so many people looking at me." Or, "I'm sorry I'm tired I was up all night working on my speech." Or "I'm sorry I have a headache and am not feeling well enough to give you my best speech delivery." Just go to the podium and deliver your speech the best you can and leave the apologies to another time when you are truly sorry about something.

Keep your introduction relatively brief, but engaging, because the core of your message comes from the body of the speech. Spend a lot of time practicing the delivery of your introduction because it will give you good momentum you can carry throughout the remainder of your speech while building your confidence. Moreover, when you are confident, your audience will have more confidence in you which will make you a more trustworthy public speaker. Your goal should be able to deliver your introduction with minimal reference to your notes so you can maintain strong eye contact with your audience. Your audience will be more engaged with a speaker who is looking at them, and your audience prefers seeing your eyes as opposed to the top of your head.

CONCLUSION

Your conclusion is your final chance to underscore your residual message. Your audience may not remember every one of your points, but they will remember their overall impression of you and your speech. Extra care will be needed when developing your final thoughts of what your audience will remember. Your conclusion has two key purposes, to signal that you will be finishing your speech, and to reinforce your central idea.

Signal the End of the Speech

One of the easiest and most obvious ways to let your audience know that you are ending your speech is to say: in conclusion, finally, one last thought, in closing, in short, in summation. These are just a few brief ways to signal your ending.

A more subtle and indirect way to let your audience know that you are ending your speech is through your delivery. By using the voice's tone, pacing, intonation, and rhythm, a speaker can build the momentum of a speech so it is clear that the speech is ending. One way of doing this is through the crescendo ending strategy. The **crescendo ending strategy** is when the speech builds to a high point of power and intensity in your delivery. Keep in mind that this does not necessarily mean becoming louder and louder; instead, it is a combination of many things, including vocal pitch, choice of words, dramatic content, gestures, pace, and pauses. On January 19, 2004, then-Governor of Vermont Howard Dean delivered a memorable speech known as the "Dean Scream" after the 2004 Iowa Caucus on his campaign to become the president of the United States. Dean placed third in the Iowa Caucus—a good showing in the eyes of his campaign. As he was addressing his supporters after the caucus he delivered a brief, but memorable, speech that started slowly but built momentum and climaxed with the "Yeah!" heard around the world.

Another strategy is to use the dissolved ending. The **dissolved ending** is a conclusion that generates an emotional appeal by fading step-by-step to a dramatic final statement. One speech that captures the idea of an emotional close is a speech delivered by President Richard M. Nixon in his "Farewell Remarks to White House Cabinet and Staff" delivered on August 9, 1974. Nixon resigned from the presidency due to mounting pressures from the Watergate scandal. This speech was delivered to his Cabinet and the staff members who worked at the White House and served the President on a daily basis. During this particular speech Nixon displays emotion, a trait he was not known for during his political career.

"And so, we leave with high hopes, in good spirit and with deep humility, and with very much gratefulness in our hearts. I can only say to each and every one of you, we come from many faiths, we pray perhaps to different gods, but really the same God in a sense, but I want to say for each and every one of you, not only will we always remember you, not only will we always be grateful to you, but always you will be in our hearts and you will be in our prayers. Thank you very much."

Both the crescendo and the dissolve endings must be worked out in great detail and care. Using these strategies requires that you practice your delivery so that the words and the delivery hit the mark.

Reinforce the Central Idea

Another purpose that needs to be met in the conclusion is the reinforcement of the central idea, and there are a variety of strategies to meet this objective. One of the most common techniques used to conclude a speech is to present a summary of your main points for your listeners. Using a summary emphasizes the most important points and reminds the listeners of your key ideas. In addition, referring back to your introduction will allow you to build a symmetrical set of bookends for your message. This may come in the form of closing a story that you started in the introduction.

A quotation is a common, but effective, strategy to conclude a speech. A good brief quote can reinforce the central idea of a speech. Another strategy that may be implemented is to visualize some type of future for your audience. In a speech in which you advocate some important changes, visualizing the results of those changes is an especially appropriate way to conclude. The visualization strategy helps your audience build a concrete visual result of your main ideas. One other way to close your speech is to challenge your audience to take a particular action, but this tactic is more applicable for persuasive speeches.

Tips for Your Conclusion

When you give your audience the cue that you will be concluding your speech, conclude the speech and do not ramble on. You may say something like: "in conclusion," "in short," "one final thought," "lastly," or "again let me stress my core points." So once you say these key verbal cues that you are finishing, your audience will not be happy about being duped that you will be finishing your speech, and have decided instead to continue on with new information. The conclusion is not the time to introduce new information. This act will bring hostility from your audience, and as a speaker it is not a good idea to upset the audience. Do not drag out your speech. Just finish the speech clearly and with poise. If you were to close your speech withy, "I think that is all I got" as you are walking back to your chair, your audience will think much less of your speech and that conclusion will leave a weak lasting impression of you as a public speaker.

Summary: Beginning and Ending the Speech

On your pathway to success you must accomplish four goals in your introduction: to get the attention and interest of your audience, reveal the topic of your speech, establish your credibility to speak about your topic, and preview the body of the speech. Some of the ways you can get and keep the audience's attention are to: relate the topic directly to your audience, startle the audience, arouse the curiosity of the audience, begin with a quote, tell a story, use humor, or ask a question.

Revealing your topic is an important task in your introduction, because if you do not, your audience will not know what your speech is all about. If the audience is confused, the probability is high they will stop paying attention to the speaker. So reveal your topic so the audience can follow along easier.

Establishing your credibility is needed so your audience perceives you to be a qualified person to speak on a particular topic. Establishing your credibility can come from first-hand personal experience, or by citing sources from reputable sources about your topic. In addition to establishing credibility, you need to create goodwill with your audience. In short, your audience needs to know that you, the speaker, are looking out for the audience and you have their best interests at heart.

Providing a preview of the main points of your speech gives the audience a road map to your pathway to success. So as you deliver your speech your audience will know what main point you are discussing, and which main points you still have yet to discuss. Additional information that you may want to provide in this part of your introduction are background information and special definitions that will help your audience have a context for your message.

Keep your introduction relatively brief and strive to be able to deliver your introduction with minimal reference to your outline. Eye contact and a carefully rehearsed delivery are powerful ways to build engagement with your audience.

Your conclusion is the final step to reinforce your residual message. Your conclusion has two key functions, the first is to signal that you are concluding your speech, and the second is to reinforce your central idea.

A few of the ways to signal the ending of your speech are to verbally state: in conclusion, in short, in summary, and so on. A more subtle way to signal the end of your speech is to use your voice such as using the crescendo ending strategy or the dissolved ending strategy. If you decide to use these strategies to signal the end of your speech, much practice is needed to master them.

The second function you need to implement in your conclusion is to reinforce your central idea. Again you want to restate the main points of your speech, so your audience remembers them. The conclusion is not the time to introduce new information, just to wrap up your speech clearly and concisely.

True-False

1. T F Goodwill is the audience's perception of whether a speaker is qualified to speak on a given topic.

2. T F The only way to convey that your speech is ending is through the use of words such as "In conclusion."

3. T F If your topic is clear in the body of the speech, there is no need to state it in the introduction.

4. T F A dissolve ending is a conclusion that generates emotional appeal by fading step by step to a dramatic final statement.

5. T F It is overly repetitious to restate the central idea in the conclusion of a speech.

6. T F Establishing goodwill is more likely to be necessary in the introduction of an informative speech than in the introduction of a persuasive speech.

Multiple Choice

7. When preparing a speech introduction, you should usually
   a. preview the main points to be discussed in the body.
   b. gain the attention and interest of your audience.
   c. establish your credibility on the speech topic.
   d. all of the above.
   e. a and b only.

8. Which of the following would you *least* likely find in a speech introduction?
   a. a preview statement
   b. a call to action
   c. a credibility statement
   d. a provocative quotation
   e. a startling statement

9. When you advocate a highly unpopular position, it is particularly important to _____ in the introduction of your speech.
   a. tell a story
   b. define unclear terms
   c. have a concise preview statement
   d. state the importance of the topic
   e. establish goodwill toward the audience

10. When preparing a speech introduction, you should usually
    a. practice the introduction no more than two or three times.
    b. make sure the introduction takes up 25 percent of the speech.
    c. complete the introduction after the body of the speech.
    d. stick with the first introduction that comes to mind.
    e. use humor to gain the audience's attention and interest.

11. Which of the following would you *most* likely find in a speech conclusion?

    a. a preview statement
    b. an announcement of the topic
    c. a lengthy quotation
    d. a reference to the introduction
    e. a statement of goodwill

12. According to your textbook, when a speaker concludes a speech by fading out on an emotional note she or he is using a _____ ending.

    a. descending
    b. crescendo
    c. cascade
    d. dissolve
    e. reflective

13. For the introduction of an informative speech, it is especially important to

    a. preview the main points to be discussed in the body.
    b. establish goodwill with the audience.
    c. use visual aids to gain attention.
    d. prepare the introduction before the body of the speech.
    e. personalize the central idea with vivid examples.

Essay Question

14. List and explain the four objectives of a speech introduction.

15. Explain the two main functions of a speech conclusion.

Pillar 4

Successfully Presenting your Message for Maximum Impact

Chapter 10

Delivery

The **delivery** of your idea embodies the nonverbal aspect of your message. Think about a storyteller you have in your life, that person may be a grandparent, a parent, a sibling, a neighbor, a coworker, a teacher, a classmate, or a friend. Ask yourself, what makes this person tell good stories? Is it the content of what they are saying or is it *how* they are telling the story that makes it an enjoyable experience? Take any comedian that you may see on television, the movies, or a comedy club, it is usually the vocal inflections, pauses, facial expressions, and gestures that make a story or joke really funny or really bad. The nonverbal component of the message clearly demonstrates how important delivery impacts the message you are delivering to your audience. The text of your speech is valuable; however, the nonverbal message of how you deliver the content carries more weight with the audience.

Think about an interaction you had with someone who left an impression on you. Maybe your boyfriend/girlfriend, husband/wife, boss or co-worker said something that made you really happy or really upset. What drove that emotion in you, was it *what* the person said, or was it *how* the person expressed the message? More times than not, it is how someone talks to us or how they interact with us that stimulates an emotional response, whether it is a positive or negative emotion. Therefore the delivery of your message impacts how your audience responds to your message. Unfortunately many beginning public speakers wait until the last minute to prepare their outlines and usually head to the podium cold, without rehearsing their speech, and that lack of preparation usually leaves the audience with a flat presentation.

A well-prepared and practiced delivery communicates the speaker's ideas more clearly and interestingly than an unprepared delivered speech. When you head up to the podium and you know that you have not practiced your delivery as much as you believe you should have, that doubt is communicated nonverbally, and your audience will pick up on that lack of confidence. The lack of confidence is usually communicated by staring down at the podium instead of scanning the room, stuttering and stammering with lots of uhms and uhs, staring in the sky for divine intervention, or delivering your speech with a monotone voice because you are reading your speech. Remember this is public speaking and not public reading.

A well-practiced speech will have you walk up to the podium with your head up and your shoulders back, and a stride that lets your audience know that you have a purpose. Your audience will usually see you before they hear you so leave a good initial impression. When delivering your speech there are numerous approaches you can use to effectively deliver your speech. You may want to consider being strong yet reserved, or more animated in your delivery. The occasion will dictate your approach for your delivery. Obviously if you are speaking at a funeral, your demeanor would be humbled and reserved, which will be reflected in how you use your voice and your hand gestures. Conversely if you just won a $300 million dollar lottery you would probably be more demonstrative and animated in your gestures and the intonation of your voice. The bottom line is you have to be yourself. Trying to present a speech like someone else may seem like a good idea, but your audience will know that you are not being authentic to yourself and will perceive you as a phony. What works for one speaker may be a colossal failure for another speaker.

The easiest way to ensure the most appropriate style of delivery is to focus on the message that you are trying to communicate to your audience. If your focal point is on delivering this message to this audience, your nonverbal messages will come naturally. By concentrating on speaking astutely, you can avoid distracting behaviors like twirling your hair or tapping the podium with a pencil. By establishing and keeping eye contact with your audience, and using hand gestures to reinforce particular points you want to stress, you will be on your way to becoming a strong public speaker. Once these basic principles are ingrained in your public speaking base you will have a good foundation to work with leading you to become a more effective public speaker. As you start to learn to become a public speaker you will be mindful of these areas to implement in your message but as you practice and gain more public speaking experience you will be doing these valuable mannerisms without thinking. In time, you may find yourself able to direct the pacing, timing, rhythm, and momentum of your speech instinctively.

METHODS OF DELIVERY

There are four major approaches to delivering a speech, speaking from a manuscript, memorizing your content, impromptu speaking, and speaking extemporaneously. The choice of method of delivery is usually based on the occasion on which you are speaking.

Speaking from a Manuscript

Speeches that are of great importance are usually reserved for the manuscript delivery method. **Manuscript** speeches are delivered word for word, and are written and re-written numerous times for absolute accuracy in content and correct word choice. For example when the President of the United States delivers the State of the Union Address, that speech is written and re-written, and the delivery is practiced for weeks before we watch the final version of the speech on television. The President's speech writing team works and plans this speech for weeks on end. Every word needs to be meticulously planned and well thought-out before making the final cut. Can you imagine the consequences of misstated words or phrases in front of the world's eyes? An error like this cannot be made in a speech of this magnitude because it can lead to an international incident.

On the surface delivering a speech from a manuscript sounds easy to do. However, delivering a speech from a manuscript is challenging, because it is so easy to just read to the audience as oppose to speaking to the audience. This is public speaking and not public reading. Some pitfalls when you read to an audience would be a monotone vocal style, a choppy rate of speech, and a glazed look in your eyes when addressing your audience. The audience needs to get the sense that you are talking to them, and not a blank wall. A properly practice speech using a manuscript should sound effervescent, appealing, and conversational.

Delivering Your Speech from Memory

Except for the shortest of speeches, it is not expected that you memorize your speech. If for example you were to say a quick congratulatory speech for someone's birthday, promotion, or token of gratitude then memorization would be appropriate. On the surface it sounds like a good idea to memorize your speech, but by using this tactic there is a tendency to not speak to your audience. When a speech is memorized there is more effort on the speaker's behalf to remember their words as opposed to communicating with the audience. Speakers who memorize their speeches characteristically are looking up to remember their words, and the audience will feel insignificant; public speaking is an audience-focused activity and they need to be engaged with eye contact.

Impromptu Speaking

Impromptu speaking is a speech delivered with little or no advance preparation. Often impromptu speeches come during a business meeting, a special occasion, or a response to a previous speaker. It is almost inevitable that you will be asked for a brief speech, so be prepared for your moment in the sun. A common phrase someone may say is "can you share your thoughts regarding this matter" and now you are expected to say something that adds to the previous discussion or setting of the situation. When faced with this situation take a deep breath, compose yourself, and think of a few words to say, say them and then sit down. Make sure your speech is relatively brief, because the longer you babble, the probability of saying something ridiculous gets higher, and your credibility in the eyes of the other people in the room will evaporate into thin air. Have you noticed that when you get nervous you tend to talk faster, and say things before thinking? In a professional setting that can get you in trouble.

If you are lucky enough to have a moment or two before speaking, use this time wisely and focus on what message you want to communicate to the audience. In contrast if your thoughts are "oh my, I can't believe I have to do this, I'm so nervous" you will be in trouble. As you collect your thoughts you can make a brief outline on a sheet of paper and use that as a memory aid. The image you want to project when delivering a speech on the spur of the moment is confidence and poise, and you do that by maintaining eye contact, an appropriate rate of speech, and clear organization of thoughts.

You may not believe this, but you have performed many impromptu speeches in your everyday life. Think about when someone stops you on campus and asks directions to the bookstore, or when you are asked by your boss why you were not able to complete an assigned task. Remember, when you are put into these situations: keep a clear head, stay confident, say a few words, and sit down. Like everything else in life the more you do something the better at it you will be, so practice.

Extemporaneous Speaking

An **extemporaneous speech** is a carefully prepared speech that is practiced ahead of time. This carries a different dynamic than the impromptu speech where you have little or no time to prepare a message. When using an extemporaneous delivery style, you will be referring to a brief set of notes (speaker's outline) as a memory aid while delivering your speech. Having a period of time before delivering your speech allows you to craft your speech and select the right words to meet your specific purpose, and practicing your speech, will allow you to work on saying each word appropriately to strengthen your message. When you practice your speech numerous times, you can test out how your message will sound by stressing particular words, and by making changes to the rate of speech, vocal variety, and volume. In addition, using the extemporaneous delivery style allows you some flexibility when you are at the podium, because you will be able to adjust your speech to your audience by observing their feedback to you at the podium.

Consider the last movie, television program, or song you saw or heard. How many times do you think the performers practiced those lines before the final cut? It is hard to guess how many times these performers took to perfect their message, yet on the final cut it sounds like they are saying it for the first time. The message has a freshness and a vibrancy that make the message sound real. You can see how these performances risk sounding tired and lifeless because of the amount of times the message has been practiced. That over-rehearsed listlessness is what you want to avoid in delivering your presentation. **Conversational quality** means that no matter how many times you have practiced your speech, it still sounds natural to the audience. When speaking extemporaneously, remember to maintain eye contact by scanning the entire room, naturally using nonverbal gestures to reinforce particular points and focusing on communicating with the audience, as opposed to at the audience. These characteristics that make a well-written speech *sound* great all lead to understanding how to use the speaker's voice.

THE SPEAKER'S VOICE

The voice is much like fingerprints—no two voices are exactly alike, so embrace your uniqueness and welcome your individuality. The speaker can control the different aspects of his/her voice to maximize the message delivered to your audience on your pathway to success. The speaker's voice embodies volume, pitch, rate of speech, pauses, vocal variety, pronunciation, articulation, and dialect.

Volume

If your audience cannot physically hear you, then even the most powerful messages will not be received by your audience. **Volume** is the loudness or quietness of the speaker's voice. On one end of the spectrum, if you speak too loudly your audience will perceive you to be unrefined or rough around the edges. Conversely if you speak so softly that no one can hear you, your audience may perceive you as not confident and not a credible person to speak on your topic. One advantage you may have in your public speaking class is that you will be delivering your speech in the same room you attend for your everyday class session. This will allow you know the size of the room; the acoustics of the room; and any outside noise, such as the foot traffic from the hallway, the door that opens and closes for the building, and so forth. Knowing these sounds will allow you to make those necessary volume adjustments while delivering your presentation. Unfortunately, when you leave your public speaking class, you will not have that luxury, so it is up to you to learn about these dynamics before heading to the podium.

Your own voice will always sound louder to you than to your audience. So if you find that your audience is leaning forward or straining to hear you, you must make the necessary volume adjustments so your audience can hear you adequately. If you are delivering a speech in a larger venue that requires you to speak in a microphone remember that you do not need to yell to be heard. If you have never spoken into a microphone before, you may want to practice ahead of time to learn the similarities and differences of speaking with and without a microphone.

Pitch

The highness or lowness of the speaker's voice is also known as the **pitch** of the speaker's voice. Changes in the speaker's pitch are referred to as **inflections**. Changing the pitch of your voice throughout your presentation adds a human quality to your message. Adjusting the pitch of your message allows you to match the mood of your speech with your voice. The inflections in your voice allow the listeners to know if you are happy, sad, mad, disappointed, lifeless, or enthusiastic. The kiss of death for a public speaker's delivery is being monotone. **Monotone** can be defined as a constant, unchanging pitch or tone of voice. Such a flat line range in your pitch is a sure way to disengage and tire the audience. Another pitch variation that will turn off an audience is a repetitive inflection pattern that does not change, regardless of the content. Each of your words, sentences, and main points have their own distinct message, and you need to reinforce those messages with how you make those statements. Remember it is not only what you say, it is also *how* you say your message that makes an impact on your audience.

Rate of Speech

It has been documented that speakers in the United States speak between 125 to 150 words per minute, but that rate allows for some flexibility based on the speaker's own communication style. The term **rate of speech** refers to how fast a person speaks. The rate at which you speak will depend on a few different factors such as the ambiance you are trying to create, the audience's command of the language, and the occasion. Think about the different rates of speech that are used in sports commentary. When Tiger Woods is set to putt, the commentator will speak at a slower rate of speech. Conversely, when two horses are neck and neck at the Kentucky Derby, the commentator will speak at a very fast rate of speech. Each of these situations will dictate the appropriate rate of speech. Your rate of speech is something you need to consider when illustrating statistics, or telling a story. The rate of speech is an important component to maximizing your message. Be mindful though not to speak slowly in the spirit of stretching out your speech to meet a time requirement. When a speaker delivers a speech that is considerably slow the audience will be left with a lot of spare time, and their minds will begin to wander, as opposed to listening to your speech. Conversely, if you are delivering a speech where your rate rivals the racers at the Indianapolis 500 your audience will be lost and not be able to digest what you are trying to communicate. Delivery cues on your speaker's outline should keep you on track regarding your rate of speech (see Chapter 8).

Pauses

The use of strategically placed pauses can catapult a good speech to a great speech. However, for most beginning public speakers this can be quite a test to implement precisely. As you gain public speaking experience placing those pauses will become more natural in your delivery. A **pause** may be defined as a momentary break in the vocal delivery of a speech. A pause can close a thought, while your audience reflects on what you have just said, or it can let a dramatic statement just sit there while the audience ponders its significance. Developing your timing with your pauses will make sense because this is something you do in your everyday conversations.

As a point of caution, when using the pause in your speech, do not fill that silence with vocalized pauses. **Vocalized pauses** are pauses that occur when a speaker fills the silence between words with vocalizations such as "uh," "er," and "um." These voiced pauses are distracting and create a perception from the audience that the speaker is not confident or competent. When hearing these voiced pauses the audience will not have confidence in you because they communicate that the speaker has not practiced or does not understand the content of the message.

Vocal Variety

Vocal variety is the changes and variety in the speaker's rate of speech, volume, pitch, and how the speaker expresses his or her thoughts through the voice. Vocal variety enlivens a speech and makes it more relatable to an audience. The easiest way to measure your vocal variety is to record your speech and listen to your speech and ask yourself, "Am I capturing and enhancing the message I'm trying to communicate with my delivery?" Remember there are similarities between your vocal variety in everyday conversation and in public speaking.

Pronunciation

Having the correct pronunciation of words is challenging. Consider how geography influences the pronunciation of words, for example the word Houston. We can refer to Houston, Texas, and Houston would be pronounced h-yous-ton. Now we travel over to New York City and refer to the infamous Houston Street. If you were to pronounce the name of the street like you would the big city in Texas, the locals would know right away you are not familiar with the City. In New York City, Houston is pronounced house-ton. Unfortunately, we do not know when we are mispronouncing our words, so it is important to run your speech by a few people before presenting it. When in doubt about the proper pronunciation of a word, just look it up in a reputable dictionary.

Articulation

A common misconception is that pronunciation and articulation are the same things. **Articulation** is the physical production of particular speech sounds. So, poor articulation is the failure to form exact speech sounds crisply and clearly. This comes from sluggishness, and from failing to control your tongue, lips, and jaw to generate the needed sounds accurately. Unfortunately, while mumbling and slurring our words is acceptable in our everyday conversations, it is not acceptable in public speaking.

Dialect

A speech **dialect** is a variety of language that is distinguished by variations of accent, grammar, or vocabulary. Dialects are primarily based on regional or ethnic speech patterns. As much as we would like to think that our own geographical dialect is best, linguists conclude that no dialect is better or worse than another. Dialects are formed by regional or ethnic backgrounds, and every dialect fits each of the communities it serves.

With the special "flavor" each of the different speech dialects represent, perceptions of those dialects will influence how an audience will interpret a speaker's message. The United States contains four major regional dialects, Eastern, New England, Southern, and General American. A speaker who has a thick dialect may have a negative response from an audience who does not share that particular dialect. As responsible listeners to public addresses, it is your responsibility to listen to the speaker's ideas and evaluate the ideas and not the speaker personally.

THE SPEAKER'S PHYSICAL CHARACTERISTICS

How you present yourself in front of your audience will impact how your audience will respond to you as a speaker. Everything from your posture, your gestures, your eye contact, what and how you wear your clothes, and your personal grooming will be judged by your audience when presenting your speech. **Kinesics** is the study of body motions as a systematic mode of communication. How you use your body at the podium—such as the position of your head, eyes, and torso—impact the speaker's

Source: Shutterstock © Yuri Arcurs

message. In the next section, we will examine how your physical mannerisms will impact your message at the podium.

Personal Appearance

How you present yourself will influence how your audience will perceive you and your message. The occasion at which you will be speaking will often determine the appropriateness of what you should wear. The clothing you wear should not detract from you the public speaker. Thus, wearing t-shirts with controversial messages should be avoided, unless the message reinforces the specific purpose of your speech. Your personal appearance should reflect the time and place of the situation and occasion. However, regardless of the speaking situation, you should do your best to keep the best impression you can with your audience.

Movement

When you get the call that it is your turn to speak remember to compose yourself as you approach the podium. When you get to the podium, remember that the podium is there for you to place your notes, and not to lean on or hold on to for dear life. Before delivering your speech scan your audience, and make eye contact with your audience just to make sure you have their attention. Once that has been established you have the green light to start your speech. After delivering your speech still maintain your eye contact for a moment. By doing this your closing line will resonate with your audience, as opposed to racing off the podium saying "that's all I got." Another tips regarding movement is to wait until you are done with your presentation before gathering your notes and props.

A common distracting mannerism behind the podium is nervous movement. Some speakers sway from left to right like a clock. Driven by the speaker's nerves, a speaker's movement behind the podium may resemble variations of the cha-cha, the hustle, or the Irish Riverdance. Other distracting movements that need to be avoided are playing with the change in your pocket, fidgeting with your outline, shifting your weight from one leg to another, and leaning on the podium. Conversely a lack of motion, much like a statue with a blank look on one's face, needs to be avoided. As you concentrate on delivering your message to your audience, a natural movement will evolve with practice and public speaking experience behind the podium.

Source:: Shutterstock © Marcin Balcerzak

Gestures

A common concern for beginning public speakers is what they should do with their hands. In your everyday conversation you use your hands to reinforce particular points you are trying to make. The same goes for public speaking. When using your hands to gesture to the audience the movements need to come across as genuine and sincere, and not forced and unnatural. The last thing you want to do with your hands is to draw attention to your hands. In other words, you do not want to look like you are guiding an airplane at the airport, or look like the main character in a martial arts movie. So make sure your hand gestures appear real, so they clarify and reinforce your ideas. The bottom line is to focus on delivering your message to your audience, and let the hand gestures take care of themselves.

Eye Contact

One of the strongest ways to develop a connection with your audience is through eye contact. On the flip side, the best way to lose your audience is to not look at them at all. This usually happens when you read your speech, stare at the ground, or stare at the ceiling. If you decide not to look at your audience, your audience will lose trust in you as a speaker, and once that bond is broken it is difficult to restore. In your everyday encounters with other people, have you noticed when people look at you, but more

Source: Shutterstock © pzAxe

importantly how they look at you? The same goes for public speaking. How is the public speaker looking at the audience, or how is the audience looking at the public speaker? How the speaker looks at the audience does impact how the audience receives the speaker's message. How would you respond if the speaker had an expressionless stare while delivering a speech? Or how about the speaker who glares at the audience as if the audience took the speaker's last beer out of the refrigerator? Other dynamics of eye contact that need to be explored are that you need to scan the entire room and not make one person the center of your attention. For example a good way to make your public speaking teacher nervous is to simply stare at him or her throughout your speech and ignore the rest of the audience.

The size of the audience will impact how you make eye contact with your audience. For smaller audiences you can actually look at your audience members, but make sure you go from one side of the room to another effortlessly. On the other hand when addressing a larger audience you can simply scan the venue because it would be difficult to make eye contact with the entire audience. Your eyes communicate confidence and purpose so use them to build a positive relationship with your audience on your pathway to success.

PRACTICING DELIVERY

Proper practice makes perfect. Tiger Woods is the best golfer on the planet, and that is not by accident. When practicing at the driving range, most golfers would address the ball, hit it, and move on to the next ball without much thought. Woods visualizes everything from where he wants the ball to go to how he will address the ball, then he takes some practice swings before he steps up to hit the ball—every time. It is this kind of diligence in his practice regime that has made him the greatest golfer.

As a beginning public speaker you can adopt some of those strategies to help you deliver the best speech you can. First spend some time going over your speaker's outline. Do your main points lead you to your specific purpose? Do your introduction, body, conclusion, and transitions fit together like a puzzle? Are your points supported well and are they accurate? Spend time going over your speech aloud. Does it sound right to the ear? Writing for the eye is different than writing for the ear, so does your speech sound as good as it looks? Once these areas have been addressed, next take a look at your speaker's outline. Will the speaker's outline help you while you are at the podium? For example, is the font large enough for you to refer to while delivering your presentation? Should you incorporate different-colored fonts to highlight your delivery cues?

Now that you have your speaker's outline up to speed, practice your speech aloud. Do not worry the first few times you practice that you will not sound like you are ready to deliver the State of the Union address—just keep at it. You must focus on gaining command of the ideas of your presentation, and not try to learn the speech word for word. If you try to memorize your speech, your message will come across as stiff and not engaging to the audience. After a few runs through your speech you will capture the main ideas, examples, and statistics of your presentation.

Now that you have your speaker's outline established and have a strong grasp of the content of your speech, you can now focus on *how* you will phrase your words and sentences. The best thing to do here is to record your speech either on video or by audio for you to capture how an audience will see and hear your message. You want to evaluate your eye contact, rate of speech, volume, articulation, pronunciation, vocal variety, and pauses. Next, ask a few of your friends, family, co-workers, or classmates to listen to your speech. Remember public speaking is an audience-focused activity so it is best to practice in front of people. At this point in the process you should feel confident about yourself and your message so carry this momentum into your presentation.

As you can see, time management is important, so start the process early. Unfortunately, many beginning public speakers start late, and spend most of their time putting together the content of their message, and little time practicing the delivery of the message. As we discussed earlier in the chapter, imagine if a comedian spent his time writing his material and immediately went on stage to try to deliver his or her routine. The probability of the routine not being funny is pretty good, because a lack of practice will hurt the most hilarious of material. Spend time practicing your delivery so you can maximize the message you want to communicate to your audience on your pathway to success.

Summary: The Delivery of Your Speech

On your pathway to success, the delivery of your speech preparation is best captured by the expression "it is not only what you say, but also how you say it." Presentation makes a big impact on your message.

The different methods of delivery for public speaking are: speaking from a manuscript, reciting from memory, impromptu speaking, and extemporaneous speaking.

Once the method of delivery has been decided, the speaker's voice allows you to control and maximize your message. The components of the speaker's voice are: volume, pitch, rate of speech, pauses, vocal variety articulation, pronunciation, and speech dialects.

In addition to your voice, there are also physical characteristics to speech delivery. Kinesics is the study of body motions as a systematic mode of communication. When you give a speech, your audience will be impacted by your physical components such as your posture, your gestures, your eye contact, your clothing, and your personal grooming.

When practicing your delivery verify the accuracy of the information on your speaker's outline. Moreover, you want to ask yourself, "Is my speakers outline easy to refer to?" "Is the font large enough?" "Do I need to add color to my outline?" and "Is it easy for me to refer to the speaker's outline from the podium?" When practicing your speech, recite to your material several times so that you have a good feel for the main ideas, and try not to focus on getting everything down word for word.

Once the main ideas are known, you now have to figure out how to say your speech effectively. So record yourself either on video or audio and study your volume, rate of speech, articulation, pauses, pitch, and vocal variety. If you are able to video yourself, also analyze how your gestures, eye contact, and mannerisms add to your message. After your self-evaluation, go ahead and practice your speech in front of real people, since your final audience will be real people.

Last but not least in preparing your delivery is to get an early start on practicing for your speech. Unfortunately, poor time management hurts a speech that is well-constructed and supported, because it was not properly practiced and rehearsed. Do not fall into this category and prepare yourself thoroughly on your pathway to success.

Name: _____

True-False

1. (T) F   Nonverbal communication is based on a person's use of voice and body, rather than on the use of words.

2. T (F)   One of the advantages of speaking from a manuscript is that it frees a speaker from the need to establish eye contact with the audience.

3. (T) F   An extemporaneous speech is carefully prepared and practiced in advance.

4. (T) F   "Conversational quality" in a speech means that the speaker talks the same as she or he would in ordinary conversation.

5. T (F)   A faster rate of speech is usually called for when a speaker is explaining complex information.

6. T (F)   Vocalized pauses are an effective way to increase a speaker's credibility.

7. (T) F   Dialects are usually based on regional or ethnic speech patterns.

Multiple Choice

8. A public speaker who frequently says "uh," "er," or "um" is failing to make effective use of

   a. vocal variety.
   (b.) pauses.
   c. pitch.
   d. rate.
   e. inflection.

9. In which situation would a speaker be *most* likely to read from a manuscript?

   a. a speech accepting an award at a school banquet.
   b. a speech in honor of a retiring employee.
   (c.) a speech on international policy at the United Nations.
   d. a speech on the activities of a church social committee.
   e. a speech of welcome to new members of the Rotary Club.

10. According to your textbook, saying "gunna" instead of "going to" is an error in

   a. accent.
   (b.) articulation.
   c. vocalization.
   d. intonation.
   e. emphasis.

11. The study of bodily motion and gestures is part of a subject called

   a. cybernetics.
   b. kinetics.
   c. cryogenics.
   (d.) kinesics.
   e. cryonics.

12. A speech that is fully prepared in advance but that is delivered from a brief set of notes or a speaking outline is called a(n) _____ speech.

    a. extemporaneous
    b. declamatory
    c. impromptu
    d. manuscript
    e. memorized

13. In which of the following situations will the personal appearance of the speaker have an impact on the audience?

    a. a politician presenting a campaign speech
    b. a business executive giving a financial report
    c. a professor giving a lecture
    d. all of the above
    e. a and b only

14. According to your textbook, the _____ speaker delivers a speech with little or no immediate preparation.

    a. colloquial
    b. extemporaneous
    c. conversational
    d. impromptu
    e. declamatory

Essay

15. Explain the importance to effective public speaking of each of the following aspects of physical delivery:

personal appearance
movement
gestures
eye contact

Chapter 11

Using Language to Maximize Your Message

Philosopher Frantz Fanon said this about language, "mastery of language affords remarkable power" and the power of your language and word choice will lead you down your pathway to success. Your choice of words influences how you see your world, and those words will influence how your audience will receive you and your message. What if you were to journal your life for the past year. What words did you use to describe your experiences? Would they be passive, active, sad, happy, angry, or even-keeled? How did those words change over time? There is a theory called the Sapir-Whorf hypothesis that suggests that our language determines our view of the world. Your word choice will influence how effective your message will be to your given audience.

In this chapter we will be analyzing how language can affect your message to your audience. Since public speaking is an audience-focused activity, you need to tailor your message to your audience. A strong understanding of who you are speaking to should guide you in your word choice. For example if you are speaking to an audience with little or no familiarity with your topic, you must use elementary terms and communicate the most fundamental issues regarding your topic. On the flip side if you used advanced terminology with this same audience, the audience would be lost and become disinterested in your presentation. Your word choice can make or break the success of your speech, so think critically about your word choice.

Language is one of the speaker's tools to build a well-supported speech that meets the needs of the audience, the occasion, and the topic. We will examine how language is symbolic, the dynamics of power and powerless language, levels of abstraction, and the need for accuracy in your word choice. Moreover, precise word selection needs to be used to communicate respect and bring life to a speech for your audience.

LANGUAGE IS SYMBOLIC

Language is symbolic. Words are random symbols that do not have any significance in and of themselves. Language uses a symbol system to arrange, classify, and communicate thought. Our words are symbolic and indicate concrete objects and abstract thoughts.

USE SIMPLE LANGUAGE

A vital characteristic to becoming a successful communicator is to think simply. In short you want your message to be clear and understandable for your audience. You never want to talk down to your audience or they will be insulted; instead speak directly to the audience using words that put across a clear and concrete message. The Gettysburg Address best captures the idea of using simple, easy to understand, yet powerful language to communicate a core message.

The Gettysburg Address is probably one of the most memorable speeches in American history. One would think that Abraham Lincoln was popular and loved by the American people while serving as the President of the United States. At the time of the Gettysburg Address nothing could have been further from the truth. Lincoln was much criticized for his position on slavery and the Civil War. As the nation looked ahead to the presidential election of 1864, Democrats and even some the representatives in his own Republican party talked about the need to get rid of the incumbent Abraham Lincoln.

Organizers came up with the idea of setting up a cemetery at Gettysburg, not only as a place to bury the war dead, but also to raise the awareness of the role of the states in supporting the Civil War. The cemetery was planned and personally completed by David Wells, an attorney who was contracted by the governor of Pennsylvania. As a token gesture organizers invited Lincoln to say a few words at the end of the program for the dedication of the new cemetery. Surprisingly, Lincoln accepted the invitation to speak.

The keynote speaker for the cemetery dedication was Edward Everett. At that time Everett was recognized as the nation's premier orator. Interestingly, the original date for the dedication of the new cemetery was scheduled for September 23, 1863, but when organizers asked Everett in July of that year to speak, he said the soonest he could be ready would be November. Organizers approved Everett's desire and the dedication for the Gettysburg cemetery was scheduled for November 19, 1863.

Over two hours and 13,607 words later, Edward Everett had delivered a speech in front of an estimated crowd of 15,000 people. Now you would think that a speech that lasted that long and had so many words would be remembered by all. However, hundreds of years later, can the average person recall the content, key phrases, key ideas, or its significance, or that Everett was even at Gettysburg?

After the two-hour address by Everett it was Lincoln's turn to speak. In a little over two minutes Abraham Lincoln's Gettysburg Address contained 268 words, and only 18 of those words were more than

In just 268 words, Lincoln's Gettysburg address impacted American history
Source: Shutterstock © Joe Gough.

two syllables. Interestingly, of the 18 multi-syllable words in Lincoln address, he used the word dedicate or dedication six times.

The point is that using simple language that an audience can easily understand and remember will impact the audience. The opening phrase of "Fourscore and seven years ago . . ." is still a phrase that is remembered in our culture. An interesting point about Lincoln's message is that he says "The world will little note nor long remember what we say here, but it can never forget what they did here." President Lincoln was wrong; after a couple of hundred years the simple 268-word Gettysburg Address is still remembered and stands the test of time as one of America's rhetorical treasures. On your pathway to success, think simple common language that will resonate with your audience.

The Gettysburg Address

Fourscore and seven years ago our fathers brought forth on this continent a new nation, conceived in liberty and dedicated to the proposition that all men are created equal. Now we are engaged in a great civil war, testing whether that nation or any nation so conceived and so dedicated can long endure. We are met on a great battlefield of that war. We have come to dedicate a portion of that field as a final resting-place for those who here gave their lives that that nation might live. It is altogether fitting and proper that we should do this.

But, in a larger sense, we cannot dedicate, we cannot consecrate, we cannot hallow this ground. The brave men, living and dead who struggled here have consecrated it far above our poor power to add or detract. The world will little note nor long remember what we say here, but it can never forget what they did here. It is for us the living rather to be dedicated here to the unfinished work which they who fought here have thus far so nobly advanced. It is rather for us to be here dedicated to the great task remaining before us— that from these honored dead we take increased devotion to that cause for which they gave the last full measure of devotion—that we here highly resolve that these dead shall not have died in vain, that this nation under God shall have a new birth of freedom, and that government of the people, by the people, for the people shall not perish from the earth.

The transcript above is known as the "Bliss" copy, the widely adopted version of Lincoln's Gettysburg Address. However, the version quoted above is likely NOT the version delivered by Lincoln.

Restate Your Message

By restating your essential messages throughout your speech, you will allow your audience to absorb the heart of the message that you want them to walk away with. Restatement is the reiteration of words, phrases, and ideas as a form of reinforcement of your message. Simply repeating yourself is not what we are getting at with restating your message; instead the idea is to articulate your central theme differently in order to progress the listener's understanding or acceptance of your central theme.

POWER LANGUAGE AND RESPONSIBILITY

American author William Feather had this to say about the power of language, "Command of English, spoken or written, ranks at the top in business. Our main product is words, so knowledge of their meaning and spelling and pronunciation is imperative. If a man knows the language well, he can find out about all else."

The Use of Power Language will Embolden Your Command at the Podium

Using language properly in combination with a well delivered speech communicates power. An audience will be more receptive to a powerful speaker than a less powerful presence at the podium. Power does not mean that you need to yell, shout, or talk *at* your audience. So how do you communicate power? You communicate power by spending time thinking about the right words for your particular audience, and delivering them with absolute conviction. Moreover the delivery of your message needs to be free of stammering, stuttering, and continuous voiced pauses, such as, "uhm" or "uh . . . ," and "like" or "you know."

Let us consider power language in the context of asking your professor for a letter of recommendation for a job.

"Hi Professor Anderson, I hope you remember me, my name is Lisa Calderon. I took Speech 100, 120, and 150 with you, and earned two "A's" and a "B" during the last two academic years. I'm applying for a job with Cooper Public Relations in the City, and would like to ask if you could write me a letter of recommendation.

Cooper Public Relations has requested that the letter should be received by the end of the month since my interview is scheduled for the first week of December. The letter may be sent to the following person and address:

Donny Hill
Human Resources Department
Cooper Public Relations
The Embarcadero
San Francisco, CA 55555

Thanks so much for your help, and I sincerely appreciate your efforts on my behalf. I'll let you know how things work out."

Obviously Lisa is assertive, but not pushy, in her request for a letter of recommendation. Her word choice communicates confidence in her relationship with her professor, and in her request. Conversely, let us look at Steven Hill in his attempt to ask for a letter of recommendation using powerless language.

"Hi yah Professor Anderson, you ah probably don't remember me, I'm Steven Hill. I think uhm . . . I took Speech 120, and 150 with you. I don't remember what I got in your class, but I thought you were a cool teacher. I was kind of wondering if you write letters of reference . . . for your students, if so could I get one? There's this job that wants at least two letters, and I'm kinda scrambln' to get'em. Let me know if this is a can-do or something. Uh . . . if not I can try to go somewhere else."

The Professor agrees to write the letter.

"You will write one?! I didn't bring the contact information because, I uh . . . , I uh . . . , didn't think . . . , that you know . . . , that you would even consider, consider my request. So I guess I could email that over to yah in the next day or two.

Gee, thanks for helping me out, I'm surprised you remembered me, I didn't really participate or anything your class . . . , but . . . I did learn a lot I guess I should go now. Oh yeah . . . , the company needs it by Friday. Uh . . . See yah."

Steven is using powerless language with the uhs and uhms in his vocabulary. Moreover, Steven is using passive language; he already seems defeated before walking into his professor's office. Steven's language does not communicate confidence, competence, or assertiveness. As you can see the language that you use strongly influences how the audience will perceive you as a speaker and as a person. Let us hope that Steven can snap out of his self-defeating funk so he can land that job!

THE LANGUAGE OF RESPONSIBILITY

When writing your speech you must think about the responsibility you are taking with your words. The responsibility of language comes in the form of analyzing words like "I," "it," "you," and "we." Understanding the responsibility of language can really assist the audience in learning about where the speaker stands with the speech topic. Taking responsibility for your language helps make the content of your message unambiguous and shape the tone of the relationship you will have with the audience.

"It" statements usually replace the personal pronoun "I." "It" statements usually avoid responsibility and ownership of the message. Using an "it" statement is an unconscious way of not taking a position.

Next is a "but" statement. A "but" statement sounds like, "You have done a great job for us here, *but* I'm going to have to fire you." The word "but" cancels the thought that came before it: "Your speech is well developed *but* was way short of the ten minute time requirement." "But" statements are a face-saving language approach for conveying the speaker's true thoughts between more pleasant ideas.

"I" language shows that the speaker is taking responsibility in relating his or her position in a speech. Moreover, using "I" language does not put his/her audience members in a defensive state, unlike the rousing "you" language.

"You" language by and large communicates a judgment of another person, which can offend an audience. Furthermore, "you" language implies that the speaker is qualified to make the judgment for another person, so let us hope you have established the necessary credibility and goodwill to speak on the particular topic.

Finally, there is "we" language that implies that the speaker is showing concern and care for the audience by building an inclusive climate.

LEVELS OF ABSTRACTION

Abstract words tend to be very general, broad, and not specific, whereas **concrete words** are specific, particular, and based on something you can see. Based on S. I. Hayakawa's ladder of abstractions, here is an example of how one can go from a very abstract idea to a specific object. When you look at how these ideas are communicated, which term in the list makes more sense to you as you try to visualize the speaker's message?

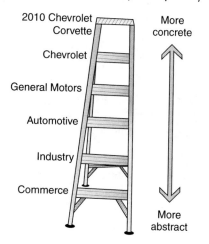

Hayakawa, Samuel I. (1978). Language in thought and action. Orlando, FL: Harcourt Brace Jovanovich

The more abstraction you use in your speech, the more you are asking your audience to use their imagination as to what you are talking about. For example, suppose I were to tell you that I saw a person wearing a casual outfit as he walked across campus. It will be up to you to fill in the blanks as to what a casual outfit would look like. Again, we would all have different definitions as to what is a "casual" outfit. However, if I were to say "a guy around nineteen years old wearing black baggy basketball shorts with a gray sweatshirt sporting the titanium Jordan XX3/XXXIII's," that description would create a picture for my audience. The more concrete and detailed your language is, the more you will remove the guesswork for your audience to interpret what you are trying to say.

Your audience will be more interested in a speech filled with concrete examples and concepts. Taking your language from the abstract to the concrete will make the speech real and tangible for the audience.

DENOTATIVE AND CONNOTATIVE WORDS

When crafting the wording for your public address, you must understand the direct and implied meanings of the words you are using. Each word carries a denotative and connotative meaning, and understanding the difference between the two will assist you in having a stronger command of your word choice. The **denotative** meaning of a word may be defined as the direct or explicit meaning or reference. When looking for the denotative meaning of a word, you may look at the dictionary definition of the word. The **connotative** meaning of a term is the suggested or the emotional tone of the word. For example the word "work" may imply feelings of drudgery, anguish, or a terrible way to spend 40 hours during a week. Whereas if you were happy about your job, the word "work" may project the feelings of excitement, adventure, challenge, or fulfillment. As you can see connotative words are highly interpretative and subjective. Not everyone in your audience will interpret your words as you intended your message to be delivered.

Moreover, make sure you know the meaning of the words you are using. If you are using a word that you do not understand, then simply look it up in a reputable dictionary. A question you want to ask yourself as you write your speech is, "is this a word my audience members may not understand?" If so, use a thesaurus and select a word that captures your point and is understandable to your audience. It is incredibly embarrassing while delivering your speech and looking at a word you have written and you have no idea what that word means, nor how to correctly pronounce it. Take the time to iron out those wrinkles in the preparation phase of your speech development.

ACCURACY OF YOUR LANGUAGE

Descriptive language depicts a specific behavior or action. Conversely, **evaluative language** witnesses a particular behavior or action, and then attaches a subjective interpretation of that behavior or action. The evaluative language can be asking for trouble because the interpretation may be inaccurate.

An interesting direction you may want to consider when accurately defining a word for your audience is to share the etymology of the word. Sharing the origin of the word will help your audience get a stronger understanding of where and how the word was derived. For example a speaker may say something like this: "The word commit comes from the Latin word committere or "to bring together." By highlighting the etymology of the word you can reinforce the audience's understanding of a key term you are defining.

As we learned earlier about concrete language, accuracy in your word choice is absolutely imperative. When you speak, your goal is to have your audience understand precisely what you are trying to say. Since words are symbolic and represent objects and concepts many of the words you may say can be interpreted in many different ways. Think about the last time you talked to your boyfriend/girlfriend or husband/wife and had the "state of the relationship" talk. Then comes the phrase "you are not committed to the relationship" and the discussion goes back and forth regarding each other's "commitment" to the relationship. Until the term "committed" is clearly defined and agreed upon by both parties this discussion will go nowhere. The same thing happens with your audience; key terms need to be defined so there is a mutual understanding of each term. Defining your key terms for your audience will build a sense of inclusion with your presentation.

Audience members need to understand the key terminology of your presentation—especially if your topic is unfamiliar to the audience. A common strategy to bring your audience up to speed is the use a dictionary definition of a term. For example, if you are discussing a topic in the medical field using the *Black's Medical Dictionary* or the *Merriam-Webster's Medical Dictionary* may be a credible choice for you to implement. Another option you have is using the **stipulative** definition, which describes the way the term will be used in a particular context. For example, "When I say 'committed to the relationship,' I mean. . ." As you can see there are numerous options as to how you can define essential terms in your speech. When making your decision as to which strategy to choose, consider your audience, your topic, and your purpose.

Using Language Respectfully

"We are at a time in our country's history that inclusive language is better than exclusive language."

—Barack Obama, President of United States

A principle that will shore up your communication skills is to learn to speak respectfully to all of the people in your audience. When addressing an audience it is important that you build the spirit of inclusion as opposed to division. Communicators are often attracted to those whose speaking styles are similar to theirs. There are numerous ways you can include your audience into your message by not dividing your audience based on the following: establishing in-group and out-group identities, or by framing negative judgments based on gender, ethnicity, sexual orientation, religious beliefs, or worldviews.

Inclusive language is language that unites an entire audience into your message, and that does not leave portions of your audience out of the mix. You can increase your chances of being inclusive by avoiding slang, because this type of language may be understood by only a small portion of your audience. Furthermore, conducting an audience survey before delivering your speech can help you find ways to build an inclusive message for your audience.

Bring Life to Your Words

Language may be both literal and figurative. Using **literal language** uses words as facts; conversely, **figurative language** compares one concept to another similar but different concept. Here are some examples of using figurative language.

Similes

When a public speaker uses a **simile**, the speaker is making a clear comparison of two things that uses the word "like" or "as." Here are some examples of similes:

I'm stiff as a board

Runs like a deer

You are slow as molasses

He is poor as dirt

Fits like a glove

Mad as a hornet

Flat as a pancake

Metaphor

A **metaphor** is the comparison of two dissimilar things in order to imply a resemblance. The etymology of the word metaphor comes from the Greek word meaning transference. So when you use a metaphor you are transferring the qualities from one thing to another while showing their similarities. Here are some examples of some metaphors:

Life is not a sprint it is a marathon.

The doctor inspected the rash like a hawk.

Fairness means leveling the playing field.

The lawyer grilled the witness on the stand.

Focus is keeping your eye on the ball.

A recipe for disaster.

Send in the heavy hitters if you want results.

A **mixed metaphor** makes irrational comparisons between two or more things. When a speaker applies a mix in their metaphors, they begin with one metaphor and then half way through switch to another.

I don't want to say they lost sight of the big picture, but they have marched to a different drummer.

Keep your eye on the ball, your ear to the ground.

Personification

A public speaker uses **personification** when he or she attributes human qualities (sight, speech, hearing, thought, emotion, action, or sensation) to animals, object, or concepts.

That chocolate cake is smiling at me.

My car loves to sleep when I need it most.

A famous use of personification is from U.S. Supreme Court Justice Earl Warren during his eulogy for John F. Kennedy, "Such acts are commonly stimulated by forces of hatred and malevolence such as today are eating their way into the bloodstream of American life."

Rhythm

Rhythm is the arrangement of words into a relationship so the sounds of the words together enhance the meaning of a phrase. Consider delivering a speech persuading your audience to go to the horse races in their free time, and you are illustrating the highs and lows of horse racing.

> *"Your heart is beating out of your chest. You are clenching your ticket for dear life. Your horse is zipping into the homestretch. He's crossing the finish line. It's a photo finish. The judges are reviewing the finish. Sweat beads come from your head. You're breathing fast. The official judgment is announced. Your horse lost by a nose."*

The rhythm is relatively quick, but because of the short sentences and a quick delivery, it can build suspense into your speech.

Parallelism

When a public speaker coordinates related words so they are balanced or arranges related sentences so that they are identical in structure, the speaker is using **parallelism**.

Not Parallel: The hiring supervisor was told to write his speech accurate*ly*, quick*ly*, accurate*ly*, and *in a meticulous way.*

Parallel: The hiring supervisor was told to write his speech accurate*ly*, quick*ly*, and thorough*ly*.

Here are some examples of parallelism in a few famous speeches.

> *"Let every nation know, whether it wishes us well or ill, that we shall pay any price, bear any burden, meet any hardship, support any friend, oppose any foe to assure the survival and the success of liberty."*
>
> —John F. Kennedy, Presidential Inaugural Address, January 20, 1961

> *". . . and that government of the people, by the people, for the people, shall not perish from the earth."*
>
> —Abraham Lincoln, Gettysburg Address, November 19, 1863

Repetition

Using repetition in your word choice can help your audience sense your cadence, and the rhythm of your linguistic structure. Using **repetition** in a speech is when the speaker repeats keywords or phrases at the beginnings or endings of sentences or clauses. In addition to your linguistic structure it is combined with the speaker's voice, rate of speech, volume, vocal variety, and pitch. Moreover, using the repetition strategy can energize your audience while helping them retain your message. Here are some examples of repetition.

> *"Mad world! Mad kings! Mad composition!"*
>
> —(King John, by William Shakespeare)

"There is nothing wrong with America that cannot be cured by what is right with America."
—(BILL CLINTON, AMERICAN PRESIDENT)

"When I was a child, I spake as a child, I understood as a child, I thought as child."
—(I CORINTHIANS 13.11)

Alliteration

Alliteration may be defined the repetition of an initial consonant. Here are some examples using alliteration:

The *b*asketball *b*ounced *b*eyond the court into the *b*arrel.

*W*hy not *w*aste a *w*ild *w*eekend at *W*oodside *W*ater *W*orld?

I don't need a boyfriend like him, they are a *d*ime a *d*ozen.

Our *c*ompact *c*ar *c*rashed on the *c*urb.

Antithesis

Using **antithesis** in a speech is when you place words and phrases in contrast or in disagreement with one another. Antithesis is perhaps more complex than parallelism and alliteration, but it still is used with great success. As you put your speech ideas together, check to see if you might be able to phrase them using the antithesis strategy.

Jim Elliot, an evangelical Christian missionary, used this antithesis, "He is no fool who gives what he cannot keep to gain that which he cannot lose."

"The Serenity Now" episode from television program *Seinfeld* used this popular antithesis quote "Serenity now; insanity later."

Imagery

Imagery can be an outstanding way to use language to connect your message to your audience's senses, to enrich their listening experience. The **imagery** descriptions would describe a human's senses: sight, sound, taste, touch, and smell.

Examples of Sound Imagery

Birds are chirping

The car roared down the street

Laughter of young children

Examples of Smell Imagery

Freshly cut grass

Fresh out of the oven bread

Spilled gasoline

Examples of Taste Imagery

Cold beer on a sweltering day

Habañero peppers

SweetTarts candy

Examples of Touch Imagery

Scraping your knee on the asphalt

Water on your feet

Walking on air

Examples of Sight Imagery

The sun setting

Snow-capped mountains

The mansion on the hill

Because of the different senses we all have, consider tapping into as many of those senses as possible in using imagery in your speech.

GENDER AND LANGUAGE

Gender-linked words are words that directly or indirectly categorize males or females, such as, policeman, fireman, congresswoman, or chairwoman. A **gender-neutral** style of language would say: police officer, firefighter, congressperson, or chairperson. As a public speaker you must not divide your audience and by using gender-neutral language you will build inclusion of your audience.

Summary: Using Language to Maximize Your Message

Language is the means in which a public speaker communicates his or her message. In order to maximize your message on your pathway to success, you must tailor your message to *your* audience. According to who your audience is, you must make the necessary adjustments to meet the needs of your audience.

Language is symbolic and words are random symbols to arrange, classify, and communicate thought. A strong principle to help you become a competent communicator is to use simple language that is easy for your audience to understand. However, you never want to talk down to your audience in a condescending way.

One strategy to that will help your message stick with the audience is using the restatement strategy, which is the reiteration of words, phrases, and ideas. In analyzing your word choice the level of the speaker's responsibility shines through, through the use of "I," "it," "you," or "we" language.

A particular strategy that helps your audience make more sense of your message is to use concrete language as opposed to abstract language. Abstract language is broad and general words to illustrate an idea; in contrast, concrete terms are very specific terms to express your ideas. Moreover, having a clear understanding of the words you are using is beneficial. For example, the denotative meaning of the word is the explicit meaning or dictionary meaning of the word. Conversely, the connotative meaning of the word is the suggested meaning or the emotional tone of the word.

A sure way to turn off an audience is to use disrespectful language in your speech. Your goal as a speaker is to use inclusive language to embrace your audience, as opposed to dividing your audience. A word choice that can build an inclusive bridge is to use figurative language. Under the figurative language umbrella, the following strategies may be used in your speech: similes, metaphor, personification, rhythm, parallelism, repetition, alliteration, antithesis, and imagery. In contrast, employing literal language uses words as facts. Another way to potentially turn-off an audience is to not use gender-neutral language. Gender-linked words are words that directly or indirectly categorize males or females such as policeman, fireman, congresswoman, or chairwoman. A gender-neutral style of language would say: police officer, firefighter, congressperson, or chairperson. As a public speaker you must not split your audience and by using gender-neutral language you will build inclusion of your audience.

On your pathway to success, making intelligent choices with your language will maximize the effectiveness of your presentation.

Name: _____

True-False

1. T (F) A speech dominated by abstract words will always be clearer than one dominated by concrete words.

2. T (F) If the meaning of a word is clear to the speaker, the speaker can assume that it is also clear to the audience.

3. T (F) The denotative meaning of a word includes all the feelings, associations, and emotions that the word touches off in different people.

4. T F The use of repetition in a speech usually results in parallelism.

5. T (F) Antithesis and alliteration are excellent ways to enhance the imagery of a speech.

6. (T) F The connotative meaning of a word is more variable, figurative, and subjective than its denotative meaning.

Multiple Choice

7. _____ is the repetition of the initial consonant sound of close or adjoining words.

   a. Antithesis
   b. Assonance
   c. Anaphora
   d. Arthimeria
   (e.) Alliteration

8. The denotative meaning of a word is

   a. what the word suggests or implies.
   b. based on the audience's sense of appropriateness.
   c. usually more abstract than its connotative meaning.
   d. often too technical to be used in a speech.
   (e.) its literal or dictionary meaning.

9. Which of the following words is the most general and abstract?

   a. skyscraper
   b. construction
   c. Empire State Building
   (d.) shelter
   e. building

10. When used effectively, repetition in a speech

   a. unifies a sequence of ideas.
   b. helps to build a strong cadence.
   c. reinforces an idea.
   d. all of the above.
   (e.) b and c only.

Essay

11. Describe the differences between gender-linked and gender-neutral language.

12. Explain how power language strengthens your command at the podium.

13. Distinguish the differences between "I," "it," "you," "we," and "but" language.

Chapter 12

Visual Aids

Adding visual aids to your speech can improve the clarity of your message. A properly used visual aid will contribute to making the speaker's ideas come alive, and assist the audience in retaining the information presented. Because of the visually stimulating world in which we live, adding visual aids can be just the touch that resonates your message with your audience. Most audiences need something real and tangible to build the necessary connection between the speaker and the topic, and a visual aid can be that bridge. For example if you are stating a demographic breakdown of a particular college, merely stating the numbers orally may be impressive to the audience, but a pie graph illustrating the breakdown would greatly enhance the impact of the numbers. Moreover, adding the visual component to the listening component will help reinforce the message you are trying to communicate, leading to stronger retention of the material by the audience.

In today's multimedia world it is vital that you know how to use visual aids in your presentations for improved persuasiveness. This skill will greatly boost your professional standing and move you up in your career and life aspirations. In short, visuals can make drab information interesting and vibrant to the audience, building a stronger relationship between the speaker and the audience.

As you go through the process of putting together a speech, when you have completed your preparation outline and are absolutely sure of the content of your speech, you can now think about how to communicate your key ideas using visual aids.

In this chapter we will be examining the different types of visual aids that you would use in a speech, as well as some guiding principles to follow regarding visual aids; in conclusion, we will give a brief discussion of the multimedia presentation software PowerPoint.

TYPES OF VISUAL AIDS TO IMPROVE YOUR MESSAGE

Adding visual aids to your speech can come in many forms such as the speaker, objects, models, photos, drawings, charts and graphs, transparencies, audio, and video. In this section we will discuss the different classifications of visual aids you may choose from and the particular dynamics used for each of these styles of visual aids.

The Speaker

The speaker can be used as a visual aid to reinforce or demonstrate a particular image. Often times the speaker may use themselves to show a dance step, a yoga position, a message in sign language, a particular cultural attire, or a tae kwon do move. When using yourself as a visual aid, spend time coordinating between you and the speaker's outline so that your visual does not drag on as you meet your desired time requirement.

Objects

Any physical object may be used as a visual aid. However, one thing to keep in mind is that the object needs to be large enough for the audience members in the back of the room to see, and small enough for you to carry around. Objects that have been used as a visual aids have ranged from rocks, to tools, to jewelry, to computers, to clocks. If the object you plan to use is small do not pass it around the room while you are speaking. The focus will now be on the object and not on you or your message. In addition, the internal noise and commotion of passing the object around will distract your audience from listening to your message.

If you consider using a live animal as a visual aid, be very vigilant for the animal's and your audience's safety. Moving an animal out of its natural element is very traumatic and may jeopardize its safety. When in doubt use a photo and please consult with your instructor or the organizers of the event where you will be speaking to find out if it is okay to use a live animal. Moreover, it is strongly recommended that you do not use prohibited objects, such as weapons or drugs, for your presentations.

Models

If you are delivering a presentation in which your item is either too big or too small to easily present, then using a model can help you visualize that item for your audience. For instance, say you were delivering a speech about the Boeing 747. Obviously that would be difficult to bring into a classroom, so you would use a model to illustrate the plane. On the other end of the spectrum, if you were delivering a presentation about ladybugs, the actual ladybug would be difficult to see, so a larger model would help show its physical characteristics. One advantage of using a model is that it is mobile and something you can use to show your audience from one end of the room to another.

Photos

Photos may be an excellent alternative to using models to help your audience visualize your topic. Photos take an abstract idea and make it real for the audience to comprehend. A few questions you want to ask yourself are: Is the photo large enough for your audience to see? Does it capture the point I'm trying to make? Should I place it on a transparency or PowerPoint for my audience to adequately see? You do not want to pass photos around the audience while you are speaking because it is distracting for the audience and speaker with all of the hullabaloo going on.

There are numerous ways to gather photos for your presentation. One, you can take pictures yourself on a digital camera and post them on a PowerPoint slide, or have them printed onto a transparency. Next, you can go on the Internet and select photos from there to use in your presentation. If you were to go to Google images and type in your subject, numerous photos will come up. When using this route to get photos for your presentation, you must credit the source of the photo in your visual aid.

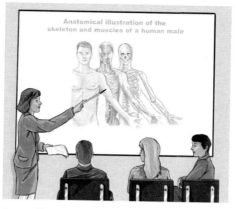

Source: Shutterstock © hkannn.

Drawings

If you are looking for a more "authentic" approach than photos, then drawings may be your best bet. By physically drawing your picture you can tailor the drawing to the specific point you are trying to make. One major drawback to drawing is that it is time consuming and that takes away from other more important aspects of the public speaking process. Another concern to consider when using drawings is that you must be very careful when transporting your drawings because they can easily be wrecked. In addition, ask yourself whether your drawings are large enough for the audience members in the back of the room to see. Moreover, will you have the necessary support to be able to display the drawings, such as tape or thumbtacks to hold up your drawing while you are presenting your speech? Holding your drawings would limit your hand gestures.

Graphs

Graphs come in handy when you are discussing statistics and numerical data in your speech. Reciting numbers to an audience is hard on the ears, but can be easy on the eyes. Graphs clarify statistics and difficult series of numbers, so as a courtesy to your audience consider graphing your numerical data. There are three kinds of graphs that you can use to illustrate your points more clearly for your audience, the pie graph, the bar graph, and the line graph.

The **pie graph** is often used to show a percentage of the whole. The visual for a pie graph is a circle showing a prearranged whole that is divided into piece wedges. Pie charts are helpful since the size of the pie pieces represent the proportion of people or items in each category. A pie graph should have between two and five wedges and no more than eight. If too many wedges are used in a pie graph, the graph will become confusing and this defeats the purpose of using a pie graph. For instance, in Figure 12.1 let us say that you want to show your audience the findings from your audience survey stating that 42% of the class purchased their textbooks from the college bookstore. Here is how that would look on a pie chart.

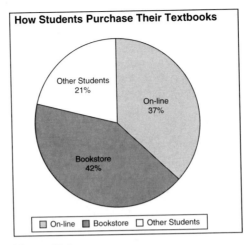

Figure 12.1

The **bar graph** may be used to show comparisons between two or more items. It usually does not matter whether you display the bars horizontally or in a column chart that displays the bars vertically on the chart. The biggest advantage of using a bar graph is that they are easy to read and to show complex ideas simply. In Figure 12.2 the bar graph shows the relationship between the age of the student body and the percentage of the student population. Rattling off the numbers to the audience may seem like a good idea, but the bar graph communicates the information more clearly, which leads to stronger audience retention of the material.

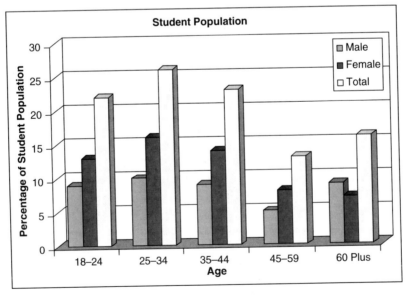

Figure 12.2

The most common graph used in a presentation is a **line graph** that uses one or more lines to show changes in statistics over time or space. The line graph uses a vertical and horizontal scale to show the correlation between the two variables. For example in Figure 12.3 the line graph shows your audience how the sales trend for the past five years has increased or decreased. The line graph would work well in demonstrating changes in statistics over time.

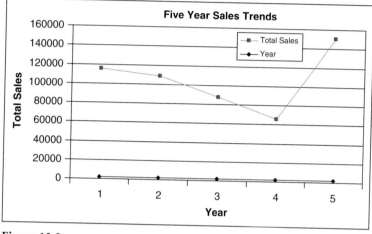

Figure 12.3

During your presentation you may use all or just one of these types of graphs to showcase your ideas. Graphing your ideas allows you to help your audience interpret challenging numerical data for the utmost comprehension. Furthermore, using graphs help you support your ideas visually in an interesting and clarifying manner.

Charts

Charts are an outstanding way to consolidate and summarize large amounts of information. Usually the amount of information that needs to be categorized would be more than you can appropriately work with in pie graphs, bar graphs, or line graphs. It is easier to just list your information on a chart and discuss the points in your presentation. Charts are particularly helpful if there is information that you think your audience may want to jot down such as key phone numbers, addresses, or Web sites. Remember that a public speaker uses visual aids to simplify and clarify complex ideas. However, using a chart may tempt you to put up too much information and to present your information in a disorganized fashion. Limit the chart to no more than seven or eight items with adequate spacing between each of your items.

An informational chart may take the form of a table. In Table 12.1 the table presents key contacts for the ACME Corporation. As you can see, the information presented in a table is presented in rows and columns.

Table 12.1

ACME Corporation Key Contacts		
Employee Name	**Department**	**Phone Extension**
Cindy McDougal	Accounting	3928
Paul Mariman	Marketing	3876
Hanah Nelson	Manufacturing	3530
Ron Carnell	Quality Assurance	3527
Patti Thornton	Sales	3958

Another kind of chart that you may want to consider for your presentation is a flow chart. A **flow chart** is a diagram that represents a process or a hierarchical structure. Figure 12.4 uses a flow chart to visually represent the hierarchy of who reports to the store manager at a local grocery store.

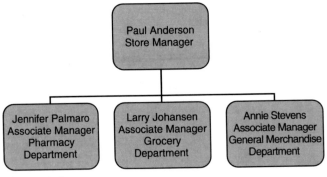

Figure 12.4

Transparencies

Using an overhead projector to display transparencies is a common tool in boardrooms and classrooms. However, as time goes by overhead projectors will soon be outdated in the modern business environment as the move to electronic means of communicating becomes more common. Transparencies displaying graphs, photos, charts, and tables are easy to use and produce. They can be made from any computer and printed onto the transparency film directly from your printer. If your printer does not have this capability, you can take your electronic files to a copy store to have them produced for you. Moreover, transparencies are easy to carry around and are difficult to damage.

When using transparencies during your speech make sure your slides are legible from the back of the room. In addition it is frowned upon to write on your slides while delivering your presentation. As part of your preparation process become familiar with the overhead projector ahead of time so when you are delivering your speech you are not trying to figure out how to use the machine in front of your audience. The image you want to project while delivering a speech is competence and confidence, and fumbling around with transparencies and the overhead will hurt that desired image.

Video

Video can be an excellent way to help you illustrate your message in motion. However, there are drawbacks to using video in your presentation. Using video can be difficult because of the frequencies of technical difficulties, and few things will hurt your confidence more than trying to figure out why the video machine is not working in front of an audience. Moreover video technical difficulties take attention away from the speaker which may hurt how the audience perceives the speaker. If you do decide to use video, your clips need to be brief, well edited, and really hit the point you are trying to make. Make sure you practice your speech with the video machine in the room you will be delivering your presentation. This will allow you to hone in your timing, be more familiar with the video machine, and build confidence in case any glitches occur. Spending a good amount of time practicing your delivery with your video clips will allow you to reap the benefits of video to support your points.

A common error for beginning public speakers is to play a video that goes on for the bulk of the time duration allotment for your speech. That is a poor use of time, because the audience is there to listen to the public speaker and not watch a video. Limit your video or audio clips to no longer than 20 or so seconds.

GUIDING PRINCIPLES FOR USING VISUAL AIDS

Preparing your visual aids is the icing on the cake in your speech presentation preparation. After you have your preparation outline complete and the foundation of your speech has been established, the thought process of using a visual aid must be developed. Your choice of visual aids must add value to your message, and not get in the way of your message. There are guiding principles for using visual aids for your speech.

Critically Think Ahead When Implementing Visual Aids

When you have finished your preparation outline, your next train of thought will be "which visual aid works best to strengthen my message?" As a public speaker you need to give yourself an adequate amount of time preparing your visual aids. Burning the midnight oil will not work for you when preparing visual aids. By spending quality time on your visual aids after arranging your preparation outline, your aids will look more creative and professional, adding a competent and confident image to you and your message.

Organizing your speech preparation timeline well will allow you to think creatively about presenting visual aids that are simple and highlight your ideas clearly and accurately. Moreover, not every point in your presentation needs a visual aid; so do not clutter your speech with visuals.

By preparing ahead of time you can adequately practice your delivery with your visual aids so that when you deliver your speech in front of your audience your speech will be delivered seamlessly between the content of your speech and your visual aids. Incorporating visual aids without the necessary practice can be potentially disastrous to your speech and your public speaking confidence.

Your Visuals Need to be Seen By Everyone

Using a visual aid that is seen by only the first two rows of an eight-row room is a sure way to turn off an audience. A guiding principle for using visual aids is that everyone needs to be able see and read your aid. Therefore, knowing the size of the room and other distinct characteristics of the room is vital when creating your visual aids. When creating a visual aid on a computer, make sure your fonts are large enough for everyone in the room to read your message. Your visual aids cannot resemble the eye charts you would see at an eye doctor, especially that last line. Recognized experts in using visual aids recommend using a 36-point font for your headings, a 24-point font for subtitles, and 18-point font for other text. Moreover, it is not recommended to use the ALL CAPS for your fonts. ALL CAPS make it difficult to read for your audience, and dilutes the importance of the words you are ALL CAPPING.

Adding color brings vibrancy to your visual aid, but be careful not to incorporate too many colors into your aids. In most cases, your charts or graphs should be narrowed to a few colors in a consistent pattern that is pleasing to the eye. The common and accepted practice is to use dark print or lettering on a light background especially if you are using poster boards or an overhead transparency. If you are using a multimedia presentation like PowerPoint you may find that light print on a dark background works better. In either case, make sure there is enough contrast between the background and the text so listeners can see everything clearly.

Presenting Your Visual Aids to Your Audience

A well thought out and carefully prepared visual aid will communicate very little if you do not know *how* to present those visual aids to your audience. Careful consideration is needed in how to properly discuss your visuals, and seamlessly implement them into your presentation.

One visual to avoid is using the chalkboard or whiteboard to present your ideas. Using the blackboard requires you to write on the board, which takes up too much time, and requires you to write legibly which can be a challenge with your audience staring at you. Moreover, your audience does not want to be watching your backside, which can be considered rude from the perspective of the audience.

An advanced scouting report of the room where you will be delivering your speech is needed. You will need to know how large the room is, and any other distinct shapes and sizes of the room so you can prepare your visual aids accurately. If you decide to use drawings or poster boards you need to know if you have clips or clamps to hold up your visual aids. Moreover, you want to position your drawings or objects so your audience can see the aid so you do not have to stand in its way.

A sure way to create a distracting environment for delivering your speech is to pass out handouts while delivering your speech. Your audience's attention will be turned to viewing and passing your visual aids instead of listening to your address. If for some reason you want your audience to have a handout, be sure to distribute the handout after you deliver your speech.

Another tip that gets overlooked is to display your visual aid only when it corresponds to what you are talking about in your presentation. Because your visual aid will draw the attention of your audience, your audience will be looking at your aid as opposed to listening to the speaker. So you will be sending mixed messages if your message does not relate to the visual aid. If you are discussing an object, chart, or photo keep it out of sight until you are ready to discuss it. When you finish your discussion regarding the visual aid, move the visual aid out of sight of the audience. If you are using PowerPoint or some other multimedia presentation software, go to a blank screen if you are not talking about the slide that is being projected. When you are done talking and referring to a visual aid, promptly remove the visual aid.

How your body is positioned is an important feature when you are utilizing a visual aid. It is okay to briefly look at your visual, but you are required to make eye contact with the audience to gather the necessary feedback from your audience. Also, make sure that the visual aid you are using is not being blocked by you or other objects like a podium; your audience needs to be able to see what you are referring to in your presentation. In addition, you never want to turn your back to the audience or talk to the visual aid. Using a pointer, a pencil, or a laser light pointer would be appropriate to focus your audience's attention on a particular portion of your visual aid.

It is not enough just to show visual aids to the audience; you also need to explain why those visuals are important and how they directly relate to the audience. Moreover, you have to let the audience know what to look for and why. Novice public speakers have a tendency to rush through the visual aids without explaining the aids to the audience. You must tell the audience what the visual aid means and its relevance to the message and how that impacts the audience.

In short, your visual aid is an added component to the preparation outline. A speech with visual aids must be practiced so that your message will be communicated flawlessly. The last thing you want to do is learn how to incorporate your visual aids into your speech for the first time in front of your audience—take care of that before heading to the podium.

Using Multimedia Software for Your Presentations

Because of the popularity and access to Microsoft products, we will discuss how you can use PowerPoint to add zest to your message on your pathway to success. PowerPoint, a proprietary presentation software used by millions of users, allows a visual aid support for speech presentations. PowerPoint can be an empowering tool to communicate your message effectively. Using PowerPoint allows you to have your visual aids all in one software package as opposed to physically carrying a poster board, or photos, or models, charts and graphs, and video tape/DVD capabilities. PowerPoint allows you to add compelling visuals in an easy-to-use format. Some of the information presented about the aesthetics of using PowerPoint may be repeated from the standards in creating visual aids. We will not get into the details of how to use the program from scratch; instead we will offer tips to implement when using PowerPoint.

A potential drawback of working with PowerPoint is that the creator of the presentation focuses on awing the audience with all of the razzle-dazzle features as opposed to using simple graphics to add value to the message. Sometimes the creators of the slide presentation think more sizzle than steak. In addition, many creators spend all of their time developing the slide presentation instead of the well-thought, well-researched, well-organized, audience-focused speech. Moreover there is an inclination to use PowerPoint exclusively for text-only presentations which allows the audience to read the speech as opposed to listening to the speech.

After completing your preparation outline you will need to think about picking and choosing your spots to use PowerPoint. When working with PowerPoint you will be working with **slides**, the single frame in a PowerPoint presentation. The main elements of PowerPoint slides are text, images, graphs, charts, sound, and video.

The use of text on a PowerPoint slide may just be the title of the slide to support a photo, chart, or image. Or you may have a slide with just bullet points of text only. When using PowerPoint you have numerous choices in font selection. There are two categories to choose from when selecting a font, serif or sans-serif. **Serif fonts** have the little tails on each of the letters, whereas **sans-serif fonts** do not have the tails. When a slide has a large amount of text the serif font is the preferred style. Conversely, the sans-serif fonts are used in slide titles, headings, and brief bulleted text-points. Titles and major headings are usually in the 46 to 36-point type range, whereas the subheads and other text are in the 32 to 24-point range. Lastly copyright credits use a 10-point font.

The Yorkshire Terrier

- Yorkshire Terrier's are easily adaptable to all surroundings, travel well and make suitable pets for many homes.

- Due to their small size, they require limited exercise, but need daily interaction with their people.

Max

A common error when using PowerPoint is to put too much information on one slide. The overload of information leads to clutter and confusion for the audience viewing the messy slide. There should be no more than six or seven lines on a slide if it is text only. If you are combining text and a graphic you may want to limit your text even further so the photo stands out and it is easy to follow for the audience. Staying with the PowerPoint default layouts will allow you to create symmetrical and visually balanced slides.

If you are looking online for photos to use in your presentation, one place to go is Pics4Learning that shows thousands of free photos with no copyright restrictions. Another place you can visit is a site called Free Stock Photos. In addition to photos the use of clip art may help illustrate your points. **Clip art** encompasses pictures and symbols representing common objects and ideas and can be retrieved from PowerPoint itself.

PowerPoint also has the capability to incorporate video and sound into your presentation. Keep in mind that you want to keep your clips brief so use no more than 30 seconds of music, video, or lyrics from an individual musical work without obtaining permission.

Consistency in color is important throughout your PowerPoint presentation. It is customary to have one color for your background, one for your title, and one color for other text throughout the presentation. The consistent color patterns unify your message into a harmonious theme both in context and aesthetics. When using a LCD projector using a light text against a dark background provides the best contrast for your visuals.

The animation of your slides can spotlight your message that you are trying to communicate. **Animation** may be defined by how objects or text enter or exit a slide while presenting your speech. If you did not use the animation feature on PowerPoint all of the information on the slide would appear at the same time once the slide was displayed. By using the animation feature you control what and when the audience sees the information on your slides as it correlates to where you are in your speech. When working on the visual aids of your speech think about ways to utilize the animation feature of PowerPoint. Again with the numerous features PowerPoint has, using too much animation can be distracting and frankly annoying for the audience to endure. Let us not agitate the audience with a gaudy slide show.

Summary: *Using Visual Aids to Support Your Main Ideas*

Visual aids in your speech can enrich the simplicity of your message. A correctly used visual aid will help your ideas flourish and assist your audience in retaining the ideas you have presented.

After you have completed your preparation outline, then you are ready to think about which visual aid will work best at reinforcing your spoken ideas. Visual aids can come in many forms such as the speaker, objects, models, photos, drawings, charts and graphs, transparencies, audio, and video. If you are discussing an object, chart, or photo keep it out of sight until you are ready to discuss it.

The speaker is an option for a visual aid. For example, the speaker may use himself or herself in demonstrating Pilates moves, cultural clothing, or a dance step. A model can illustrate an object that is either too big or too small to use in a classroom or boardroom setting. For example, if you were delivering a speech about the Golden Gate Bridge, it would be difficult to bring the actual bridge into your classroom, so a model would have to do. Photos are another effective way to take your abstract ideas and make them more concrete. If you are looking for a more "authentic" approach than photos, drawings may be your best bet. One major drawback to using a drawing is that it is time consuming to prepare and can take away from other more important aspects of the public speaking preparation process.

There are three forms of graphs that you can use to embody your points more evidently for your audience, the pie graph, the bar graph, and the line graph. The pie graph is frequently used to show a percentage of the whole. The diagram for a pie graph is a circle showing a whole that is divided into sectioned wedges. The bar graph may be used to show relationships between two or more items. It usually does not matter whether you display the bars horizontally, or in a column chart that shows them vertically. The most frequent graph used in a presentation is a line graph that uses one or more lines to show adjustments in statistics over time or space. Charts are an outstanding way to consolidate and summarize large amounts of information. A flow chart is a map that represents a process or a hierarchical structure.

Now that you have these options at your fingertips, you need to consider how to present those options. You may want to use transparencies because are easy to use and can be printed directly from any computer. Perhaps you would consider the accessible presentation software PowerPoint from Microsoft to use as a visual aid tool.

Another option you have is to bring your ideas to life is using video or audio. The challenge to using audio or video is the high probability of technical difficulties in the middle of your presentation. Your video or audio clips need to be brief, well edited, and really achieve the point you are trying to make. Moreover, your video or audio clips must be no longer than 20 or so seconds.

Other tips to maximize your visual aid is that everyone needs to be able see and read your aid. Recognized experts in using visual aids recommend using a 36-point font for your headings, a 24-point font for subtitles, and 18-point font for other text. Moreover, it is not recommended to use the ALL CAPS for your fonts. Adding color to your visual aid produces a liveliness in your message. However, do not get carried away by using too many colors that can be interpreted as an eye sore.

A sure way to create chaos is to distribute a handout while you are delivering your presentation. Your audience's attention will be turned to viewing and passing your handouts instead of listening to your address. If it is absolutely necessary for you to have handouts wait until after your presentation to distribute them. On your pathway to success visual aids will clarify and strengthen your message and fulfill your purpose behind the podium.

Name: _____

True-False

1. T F   One of the reasons to use visual aids in a speech is that you can break eye contact with the audience while discussing the aids.

2. T F   If the object you want to speak about is too large, too small, or unavailable to use as a visual aid, you should change the topic of your speech.

3. T F   Because a picture is a valuable visual aid, it is a good idea to pass photographs among the audience in order to illustrate your point.

4. T F   When presenting your speech it is usually a good idea to write or draw on an overhead transparency while you are speaking.

5. T F   Printing your visual aid in ALL CAPITAL letters is a good way to make sure it will be easy for the audience to read.

6. T F   You can use yourself as your own visual aid.

Multiple Choice

7. When using visual aids in a speech, you should
   a. display visual aids only while discussing them.
   b. draw graphs and charts on the chalkboard.
   c. pass aids among the audience at the start of the speech.
   d. not worry about maintaining eye contact with the audience.
   e. display visual aids to the left of the lectern.

8. When you are going to give an audience material to take home from a speech, you should distribute the material
   a. as the audience arrives for the speech.
   b. at the beginning of the speech.
   c. at the time you discuss it during the speech.
   d. during the conclusion of the speech.
   e. after the speech.

9. When using a visual aid in a speech, you should display the aid
   a. on the left side of the lectern.
   b. so everyone in the room can see it.
   c. throughout the speech.
   d. all of the above.
   e. a and b only.

10. A _____ graph is best suited for illustrating simple distribution patterns.
   a. pie
   b. line
   c. parallel
   d. ratio
   e. bar

11. When making a multimedia presentation, you should
    a. limit yourself to showing charts, graphs, photographs, and drawings.
    b. be prepared to give your speech even if the equipment malfunctions.
    c. use a different set of fonts for each chart to keep the audience interested.
    d. reduce the number of main points to make sure you do not run out of time.
    e. tell your audience which software program you are using for the speech.

12. Visual aids can be very useful to a speaker because they
    a. often take the place of statistics.
    b. enhance the clarity of a speaker's ideas.
    c. can be passed among members of the audience.
    d. do not require a great deal of explanation.
    e. all of the above.

13. As your textbook explains, if you plan to use a photograph as a visual aid in a speech, you should
    a. convert it to a transparency and show it with an overhead projector.
    b. pass the photograph among the audience so everyone can look at it.
    c. use a photograph in an oversize book and hold it where it can be seen.
    d. all of the above.
    e. b and c only.

Essay

14. What are the three kinds of graphs discussed in your textbook? Give an example of each.

15. If you are planning to use a video as a visual aid in your speech, what steps should you take to make sure the video will enhance the speech?

Pillar 5

Ranges of Public Speaking Avenues for Communicating Your Message Successfully

Chapter 13

Speaking at a Special Occasion

On your pathway to success you will be required to speak at numerous special occasions. It is those special occasions that will serve as your hallmarks in your personal and professional development. Special occasions may include presenting an employee of the year award, or receiving an Oscar, Emmy, or a Pulitzer Prize. In addition, a special occasion may occur when presenting a toast at your best friend's wedding, or eulogizing a dear friend at their funeral. Perhaps you will be delivering an after dinner speech at a civic organization. Other examples of a special occasion speech would be delivering a speech at graduation, commemorating a new building, bidding farewell to a longtime employee at your company, or welcoming a group of conventioneers at a trade show. All of these special occasions are well within your grasp to be a part of on your pathway to success.

As you can see, these speeches are delivered in a more "social" setting, but these speeches require you to be more formal because of the importance of those occasions. Special occasions generally call for a more formal presentation than a persuasive or informative speech. For example, weddings, funerals, building dedications, and retirement parties become the foundation of a particular community and will live on forever in the memories of all those present.

The formality of your presentation in a special occasion should not be interpreted as being stiff and impersonal. To the contrary as a speaker you must be flexible enough to identify and adapt to the occasion to meet the desired expectations of the occasion. Speeches at funerals, weddings, memorials, awards ceremonies, and tributes all require a specific language and tone to meet the appropriate expectations that each of these occasions entail. In short these occasions are memorable and special, and those moments and events stand out in the lives of the people who are affected by the occasion.

The ancient Greeks labeled special occasion speeches an *epideictic*. An **epideictic** is a speech that one would deliver when you pay tribute to someone, present or accept an award, or acknowledge some kind of special occasion or event. Ceremonial or special occasion speeches add to the backbone and way of life of society. Through the special occasion speech we are reminded of our culture, traditions, individual champions, and shared social values while offering inspiration and strength. We will be exploring the following different special occasion speeches: welcome and farewell speeches, commemorative, speech of introduction, receiving or accepting an award, and the after dinner speech.

WELCOME AND FAREWELL SPEECHES

Speeches that welcome are geared to set the tone of warmth and inclusion to a person or a group of people at a convention, conference, or some other social gathering. The key is to set a friendly and welcoming attitude for the collection of people. Thoughtful reflection on word choice and nonverbal gestures are necessary before delivering a welcome speech. The welcome speech must be brief and concise because the audience will be focused on the main events or activities of the occasion's purpose. When delivering a welcome speech, two messages need to be communicated. First, the presenter needs to recognize the honored guests and key people who are in attendance. Next, briefly share with the audience the purpose of the occasion. Again the presenter must be mindful of the mood he or she wants to set in the welcome address.

Here is a sample of a welcome speech for a conference of the Note Singers Society presented by be the President of the Note Singers Society.

Welcome to the 9th annual jamboree of the Note Singers Society. It is great to see so many singers here to join together and collaborate in our quest to sing the perfect song. It was just nine years ago we were ten singers, and today over 2,000 are gathered!

The Note Singers Society is proud to have everyone here in San Francisco. I know that many of you have traveled from quite a distance and I'd like to acknowledge our members from Iceland, France, and even Australia who have made this long trip to participate in the largest singing conference in our nine year existence.

Among the activities we have planned are workshops about singing in quartets, country and western singing, and the introduction of opera singing.

Please refer to your conference brochures for specific activities. In the exhibition hall you will be able to consult with singing coaches and agents looking for new talent to represent. Remember to enter our raffle for two tickets with backstage passes to the San Francisco Opera. Tonight you will enjoy our opening dinner with our special keynote speaker, Grace Bird.

I know most of you are already members of the Note Singers Society, but for those of you who aren't I encourage you to fill out a membership application so that you can benefit from all the perks that our members enjoy at a discounted price.

To all of you, thank you for being here and for supporting the Note Singers Society. Welcome to our annual conference and enjoy the festivities.

Farewell speeches occur when a longtime employee or member of an organization leaves the company or organization. There are two different perspectives from which a farewell speech may be delivered. One, the farewell speech may be delivered from the group who are staying in a particular place. If you are saying goodbye to someone, create a brief introduction and create the emotional tone of the event. Next express the contributions the person may have had in the organization. Finally, wish the person well in their new life. The general theme in a farewell speech is to show gratitude for the person's contributions to the organization.

Here is a sample farewell speech on behalf of a company to an employee who is retiring after forty years of service. The CEO of Acme Construction Company is presenting the farewell on behalf of the company.

Welcome, everyone, to this very special celebration. Our occasion is a very joyous occasion, but also a very sad occasion in our company's history. We are gathered to say goodbye to our third employee ever in our 40-year history—Kathy Jacobs.

Kathy has been the pillar of consistency and loyalty over the span of 40 years to Acme Construction Company. Without the contributions of Kathy I doubt that Acme would have lasted this long, or would have been this prosperous in this competitive industry.

Acme will be a much emptier place without her, but her legacy will live on. Although we are saying good-bye to Kathy, her contributions will be felt for many years. Instead of having to deal with us on a daily basis, Kathy will have time to pursue her passion for golf and to spend time with her grandchildren.

So on behalf of Acme Construction I would like to present you a seven-day golf vacation at the resort at Myrtle Beach, South Carolina.

Finally, I would like to wish you the very best on behalf of all of us and have a great life! Good luck to you Kathy! So let us all now raise our glasses in Kathy's honor for 40 years of service.

Another perspective on a farewell speech will be delivered by the person who is leaving and that person would be addressing the people who will be remaining at the company or organization. That person should talk briefly about their time at the organization and perhaps share stories, and thank those people who made their stay a good one.

Here is Kathy's Farewell speech in response to the send off on behalf of her company Acme Construction Company.

Oh my gosh, I can't believe this incredibly generous gift of golf in South Carolina, and thanks so much for this fun and amazing celebration.

I have been wrestling with this decision to retire for about five years and finally decided to take the plunge. I'm feeling so many mixed emotions about this decision. I have been with Acme Construction for all of my adult life, and during my forty years I got married, had kids, had grandchildren, purchased a home, and became a part of a larger family with Acme.

I'm going to really miss all of the fantastic people I have worked with over the years, and their contributions to my personal development are immeasurable. The times shared and the inconceivable successes that we have enjoyed with the company have been an extraordinary part of my life.

I am very proud of what we have achieved and I have had the best time of my life working here at Acme. I wish all of you every success for the future!

COMMEMORATIVE SPEECHES

A commemoration is a ceremonial speech that marks an important date or event, and is usually presented at an event like a graduation, holiday, or a special local occasion to a particular community. Careful consideration of the situation and audience during the preparation for a commemorative speech is paramount. The emotional tone of the occasion will dictate your word choice and the length of the address. When commemorating, analysis needs to be done in evaluating which specific values need to be highlighted in the address. Furthermore, your purpose is to articulate and reinforce existing social values. The aim is to give an eloquent expression to the beliefs and values already held by the audience.

Here is a sample of a University graduation speech presented by a graduating student capturing the activities and spirit of the past four years while providing wisdom for the graduating class.

Are you better off?

Parents, faculty, administrators, and the State University graduating class, are you better off as a result of the experiences shared at this fine institution over the course of the past four years, or in some special cases the past seven years? Over the past four years being away from home, I'm better now that I know not to mix my red t-shirts with my white clothes. It really sucked being known as the guy who wore the pink clothes around campus for a couple of semesters, but I'm better off because of the ridicule. Due to this ridicule I plan on opening a chain of dry cleaners after graduation; I figure it is a good, clean business to get into. Will I be better off going in this direction? For now it is still too early to tell.

Over the past four years our country has spent over $12 trillion, and is our country better off due to our spending? Conversely, our parents and many of you graduates have spent over $75,000 on our education over the course of the past four years; or for those of you on the seven-year plan, I'll let you figure out that cost. Are WE better off that we have spent that time and money toward our education? I stand here before you to say, absolutely we are better off by spending our time and money at State University!

Over the past four years I have met interesting people from around the world and have learned about many cultures I never heard of even from the first day I stepped on campus. Over the past four years I have been exposed to amazing teachers who really get into their subject matters, and that energy was simply contagious. Over the past four years I have fallen in love, fallen out of love, and back in love again, and out of love once more. Over the past four years we have rooted for our division championship football team, and suffered together through four long basketball seasons. Over the past four years we have raised thousands of dollars to aid orphanages overseas, and together we mourned the death of our popular history professor John Davidson. In the past four years we have experienced life's highs and lows, and I can say I'm better for these experiences in preparation for life after State University.

All of this leads me to my final thought: let the question "am I better off" be your guiding light in life's difficult decisions. Am I better off marrying this person, am I better off in this chosen profession, am I better off starting a business, am I better off living in xyz town, am I better off hanging out with these friends—am I better off?

I'm better off because of my time at State University, I'm better off because of the guidance of my parents, I'm better off because of my dedicated teachers, and I'm better off because of my awesome classmates right here at State University!

Pay Tribute

Tribute speeches are another type of commemorative speech that are intended to honor, commend, and observe a person, a movement, or an organization. Presentations of tributes are usually offered at retirement parties, funerals, weddings, anniversaries, or birthday celebrations. Anecdotes and narratives are terrific ways to pay homage to the group or person being celebrated. In addition, it is appropriate to give some biographical information, but stories using thoughtful language that reveal the person or group's moral fiber and individuality carry a tenor that will stick with the audience. The speech that pays tribute must convey appreciation, value, or respect to the person, occasion, or organization. When delivering a speech that pays tribute the attitude needs to be constructive, and not speak to any negative relations, dealings, or quarrels.

One type of tribute speech is the eulogy. A eulogy praises a friend, relative, or colleague who has died. When crafting the text and tone of a eulogy speech, the dignity for the deceased needs to be at the forefront. The person delivering the eulogy is in the pole position to give a voice to the collective mind-set of love and loss held by the audience. The challenge for the speaker is to capture the right words for the feelings being experienced by those in attendance such as family and friends.

When preparing for a eulogy speech, the focus needs to be geared to the significance that the deceased person has had in their actions and their relational influences on their respective families and communities. In short, sharing only biographical information does not capture the magnitude of the person's contribution and how the deceased person enriched the lives of others. Moreover, ethical, moral, and character lessons delivered through stories can motivate the audience to carry forth prominent traits of the deceased. In addition, paying tribute to those who have passed often defines the personal virtues and social values that we admire most. Furthermore, it is those personal traits that will inspire the future generations to bring those admirable traits into their daily lives.

Here is a sample of a eulogy speech.

> We are gathered here today to celebrate the life and the tragic death of our good friend Steven Richards. I have been lucky to say that I have been Steve's best friend for twenty out of my twenty-four years. We met out in a playground at Central Park in San Mateo, California. Our moms went to high school together and randomly met up at the park, and from there a friendship was born.
>
> My fondest memory with Steve is when we took our first road trip to Las Vegas when we both turned twenty-one. Our car overheated and we did not have water to put in the radiator, but we did have a gallon of lemonade and used that instead. The car smelled like lemons and brought the cliché "when you have lemons make lemonade," an inside joke between us. We lost our shirts at the crap tables, but forged a bond in our friendship that would never be broken. And to this day I still smell lemons in the car.
>
> When I heard the news of Steve's passing I was shocked and could not believe his death really happened, and it's now a reality. Steve was well-liked, loved, and made so many contributions to our community. I will forever be grateful to be Steve's best friend and to have had the many memories I shared with Steve.
>
> Steve is in another place right now and we are here on earth. Steve touched so many lives and I encourage all of us to carry Steve's spirit, kindness, and generosity in our daily lives. I think that is the best way to honor Steve's memory.
>
> Steve, I will miss you very much and thanks so much for being my friend. I love you, Steve, may you rest in peace.

SPEECH OF INTRODUCTION

The purpose of a speech of introduction is to have the presenter deliver a brief introduction of the main speaker to an audience. The focus must be on the main speaker and *not* on the presenter introducing the main speaker. More than likely these speeches will surface at civic meetings, conferences, conventions, and congregations at religious organizations. The principle of the speech of introduction is to share the main speaker's credentials, give a brief description of what the main speaker will be talking about, and generate great enthusiasm for both the person and the event. Moreover, a welcoming theme for the main speaker needs to be established. A mindset that is helpful when delivering an introduction speech is to see yourself as a host or hostess welcoming the main speaker.

When introducing the main speaker being brief is important, so your introduction should not last longer than two minutes. It is also a good idea to introduce yourself and how you fit in the occasion. This allows the audience to have some context as to where you fit in the organization and planning of the occasion.

A critical point in the speech of introduction is to pronounce the main speaker's name correctly, so you do not embarrass yourself and the main speaker. Moreover, absolute accuracy is needed when sharing the speaker's credentials and experience. It is strongly suggested that you discuss your introduction with the main speaker before delivering your introduction. Nothing will break the main speaker's momentum than having to correct the introducer's errors. If the speaker you are introducing is not well known to the audience, a more detailed introduction highlighting the speaker's achievements and milestones will be necessary.

Following the establishment of the speaker's credibility to speak to this particular audience, you will briefly share the general theme that the speaker will be talking about and build a brief bridge between the theme and how that pertains to the audience and the occasion.

Finally you will have a closing comment and welcome the main speaker to the podium. The tone and content of your introduction needs to be appropriate for the speaker, the occasion, and the audience.

Another point to remember when delivering a speech of introduction is to not embarrass the speaker, where the speaker will feel uncomfortable delivering his/her speech. For example, a sure way to make the main speaker feel uneasy is to bring up potentially embarrassing situations from the speaker's childhood or personal or professional life. Furthermore, another way to make the main speaker feel uncomfortable is to exaggerate the speaker's personality like saying "this is the funniest person you will ever meet," or "here is the most brilliant person on the planet." By making these kinds of declarations, you may lead the main speaker to feel anxious about fulfilling those unrealistic expectations.

Here is a sample speech of introduction:

> *"Good evening everyone, we're in for an inspirational message from our keynote speaker. My name is Larry Combs and I am the president of the southern chapter of the Small Business Coalition and the organizer for tonight's festivities. Our speaker is a man who has been the voice for small business owners throughout the country. Tonight's presenter has started five small businesses that have grown to become Fortune 500 companies in the past twenty-five years. He has earned an MBA from the University of Texas at Austin and will be talking about the importance of personal development for your small business success. Please join me in giving a very warm welcome to Bruce Bevo."*

ACCEPTANCE OR PRESENTATION OF AN AWARD OR OTHER FORM OF PUBLIC RECOGNITION

If you are given an award, or a promotion, or some other form of public recognition, an acceptance speech may be in order. The goal of the acceptance speech is to give thanks to those who helped you earn the award, and thank the organization that is presenting the award. Now it is easy to start thanking your fifth grade teacher who was kind to you, or the check-out person at the grocery store who always greets you with a smile, but if these people were not instrumental in your achievement of the award, your acceptance speech is not the place to bring those nice people up. Moreover, it can be easy to get carried away with how much the award means to you. If you are way over the top and say that, "my life is now complete, and I can die now" since winning the award, unless you really mean it, the audience will sense that you are not sincere. Another important point to remember when accepting an award is to be brief. Often, when a recipient at an awards show goes over the allotted time parameters, the organizers will start the music as a "subtle" hint to stop talking. Again be brief, clear, and concise in your statements when accepting an award or some other form of public recognition.

Speeches of presentation have two purposes. The speech of presentation needs to address the purpose of the award and information about the person receiving the award. First, the presentation of an award should embody any background information about the recipient that will help the audience understand the purpose or circumstances of the award so they have the appropriate context. Next, the speaker would explain the criteria used to select the recipient of the award. Subsequently, the audience needs to hear the personal characteristics of the recipient, and how they are in sync with the parameters of the given award. Finally, share the achievements of the person receiving the award. Moreover, it is common to save the speaker's name for last as a way to build up suspense as to who will be the recipient of the award.

Tonight the Commerce Association will present the "Business Person of the Year Award" to a worthy recipient. Our award is given to an individual who displays good business ethics and involvement in the community.

This year's recipient owns the local hardware store that supplies our community with parts and expertise so our residents can maintain their homes. Our recipient also provided the supplies needed to rebuild homes lost in last winter's terrible flood that displaced many families in our community. In addition, you can see our recipient at Lincoln Elementary school teaching grade school kids about being responsible corporate citizens and entrepreneurs. Moreover, this year's recipient can be heard as a regular on Isabella Stapleton's local radio talk show.

I am proud to present this year's "Commerce Association's Business Person of the Year Award" to Joel Shelley. Congratulations, Joel, and come on up for your award!

SPEECHES TO ENTERTAIN (AFTER DINNER SPEECHES)

"The sense of humor is the oil of life's engine. Without it, the machinery creaks and groans. No lot is so hard, no aspect of things is so grim, but it relaxes before a hearty laugh."
—GEORGE S. MERRIAM AUTHOR

Speeches to entertain are used to make a point via humorous and thought provoking means. Speeches to entertain are also called "after dinner speeches" so those two terms may be used interchangeably. One reason the term "after dinner speeches" is used is because these speeches come after a meal whether that would be a business lunch, or after a dinner as part of a social time, convention, or banquet.

After dinner speeches can take on a serious message but must be delivered in a light- hearted tone. The after dinner speech is different than an informative or persuasive speech, because your goal is not to inform or persuade, but to facilitate a diversion and offer food for thought in an interesting manner. Elements of an informative or persuasive speech do play a role in the after dinner speech, but the goal is to share a message in an way that is easy to hear. Once you have determined the message you want to deliver, the next challenge is to weave humor into your presentation that will be appropriate to the occasion and the audience. Practicing your delivery is essential here, because it is not only what you say, but how you say it, so maximize that opportunity to deliver a strong message.

THE BABIES

(Speech of Samuel L. Clemens [Mark Twain] at a banquet given by the Army of the Tennessee at Chicago, Illinois, November 13, 1877, in honor of General Grant on his return from his trip around the world. Mark Twain responded to the toast, "The Babies: as they comfort us in our sorrows, let us not forget them in our festivities.")

Mr. Chairman and Gentlemen: "The Babies." Now, that's some-thing like. We haven't all had the good fortune to be ladies; we have not all been generals, or poets, or statesmen; but when the toast works down to the babies, we stand on common ground—for we've all been babies. (Laughter) It is a shame that for a thousand years the world's banquets have utterly ignored the baby, as if he didn't amount to anything! If you, gentlemen, will stop and think a minute—if you will go back fifty or a hundred years, to your early married life, and recontemplate your first baby, you will remember that he amounted to a' good deal—and even something over. (Laughter)

You soldiers all know that when that little fellow arrived at family headquarters, you had to hand in your resignation. He took entire command. You became his lackey, his mere bodyguard; and you had to stand around. He was not a commander who made allowance for the time, distance, weather, or anything else. You had to execute his order whether it was possible or not. And there was only one form of marching in his manual of tactics, and that was the double-quick. (Laughter) He treated you with every sort of insolence and disrespect, and the bravest of you did not dare to say a word. You could face the death-storm of Donelson and Vicksburg, and give back blow for blow, but when he clawed your whiskers and pulled your hair, and twisted your nose, you had to take it. (Laughter) When the thunders of war sounded in your ears, you set your faces towards the batteries and advanced with steady tread; but when he turned on the terrors of his war-whoop (Laughter) you advanced in—the other direction, and mighty glad of the chance, too. When he called for soothing syrup, did you venture to throw out any remarks about certain services unbecoming to an officer and a gentleman? No; you got up and got it! If he ordered his pap bottle, and it wasn't warm, did you talk back! Not you; you went to work and warmed it. You even descended so far in your menial office as to take a suck at that warm, insipid stuff yourself, to see if it was right!—three parts water to one of milk, a touch of sugar to modify the colic, and a drop of peppermint to kill those immortal hiccoughs. I can taste that stuff yet! (Laughter)

And how many things you learned as you went along! Sentimental young folks still take stock in that beautiful old saying, that when baby smiles in his sleep it is because the angels are whispering to him. Very pretty, but "too thin"—simply wind on the stomach, my friends. (Laughter) If the baby proposed to take a walk at his usual hour—half-past two in the morning—didn't you rise up promptly and remark (with a mental attitude which wouldn't improve a Sunday school much) that that was the very thing you were about to propose yourself? Oh, you were under good discipline. And so you went fluttering up and down the room in your "undress uniform"; (Laughter) you not only prattled undignified baby-talk, but even tuned up your martial voices and tried to sing "Rock-a-Bye Baby on the Tree-top," for instance. What a spectacle for an Army of the Tennessee! And what an affliction for the neighbors, too, for it isn't everybody within a mile around that likes military music at three o'clock in the morning. (Laughter) And when you had been keeping this thing up two or three hours, and your little velvet-head intimated that nothing suited him like exercise and noise, and proposed to fight it out on that line if it took all night—"Go on." What did you do? You simply went on till you dropped in the last ditch! (Laughter)

I like the idea that a baby doesn't amount to anything! Why, one baby is just a house and a front yard full by it-self; one baby can furnish more business than you and your whole interior department can attend to; he is en-terprising, irrepressible, brimful of lawless activities. Do what you please you can't make him stay on the reservation. Sufficient unto the day is one baby. As long as you are in your right mind don't ever pray for twins. Twins amount to a permanent riot; and there ain't any real difference between triplets and insurrections. (Great laughter)

Among the three or four million cradles now rocking in the land there are some which this nation would preserve for ages as sacred things, if we could know which ones they are. For in one of these cradles the unconscious Far-ragut of the future is at this moment teething. Think of it! and putting a word of dead earnest, unarticulated, but justifiable, profanity over it, too; in another, the future renowned astronomer is blinking at the shining Milky Way with but a languid interest, poor little chap, and wondering what has become of that other one they call the wet-nurse; in another, the future great historian is lying, and doubtless he will continue to lie until his earthly mis-sion is ended; in another, the future president is busying himself with no profounder problem of state than what the mischief has become of his hair so early; (Laughter) and in a mighty host of other cradles there are now some sixty thousand future office-seekers getting ready to furnish him occasion to grapple with the same old problem a second time! And in still one more cradle, somewhere under the flag, the future illustrious commander-in-chief of the American armies is so little burdened with his approaching grandeurs and responsibilities as to be giving his whole strategic mind at this moment, to trying to find out some way to get his own big toe into his mouth, an achieve-ment which (meaning no disrespect) the illustrious guest of this evening also turned his attention to some fifty-six years ago! And if the child is but the prophecy of the man, there are mighty few will doubt that he suc-ceeded. (Laughter and prolonged applause)

Summary: Tips for Preparing for a Special Occasion Speech

Special occasion speeches are delivered in a more "social" setting, but the speeches you deliver require more formality because of the importance of those occasions. For example, weddings, funerals, building dedications, retirement parties become the fabric of a particular community and live on forever in the memories of the attendees. Special occasion speeches come in many forms such as the welcome/farewell speech, the commemorative speech, the speech of introduction, presenting or receiving an award, and the after dinner speech.

A welcome speech will serve you on your pathway to success when welcoming or introducing a new employee to your department or company. Conversely the farewell speech may take place in two differ-ent forms. One form is given by the group who is staying at the organization to address the person leaving. The other is made by the person who is leaving the organization addressing his/her colleagues who are staying.

A commemoration is a ceremonial speech that marks an important date or event, and is usually pre-sented at an event like a graduation, holiday, or a local occasion that is special to a particular commu-nity. The emotional tone of the occasion will dictate your word choice and the length of the address. Tribute speeches are designed to honor, praise, and celebrate a person, a cause, or an organization and are usually offered at retirement parties, funerals, weddings, anniversaries, or birthday celebrations.

The purpose of a speech of introduction is to have the presenter deliver a brief introduction of the main speaker to an audience. The objective of the speech of introduction is to help create the main speaker's credibility and credentials and provide a brief description of what the main speaker will be talking about. Moreover, a welcoming tone needs to be established.

If you are given an award, or a promotion, or some other form of public recognition, an acceptance speech may be in order. The goal of the acceptance speech is to give thanks to those who helped you earn the award, and thank the organization that is presenting the award. Speeches of presentation have two purposes. The speech of presentation needs to address the purpose of the award and to give information about the person receiving the award.

Speeches to entertain are also called "after dinner speeches" so those two terms may be used interchangeably and are used to make a serious point via humorous and thought-provoking means.

On your pathway to success speaking at special occasions will be required and your opportunity to shine in front of influential people in your professional and personal life. So when you are called upon, remember that these opportunities to speak at a special occasion should not be taken lightly and will require your best effort.

Name: _____

True-False

1. T F   The primary purpose of a special occasion speech is to communicate information to an audience.

2. T F   The purpose of a speech of introduction is to introduce the person receiving an award or an honor.

3. T F   When giving a speech of presentation, you should usually explain why the recipient is being given his or her award.

4. T F   "To persuade my audience that Howard Johnson did not write the plays attributed to him" is an example of a specific purpose statement for an after-dinner speech.

5. T F   The basic purpose of an acceptance speech is to give thanks for a gift or an award.

6. T F   Even though humor is an important element of an after-dinner speech, the speaker should still strive to provide special insight into the topic.

Multiple Choice

7. The main purpose of a speech of presentation is to present

   a. the main speaker to the audience.
   b. thanks for a gift or an award.
   c. the reasons why a person deserves commendation.
   d. information about the importance of the occasion.
   e. a gift or an award to the recipient.

8. A speech in which an individual gives thanks for a gift or award is termed a(n)

   a. speech of presentation.
   b. commemorative speech.
   c. after-dinner speech.
   d. acceptance speech.
   e. speech of introduction.

9. After-dinner speeches are best thought of as a kind of speech to

   a. entertain.
   b. inform.
   c. persuade.
   d. commemorate.
   e. eulogize.

10. When Andy Michaels was presented the Alumni of the Year award at his alma mater's annual award dinner, he gave a speech thanking the school for recognizing his work. What kind of speech did Andy give?

   a. an acceptance speech.
   b. a speech of introduction.
   c. a commemorative speech.
   d. a speech of presentation.
   e. an informative speech.

Essay

11. Define and give an example of each of the following:

    speech of introduction
    speech of presentation
    acceptance speech
    commemorative speech
    after-dinner speech

Chapter 14

Speech to Inform

While on your pathway to success delivering a speech to inform happens in everyday situations. Think about the last time you offered someone directions to the mall, or informed your co-worker about the progress of a particular task at work so they could finish up where you left off. Moreover, speaking to inform takes place when you report to your co-workers of a new product launch, or tell them how to carry out a specific work task. Speaking to inform comes in forms that range from briefings, to classroom lectures, to sharing health ailments with your doctors.

The purpose of the informative speech is to convey information or knowledge so your audience understands your topic more comprehensively. Often times you will be passing on new information, so you can help others understand something they have had little or no experience with before. Conversely, you may be informing a group where the audience has a great deal of experience and knowledge with the topic that you are presenting. In addition, you may also want to inform an audience about a particular topic just to raise the audience's awareness of a particular situation. In short the informative speech can raise awareness, awaken interest, and enlighten your audience.

However, an important guideline for the informative speech is that it does not persuade or advocate for a particular cause or purpose. The informative speech needs to be communicated clearly, accurately, and grippingly to your specific audience. The precision and accuracy of the information you are presenting must be top priorities when delivering an informative speech. Having quality information will protect and enhance the speaker's credibility and integrity. In addition, when delivering an informative speech, using concrete and specific examples will help your audience grasp your message quickly and comprehend it clearly. Your audience needs to firmly believe that you are well informed and connected to your speech topic, and that the information you are presenting to them is relevant to their lives. Public speaking is an audience-focused activity so your message needs to meet the needs of your specific audience.

There are four kinds of informative speeches that we will be discussing in this chapter: descriptions/objects, processes, events, and explanations/concepts.

INFORMATIVE SPEECHES ABOUT DESCRIPTIONS OR OBJECTS

Many of your informative speech topics will be derived from some sort of object, which may be defined as something that is tangible and secure in form. Objects may be people, places, things, animals, building, structures, or cars—just to name a few.

For example, if you decide to explain the evolution of your object you may want to consider organizing your speech chronologically.

Specific Purpose: To inform my audience of the career achievements of former New Jersey Senator Bill Bradley.

Central Idea: Bill Bradley earned his degree and became an All-American basketball player at Princeton University, moving on to lead the New York Knicks to two NBA championships, before becoming a Senator representing the state of New Jersey.

Main Points:

    I. Bill Bradley, a Rhodes Scholar, earned a Bachelor's degree in American History from Princeton University while earning three All-American awards in basketball.

    II. Bill Bradley was instrumental in helping the New York Knicks win two NBA championships during the 1969–70 and 1972–73 seasons.

    III. Bill Bradley transitioned from a professional basketball star to become a U.S. senator representing the state of New Jersey.

If you decide to describe particular features of your object, consider using the spatial (directional pattern) order to organize your speech.

Specific Purpose: To inform my audience of the three components that make up a cigar.

Central Idea: There are three parts to the construction of a cigar, the filler, the binder, and the wrapper.

Main Points

    I. The center of the cigar is known as the filler.

    II. The next layer on top of the filler, which keeps the filler in place, is known as the binder.

    III. Finally the wrapper wraps around the filler and the binder, creating the finished look of the cigar.

Generally speaking, many of the informative speeches that fall under the object category will be organized using the topical order.

Specific Purpose: To inform my audience of the main components to bear in mind when purchasing a desktop computer.

Central Idea: The main components you must consider when purchasing a desktop computer are: costs, speed, hard drive capacity, and included software.

Main Points

    I. The first component to consider is the cost of the computer and your budget parameters.

    II. Secondly, consider the speed of the processor you will need to adequately run the programs you will be using.

    III. Next you will have to gauge the amount of hard drive space you will need to store your programs and files.

    IV. Finally, inquire about any software that may be included in your desktop purchase.

When delivering a speech about an object/description, do your best to describe the subject of your speech with comparisons, contrasts, and many relevant examples. Furthermore, adding visual aids will help your audience capture the object/description better than words.

INFORMATIVE SPEECHES ABOUT PROCESSES

When delivering a speech about a process you are expressing a chain of actions that lead to an outcome, result, or product. The process speech clarifies how something is done, made, or how something works. There are two different directions you can take the process speech. The first direction is to explain the steps of the process and how those steps relate to each other, and how that leads to a final output. The second direction you can take a process speech would be to explain how to *perform* the respective steps of the process that lead to an end result. When delivering a process speech that explains how to *perform* a particular task, more detailed decriptions of the steps will be required. On your pathway to success, the process speech will come in handy when sharing how to perform a specific job task or implement a new company strategy.

When delivering the process speech, the strongest organizational strategy to use would be the chronological order, which starts at the beginning of the process and goes through each of the steps involved, until you reach the end of the process and the final output.

Specific Purpose: To inform my audience of the process of writing a song.

Central Idea: Writing a song requires you to establish a verse, a chorus, and a bridge.

Main Points

    I. The first area you need to develop when writing a song is the verse.

    II. Next, creating the chorus will generate the catchiness to your song.

    III. Finally, the bridge will bring together both the verse and the chorus.

INFORMATIVE SPEECHES ABOUT EVENTS

An informative speech about an event may be defined as a happening. If you decide to talk about a historical event you would arrange the event using the chronological order and relate the events one after another in the order in which they transpired. Another direction you can take a speech about an event is to discuss the cause and effects of an event. Therefore the causal organizational strategy would be appropriate for this kind of speech. The key in informing your audience about an event is to emphasize the meaning of the event in language that helps your audience understand its true level of importance. Here is an example of an informative speech for an event.

Specific Purpose: To inform my audience of the Woodstock Music and Art Fair of 1969.

Central Idea: The creators of the Woodstock Music and Art Fair of 1969 attracted top performers and left a lasting legacy on American culture.

Main Points

    I. The Woodstock Music and Art Fair of 1969 was originated by Artie Kornfield, Michael Lang, John Roberts, and Joel Rosenman who wanted a festival to embody the counterculture of the late 1960's.

II. The promoters of Woodstock were able to attract top musical talents like The Who, Janis Joplin, the Grateful Dead, and Jimi Hendrix.

III. Woodstock became synonymous with the counterculture movement in the United States in the 1960's leaving a legacy on American culture.

On your pathway to success you may also be asked to deliver an oral report in a professional or community setting about an event. In some cases these reports about an event may be informally presented to a couple of people and should be brief. In other cases, depending on the occasion, you may be asked to deliver a more formal address regarding a milestone event that has taken place. For example, if you were the CEO for an airline and there was a crash you would be needed to talk to the shareholders, media, and other government agencies. When delivering such an oral report, the speech for an event in the professional or community setting shares discoveries, recent developments, or vital information with a particular audience.

INFORMATIVE SPEECHES OF EXPLANATIONS OR CONCEPTS

When we discussed speeches about objects we looked at topics that one could see or touch, but with concepts the topics are more abstract in form. Speeches about concepts embrace theories, ideas, principles, and philosophies. Because the discussion about abstract ideas may be difficult for your audience to grasp, special consideration to use visual aids would help your audience understand your message easier. If you are discussing an explanation/concept topic you must be able to define the concept's main points or parts, its significance, and concrete examples to make it more real for your audience to comprehend. In addition, when delivering a topic that is more abstract, make it a priority in your preparation by providing definitions and clearly using concrete examples to help visualize the concepts presented for your audience.

Specific Purpose: To inform my audience of the impact of the philosophy of game theory.

Central Idea: The Game theory came to international prominence with the book Theory of Games and Economic Behavior, which sues mathematics to depict premeditated situations in making choices, which has yielded theorists who have won Nobel Prizes in Economics.

Main Points

I. Game theory came into international prominence in the 1944 book *Theory of Games and Economic Behavior* by John von Neumann and Oskar Morgenstern.

II. "Game theory" is a mathematical approach of analyzing the tactics that different "players" choose to achieve the best possible outcome for themselves in a given transaction.

III. Game theory has yielded numerous theorists who have won Nobel Prizes in economics.

Guidelines for Choosing an Organizational Strategy for your Informative Speech		
Organizational Strategy Chronological	*When it is Applicable* Discussing an event, trend, or theory over time or demonstrating a step-by-step sequence	*Prospective Topics* • Developments in the automotive industry over the last 75 years • The evolution of the student demographics at your college • How to make homemade beer
Spatial	Assisting your audience to envision something you are describing and/or you want to describe something directionally by moving from point to point through space (up/down, left/right, inside/out).	• The layout for new walking trails in our town • Expenditures for educational financial aid, based on the individual states • The architectural design for the proposed high rise downtown
Categorical or Topical	Underscoring the impact of the categories or divisions of a topic—the most flexible approach to organization of a speech	• Strategies for treating diabetes • Transportation options for protecting the environment • Innovative programs serving college ESL students
Causal	Understanding the causes that lead to some result (effects) or assisting your audience to understand the impacts of some problem or occurrence.	• The relationship between fast food and obesity • Educational levels and salary levels • Car insurance rates and age

GUIDELINES FOR INFORMATIVE SPEECHES

Before delivering your informative speech conduct an audience analysis so that you can tailor your message to meet the needs of the audience. It is essential that you know the level of knowledge your audience may have about your topic, so that you know what and how to present your information. Conducting an audience analysis will allow you to not make any assumptions about their knowledge base so they will have a better chance of understanding your message. Other findings you can learn from your audience survey will help you build a bridge between your topic and the relevance of your topic to the audience's interests and needs. The stronger you establish your credibility with your topic the more your audience will respond favorability to your presentation.

Word choice when creating your informative speech is paramount to get your point across clearly and accurately. As a word of caution: do not fall into the trap of trying to use big words to impress your audience. Use words that are simple and understandable to you and your audience. The goal as a public speaker is to take the most complex ideas and simplify them for your audience by using understandable words.

Special care is needed about how you will relate your topic to the audience to build on the core themes your audience is familiar with, which will lead to a higher retention of your material for your audience. Your audience will be thinking "what's in it for me?" and your job is to fill in those blanks and answer that question for them. If you are able to relate your speech specifically to the needs of your audience, you will be a very successful public speaker. People are interested in people especially if they are sitting next to those people.

A common error made by public speakers is delivering an informative speech that tries to pack in too much information that an audience member cannot realistically absorb. Limiting your main points to between two and five will allow you to not overwhelm your audience with too much information. When delivering new information to an audience the soundest strategy is to present your information effectively, clearly, use visual reinforcement, and use language that is adapted to the newbie's perspective on the topic. When delivering an informative speech, information that is restated or repeated tends to be received better by the audience. By providing emphasis, restatement, and repetition, the speaker will help his/her ideas and information stick in the minds of the audience.

The quality of your information in your speech needs to be accurate and timely. You need to ask yourself, is your information accurate, verifiable, and stated in the correct context? More importantly, as an informative speaker your audience is looking to you for correct information, so do not make things up. Once you have been found out passing made-up information your credibility and professional reputation will be tarnished. In addition, take extra care in citing your sources accurately and quote your material in its proper context.

Summary: Tips for Your Speech to Inform

There are four types of informative speeches: descriptions/objects, processes, events, and explanations/concepts. When preparing for an informative speech, your purpose will be to pass on knowledge and information to your audience or raise the awareness of a particular situation. During your preparation phase you will need to know what your audience's knowledge, interest, and attitude base is for your topic so that you can address them at the appropriate terminology level.

Your credibility and your goodwill will be evaluated by the audience so special measures will be needed to directly relate your topic to your own personal experience and how the topic will relate to the audience. Again your audience will be thinking "what's in it for me?" and it is your job to answer that question.

Finally, the information presented to the audience must be accurate, verifiable, and stated in the correct context. On your pathway to success you will be asked to inform an audience on your particular realm of expertise, so follow these tips and you will enhance your professional and social standing of your choice.

Sample of an Informative Speech

Specific Purpose: To inform my audience of the upbringing and legacy of Civil Rights leader Rosa Parks.

Central Idea: From humble beginnings, Rosa Parks rose to become a leader in the American Civil Rights Movement by refusing to forfeit her seat on a Montgomery, Alabama bus, leading to a legacy that is still remembered today.

Introduction

I. "The only tired I was, was tired of giving in."

    A. This well-known quote by Rosa Parks during her arrest has been heard around the world and changed the world forever.

II. According to my in-class survey, only 65% of you knew of the cultural climate of the United States that eventually made Rosa Parks a prominent figure in the American Civil Rights Movement.

    A. Rosa Parks became a leader in the Civil Rights Movement and impacted American history by refusing to leave her seat on a crowded bus in Montgomery, Alabama when she was asked to move because of her skin color.

III. Today I will share Rosa Parks' background, the incident on a Montgomery bus that moved the American Civil Rights Movement forward, and the legacy of Rosa Parks that still lives on today.

(Transition: Let's start with the beginning of Rosa Parks' upbringing.)

Body

I. Rosa Parks was born to into a working class family in 1913 in Tuskegee, Alabama.

    A. Parks' father was a carpenter, and her mother was a teacher; education was stressed in the family.

        1. During this time there were limited educational opportunities in their local area offering education to African-American children.

        2. Parks was home schooled by her mother until she was eleven years old.

    B. But her parents were determined to have Rosa go to school, so they found her a school where there were programs that taught young African-American women.

        1. Rosa enrolled at the Montgomery Industrial School for Girls, and later graduated from the all-African-American Booker T. Washington High School in 1928.

        2. After graduating from Booker T. Washington High School, Parks attended Alabama State College briefly where she cleaned classrooms in order to pay her way through school and became a teacher.

        3. Rosa excelled in her studies and though she had to take a leave of absence from school to help her ailing grandmother, she still had the motivation to go back and finish.

    C. With a high school diploma in hand she set off to find a job where she could use her newly developed skills.

        1. She worked at a shirt factory, a hospital, and other small jobs until she got hired into a well-known department store as a seamstress.

II. History would be made on December 1, 1955, when Rosa Parks left work as a seamstress and walked to the bus stop where she would take a bus ride home.

    A. Little did she know that on this bus ride home she would kick off a new period in the Civil Rights Movement.

        1. During this time in American history, buses were set up in two sections, the front of the bus was for Caucasians, and the middle and back of the bus were designated for African-Americans.

        2. Parks boarded the bus and saw that the back of the bus was crowded, so she found a seat in the middle of the bus right behind the section designated for Caucasians.

           a. As more people got on the bus it became more and more crowded.

    B. The bus driver noticed that a Caucasian man was standing and, since Caucasians were the dominant race, the bus driver requested that all African-Americans sitting in the middle area move to the back of the bus even though there was no room.

        1. Everyone complied except for Rosa Parks who did not surrender her seat.

           a. Soon after the confrontation, Parks was arrested for not giving up her seat on the bus.

        2. Years later, in recalling the events of the day, Parks said, "When that white driver stepped back toward us, when he waved his hand and ordered us up and out of our seats, I felt a determination cover my body like a quilt on a winter night."

    C. According to the book *Bus Ride to Justice* by Fred Gray, Parks was arrested for disorderly conduct, and not for violating the segregation laws.

        1. After Rosa Parks was arrested the National Association for the Advancement of Colored People, also known as the NAACP, took action in support of Parks.

    D. On December 4, 1955 plans for the Montgomery Bus Boycott were announced at black churches and members began to disperse leaflets telling black people to boycott the bus on the day of Rosa Parks' trial.

        1. According to the book, *Freedom Walkers: The Story of the Montgomery Bus Boycott*, by Russell Freedman the leaflets said, "Another Negro woman has been arrested and thrown into jail because she refused to get up out of her seat on the bus for a white person to sit down . . . If we do not do something to stop these arrests, they will continue. The next time it may be you or your daughter or mother. This woman's case will come on Monday. We are therefore asking every Negro to stay off the buses on Monday in protest of the arrest and trial."

        2. On the day of Rosa Parks' trial, the buses were empty, demonstrating the solidarity in the African-American community.

III. Through her actions, Rosa Parks left a legacy and recognition for the Civil Rights Movement in the United States.

    A. Rosa Parks received America's highest civilian award, the Congressional Gold Medal of Honor, in 1999.

        1. Parks was quoted in *Jet* magazine saying, "This medal is encouragement for all of us to continue until all people have equal rights."

B. At Troy State University in Montgomery, Alabama they dedicated a library and museum in Parks' honor in December of 2000.

    1. The museum shows a replica of the infamous Cleveland Avenue bus from 1955.

C. In 2001, the actual bus was purchased by the Henry Ford Museum in Dearborn Michigan for $492,000.

    1. The Henry Ford Museum promised Parks that they would restore the original bus to its authentic 1955 fashion, which they did in 2003.

D. The milestone event of Parks' legacy lives on through books and movies.

    1. Parks published a children's book in 1992 entitled *My Story* explaining the events of the 1955 bus incident.

    2. A 2002 television movie called *The Rosa Parks Story* starred Angela Bassett and aired on CBS.

        a. The film described her early years, her confrontation on the Montgomery bus in 1955, and her role in the Civil Rights Movement.

(Transition: As we have seen, Rosa Parks changed the world of the American Civil Rights Movement.)

Conclusion

I. Rosa Parks passed away on October 24, 2005.

II. The world will still continue to evolve, and by knowing what Rosa Parks did to better her race, we in this classroom can follow her path and help advance the world we live in today.

    A. Parks' legacy still lives on today for Americans of all races, faiths, and backgrounds.

Works Cited (MLA Format)

Bailey, Ruby L. "Bill to honor Parks gets complex." *Detroit Free Press (Detroit, MI)* (Oct 28, 2005): NA. *General OneFile*. Gale. Skyline College Library. 2 May 2008 <http://find.galegroup.com/ips/start.do?prodId=IPS>.

Freedman, Russell. *Freedom Walkers: The Story of the Montgomery Bus Boycott*. New York, NY: The Holiday House, 2006.

Giovanni, Nikki. *Rosa*. New York, NY: Henry Holt Company, 2005.

Gray, Fred. *Bus Ride to Justice: Changing the American System by the System*. Montgomery, AL: The Black Belt Press, 1995.

The Henry Ford: America's Greatest History Attraction. 2002. The Henry Ford Foundation. 3 May 2008 <http://www.hfmgv.org/exhibits/rosaparks/faqactual.asp>.

Kinnon, Joy Bennett. "The Rosa Parks and Martin Luther King Jr. Connection." *Ebony* Jan. 2006.

Parks, Rosa. *Rosa Parks: My Story*. New York, NY: Dial Books, 1992, 116.

Shipp, E.R. "Rosa Parks, 92, Founding Symbol of Civil Rights Movement, Dies." *New York Times* 25 Oct. 2005: A1.

Troy State University Rosa Parks Library and Museum. Troy State University. 3 May 2008 <http://montgomery.troy.edu/rosaparks/museum/>.

Wong, Jennifer. In Class Audience Survey. Raw data. 5 May 2008.

Bibliography (APA Format)

Bailey, R. (2005, October 28). Bill honoring Parks complicated. *Detroit Free Press.*

Freedman, R. (2006). *Freedom walkers: The story of the Montgomery bus boycott.* New York, NY: The Holiday House.

Giovanni, N. (2005). *Rosa.* New York, NY: Henry Holt Company.

Gray, F. (1995). *Bus ride to justice: Changing the American system by the system.* Montgomery, AL: The Black Belt Publishers.

The Henry Ford Foundation. (2002). Retrieved May 3, 2008, from The Henry Ford: America's Greatest History Attraction Web site: http://www.hfmgv.org/exhibits/rosaparks/faqactual.asp

Kinnon, J. B. (2006, January). The Rosa Parks and Martin Luther King Jr. connection. *Ebony.*

Parks, R. (1992). *Rosa Parks: My story.* New York, NY: Dial Books.

Shipp, E. R. (2005, October 25). Rosa Parks, 92, founding symbol of Civil Rights Movement, cies. *New York Times*, p. A1.

Troy State University Rosa Parks Library and Museum. Retrieved May 3, 2008, from Troy State University Web site: http://montgomery.troy.edu/rosaparks/museum/

Wong, J. In Class Audience Survey. Raw data. 5 May 2008.

Sample Speech to Inform

Specific Purpose: To inform my audience of the prominence of human trafficking in San Francisco.

Central Idea: Human trafficking is modern day slavery that weaves itself in many ways and into many industries, and is prevalent in many spots in the city of San Francisco.

Introduction

I. Let me share the story of a girl named Duan with you.

    A. Born in a poverty-stricken part of Thailand, Duan's parents always struggled to support their eight children.

        1. Things got so hard for the family that they were forced to make a difficult decision: either to watch their children slowly starve or to sell one of their children so their family could survive.

        2. In the end, they chose to sell Duan.

    B. The family was devastated to have to part with Duan, but the smiling woman who bought Duan vowed that she would have a bright future with a well-paying job.

        1. Unfortunately, this promise was a lie.

            a. Instead, Duan lost her innocence and her life turned into a nightmare because she was forced to live and work in a brothel.

            b. Duan was raped 6 to 12 times a night, and was beaten if she failed to satisfy her "customers."

    C. It didn't stop in Thailand; Duan was eventually trafficked into the United States, and wound up in one of the country's human trafficking hot spots: San Francisco.

II. The fact that humans are trafficked in a city situated about 8 miles from this campus is unsettling.

    A. According to my audience survey, everyone in this class goes into San Francisco at least monthly, and half of this class goes there every day or every few days.

        1. That means that this issue literally does hit close to home.

(Transition: Today I'm going to share with you that human trafficking is modern day slavery that weaves itself in many ways and industries, and is prevalent in many spots in the city of San Francisco.)

Body

I. Human trafficking is modern-day slavery.

    A. According to the U.S. Department of State, human trafficking is "modern-day slavery, involving victims who are forced, defrauded or coerced into labor or sexual exploitation.

        1. Annually, about 600,000 to 800,000 people, mostly women and children are trafficked across national borders."

B. Contrary to popular belief, as reflected in my audience survey, human trafficking is not the same as prostitution or the smuggling of humans.

    1. While many victims of trafficking end up in the sex trade, the key difference is that, unlike prostitutes, they are forced to sell themselves.

    2. As far as human smuggling goes, the August 14th 2008 issue of *The Economist* stressed the difference between the smuggling and the trafficking of humans in one of its articles.

        a. The article said that when a person is smuggled, he or she pays a smuggler to safely get him or her into another country; it is a business relationship that ends once the transaction is complete.

        b. Human trafficking, on the other hand, involves moving people against their will or under false pretenses for the profit of the trafficker.

II. Humans are trafficked into San Francisco in a variety of ways.

    A. Traffickers most commonly lure victims from poverty-stricken countries.

        1. For example, a woman in Romania may be promised a well-paying job as a waitress or model in America, an exciting opportunity that will enable her to send much-needed financial aid to her family back home.

            a. Little does she know that she is walking into a trap set by traffickers.

            b. The next thing she knows, she is forced to work in horrific circumstances, and her traffickers threaten that if she resists in any way or tries to escape, her family back home will be harmed.

        2. Children in poor countries are usually victimized in one of two ways.

            a. Like in the story I shared at the beginning of this speech, children are often sold to traffickers by families in desperate need.

            b. Others are kidnapped off the street.

        3. Once in their trafficker's grasp these victims are either flown into the United States with a fake passport and I.D. or are snuck into the country from Mexico or Canada.

    B. However, victims aren't all from other countries.

        1. Author David Batstone in his book, *Not for Sale*, tells about girls as young as 13 from the Midwest being kidnapped and then forced to work in brothels.

        2. Additionally, runaway American girls are often lured romantically by A pimp, and then are convinced that if they really love him, they will do what he says.

III. Once in San Francisco, victims of human trafficking are forced to work in a variety of industries.

    A. The sex trade is recognized as the primary industry in which human trafficking shows up.

        1. The *San Francisco Chronicle* reports that there are thousands of trafficked women in San Francisco.

2. The average age a girl becomes involved in the sex trade is 14 years old, and according to the FBI, more and more young males are being forced into the commercial sex industry as well.

B. As listed in the book *Not For Sale*, other industries in which humans are trafficked include domestic service such as housekeeping, nanny services, agriculture, sweatshop/factory work, restaurant work, and hotel work.

    1. Moreover, David Batstone, a professor at the University of San Francisco and the author of the book I referred to earlier, *Not for Sale*, learned about human trafficking very abruptly.

        a. In the introduction of his book, the modern-day abolitionist wrote about how shocking it was to read in the newspaper that one his favorite restaurants in the Bay Area harbored slaves.

        b. The owner of the Indian restaurant had trafficked Indian girls for sex and for free labor in his restaurant.

        c. His actions were uncovered when one of the girls, who was 17 years old had died of carbon monoxide poisoning in one of his apartments.

    2. Discovering that such a horrific practice was going on so close to home shocked and unsettled Professor Batstone.

IV. Human trafficking occurs in a variety of places in San Francisco.

A. Since we all have spent time in San Francisco, it can be hard to believe that human trafficking really happens there today, but it does.

    1. One has to wonder where these victims of human trafficking are located.

B. Victims of the sex trade are held in underground brothels that operate from locations like apartments, houses, and massage parlors.

    1. Just last year, the *San Francisco Chronicle* reported that 17 massage parlors were closed due to suspicions of involvement in the trafficking of Asian women.

C. As far as labor trafficking is concerned, victims can be found working in restaurants, agricultural fields, factories, hotels, and homes.

    1. As mentioned earlier Professor Batstone discovered that human trafficking happened at his favorite restaurant.

    2. He assumed that the girls waiting his table were free, and it is easy for anyone to assume the same thing when they see their janitorial service in a hotel or their next-door-neighbor's nanny.

    3. Have you thought about whether the staff at your favorite restaurants, hotels, or service stops are there on their free will?

(Transition: Learning that human trafficking is such a prevalent problem in San Francisco and that it happens so close to many of our homes and just 8 miles from campus should raise our awareness to this horrifying human rights issue.)

Conclusion

I. In closing, we can see that human trafficking isn't just something that happens in other countries or in history books or in someone else's backyard.

    A. In an essay written by Jonathan Tran published in the magazine *Christian Century,* he writes ". . . the Vatican declared that human trafficking in our time is a greater scourge than the transatlantic slave trade of the 18th century."

        1. It really is a modern-day slave trade, and today I have shared that slaves are trafficked from a variety of places in a variety of ways.

        2. They are forced to work in horrible conditions, and they seem invisible despite the fact that they exist all over San Francisco.

    B. Learning about this issue opened my eyes, and I hope that it has opened yours as well.

        1. In the words of Simone de Beauvoir, "I wish that every human life might be pure transparent freedom."

Bibliography (MLA Format)

Batstone, David. *Not for Sale: The Return of the Global Slave Trade—and How We Can Fight It.* New York: Harper San Francisco, 2007.

Beauvoir, Simone de. *The Blood of Others.* New York: Pantheon, 1984.

Cabanatuan, Michael. "100 arrested in Bay Area in prostitution sting." *San Francisco Chronicle* 28 Oct. 2008: B1.

"Drawing lines in a dark place; People-trafficking and people-smuggling." *The Economist* 14 Aug. 2008. 31 Oct. 2008. *General OneFile.*

Elhardt, Twyla D. Audience Survey: Those surveyed confused human trafficking with human smuggling and prostitution in response to open-ended question. Raw data. 28 Oct. 2008.

Facts About Human Trafficking. United States. Department of State. Office to Monitor and Combat Trafficking in Persons. 7 Dec. 2005. U.S. Department of State. 2 Nov. 2008 <http://www.state.gov/g/tip/rls/fs/2005/60840.htm>.

"Human Trafficking—An Intelligence Report." *FBI.gov.* 6 Dec. 2006. Federal Bureau of Investigation. 31 Oct. 2008 <http://www.fbi.gov/page2/june06/human_trafficking061206.htm>.

May, Meredith. "SEX TRAFFICKING / San Francisco Is a Major Center for International Crime Networks that Smuggle and Enslave." *San Francisco Chronicle* 6 Oct. 2006: A1.

Tran, Jonathan. "Sold into Slavery: The Scourge of Human Trafficking (Essay)." *The Christian Century* 124 (2007): 22+. 27 Nov. 2008.

Name: _____

True-False

1. T *F*   The four kinds of informative speeches are—speeches about descriptions/objects, speeches about explanations/concepts, speeches about processes, and speeches about events.

2. T *F*   One of the biggest barriers to effective informative speaking is using language that is too simple for the audience.

3. T *F*   "To inform my audience how to create their own Web pages" is a specific purpose statement for an informative speech about a process.

4. *T* F   Abstract language is especially helpful for clarifying ideas in informative speeches.

5. *T* F   A summary is rarely necessary in the conclusion of an informative speech.

Multiple Choice

6. Informative speeches about processes are usually organized in the _____ order.
   a. causal or spatial
   b. topical or spatial
   c. causal or topical
   d. spatial or chronological
   e. chronological or topical

7. If your specific purpose statement were "To inform my audience about the major landmarks of the San Francisco Bay Area," you would probably organize your speech in _____ order.
   a. topical or causal
   b. spatial or comparative
   c. comparative or chronological
   d. chronological or causal
   e. spatial or topical

8. If your specific purpose were "To inform my audience of the major steps in an effective weight loss program," you would probably organize your speech in the _____ order.
   a. comparative
   b. spatial
   c. chronological
   d. causal
   e. illustrative

9. Speeches about _____ are often more complex than other types of informative speeches.
   a. objects
   b. events
   c. processes
   d. functions
   e. concepts

10. Which of the following is an occasion of informative speaking?
    a. a lawyer pressing a jury not to convict her client
    b. a teacher influencing colleagues to adopt a new policy
    c. a banker explaining how the stock market operates
    d. all of the above
    e. a and c only

Essay

11. What are the four types of informative speeches discussed in the text? Give an example of an effective specific purpose statement for each type.

Chapter 15

Speech to Persuade

"My most brilliant achievement was my ability to be able to persuade my wife to marry me."
—Sir Winston Churchill (British Prime Minister, 1874–1965)

PERSUASION IS USED EVERY DAY

Think about how many times you persuade people to do something for you in a given day. How many times have you asked your parents, friends, or co-workers for money? Or how about persuading your teacher for an extra point so your grade will increase by a level? Or, in Winston Churchill's case, persuading his wife to marry him may have been a tall order to accomplish. On your pathway to success the ability to persuade people will take your career and/or personal life to the next level; the art of persuasion is an essential skill that must be continuously polished.

When you are persuading an audience, your purpose is to have your audience agree with you and your position, and/or take action on behalf of your message. Persuading your audience obliges you the speaker to communicate information clearly, correctly, and convincingly to influence the listener's opinions, ethics, and actions.

In order to be a truly effective persuasive public speaker it is your responsibility to know all sides of the issue and not just the position you are advocating. Because your audience will have diverse viewpoints on your persuasive topic, by understanding the entire scope of the issue you can better tailor your message to meet the needs of the audience. In addition, by understanding the wide range of perspectives of the issue, you will be able to address the opposing points of view that may be shared by the audience, only to disprove them. Moreover, your audience may be skeptical about particular parts of your speech, but by knowing the different facets of the topic you can proficiently address that skepticism, and in the process gain the credibility and respect of your audience by doing your homework.

CREDIBILITY

A key ingredient to successful persuasive public speaking is establishing yourself as a credible person to speak on this particular topic to this particular audience. Generating your "ethos" is a two-pronged approach: 1) establishing your expertise and knowledge base regarding the given topic and 2) developing your character or goodwill toward the audience with your speech.

Your audience needs to know that you have some first-hand experience or have utilized reliable sources and/or are using highly regarded testimony for your given topic. David Ogilvy, also known as the "Father of Advertising," said it best about personal experience enhancing persuasiveness, "I have a theory that the best ads come from personal experience. Some of the good ones I have done have really come out of the real experience of my life, and somehow this has come over as true and valid and persuasive." If you have personal experience with the topic on which you are trying to persuade your audience, by all means state it in your presentation particularly in your introduction. For example, let us say that you are an auto mechanic and you are going to persuade your audience to start using synthetic oil instead of the petroleum-based oil that is commonly used in our cars. You will strengthen your believability and enhance your credibility to the audience if you state that you are an auto mechanic with x number of years' experience, and that you are here to persuade the audience to start using synthetic oil in their cars the next time they need to change their oil. Now imagine if you tried this approach, "I have been with the San Francisco Opera for the past five years and am here to persuade you to start using synthetic oil the next time you need to change the oil in your car." That would be a tough sell, unless you did oil changes between scenes at the opera.

Another concern that may arise is "how about if I don't have first-hand experience with my subject matter, how am I supposed to sound credible to my audience?" A couple of different approaches can work to remedy this situation. The quality of research sources you use to support your message becomes more important. By using highly respected and well-known experts in the field as your expert testimony and including the views of others who have first-hand experience, you can boost your peer testimony which will serve you well as you advocate for a particular issue. In addition, thorough audience analysis and the implementation of the findings you may have from your questionnaire will boost your credibility with the audience.

Again, remember the quote from our friend David Ogilvy the father of advertising, ". . . the best ads come from personal experience. Some of the good ones I have done have really come out of the real experience of my life, and somehow this has come over as true and valid and persuasive." Nothing beats having first-hand experience with a subject matter you are advocating.

The combination of having first-hand experience and goodwill for your audience will put you on your pathway to success in persuading your audience. CBS broadcast icon Edward R. Murrow said this about credibility, "to be persuasive we must be believable; to be believable we must be credible; to be credible we must be truthful." The millions of audience members who tuned in to Murrow's nightly newscast believed he was a man whom they could trust, and your audience needs to get that same sense from you the speaker. In short, Murrow instilled in his audience that he had *their* best interest at heart when he was reporting the news from around the world. Your audience needs to have that same feeling from you when you deliver your persuasive speech. When your audience believes and senses that you are looking out for *their* best interest, they are sure to follow along with your message. Now the question you are probably asking yourself is, "How do I communicate the characteristic of trustworthiness to my audience?"

A sure way to build that strong relationship with your audience is to be honest in what you are presenting, and stay away from clever ways to deceive and misguide your audience. For example, not distorting your statistics or quoting experts out of context is a sure way to build an honorable relationship with your audience. Moreover, during your data gathering stage in your speech development process you should ask yourself, "Am I using the most accurate information?" "Am I using the most reliable sources to support my ideas?" "Is the information I'm using timely, or is this outdated?" "Am I accurately reflecting the responses from the feedback from my audience survey?" All of these questions go back to the opening statement in this paragraph, "be honest in what you are presenting."

Moreover, you can communicate goodwill for your audience by presenting their thoughts, feelings, and concerns in your presentation from their feedback from their surveys. By doing this, your audience will get the sense that you listened to their concerns, fears, and anxieties regarding your topic. Listening is probably the most powerful gesture you can do for a human being. Once a person feels that they have been heard, the communication channels between the speaker and the audience are now open, and your audience will be more inclined to be receptive to your message.

So let us say that you are delivering a speech in support of the right to carry guns, and you are delivering this speech to the Free Love and Peace Association at their annual convention. As you can see, this can be a recipe for resistance and conflict between the speaker and the audience. Instinctively, we can see how the main speaker may chastise the audience for not carrying guns and that they are "less than" for not carrying weapons. This strategy will build tall walls and little will be accomplished, and the speaker would have failed at his attempt to persuade this audience to start carrying guns.

In contrast by demonstrating goodwill and respect towards the audience's values and beliefs for not carrying guns, the speaker will have a higher probability of success. The speaker would start off by stating the mission of the group (Free Love and Peace Association), and how carrying guns will support and strengthen their group's safety. Another tactic may be to share how there is more crime in the area where the group congregates, and by carrying guns, they can protect each other and embolden the group to maintain and extend the association's love and peace philosophy into the neighborhood. More than likely the audience would be more willing to listen to the speech, maybe not to agree or completely change their position, but at least listen to the message and reconsider their strong points of view. In addition, the audience will sense that the speaker is respecting them and likely will reciprocate that gesture back to the speaker. When facing a hostile audience (not our friends at the Free Love and Peace Association) or an audience who adamantly opposes your position, demonstrating goodwill and respect towards your audience is a top priority to build bridges and not walls.

PERSUASION IS MORE DEMANDING THAN INFORMING AN AUDIENCE

Persuading your audience is much more demanding than informing an audience. The test comes in the area of audience analysis, which requires more scrutiny of what makes your audience tick. Understanding your audience's attitudes, values, and beliefs will give you the competitive edge when persuading your audience.

Another dynamic that distinguishes a persuasive speech from an informative speech is that not everyone in your audience will agree with your position. With that said, when entering into your persuasive speech, have a realistic approach as to what you can achieve with your presentation. For example, if you find through your audience survey that not one person is in agreement with your position, do not expect that you will convert an entire audience to your side of the issue. In this case, if you were able to have a few audience members re-evaluate their opinions and beliefs, then you would chalk that up as a successful speech. Because public speaking is an audience-focused activity, you must tailor your message to your audience; therefore strong findings from your audience survey must be utilized to help you reach your specific purpose.

Dean Rusk, the Secretary of State under Presidents John F. Kennedy and Lyndon B. Johnson, said this about the importance of listening in the art of persuasion, "the best way to persuade people is with your ears—by listening to them." In the world of public speaking the findings from your audience survey will allow you to get in the heads of your audience members, especially those whom you want to persuade most. While listening to your presentation, your audience will be continuously judging you by the quality of your arguments, your evidence (examples, statistics, and testimony), your sources, your emotional appeals, and your delivery. In addition, the listeners are expecting you to answer their skepticism about you the speaker and your speech topic. If you do not address the elephant in the room regarding your topic, your audience will discredit you instantly, and from there no matter what you say you will not be fully received by your audience. Moreover, the audience survey allows you to put yourself in the perspective of the audience, providing valuable insights on how to approach your persuasive speech.

THREE CATEGORIES OF AUDIENCE MEMBERS

Regardless of the amount of effort and passion you put into your persuasive speech, you will not persuade everyone in the audience. However, through the findings of your audience survey you will be able to divide your audience into three distinct camps. The first camp will be in support of your position, the second camp will be those undecided to your position, and the third camp will be those who are adamantly against your position. By distinguishing the three sets of people in your audience you can now tailor your message to the group who is most persuadable, the undecided group. The undecided group is also known as your **target audience**. You never want to disregard any part of your audience, but special attention is needed in analyzing the group in the undecided camp. Extra care is needed when at looking this group's attitudes, values, beliefs, and knowledge base of your speech topic.

An area that is helpful in persuasion is to gauge the audience's previous pattern of changing attitudes, values, and beliefs. When developing your audience survey you may want to ask questions that will help you get a sense of previous behavior which can forecast future behavior. A familiar slip-up made by persuasive speakers is to ask for radical changes of their audience. A more prudent approach would be to request small, doable, and incremental changes to their actions, values, or beliefs.

TYPES OF PERSUASIVE SPEECHES

There are three types of persuasive speeches, the question of fact, the question of value, and the question of policy. We will discuss in depth the three different types of persuasive speeches as well as the organizational strategies to help you achieve your goals in using the three types of persuasive speeches.

Questions of Fact

Who scored the most touchdowns in Arizona State University football history? What was the winning finishing time for the 2008 New York City marathon? Who won the 1968 presidential election? These are questions of facts that can be answered undisputedly. However, many questions of fact cannot be answered definitively, and are in the form of predictions. For example: will the Dow Jones Industrial hit 15,000 by 2011? Will a Category 5 hurricane strike the Gulf Coast during the next hurricane season? Other questions of fact deal with occurrences where the facts are not clear and the lines are blurred. What specifically happened in Dallas the day President John F. Kennedy was assassinated? How exactly did John F. Kennedy Jr. lose control of his airplane that crashed? These questions have continued to spark debate because of their inconclusive and speculative nature. When delivering a question of fact type of persuasive speech you are presenting your speech from the place of a promoter and supporter of your specific purpose.

A frequent organizational strategy for a question of fact is the topical strategy. For example if you decided to persuade your audience that a Category 5 hurricane will hit the Caribbean Sea during the next hurricane season, the outline would look like something like this:

Specific Purpose: To persuade my audience that a Category 5 level hurricane will hit the Caribbean next year.

Central Idea: Warm surface layers that run deep in the Caribbean and the northward extension of the loop current will lead to a Category 5 hurricane next year.

Main Points:

I. The warm surface layer extends much deeper in the Caribbean than in the Gulf, which is why Category 5 hurricanes are much more common in the Caribbean.

II. The northward extension of the loop current is a trend that will likely to continue into the Caribbean and was the most likely reason that Katrina and Rita intensified to Category 5 hurricanes.

Another organizational strategy that may be beneficial for the question of fact is to use the spatial order.

Specific Purpose: To persuade my audience that all states must have a mandatory motorcycle helmet law.

Central Idea: There are three states that need to implement the mandatory motorcycle helmet law, Illinois, Iowa, and New Hampshire.

Main Points:

I. The state of Illinois must implement a mandatory motorcycle helmet law immediately.

II. Staying in the mid-west, Iowa is another state that must implement a mandatory motorcycle helmet law.

III. Moving from the mid-west to the east, the state of New Hampshire must implement a mandatory motorcycle helmet law.

The goal of the question of fact speech for these examples is to persuade the audience to accept a specific point of view regarding each of the topics. Whatever your specific purpose is for your question of fact presentation, relevant examples, trustworthy statistics, and believable testimony are needed to support your specific purpose.

Questions of Value

The question of value is based on a value judgment, based on the speaker's belief about what is fair or unfair, right or wrong, correct or incorrect, good or bad, moral or immoral, just or unjust. Examples that fall under the question of value umbrella would be: is doctor-aided suicide moral or immoral, is Magic Johnson the best point guard in NBA history, was the American invasion of Iraq fair or unfair? When answering these questions, you are tapping into your critical thinking skills, supporting your ideas with credible sources, but also investigating your values. It is important to remember that when addressing the question of value, you are not merely spouting your opinions with little or no supporting materials to strengthen your argument. Strong sources of information and a well-organized speech will enhance your status in the eyes of the audience. It is not the facts that are in disagreement, but how those facts are applied to values being persuaded.

When delivering a question of value speech, specific thought must be considered towards the standards you have established in your value judgment. Moreover, after identifying those standards, how will those standards be implemented to support your arguments? A common organizational strategy that is used for a question of value is the topical order.

> **Specific Purpose:** To persuade my audience that school uniforms should be implemented in our local junior high schools.

> **Central Idea:** Having junior high school kids wear uniforms will allow them to go to school without being judged by their clothing, help the kids parents save money, and allow the community to know which school the children attend.

Main Points:

    I. Junior High School children should wear uniforms because it serves numerous purposes that enhance the success of the child.

        A. The student will be judged on their personality and academic merits and not by their fashion sense.

        B. School uniforms are a more cost-effective alternative.

        C. The school uniform can represent to the community which school each child attends.

    II. School uniforms for Junior High School children are a better alternative to meet numerous purposes to best serve the student and their respective communities.

        A. Wearing a school uniform allows kids to not be judged by the caliber of the labels worn on their clothes but rather by their personality and academic merits.

        B. Wearing a school uniform is a cost-effective tool for the parents to clothe their kids for school as opposed to purchasing the latest fashions for the new school year.

        C. In case of an emergency, each school uniform will represent to the community which school each child attends. This is a safety issue.

Delivering the question of value speech discusses values but is careful *not* to advocate your audience to take a particular course of action as a result of your speech. Again the function of the question of value is to argue about what is fair or unfair, right or wrong, correct or incorrect, good or bad, moral or immoral, just or unjust.

Questions of Policy

Unlike the question of value, the question of policy speech demands a specific course of action from the audience. However, what distinguishes the question of policy from the question of fact and the question of value is that something should or should not be done. There are two types of agreement that you will need to decide on for your question of policy, passive agreement or active agreement. If your aim is to have your audience reach **passive agreement** with you, you want the audience to concur that the policy you have selected is desirable, but you will not have your audience do anything to realize the particular policy. When pushing for the passive agreement you are articulating that the speaker's policy is needed and sensible. Again no action is being asked from the audience.

When crafting your specific purpose for the question of policy the word "should" is usually used in your statement. For example:

To persuade my audience that the freeway speed limit should be reduced from 65 miles per hour to 60 miles per hour.

To persuade my audience that the federal government should increase the NASA budget by 10 percent over the next five years.

The other choice for the speaker delivering a question of policy speech is to ask for **immediate action** as opposed to passively agreeing to the speaker's idea. When crafting this type of speech your goal is to prompt your audience to take immediate action for your call to action. Here are some examples that would fall under the immediate call to action:

- To persuade my audience to donate blood at the College regional blood bank.
- To persuade my audience to register to vote for the gubernatorial election.
- To persuade my audience to register for Sociology 270 before the 4:00 PM deadline today.
- To persuade my audience to donate $15 toward the Michael Canfield presidential campaign fund.

When delivering a speech for immediate action you want your audience to be able to do something that is simple and doable so that they will be committed to the cause. If you find that you can have your audience do something in support of your call to action, they will be more than likely be committed to the issue that you are advocating. When making your call to action, be as specific as possible as to what you want your audience to do. In addition, make the specific action simple and easy to do, for example, sign this petition, drop $5 in the hat in the back of the room on your way out, or wear this badge for the rest of the day.

Requirements for the Question of Policy: Address the Need, Plan, and Practicality

The first area you need to address in a question of policy is the *need*. Your audience needs to get a sense that a change to an existing policy is needed and it is your job to illustrate that point. If there is no need to change a policy, why would one want to fix something that is running well? So the first step in your speech development is to clearly identify and explain the need to change some problem. The burden of proof will sit squarely on the shoulders of the speaker that there is a need to change. The **burden of proof** may be defined as "the responsibility of the persuasive speaker to establish that a change from an existing policy exists." After explaining and describing the need there should be no doubt in the audience's mind that a need for change is necessary.

The next area to address in a question of policy is the *plan* to change an existing policy. With most plans that are proposed there will be gaps from the audience's perspective that need to be addressed. As a responsible and ethical pubic speaker, you must highlight the audience's skepticism directly. Therefore understanding the issue from many perspectives will allow you to tackle this tall task head-on.

The final piece to address in a question of policy will be the *practicality* of the plan for the speaker's new policy. Your new plan is going to have to stand up to this question, "will this plan solve the problem, or will it create even more problems?" Anytime something "new" is proposed a red flag will be raised from the audience. Hence, when presenting your new plan, underscore that your plan is reasonable and practical. A proven tip when proposing a new course of action is to research if a similar plan has been implemented somewhere else that would be applicable to your situation.

When delivering your question of policy speech, you have four options that will help you organize your speech effectively. Common organizational strategies used are: problem-solution, problem-cause-solution, comparative advantages order, and Monroe's motivated sequence.

Problem-Solution Order

The problem-solution order has two main points. The first main point addresses the problem, or the need that a problem does exist. The second main point examines the plan for the solution to the problem and the practicality of your plan.

> **Specific Purpose:** To persuade my audience that the city needs to implement a 10:00 PM curfew for minors (under 18) in the downtown area to cut down on crime.

> **Central Idea:** 70% of the crimes committed downtown are by minors and the city needs to enforce a curfew to combat crime for a safer downtown.

Main Points:

    I.   According to police reports 70% of all crimes committed downtown are carried out by minors after 10:00 PM.

    II. The city must implement a 10:00 PM curfew for all minors in the downtown area to create a safer downtown.

The Problem-Cause-Solution

The problem-cause-solution order produces three main points to persuade the speaker's audience to take a specific course of action. The first main point speaks to the problem, the second main point accounts for the causes to the problem, and the third main point offers a solution to the problem in the specific purpose.

> **Specific Purpose:** To persuade my audience to reject television programs, movies, and music that portray women in a negative light.

> **Central Idea:** To put a stop to the increase in violence toward women, we must shun the consumption of media that celebrates negativity toward women.

Main Points:

    I.   Harmful attitudes and violent behavior towards women have increased among men from the ages of 18 to 25 years old.

    II.   Media such as television, movies, music, and music videos that objectify women have led to the increase in violent behavior towards women.

    III. You must refuse to watch or purchase work from artists who negatively present women in their bodies of work.

The Comparative Advantages Order

The comparative advantages order occurs when your audience is in harmony that a problem exists and needs to be remedied. Since there is agreement that a problem exists, your efforts and speech development can be focused on the advantages and disadvantages to a particular plan of action to solve a specific problem. When using the comparative advantages order organizational strategy, each of your main points will be amplifying why your solution is favorable to other proposed solutions.

Specific Purpose: To persuade my audience that financial literacy programs must be implemented into the K–12 curriculum.

Central Idea: Mandating financial literacy programs in grades K–12 will lead children to become more familiar with financial consequences of credit card debt and the skills to make wiser financial decisions for a more prosperous society.

Main Points:

    I.   Financial literacy programs for students in grades K–12 will allow them to become more familiar with financial consequences of credit card debt than the existing financial education of our youth.

    II. Financial education in grades K–12 will allow America's youth to make wiser financial decision leading to a more prosperous nation that will benefit more people around the world.

Monroe's Motivated Sequence

Monroe's motivated sequence was developed by Alan Monroe from Purdue University in the 1930's. There are five points to cover in the Monroe's motivated sequence strategy.

1.   Attention

2.   Need

3.   Satisfaction

4.   Visualization

5.   Action

The first point to cover is to gain the *attention* of the audience. Gaining the attention of the audience is a sound strategy to implement in the introduction of the speech. The second point in the Monroe's motivated sequence is to address is the *need* for a new policy. Once you have captured the attention of the audience you must now demonstrate a need for a policy change. Again the more you can tailor your arguments to the needs of the audience during this phase of your speech the more your audience will be engaged in your message. The need must be so real for the audience that they are genuinely concerned.

Now that the need is clearly articulated you now have to supply a *satisfactory* resolution to the problem. In addition to presenting a solution, you also need to share how this plan will work, so noticeably that the audience can envision the benefits of the plan of action. At this juncture, focus your rhetoric towards how your audience will specifically benefit from the solution of your plan.

The final and most important push is to clearly spell out what course of action you want your audience to take as a result of your speech. Again when making a request for action from your audience, be as specific as possible and make the plan of action as doable as possible. The more hoops you make your audience jump through, the less likely your audience will support your speech.

The breakdown of how to use the Monroe's motivated sequence for your complete sentence outline would look like this:

Specific Purpose:

Central Idea:

Introduction

(Attention)   I.

Body

(Need)   I.

(Satisfaction)   II.

(Visualization)   III.

Conclusion

(Action)   I.

Summary: Tips for your Speech to Persuade

On your pathway to success learning the art of persuading people will propel your personal and professional success into the stratosphere. A successful persuasive public speaker knows all sides of the topic and not just the stance he or she is supporting. Because your audience will have different views on your persuasive issue, by comprehending the entire scope of the issue you can better meet the needs of your audience.

Your audience will be composed of three distinct groupings, those for your position, those against your position, and those who are undecided on your position. The undecided group is also known as your target audience. It is never recommended to ignore any faction of your audience; however, further study is required for the group who are undecided on your position. From there, you can really channel your energy into the attitudes, values, and beliefs of the target audience since they will be more inclined to be persuaded.

There are three types of persuasive speeches, the question of fact, question of value, and the question of policy. The question of policy is distinct because it calls for the speaker to address three vital details in your speech, the need, plan, and practicality.

Common organizational strategies used for a persuasive speech are: topical, spatial, problem-solution, problem-cause-solution, comparative advantages order, and Monroe's motivated sequence. When using the Monroe motivated sequence strategy, these five areas need to be addressed in your speech:

1. Attention

2. Need

3. Satisfaction

4. Visualization

5. Action

When delivering a persuasive speech, it is important to remember that how you deliver your speech carries a lot of weight as to how your audience perceives your message. In short communicate your message passionately and vibrantly utilizing vocal variety, pacing, and variations to your volume. Speak with conviction and confidence but be careful not to cross the line over to arrogance or being obnoxious. In short, quality practice with your delivery could be the difference between getting what you want and falling short of your persuasive goals.

On your pathway to success, having the skills to persuade will prove to take your personal and professional success to places you have never imagined.

Sample Speech to Persuade Outline

Specific Purpose: To persuade my audience not to buy organic foods because they do not have a comparative advantage to non-organic foods.

Central Idea: We should stop buying organic foods because they are not more nutritional, safer, healthier, or environmentally friendly than non-organic foods.

Introduction

I. The organic food market has grown 132% between 2002 and 2007 according to the April 2008 issue of *Prepared Foods*.

   A. The marketing of organic food is very effective at convincing consumers to buy their products.

   B. It is assumed that organic products are healthier and that they provide other benefits due to the way they are grown and processed, but there is no evidence that proves organics to be disease-free food.

II. The sales of organic foods remain high despite consumers having to pay considerably more for them.

   A. Even with our current economy with increasing food and gas prices, consumers are still leaning towards these pricey alternatives.

      1. According to my audience survey, 50% of the class buys organic foods and they prefer them over non-organic foods because they believe that organic is a safer and healthier alternative.

      2. The other 50% of the class had no preference.

   B. Consumers choose organic foods for safety and nutritional reasons, while choosing non-organic foods for the cost.

      1. According to the U.S. Department of Agriculture, organic food is defined as "food produced without using most conventional pesticides and does not come from animals that are given antibiotics or growth hormones."

   C. Why are consumers still willing to spend twice as much for essentially the same products?

      1. Let's say that you and your family normally drink one gallon of milk per week.

      2. In this week's Safeway ad, one gallon of milk goes for about $3.00 and one gallon of organic milk normally runs about $6.00.

      3. In the span of a year you will be spending an extra $200 by choosing organic over the non-organic option for milk.

      4. Now imagine buying other organic products besides milk and think about the amount of money you could save if you chose the non-organic option.

III. There are three main reasons why a consumer would choose organic foods over non-organic foods.

    A. One, consumers believe that organic foods provide better nutritional value.

    B. Two, consumers unconditionally accept that organic food is safer than non-organic food.

    C. And thirdly, consumers have faith that the production-process of organic food is more environmentally friendly.

        1. However, there is no clear evidence of organic foods having a comparative advantage over non-organic foods.

(Transition: I will tell you the hideous side to organic products and why it is not practical to buy or continue buying them.)

Body

I. According to my in-class survey the most common reason why you prefer organic food is because you think that it is healthier and more nutritious than non-organic food.

    A. However, is it really more nutritious than conventional foods?

        1. According to the June 2006 issue of *Men's Health Advisor,* most studies have shown little difference nutritionally between organic and conventional produce.

        2. People believe that just because the foods are pesticide-free that they are somehow healthier for you.

    B. However, studies show that the trace amount of pesticide residues found in conventional foods does not pose a hazardous risk to people.

        1. In fact, researchers are still looking for the first human death associated with pesticides.

        2. Today's use of pesticides in farms is carefully monitored and never exceeds the safety limit.

        3. Of course pesticides are dangerous in high concentrations but often times when our foods are tested for levels of pesticide residue, the amount found in both organic and conventional samples are almost zero.

        4. For that reason, the danger of pesticides to human and wildlife is minimal.

            a. Dennis Avery, author of *The Hidden Dangers of Organic Foods,* states that in order for the presence of pesticides to be at a cancer-causing level, we must drink 150,000 billion gallons of water with trace amounts of a common pesticide for about 70 years for it to affect us.

    C. Whether or not there is a presence of pesticides in our foods does not make a significant difference in its nutritional value and safety.

        1. As a matter of fact, it can be even more dangerous without the use of pesticides on our crops.

2. Because no pesticides are used in organic farming, their crops cannot naturally ward off insects so they are destroyed by insects and rodents where fungi can enter.

    a. As a result, they produce toxins which can possibly be cancer-causing and even fatal if consumed.

3. The FDA regularly tests organic crops and often finds these toxins present.

4. So, in reality, the nutrition you think you may be getting from organic foods may very well have been infested with these toxins.

II. The second reason why consumers choose organic foods is because they believe that organic foods may be safer for them and their families.

    A. Did you know that 73,480 Americans got sick from a food-born illness that is caused by a strain of E. coli which is found in our organic crops?

        1. Organic produce like lettuce and spinach are commonly grown in soil which contains cow and human manure.

        2. Since manure is a breeding ground for E.coli, it lives and proliferates there, entering crops and later affecting consumers.

        3. This strain of E. coli is so dangerous that if consumed can cause acute kidney damage, liver damage, and even death.

    B. In 1996, a family in Connecticut was affected by this dangerous bacterium.

        1. Three out of the five family members got sick and still suffer from kidney damage and vision problems.

            a. In the end, this incident was traced to organic lettuce.

    C. Consumers think that just because these products are pesticide-free that they are purer and safer.

        1. But it is obvious that they are actually making them sick.

        2. According to the U.S. Centers for Disease Control and Prevention, people who eat organic are eight times as likely as the rest of the population to be attacked by the strain of the E. coli bacterium.

    D. While researchers are still looking for the first human fatality caused by pesticides, the E. coli found in manure has claimed many lives already.

III. Besides nutrition and food safety, the third most popular reason why consumers choose organic foods over non-organic foods is that they believe the production of organic products is better for the environment.

    A. Carol Reiter, a writer for the *Merced-Sun Star*, says that "consumers want to eat food they know has not harmed the Earth."

        1. Automatically, people think that the use of pesticides are bad for the environment, but little do they know that organic production methods are just as bad.

B. You may think that we are being greener by supporting organic farming but it is actually harming the environment.

    1. Organic farming actually yields fewer crops than conventional farming meaning that more land is needed for more crops.

    2. This risks the habitats of wildlife, decreases biodiversity, and contradicts the purpose of buying organic, which is to be more "green and earth friendly."

C. Unless we stop buying these products, we will lose a lot more than we are actually getting.

    1. That is, we will pay twice as much to grow these low-yielding crops, only resulting in a tremendous loss of forests and wildlife habitats.

(Transition: Now that we know the reality of organic products, there really is no advantage to buying them.)

Conclusion

I. Organic products are over-priced for something that claims to have the job of providing nutritional value, but there is no evidence that proves this to be true.

II. Consumers believe that organic foods are a safer alternative to conventional food due to pesticides used in conventional farming.

    A. In actuality, the toxin and bacteria found in organic foods can be even more dangerous, and Americans are just as likely to be exposed to health risks that they may be concerned about with conventional foods.

III. In short, it is not practical to invest hundreds and thousands of dollars a year in organic products that do not do what they promise.

    A. Instead, they are costing consumers their money, their health, and the environment.

    B. So save money without comprising your nutrition and stop purchasing organic food at once!

Works Cited (MLA Format)

Burke, Cindy. *To Buy or Not To Buy Organic.* New York, NY: Marlow and Company, 2007.

Cho, Irene. In-Class Audience Survey. Raw data. 5 May 2008

"Consumers Still Buying Organic and Living Green Despite Economy." *PRNewswire* 29 Apr. 2008.

Cothran, Helen. *Global Resources: Opposing Viewpoints.* Framingham Hills, MI: Greenhaven Press, 2003.

Howie, Michael. "Industry Study on Why Millions of Americans Are Buying Organic Foods." 29 Mar. 2004. 05 May 2008 <http://www.organicconsumers.org/organic/millions033004.cfm>.

"Organic is the Thing, but is it the Right Thing." *Merced Sun-Star* 22 Mar. 2008.

"The organic option it costs more but is organic produce safer and more nutritious than its conventional counterpart." *Men's Health Advisor* June 2006.

Pence, Gregory E. *Designer Food.* Boston, MA: Roman & Littlefield, 2002.

Sample Speech to Persuade

Specific Purpose: To persuade my audience that they should start drinking tap water instead of consuming bottled water.

Central Idea: Consuming tap water is safer, more economical, and more environmentally friendly than drinking bottled water.

Introduction

I. Usually after speech class I head over to the vending machine and buy a bottle of water for the walk over to the student union.

    A. This has become a ritual for me this semester, and according to my in-class survey 78% of the class prefers bottled water over regular tap water, 8% preferred tap water over bottled water, and 14% of class is undecided about their preference.

        1. Some responses from the survey say that "bottled water is safer and tastes better" and that "bottled water is much more convenient" than tap water.

    B. Contrary to your bottled water preference, tap water is the better alternative.

        1. I will be persuading you that tap water is safer than bottled water, tap water is more economical than bottled water, and that tap water is the superior choice for being environmentally friendly than bottled water.

(Transition: Let's start with safety.)

Body

I. In contrast to your response to the audience survey, tap water is safer than bottled water.

    A. Many bottled water companies suggest that their water comes straight from glaciers in pristine mountain environments.

        1. Consumers believe that their water must be pure since it came straight from the source and hasn't been exposed to any kinds of contaminants.

           a. However this simply is not the case.

    B. The class survey conducted just last week revealed that 85% of the class identified that Aquafina and Desani bottled water are your preferred brands of bottled water.

        1. In an article entitled "H2O U" in the November 3rd issue of the *Chronicle of Higher Education*, author Annie Shuppy writes that the source of 25% of all bottled water is indeed tap water.

        2. Reinforcing the idea that tap water is used in bottled water brands like Aquafina, the companies state on their labels that their water comes from public water sources.

C. 98% of those surveyed in this class did not know that bottled water is not held to the same strict regulation as tap water.

    1. *The Clean Water Report* newsletter published an article entitled, "Bottled Water Needs More Oversight" and it clarifies that tap water is monitored by the Environmental Protection Agency (also known as the EPA), while bottled water is monitored by the Food Drug Administration (known as the FDA).

    2. The EPA requires that tap water be tested multiple times a day and that all of the test results be made public.

    3. The FDA, on the other hand, only requires bottled water to be tested a few times a year, and doesn't require bottled water companies to make their results public or to submit them to the government.

    4. Shuppy's article in the *Chronicle of Higher Education* says that there are 20 contaminants that are required to be inspected in tap water but not in bottled water.

II. Next, tap water is more economical than consuming bottled water.

  A. Many brands of bottled water are merely glorified tap water.

    1. To that end, often the only difference between bottled water and the water that comes out of your faucet at home is the hefty price tag.

  B. When you buy a bottle of water from the nearby vending machine on campus it is easy to overlook the hefty price you are paying.

    1. How often have you said to yourself, "Oh, it's just a dollar seventy-five in loose change."

    2. On average this class consumes four bottles of water a week at a dollar seventy-five a pop.

    3. Our semesters lasts 17 weeks, so over the course of 2 semesters the class averages $238 per school year on just bottled water.

    4. With that money you could purchase an ipod touch digital player, a couple of pairs of Air Jordan's, or two premium field club tickets when the San Francisco Giants host division rivals the Los Angeles Dodgers.

  C. Conversely, tap water will set you back a whopping .002 cents per gallon.

    1. Compare the $1.75 for 20 ounces out of the vending machine to .002 cents for an entire gallon of nature's fruit juice.

    2. This startling fact is highlighted in the book *Introduction to Water in California* where author David Carle says that bottled water is between 240 and 10,000 times more expensive than tap water.

    3. For purified bottled tap water in particular, this mark-up in price seems quite extreme.

    4. Whether you choose to filter your tap water, or drink it straight from the faucet, tap water tastes great and is inexpensive.

III. Finally tap water is more environmentally friendly than bottled water.

    A. When it comes to a carbon footprint, bottled water should be known as Big Foot.

        1. Let's start with the making of those plastic bottles. According to a June 2008 magazine article in *The American Prospect*, writer Karl Flecker says that it took about 17 million barrels of oil to make just the actual plastic bottles for the water that Americans drank in the year 2006.

        2. The magazine, *Natural History* in the February 2008 issue estimates that a mere 20% of those bottles are recycled, and that it takes three liters of water to produce a one-liter bottle of water.

        3. Moreover, the total estimated energy needed to make, transport, and dispose of one bottle of water is equivalent to filling the same bottle one-quarter full of oil.

        4. The point of sharing these statistics is to emphasize the tremendous Burden that just making the bottles has on the environment.

    B. The next time you take a hike in the mountains, walk through the college courtyard to the student union, or stroll on the beach you will notice emptied water bottles that clutter our natural beauty. Now think about all of the natural resources needed for those bottles that we are wasting by consuming bottled water.

        1. Are you guilty of contributing to the destruction of our precious natural resources—our environment?

Conclusion

I. In conclusion bottled water may be very convenient in our busy lives; however, don't let the fancy packaging seduce you.

    A. Bottled water is simply purified tap water and is not strictly regulated for your safety.

        1. On the other hand, tap water adheres to strict government regulations for the betterment of your safety and health.

II. Bottled water is also much more expensive than tap water and is a detriment to the environment.

III. With the information presented you have learned that tap water is safer, less expensive, and more environmentally conscious than bottled water.

    A. Make tap water a normal part of your routine by walking past the vending machine and straight to the water faucet.

        1. Have good taste and follow the green movement in cash savings and in preserving the environment by drinking tap water.

Works Cited

"Are Consumers Daft? Spotlight on Bottled Water.(Aquafina and Dasani from Coca-Cola Co)." *The Economist* 4 Aug. 2007.

"Bottled Water Needs More Oversight, NRDC tells Senate panel." *Clean Water Report* 46 (18 Sept. 2008): 19.

Carle, David. *Introduction to Water in California (California Natural History Guides)*. New York: University of California P, 2004.

Flecker, Karl. "Backlash against bottled water." *The American Prospect* June 2008.

"Message in a Bottle." *Natural History* Feb. 2008.

Niman, Michael. "Bottled Insanity." *The Humanist* May/June 2007.

Shuppy, Annie. "H2O U." *The Chronicle of Higher Education* Nov. 2006.

Student, Sandy. In-Class Audience Survey. Raw data. Skyline College, San Bruno. 20 Nov. 2008.

Name: _____

True-False

1. (T) F   Questions of policy usually include the word "should."

2. T (F)   Monroe's motivated sequence is most appropriate for persuasive speeches on questions of value.

3. T (F)   The burden of proof rests with the persuasive speaker who opposes change.

4. T (F)   Persuasive speeches on questions of value usually argue directly for or against particular courses of action.

5. (T) F   Persuasion is a psychological process in which listeners engage in a mental dialogue with the speaker.

Multiple Choice

6. The _____ is that segment of the entire audience that the speaker most wants to persuade.

   a. core audience
   b. target audience
   c. projected audience
   d. intended audience
   e. focus audience

7. "To persuade my audience that a major earthquake will hit San Francisco before the year 2030" is a specific purpose statement for a persuasive speech on a question of

   a. fact.
   b. attitude.
   c. value.
   d. policy.
   e. opinion.

8. Persuasive speeches on questions of fact are usually organized in _____ order.

   a. topical
   b. problem-solution
   c. comparative advantages
   d. problem-cause-solution
   e. descriptive

9. "To persuade my audience that an increase in California's sales tax should be adopted to pay off the current deficit" is a specific purpose statement for a persuasive speech on a question of

   a. fact.
   b. attitude.
   c. value.
   d. policy.
   e. opinion.

10. Which of the following is the *third* step in Monroe's motivated sequence?

    a. need
    b. action
    c. visualization
    d. attention
    e. satisfaction

11. If you want to persuade a skeptical audience, you need to

    a. Organize the speech in Monroe's motivated sequence.
    b. Urge the audience to take immediate action.
    c. Circulate an audience-analysis questionnaire.
    d. Answer the reasons for the audience's skepticism.
    e. Focus your speech on questions of practicality.

12. "To persuade my audience that Bill Clinton deserves to be rated as a great President" is a specific purpose statement for a persuasive speech on a question of

    a. fact.
    b. attitude.
    c. value.
    d. policy.
    e. opinion.

13. Regardless of whether your aim is to encourage passive agreement or immediate action, you must deal with three basic issues whenever you discuss a question of policy. They are

    a. cause, effect, and practicality.
    b. evidence, practicality, and reasoning.
    c. need, action, and reaction.
    d. problem, plan, and solution.
    e. need, plan, and practicality.

Essay

14. Explain the distinctions among questions of fact, value, and policy. Give an example of a specific purpose statement for a persuasive speech on each question.

15. What is the target audience for a persuasive speech? Why is determining and analyzing the target audience so important to effective persuasive speaking?

Chapter 16

Techniques of Persuasion

FACTORS OF CREDIBILITY

On your pathway to success persuading people will be a situation in which you will often find yourself. Competence and character are two primary traits that are often evaluated when persuading another person. Character and competence are the cornerstones of the principle of *ethos* from the great Greek philosopher Aristotle. **Competence** is how an audience regards the speaker's intelligence, expertise, and knowledge of the subject matter. In reference to the Speech to Persuade chapter (Chapter 14), your audience will be more confident about the speaker's competence if the speaker clearly states his/her first-hand experience or exposure to the subject matter. It is critical, especially in the introduction of your speech, to announce your expertise with your speech topic. Make this point clear so that your audience receives the message of your competency loud and clear.

Character is the next criterion the audience will be looking at in relation to establishing the speaker's credibility is how well the speaker demonstrates concern for the audience's best interest. The audience will continuously be assessing the speaker's honesty, trustworthiness, and believability, including whether the speaker has the audience's best interest at heart. Moreover, the audience needs to believe that the speaker is authentic in their credentials, goodwill, and their delivery. If the audience senses that the speaker is being a phony in their attempt to have the audience do something, or reconsider their attitudes, values, or beliefs or perhaps take action on a cause, the speaker will fail in his or her efforts. Credibility must pass the audience's judgment of legitimacy and authenticity and not the speaker's belief in their own credibility. The more your audience believes that you are the appropriate person to speak on the particular topic, the more the audience will be receptive to your message.

An interesting caveat about credibility is how speakers may be considered competent and even admired when they are discussing their topic of expertise with a particular audience, but then fall flat when addressing a topic and audience outside their competency. Let us think about a hypothetical example of the credibility Steve Jobs of Apple brings to the table when addressing the audience at the annual Macworld Conference and Expo. As a co-founder of Apple, and after the contributions he has made to the company and the world of computers, the audience is captivated by Jobs' message and his presence when discussing the latest Apple developments. Now let us look at how this powerful presence and credibility will head south if he were to address an audience filled with triathletes who are present to hear advanced techniques for training for the Ironman Triathlon. Since Jobs is not an active triathlete, his credibility to speak about this topic would be very low, yet when addressing the Macworld audience, his credibility would be very high.

PHASES OF CREDIBILITY

There are three phases of credibility that transition throughout the duration of a speech. The first phase of the evolution of credibility in a speech is the **initial credibility**. Initial credibility is the credibility of the speaker *before* he or she starts to deliver their speech. In every speech you deliver, there will be some measure of initial credibility. For example, when delivering your speech for your class, your initial credibility will be derived from your personality, comments made in class, and how your classmates and teacher perceive you as a member of the class. As you deliver speeches in class your initial credibility will be highlighted by the job you did with your previous speech.

As the speaker delivers his/her message the next phase of credibility is the **derived credibility**. Derived credibility is the credibility formed from the time the speaker starts his/her speech to the time the speech is completed. The audience will scrutinize the speaker's message, strength of evidence and support, emotional appeals, organization, audience adaptation, quality of research, catchiness of the introduction and conclusion, and the fluidity of the speaker's delivery. The derived credibility phase is the most pivotal period for speakers because it may either enhance or diminish their credibility with their audiences. Again, credibility must go through the perceptual filters of the audience and not the speaker's own self-perception.

Last but not least is **terminal credibility**, which occurs after the speech is complete and the entire presentation is marinating with the audience. Terminal credibility is the aftertaste of the speech and the impression left on the audience. It is the aftermath of the speech that audience will remember most, and will serve as the speaker's basis for their initial credibility at a future public speaking occasion. When speaking in a classroom setting, if your classmates and teacher see you as prepared, authentic, and proficient at one presentation, they will be more responsive to your future presentations.

BUILDING THE HUMAN CONNECTION WITH YOUR AUDIENCE

When developing strategies to strengthen your credibility remember that your audience will be judging everything you say and how you say your message including your facial expressions, posture, and non-verbal gestures. Building a strong connection with your audience is needed in bolstering your credibility. Essentially, ask yourself "how can I connect with this audience on a human being level?" Creating a common ground with your audience is essential in a speech to persuade setting. If you are able to identify with your listeners, then your listeners will be more inclined to listen to your message. By stressing the common understanding of the predicament, the speaker will hit it off with the audience, and once that commonality is established, it is easier to move into more controversial points to your persuasive speech. In addition, building a human connection with your audience will lead you in your word choice, supporting materials, and emotional appeals tailored for your specific audience.

HOW DELIVERY IMPACTS PERSUASION

A common pitfall for many public speaking students is that they do not spend much time practicing their delivery of their persuasive speech, therefore softening the impact of a well-written speech. Researchers have made the observation that faster and more fluid speakers are by and large seen as more competent and convincing than slower incoherent speakers. By no means does this mean you should race through your speech so that when you are finished the checkered flag drops. However, using vocal variety surely adds value to your persuasiveness as opposed to a monotonous tone of voice. The kiss of death in poor delivery is the speaker who consistently loses his/her place, hesitates, and masters the vocalized pauses such as "uhm, uh, er . . ." your audience will discredit you in a heartbeat. In addition, your audience will not see you as competent, well-practiced, or well-prepared, which clearly communicates a lack of regard for your audience. Your persuasive message must be delivered with maximum fluency and conviction.

Practice is mandatory to really make your well-supported, well-written, and well-organized speech persuasive for your audience. When you diligently practice your delivery, you will then be able to speak with conviction. If you do not sound like you believe in your message, you can be sure that your audience will not believe your message either. Remember that the emotion and conviction you communicate through your message will be monitored by your audience.

IMPROVING YOUR CREDIBILITY THROUGH THE USE OF SOUND EVIDENCE

"All credibility, all good conscience, all evidence of truth come only from the senses."
—FRIEDRICH NIETZSCHE (GERMAN PHILOSOPHER AND CLASSICAL SCHOLAR)

The supporting materials in your speech, such as the examples, statistics, and testimony, will be your tools to prove or disprove the ideas in your persuasive speech. There is a strong need from your audience to rationalize your claims with strong supporting materials. Quality evidence is particularly important in classroom speeches since the probability at this point in the speakers' development is that they are not recognized as experts in their field. (That is not to say that in time you will not be a recognized expert in your desired field.) However, when using evidence in your persuasive speech, the more specific your support is the more influence you will have on your audience.

By having strong evidence as opposed to merely spouting off your opinions, you will have a stronger impact in your quest to persuade your audience. The evidence you decide to use must fulfill the mission of your specific purpose. When analyzing your supporting materials during the research phase of your preparation you must continuously ask yourself, "Do these examples, statistics, and testimony support my specific purpose?" Again the specific purpose is your anchor asking what you (the speaker) hope to accomplish with your speech. In addition, when looking at the credibility of your evidence using specific evidence is more convincing than making generalizations. Your audience will be distrustful of the speaker when the evidence used to support his/her arguments looks to be partial or self-interested. The stronger road to travel when persuading an audience is to use evidence from unbiased and neutral sources.

EMOTIONS AND THE PERSUASIVE PLEA

"People mistakenly assume that their thinking is done by their head; it is actually done by the heart which first dictates the conclusion, then commands the head to provide the reasoning that will defend it."

—ANTHONY DE MELLO (JESUIT PRIEST AND AUTHOR)

When persuading an audience you must appeal to the intellect of the audience as well as the heart of the audience. Therefore, to be a more persuasive speaker you must incorporate an emotional appeal with your reasoning. Tapping into the emotions of the audience, such as feelings of sadness, happiness, anger, or sympathy, will likely move the audience towards a specific course of action or a change in position or point of view. When preparing your speech to persuade, careful thought and consideration are needed as to the most appropriate emotional appeal for your presentation.

A way to generate the necessary emotional appeal is through your choice of language in your speech. The use of language can create clear vivid examples for your audience to follow with your line of reasoning which can resonate with your audience. However, using too many emotionally charged words in a short span of time can put off many listeners or weaken your message, so use them sparingly. In addition to emotionally charged language, the nonverbal aspect of your message can effectively communicate those emotions. The emotional appeals may also be communicated in your delivery through your voice, posture, eye contact, and nonverbal gestures.

A point that must be addressed when using emotional appeals is to use them ethically. For instance, when delivering a question of fact, using emotional appeals is usually not ethical. That is because with questions of fact speeches, your focus is on specific information and logic with little emotional appeal. Conversely, if you want to move listeners to act on a question of policy, emotional appeals are not only legitimate but perhaps necessary. If you want listeners to do something as a result of your speech you may need to plead to your audience's hearts as well as their heads.

The underlying purpose of emotional appeals is to complement your evidence and reasoning and not use emotional appeals as a substitute for persuasion. The construction of your persuasive speech needs to be built on the groundwork of facts and logic. This is important not just for ethical reasons, but for practical reasons as well. Unless you prove your case carefully, listeners will not be moved by your emotional pull. You need to build a good case based on reason and evidence to stir up the emotions of your audience.

REASONING

"Don't leave inferences to be drawn when evidence can be presented."
—RICHARD WRIGHT (AMERICAN AUTHOR)

As a speaker it is your responsibility to walk your audience through your thoughts which led to the desired conclusion or outcome of your persuasive speech. Moreover, it is up to the speaker to draw the necessary conclusions you want your audience to get as a result of your evidence. **Reasoning** may be defined as the process of drawing a conclusion on the basis of evidence. In persuading your audience, your reasoning must be sound so that your audience will agree with your train of thought. We will examine basic methods of reasoning and how to incorporate them into your speeches.

Reasoning from Specific Instances

"Reasoning draws a conclusion, but does not make the conclusion certain, unless the mind discovers it by the path of experience."
—ROGER BACON (ENGLISH PHILOSOPHER)

When you reason from a specific instance, you take a few particular instances, and then make a general conclusion based on those specific instances. Reasoning from specific instances to general conclusions is also known as **inductive reasoning**. The following example moves from a specific instance to a general conclusion. The agricultural chemical industry contends that restraining pesticide use does not hold back the food supply. Argentina has reduced its pesticide use by 75 percent over the last few years with a minimal decrease in its harvest. The Skynyrd Agricultural Company does not use any pesticides in their strawberry crops grown in Florida, and they harvest as much fruit as ever. Many farmers from Arizona who utilize pesticide-free farming have encountered an escalation in their crop returns.

A common error that occurs is when one would make an impulsive conclusion from a specific instance to a sweeping generalization. It is easy to jump to conclusions based on a limited amount of exposures to particular evidences. When imparting your evidence (examples, statistics, and testimony) from a specific instance due diligence is needed that your instances are just, fair, and representative. Furthermore, your audience will be skeptical if they hear reasoning that sounds unrepresentative, and will likely dismiss your reasoning as sensational and extreme.

The credibility used from using inductive reasoning (reasoning from a specific instance) comes from the number of occurrences researched, and the representativeness of those occurrences. Gaining a strong grasp of representative samples is challenging since it forces the speaker to make a hypothesis about the distinctiveness that might be most significant to the generalization. A couple of key questions that will anchor you in your quest for accurate inductive reasoning are: "How many examples shore up the generalization?" "And is that a satisfactory number of instances to warrant the generalization?" "Are the instances appropriately chosen?" "Are there significant exceptions to the generalization or claim that must be scrutinized?"

When reasoning from a specific instance you can either state your conclusion, then give the specific instances on which it is established, or give the specific instances and then draw your conclusion. Either way works regardless of the order as long as your facts support your conclusion.

Reasoning from Principle

Reasoning from principle progresses from the general to specific, just the opposite from reasoning from specific instances. Reasoning from principle is also known as **deductive reasoning**. A sound argument from principle is one in which the reason is valid and all of the premises are true. For example: In order to purchase alcohol you must be 21 years of age or older. Jimmy Johnson headed over to the grocery mart and purchased a 12 pack of beer. Therefore, Jimmy Johnson is at least 21 years of age. The logic moves through three phases, the general principle (In order to purchase alcohol you must be 21 years of age or older.), to the minor premise (Jimmy Johnson headed over to the grocery mart and purchased a 12 pack of beer.), to a conclusion (Therefore, Jimmy Johnson is at least 21 years of age.).

Causal Reasoning

Causal reasoning is when the speaker attempts to create a relationship between the causes and effects of a given situation. There are two common errors to avoid when using causal reasoning. The first is the fallacy of false cause which is often referred by its Latin name, *post hoc, ergo propter hoc*, translated as "after this, therefore because of this." In other words, the fact that one episode happens after another does not mean that the first episode is the sole cause of the second episode.

The second error to avoid in causal reasoning is assuming that events have only one singular cause. An ordinary approach to causal reasoning is to assign an event to a single remote cause, yet the majority of events may have numerous causes. The responsible advocate qualifies his/her statements and admits that there is not a single or exclusive cause to the complex problem. When analyzing your evidence for causal reasoning here are some helpful questions to ask: "Did superseding events or persons prevent a cause from having its normal effects?" "Can you detach the causes and effects?" "Could any other cause have produced the effect?"

For example, a student may say that they failed their public speaking exam because they went to the big football game against rival State over the weekend. Now upon closer examination, there could have been many reasons why this student failed the public speaking exam. Maybe the student did not attend class regularly, or did not take good notes on the day of the review, or perhaps the public speaking class was a low priority item behind such things as video games, drinking games, and sleep. So, it really is not accurate to pin the one cause, attending the football game, to the result of a failed exam.

Analogical Reasoning

Analogical reasoning examines whether the two instances being compared are fundamentally the same. If the two instances are fundamentally the same, the analogy is valid. On the other hand if the two instances are not fundamentally the same, the analogy is invalid. Reasoning from analogy is applied regularly in persuasive speeches focusing on the question of policy. When making a case for a new policy, you should find out whether a similar policy has been implemented in a situation that is similar to the current problem. You are more likely to persuade your audience if the analogy confirms a truly similar situation. Analogical arguments ought to be modified at the appropriate point of certainty. In essence, if a policy worked in the past in a similar situation, that policy will more than likely work with this situation. For example, "the town of Lightville cut their crime rate by 20% by instituting a video surveillance system in the downtown area. Since the video surveillance system worked so well in Lightville, such a video surveillance system can work in our downtown area to reduce our crime rate."

Your analogical reasoning will gain traction and be more persuasive the more clear-cut the analogy is to a comparable situation.

FALLACIES

A **fallacy** is an error in reasoning or evidence. Fallacies often occur when the speaker states unconnected conclusions, applies flawed reasoning, presents poor evidence, or succumbs to personal attacks. We will take a look at some common fallacies used in persuasive messages.

Red Herring

The **red herring fallacy** brings up an unrelated issue simply to divert attention from the argument or point that is being discussed. Often times using the red herring fallacy in a persuasive speech is an attempt to throw an audience off-target with an emotional matter that prevents the heart of the issue to be analyzed by the audience. For example, "the council acknowledges that this ballot measure is all the rage. But we also ask you to remember that there are so many bond initiatives already on this ballot that the whole thing is getting out of hand." The ballot measure is popular, but the council is introducing the idea of the numerous other bond measures that will dilute the popular measure.

Ad Hominem

The **ad hominem fallacy** refers to the fallacy of attacking the person rather than taking up the real issue in the debate. In political elections, the integrity and character of a candidate is often addressed. However, the ad hominem attack occurs when the candidates may be debating health care, and one of the candidates goes off on a tangent and attacks his or her opponent on a personal level.

We often see the ad hominem attack in our everyday lives. For example, say you go to the doctor, and the doctor says that you should start an exercise and nutrition program to lose weight. You then respond "why should I listen to you, you could stand lose 35 pounds yourself." Again the issue is that you the patient needs to embrace the exercise and nutrition program for your well-being and not personally attack the messenger.

Bandwagon

The **bandwagon fallacy** assumes that because something is popular, it must be good, appropriate, or advantageous. Widely held opinion cannot be taken as proof that an idea is right or wrong. Individuals may be tempted to follow the crowd, and this tendency is understood by some public speakers who take advantage of this herd mentality by encouraging the audience to do something because everybody is doing it.

We often see the bandwagon fallacy with our local sports teams. Your local team may be a doormat of the league, and have little support in the community. Yet they may have a season where they make a run for the championship and you will see the community wearing the team's colors and merchandise. Because the team is doing well, everyone will join the crowd to be a part of the winning team.

Slippery Slope

A speaker who commits the **slippery slope fallacy** suggests that taking a first step will lead to a second step and so on all the way down the slope. For example, a common slippery slope fallacy is "If we legalize marijuana, the next thing you know we'll legalize heroin, crystal meth, and ecstasy."

The Hasty Generalization

The **fallacy of hasty generalization** occurs when a generalization of a claim is made based on too-little evidence. For example, Tony has been to Austin, Texas three times, and the weather conditions were always ideal, blue skies and lots of sunshine. Therefore, Tony makes the hasty generalization that the weather in Austin, Texas must be perfect all of the time.

Guilt by Association

Guilt by association occurs when we judge a program, a proposal, or a person exclusively on their association with other programs, proposals, or persons. We often see the concept of guilt by association when examining the political field in our country. For example, if you see yourself as politically "liberal," information being presented by traditionally "conservative" politicians, commentators, or outlets may be immediately dismissed without listening to the message. Unfortunately one may reject an otherwise good idea simply because of guilt by association.

The Final Word on Fallacies

Fallacies generate conclusions that do not flow rationally from the evidence presented. Fallacies are merely a way to divert attention from the real issue at hand. Advertisers use fallacies in their commercials so consumers will purchase their products over their competitors' products. As critical thinkers we need to be able to identify that a fallacy has been presented, and base our final decisions on quality evidence, logic, and reasoning.

Summary: Techniques of Persuasion

On your pathway to success you will need to have the ability to persuade people to help you achieve your goals. Your ability to persuade people will depend on your initial, derived, and terminal credibility with your audience. Furthermore, it will be your responsibility to clearly demonstrate to your audience that you are competent with your subject matter, and that you have the audience's best interest at heart. A wise path to persuade your audience is to build a common connection with the audience based on the findings from your audience analysis. Once that common connection has been established, from there it is easier to introduce differences to persuade your audience.

A conversational style of delivery will add a believability factor to your persuasive speech. The lesson here is, it is not only what you say, it is also how you say it that can either make or break your persuasiveness. The audience will be assessing everything from your eye contact to your posture, your vocal variety, and your nonverbal gestures. The confidence you have in your message, and in yourself, is communicated nonverbally to your audience.

When composing your persuasive message, the more specific your evidence is using examples, statistics, and testimony, the more credible and believable you will come across as with your audience. The actual reasoning, the drawing of conclusions on the basis of evidence, is necessary to persuade your audience; therefore, connecting those dots for your audience is paramount for maximum persuasiveness.

There are four distinct reasoning strategies that may be implemented in your persuasive speech:

1. Reasoning from specific instances
2. Reasoning from principle
3. Causal reasoning
4. Analogical reasoning

Fallacies often creep up in persuasive messages, and a fallacy may be defined as reasoning that is not rational, because it buries important evidence, includes debatable premises, or is simply unsound. Fallacies that are frequently used in persuasive messages are: the red herring fallacy, the ad hominem fallacy, the bandwagon fallacy, the fallacy of hasty generalization, and guilt by association. This is not a comprehensive list of all of the available fallacies, but just a few common fallacies to keep in mind.

On your pathway to success using the techniques of persuasion will become routine when you are persuading customers, professional colleagues, and potential investors to help you achieve your goals and aspirations. We have highlighted several persuasive tools you can put in your communication tool belt as you build your public speaking success skill set.

Name: _____

True-False

1. (T)F   Competence and character is a direct factor of affecting a speaker's credibility.

2. T(F)   The credibility of a speaker before she or he starts to speak is called derived credibility.

3. T(F)   Speakers with high initial credibility need to use more evidence than speakers with low initial credibility.

4. T(F)   When you reason from specific instances in a speech, you move from a general example to a specific conclusion.

5. T F   When you reason from principle in a speech, you move from a specific principle to a general conclusion.

Multiple Choice

6. An either-or fallacy

   a. presumes that because two things are associated in time, they are causally linked.
   b. attacks the person rather than coping with the real issue in disagreement.
   c. raises an irrelevant issue to divert attention from the subject under discussion.
   d. forces listeners to choose between two alternatives when more than two alternatives exist.
   e. assumes that because something is popular, it is therefore good, correct, or desirable.

7. A slippery slope fallacy

   a. assumes that taking a first step will inevitably lead to other steps that cannot be prevented.
   b. raises an irrelevant issue to divert attention from the subject under discussion.
   c. assumes that because something is popular, it is therefore good, correct, or desirable.
   d. forces listeners to choose between two alternatives when more than two alternatives exist.
   e. assumes that because two things are related in time, they are causally linked.

8. The *ad hominem* fallacy

   a. attacks the person rather than dealing with the real issue in dispute.
   b. presumes that complex events have only a single cause.
   c. assumes that because something is popular, it must be correct.
   d. none of the above.
   e. b and c only.

9. A bandwagon fallacy

   a. assumes that taking a first step will inevitably lead to other steps that cannot be prevented.
   b. introduces an irrelevant issue to divert attention from the subject under discussion.
   c. assumes that because something is popular, it is therefore good, correct, or desirable.
   d. forces listeners to choose between two alternatives when more than two alternatives exist.
   e. assumes that because two things are related in time, they are causally linked.

10. When reasoning analogically, you conclude that
    a. a causal relationship can be established between two or more events.
    b. what is true in one case will also be true in a similar case.
    c. a general principle is validated by a question of fact.
    d. your position is true because it is demonstrated by statistical trends.
    e. a specific conclusion is true because it is verified by a general principle.

11. *Post hoc, ergo proper hoc*, meaning "after this, therefore because of this," is a fallacy associated with
    _____ reasoning.

    a. parallel
    b. deductive
    c. comparative
    d. descriptive
    e. causal

Essay

12. What is causal reasoning? Explain inaccuracies in causal reasoning speakers should avoid in their speeches.

13. What is analogical reasoning? How do you assess the validity of an analogy?

Chapter One

A Positive Mental Attitude: Your Gateway to Success in Public Speaking

Your Mental Attitude Creates Your Public Speaking Experience

- There are three areas where you have complete control on your pathway to success, your thoughts, the mental pictures you create, and your actions.

- It is your responsibility to create a dynamic public speaking experience for yourself and your audience.

- Proficiency in public speaking will advance you in your formal education, and in your chosen profession.

Embrace the Process of Learning a New Skill

- Anytime you learn a new skill you will encounter four different stages of development.
    1. Beginning Awareness
    2. Awkwardness
    3. Skillfulness
    4. Integration

- **Beginning awareness** occurs when you learn that there is a specialized and more authoritative way of doing something.

Embrace the Process of Learning a New Skill (Continued)

- Anytime you learn something new, your initial attempts may be **awkward** and uneasy.
  - This happens to beginning public speakers as they learn how to use a speaker's outline, correctly cite their sources orally, implement findings from an audience analysis survey, and maintain eye contact with their audience while standing at a podium.

Embrace the Process of Learning a New Skill (Continued)

- The **skillfulness phase** of your development allows you to handle yourself well enough to do the task, but you are still thinking about the appropriate actions to do the task.

- During the **integration phase** you are delivering a speech, and all of those thoughts you had of doing particular actions during the skillfulness stage will come naturally and automatically, so your focus now is on delivering a well-thought-out address for your audience.

Goal Setting

- Ask yourself:
  - "What do I want to accomplish in my public speaking course?"
  - "What do I want to be able to do as a result of my public speaking experience?"
  - " How can I develop the necessary skill-set to deliver my upcoming _____ speech?

- One thing to keep in mind about goals and the direction of your life is that you may not be able to arrive at the desired destination in an instance, but you can change the direction towards your desired outcome immediately.

The Goal Setting Process

- In short, write down the goals that you want to achieve.
  - Be realistic as to what you can achieve.
  - Ideally any goal that you establish should be measurable (minutes, number of orally cited sources, number of people in the audience), and have a deadline (a specific day and time).

- Next write a short description as to why you want to achieve your particular goal, what you would miss if you did not achieve this goal, and what you would gain from the achievement of the goal.

- Third, revisit your written goals and your "why" description at least twice a day.
  - Wake up with a purpose, go to sleep with an accomplishment.

The Goal Setting Process

- Fourth, think about how you can surround yourself with the appropriate people who can help you attain your goal.

- Once you have documented your goals and why you want to achieve them, and allocated time to review your goals, it is now time to develop action plans to achieve your goals.

- By consistently referring to your written goals from a 3X5 card you will have that extra motivation to take the appropriate action to meet your desired results.

The Goal Setting
Overcoming Obstacles

- You can be sure that roadblocks and barriers will visit you on your pathway to success.
  - For example, when establishing a goal thoughts now turn to "boy I'm going to have to stay late at the library," or "I now have to get my computer fixed so I can work on my outline."

- It is good to address these doubts head-on and write them out on paper, so that now you can confront and overcome those limiting beliefs analytically and not emotionally.

- Do your best to think ahead and anticipate life and prepare for those unfortunate life experiences.

- That is why the sage advice of starting your speech preparation early usually off-sets many of these "last minute" derailments in achieving your public speaking goals.

Visualization

- Take the time to close your eyes and visualize yourself delivering a high-quality speech, and allow those images to be absorbed by your subconscious mind.
- Picture yourself standing in front of your audience to receive their applause as you get ready to say your opening line of your introduction.
- The more you can visualize your speech by capturing all of your senses in a movie format, the more real your public speaking experience can become.

Affirmations

- In conjunction with the process of visualization you can create written affirmations to support your efforts at delivering a successful speech.
- Start with "I am," affirm what you want and *not* what you do not want, and keep it short and precise.
- Furthermore, with your positive affirmation in hand you can now *believe* that you have already delivered an engaging speech to inform that was well prepared, well researched, and well delivered.
- Another added-value characteristic of the visualization and affirmation process is that it creates positive expectations of yourself and the presentation of your public address.

Self-Fulfilling Prophecy

- A **self-fulfilling prophecy** happens when one's expectations of an event affect the person's behavior in that given event.

- There are four phases to a self-fulfilling prophecy:
  1. Clutching onto an expectation for yourself or others
  2. Acting in harmony with that expectation
  3. The expectation becomes realized
  4. The original expectation is supported and strengthened

- So to help you in the mental aspect of delivering a well-thought-out address, first "be" the proficient public speaker, then "do" the necessary tasks required to be a proficient public speaker, and soon you will "have" everything come together as a public speaker.

Enthusiasm is the Fuel to a Positive Mental Attitude

- Enthusiasm is a characteristic that is needed at the podium, but it is even more important during the preparation process.
- No one wants to listen to someone who comes across like they are simply going through the motions, so have some enthusiasm.
- In short, your enthusiasm for your topic, your audience, and the work behind the scenes is contagious.
- Enthusiasm and passion will overpower talent any day.

Modeling Successful Public Speakers

- By watching world-class speeches, you will be able to see how top notch public speakers deliver their message, frame their emotional appeals, organize their thoughts, and present themselves as leaders.
- When studying other public speakers you want to look for traits you can implement in your public-speaking skill-set and that can help you become a better public speaker.
- Conversely, watching speeches by those whose talent and skills may not lie in public speaking can also give you tips as to what *not* to do.
- Modeling is a proven activity to get you to where you want to go in a shorter amount of time.

You Have 1,440 Minutes a Day

- The one thing we have in common with the world's most influential people is that all of us have 1,440 minutes in a day.
- Unfortunately in the realm of beginning public speaking, many students do not maximize their daily 1,440 minutes to the fullest and demonstrate the fruits of their poor time management at the podium in front of an audience.

Have a Clear Purpose

- Not having a clear purpose of what your desired outcome is in a given day is a sure way to waste time.

- Having a strong sense of urgency in using your time wisely is important in preparing for a speech, so **START EARLY!**

Learn to Say "No"

- In order to use your time wisely, you will have to learn to say the word "no."

- Also, saying "no" to these time-robbers like your cell phone, text messaging, video games, and email/web surfing activities while preparing for your speech will keep you focused and in a position to be fully prepared for your upcoming speech.

- Moreover, by saying "no" you are saying "yes" to your success and your individual achievement towards your given goals, such as earning an "A" in your public speaking course.

- One way to maximize your time is to create deadlines for yourself, like "in the next 30 minutes I will select a topic and write a specific purpose for my upcoming persuasive speech."
  - While doing this activity you will have a timer that will count down from 30 minutes to 00:00.

The Preparation Process
"The more you sweat in peace, the less you bleed in war."
General George S. Patton, Jr.

- Step 1: Select a topic
- Step 2: Determine a general purpose
- Step 3: Formulate your specific purpose
- Step 4: Document a central idea that accurately reflects the main points of the speech
- Step 5: Conduct an audience analysis survey
- Step 6: Research your topic using the library, the Internet, and field studies
- Step 7: Support your ideas using examples, statistics, and testimony
- Step 8: Organize the body of your speech
- Step 9: Create a catchy introduction and conclusion
- Step 10: Develop and proofread a preparation and speaker's outline of your speech
- Step 11: Analyze the word choice in your speech, refine and edit
- Step 12: Implement appropriate visual aids that reinforce and add value to your message
- Step 13: Practice your delivery

Chapter Two

Strategies to Combat Your Stage Fright

Action and Training Will Help You Combat Stage Fright

- Public speaking gets a bad rap because we are often asked to deliver a speech with little or no training.

- Remember, your audience members are real live human beings with thoughts and feelings like yourself, and they want to see you do well.

- Dale Carnegie had this to say about fear, "Inaction breeds doubt and fear. Action breeds confidence and courage. If you want to conquer fear, do not sit home and think about it. Go out and get busy."

Turn Those Unknowns Into Knowns

- As a critical thinker and a trained public speaker, it is your job to be able to identify the unknowns and turn those unknowns into knowns.

- The higher the uncertainty of the situation, the higher the anxiety one would experience in that given situation.

- So the lesson here is to minimize as many of the uncertainties as you can so that they become certainties.

Facilitative and Debilitative Emotions

- If you are feeling nervous before a speech consider yourself normal.
- Being nervous before a speech is an appropriate feeling to have, and it is those exact nervous feelings inside that bring out the best in world-renowned athletes, musicians, artists, lawyers, and business people before big events.
- It is important to note the distinction between facilitative and debilitative emotions.
  - **Facilitative emotions** are feelings that spur you on to do good, positive, and inspiring things.
  - Conversely, **debilitative feelings** paralyze competent people to underachieve.

Continuous Practice Helps Minimize Nervousness

- It will be your responsibility to harness that nervous energy to catapult yourself to do your best behind the podium.

- The key to conquering potentially debilitative emotions of nervousness in public speaking is to practice delivering as many speeches as you can.

Be Fully Prepared for Your Speech

- Selecting and narrowing of a topic
- Writing a clear specific purpose
- Having a precise central idea,
- Conducting an accurate audience analysis, accumulating valid materials
- Supporting your main ideas, creating an easy–to-follow organization
- Using suitable language, writing a catchy introduction and conclusion
- Making value-added visual aids, and learning practiced delivery

Other Preparation Tips

- Selecting a topic you are familiar with will give an edge to combat nervousness.
- Another tool you may use to overcome your nervousness is to visualize yourself delivering a successful speech.
  - It is important to really see yourself, like in a movie, delivering a well-thought-out speech, and watching your audience really enjoying your public address.

Other Preparation Tips (Continued)

- In addition to visualization and being fully prepared for your speech, most of your nervousness is not visible.
- Beginning public speakers need to have a realistic outlook as to what you can accomplish with your speech, which helps manage your nervousness.
- Unfortunately, many beginning public speakers expect perfection in their early speeches and apply too much pressure on themselves.
- Your audience will expect that you are fully prepared, and that you will deliver an enthusiastic message, both of which are doable for beginning public speakers.

Other Preparation Tips (Continued)

- Another tip in managing your nervousness is to spend a lot of time working on your introduction.
  - Much like an Olympic sprinter getting off the blocks cleanly for a good race, a public speaker also wants to get off the blocks (your introduction) cleanly.
- A well-practiced and interesting introduction will allow you to maintain strong eye contact while immediately engaging your audience right at the start.
- As you gain public speaking experience and confidence your focus will be more on delivering your message to your audience than it is on being self conscious about how you are being perceived by your audience members.

Building on Your Current Conversation Skills to Strengthen Your Public Speaking Skills

- How you address your best friend of ten years would be different from how you interact with your parents, which would be different from how you interact with your co-workers, which would be different from how you interact with your boss.
  - The message here is that you have customized your message to a "particular" audience, a skill and mindset imperative in public speaking.
  - Public speaking is an audience-focused activity so your message, delivery, and appeals must be tailored to your specific audience.

Building on Your Current Conversation Skills to Strengthen Your Public Speaking Skills

- Lastly a key similarity between your current conversational skills and public speaking skills is the power of feedback and how that shapes our conversation.
  - Feedback comes in two forms, verbal feedback and nonverbal feedback. In observing **nonverbal feedback** from your audience you will notice the audience members' postures in their seats, eye contact, facial expressions, and gestures.
  - When chatting with your friends, **verbal feedback** would come in the form of probing questions, direct requests for clarification, or simply a response to what was asked by your conversational partner.

Key Distinctions Between Conversation Skills and Public Speaking Skills

- More planning is needed in what you will say in a public speaking venue as opposed to a conversation with your friends.
- Next, there is usually a time limit in public speaking as opposed to an everyday conversation.
- In your conversations with the people you interact with regularly, it may be common to hear many voiced pauses, like: "uhm," "uhrr," "like," and "kinda."
  - In public speaking, those voiced pauses will detract from your believability and credibility with the members of your audience.

The Speech Communication Process

- The **speaker** is the driver of the process. Without the speaker the process will not start and generate the momentum needed to move the speech communication system.

- As the driver of the process, your credibility, your delivery, your preparation, and your audience analysis will be evaluated and rest squarely on the speaker's shoulders.

The Speech Communication Process (Continued)

- The **message** is the point you want to communicate to your audience.

- An additional component that needs to be acknowledged is the congruency between your verbal message and your nonverbal message.

- Messages contain the verbal component (subject matter) and the nonverbal component (emotions and relational aspects to a message) and they must be in sync for your audience to believe in your message.

The Speech Communication Process (Continued)

- The **channel** is the means by which a message is communicated.

- The channel may come in many forms, such as the television, radio, Internet broadcast, telephone, or simply by your voice, which is the most common channel used in a public speaking course.

The Speech Communication Process (Continued)

- The **receiver** or listener of your message would be your audience.
- The real challenge in human communication is that every one of us carries different life experiences, areas of intellectual expertise, interests, values, and beliefs.
- As a public speaker and communicator, our message needs to penetrate through all of those perceptual filters that our audience members may have.

The Speech Communication Process (Continued)

- **Feedback** regularly occurs in two-way communication and is delivered back to the speaker both verbally and nonverbally.
- You will be observing how your audience is responding to your speech by how they are positioned in their seats, so if they are leaning forward at the edge of their chairs, it may be interpreted that they are interested in your message.

The Speech Communication Process (Continued)

- **Interference** is anything that gets in the way of communication between the speaker and the listener.
- Interference or noise can come in many different forms, and from both the speaker and the audience.

The Speech Communication Process
(Continued)

- The **environment** embodies all of the players involved in the speech communication process in addition to the time and place of the speech.

- The sum of all of the parts in the speech communication process makes up the environment.

Knowing the Ethical Rules
of the Game

- Your audience must have no doubt in their minds that the speaker has their best interest at heart. Moreover, the audience will expect you to be honest in your words, and in the integrity of your evidence that you present to them.
- A speaker may demonstrate dishonesty in other ways such as through the manipulation of statistics.
  - Once the audience learns how that statistic was derived, the audience will discount the speaker's ideas and evidence, not only for that speech presented then, but will also have a cynical eye for all future speeches presented by this specific speaker.

Knowing the Ethical Rules
of the Game (Continued)

- Additional ethical rules that must be obeyed are the careless use of racist, sexist, and other demeaning language in public speaking.
  - These principles also apply to religious beliefs, sexual orientations, and physical or mental disabilities.

Knowing the Ethical Rules
of the Game (Continued)

- Another ethical guideline that must be followed is being completely prepared for your speech.
- The process of being prepared includes: selecting and narrowing a topic, crafting a specific purpose, having an accurate central idea, carefully compiling audience analyses, accumulating valid materials, using appropriate supporting materials, building a logical organization, using refined language, writing catchy introductions and conclusions, making value-added visual aids, and speaking with practiced delivery.

Plagiarism

- **Plagiarism** may be defined as the unauthorized use or close imitation of the language and thoughts of another author and the representation of them as one's own original work.

Types of Plagiarism

- **Global plagiarism** is when a speaker takes a speech in its entirety from a single source and passes it off as his/her own.
- **Patchwork plagiarism** occurs when the speaker directly takes materials from two or three sources verbatim, combines them, and then passes them off as his or her own work.
- **Incremental plagiarism** occurs when the speaker fails to give credit for particular parts of a speech that are borrowed in increments from other people.

Ethical Listening

- As public speakers your ethical responsibility is not only behind the podium but also as an audience member.
- The key principles for ethical listening are to give your complete and undivided attention to the speaker, to avoid making quick unsubstantiated judgments about the speaker before listening to them, and to keep an open mind.

Ethical Listening and Learning

- Paying attention to the main speaker sets the tone for a safe, supportive, and encouraging environment.
- By actively listening to the main speaker you are instilling confidence in them, and in turn, the speaker will produce a stronger speech.
- Moreover, taking a public speaking course is fertile territory for learning.
  - Not only will you be learning the techniques of public speaking from your instructor, you will be learning about subject matter that you may have never been exposed to in your previous learning experiences.

Ethical Listening Obligation

- An unfortunate characteristic of unethical listening is making a quick unsubstantiated judgment about the speaker or the topic based on inaccurate and sometimes silly perceptions.
  - As a listener you have an obligation to honestly "hear out" what the speaker has to say without any prejudgments.
- If the speaker has honored his/her obligation to deliver an honest speech using reliable evidence from trustworthy sources, tailored his/her message to the audience, and has practiced his/her delivery, you have an obligation to listen.
- Once the speech is concluded, and you have paid attention to the speech in its entirety, then it is appropriate to make judgments about the speech in its proper context.

Chapter Three

Multicultural Component
to Public Speaking

**Multicultural Component
to Public Speaking**

- Business is no longer limited to the boundaries of our national or state borders; in today's economy, business has gone global.
- There is an assumption now that all of us must be able to meet the global challenges set before us.
- Moreover, by being mindful of these multicultural principles you will put yourself in a place to be a difference maker while connecting with another human being on a global level.

Worldview

- Studying your **worldview** will allow you to see how you perceive the world and how that impacts the communication you may have with others, both as a public speaker and as an audience member.
- In their book *Cultural and Social Anthropology*, authors Edward Hoebel and Everett Frost define worldview as "the human being's inside view of the way things are colored, shaped, and arranged according to personal cultural preconceptions."
- As a public speaker who is addressing a multicultural audience it is good to know how your worldview impacts your message, your word choice, your delivery, and your perception of your audience members.

Ethnocentrism

- Ethnocentrism may be defined as "when one holds the mindset that one's own culture is superior to others'." Someone who is ethnocentric reasons that anyone who does not belong to his or her in-group is somehow wrong or even inferior.
- As a public speaker you can avoid the negative effects of ethnocentrism by respecting the dignity of the values and beliefs of our multicultural society.
- You may not agree with others' values and beliefs, but the demonstration of respect of those values and beliefs will go a long way.
- By signifying respect for the diversity of your audience, you will create a more open line of communication between the speaker and the audience.

Stereotyping

- **Stereotyping** is categorizing individuals according to a set of characteristics assumed to belong to all members of a group.
  - Categories of stereotyping may include race, age, gender, occupation, religion, disability, socio-economic status, educational level, and region of residence.
- **Decategorization** is the process of treating the person as an individual instead of assuming that they possess the same characteristics as every other member of the group to which you have assigned them.

The Work of Geert Hofstede

- Hofstede's work can be studied in greater detail in his book, *Culture's Consequences: International Differences in Work-Related Values* Hofstede's research yielded four themes:
  1. Individualism versus Collectivism
  2. Power Distance
  3. Masculinity
  4. Uncertainty Avoidance

Individualism and Collectivism

- On the individualism end of the spectrum would include: the United States of America, Australia, Great Britain, Canada, and the Netherlands.

- Countries listed on the collectivist end of the spectrum would include Venezuela, Colombia, Pakistan, Japan and the territory of Hong Kong.

Individualism

- People in countries representing the **individualistic** category see their own personal goals as being more important than the goals of a particular group.
- An "I" philosophy is prevalent in their behavior and thought.
- In short, people in the individualistic cultures look out for number one, and place their own goals and needs above a group, or membership objectives.
- Moreover, those in the individualistic cultures thrive on competition and the achievement of personal goals, as opposed to cooperation, and the attainment of group goals and a group's purpose.

Collectivism

- In the **collectivist** culture, the group's goals are more important than those of the individual.
  - A "we" philosophy is the driver of behavior and thought.
- In the collectivist culture there is a strong distinction between the members of the in-group (families, organizations, or groups) and members of the out-group (those not in the family, organization, or group).
- There is a stronger sense of loyalty to the hierarchy and the in-group dynamic whether it is in the form of family or company, as opposed to those belonging to the out-group.
- Moreover, it is understood that there is a strong need for cooperation, as opposed to competition, in dealings with others.

Power Distance

- **High-power distances** would represent those who hold high power and the wide separation between the decision makers and those implementing the decisions.

- On the other hand, **low-power distance** is the narrow distance between those in power and those implementing the decisions.

High Power Distance

- Countries that would fall in the high-power distance category would be Venezuela, Brazil, Mexico, and India.

- Since there is a large gap between the decision makers and those implementing those decisions, more formality is shown in how one would address another person in a company, organization, or family.

Low Power Distance

- The low-power distance philosophy believes that the disproportion of distance should be minimized as much as possible.
  - Countries that would fall under the low-power distance category would be New Zealand, Austria, Finland, and Denmark, just to name a few.
- The philosophy in the workplace in these countries says that subordinates consider superiors to be on the same level in their interactions and status of importance to the organization or group.

Masculinity and Femininity

- **Masculinity** refers to the values and beliefs of a country's society in the areas of achievement, attainment of money, and accepted male-oriented roles.
    - Countries that embody masculine worldviews would be South Africa, Japan, Italy, Mexico, and the Philippines.
- Masculine societies teach men that they are the central dominant figures, and women are expected to be encouraging and supportive of men.

Femininity

- Cultures that embrace **femininity** value more caring and nurturing behaviors.

    - Countries that embody the femininity values would be Finland, Sweden, the Netherlands, and Norway.

- It is validated that men do not need to be assertive, and can accept caring and nurturing roles in society.

High-Uncertainty Avoidance

- The direction of Hofstede's ideas about uncertainty avoidance is how a particular culture feels about uncertain and ambiguous situations.
- **High-uncertainty-avoidance** cultures work at avoiding uncertainty by utilizing written rules, regulations, and a strong structure in their daily lives.
    - Countries that fall under the high-uncertainty-avoidance category would be Japan, Belgium, Portugal, and Greece.
- High-uncertainty-avoidance groups move at a slower pace and spend more time in the planning and detailing phase when making decisions.

Low-Uncertainty Avoidance

- On the flip side the **low-uncertainty-avoidance** cultures accept the uncertainty in life.
  - Countries that are considered low-uncertainty-avoidance cultures are the United States, Netherlands, Ireland, Singapore, and Sweden.
- Low-uncertainty-avoidance cultures are willing to take risks, are not in favor of rigid protocols, and are comfortable with the unusual.
- Low-uncertainty-avoidance cultures run at a faster pace and make decisions more quickly.

High-Context Communication

- In **high-context** cultures tradition and history are consistent over time. In the high-context culture the message is communicated through nonverbal gestures, proximity, and silence.
- In addition, the high-context cultures demonstrate a stronger awareness of the overall background of the environment of the communication, as opposed to words alone.

Low-Context Communication

- In **low-context** cultures the verbal message is the driver of the message and little "context" is incorporated into the meaning of the message.
- Low-context cultures would include America, Germany, and Switzerland. Communication tends to be direct and unambiguous, so the message is clearly stated with little "context."

Chapter Four

Know Your Purpose and Select a Topic

Selecting a Topic

- Selecting a topic may be the hardest step in the speech communication process.
  - One of the biggest tips for a public speaker is *not* to procrastinate at this phase of the process of building a speech.
- By postponing the start of your speech development process you are shrinking the window of time for developing an effective speech.
- In addition, by delaying the first step, you are minimizing the time available to adequately research, organize, and practice your speech before getting up in front of your classmates to delivering your presentation.

Selecting a Topic

- Speech topics are determined by the occasion, the audience, and the speaker's qualifications.
- Another strategy for helping you decide on a topic is to keep a page in your notebook titled "Potential Speech Topics."
  - As you go through your speech class, many in-class discussions may occur that are potential speech topics, so you can jot those down in your log.

The Process of Self-Evaluation

- The process of self-evaluation has you explore topics that you know a lot about, and topics you would like to know more about.
- Begin by asking yourself some of the following questions to get a sense as to what you know a lot about:
  - What are my interests?
  - Where have I traveled?
  - What jobs have I held?
  - What is my major?
  - What is my cultural background?
  - Where are the different parts of the world, country, state, or city I have lived?
  - What do I do in my free time?

Brainstorming For Topics

- Your prompts will range from personal interests, grouping, and reference searches to an Internet search.
- The goal of brainstorming is to try to think of as many topics as you can in a brief amount of time.
- During this phase of the creative process, judging and criticizing your ideas is not appropriate.

Personal Interests

- Think about your life experiences, interests, hobbies, skills, attitudes, values, beliefs, and write those down.
  - Do not let your pen stop; just keep writing and be creative in your thoughts regardless of how ridiculous some of your thoughts may be, just keep writing.

Grouping

- Take a sheet of paper, pencil-in six columns and label those columns with these headings: people, places, things, events, processes, and concepts.

People	Places	Things	Events	Processes	Concepts

Reference Search

- Another technique is to use the reference area in your library and look through an encyclopedia, a periodical database or some other reference work until you find a good speech topic.

Internet Search

- One of the easier ways to find a speech topic is to hop on the Internet and conduct a web directory search on either Google or Yahoo!.
  - Go to either the Yahoo! or Google home page and type in "Web Directory Search"

Determining the General Purpose

- The general purpose may be defined as the broad goal of your speech, and there are three kinds of general purposes in public speaking:
1. To entertain
2. To inform
3. To persuade

The Special Occasion Speech (To Entertain)

- The **special occasion speech** is a speech that concentrates on a special event.
- Special occasion speeches include presentations that have their purpose to introduce the main speaker; present an award or public recognition; accept an award; commemorate by paying tribute to a person, group institution, or an idea; and give an after dinner speech.

The Special Occasion Speech (To Entertain)

- Other common special occasion speeches are made at weddings when presenting the bride and groom a toast.
- They also happen at retirement parties, when a company representative bids farewell to the loyal employee.
- We see the speech to entertain during award shows when our favorite entertainers accept an Oscar, Emmy, or MTV Award for their work.
- Special occasion speeches are also prominent at funerals when one delivers the eulogy for the deceased.
- On a happier note, a special occasion speech occurs when you salute and toast an important person in your life at his or her birthday party.
- As you can see these speeches are delivered in a more "social" setting, but the speeches you deliver in this setting are noticed by all who are in attendance.

Speech to Inform

- When your general purpose is to inform, your objective is to enhance the audience's awareness, understanding, or knowledge about a topic.
- You do this by communicating the information clearly, correctly, and interestingly.
- In a speech to inform, **you do not** try to persuade your audience to do or believe something as a result of your speech.

Speech to Persuade

- The **speech to persuade** needs to influence, strengthen, or change the audience members' attitudes, values, beliefs, or behaviors.
- The persuasive speaker attempts to modify how the audience feels about what they know and in the end how they behave.

The Specific Purpose

- The **specific purpose** is a single sentence that specifically states what the speaker hopes to accomplish in his or her speech.
- During the speech preparation process it is easy to get sidetracked and distracted, but establishing your specific purpose will keep you anchored and on track.

Formatting the Specific Purpose

- The first step is to state your general purpose.
  - You have three options here; it is to entertain, to inform, or to persuade.
- The second part of the sentence is *always* "my audience," regardless of what kind of speech you are delivering.
  - You must think of the audience at every step of the speech preparation process.
- The third part of your specific purpose statement is the piece where you express what you hope to accomplish.

Example of the Specific Purpose

- To inform my audience so that they will be able to distinguish between legal and illegal street-car racing.
- (General Purpose) To inform (my audience) my audience (specific goal to be accomplished) so that they will be able to distinguish between legal and illegal street-car racing.

Rules for the Specific Purpose

- Again the specific purpose is a single sentence that specifically states what the speaker hopes to accomplish in his or her speech.
- Additional guidelines for the specific purpose are:
1. the purpose statement must *not* be a fragment,
2. must *not* be in the form of a question,
3. must avoid using figurative language,
4. and must present *one* clear-cut idea.

The Purpose Statement
Must *Not* be a Fragment

- Poor Specific Purpose: Watches
- Appropriate: To inform my audience of the declining demand for wristwatches due to the popularity of cell phones.

Must *Not* be in the Form
of a Question

- *Write your specific purpose statement as a statement NOT as a question.*
- Poor Specific Purpose: Are the New York Yankees the best MLB franchise?
- Acceptable: To persuade my audience that the New York Yankees are the greatest MLB franchise in history.

Must Avoid Using
Figurative Language

- Weak Specific Purpose: To inform my audience that bicycle riding is trendy due to the high price of gasoline.
- Acceptable: To inform my audience of the cost effectiveness of bicycle riding.

Must Present *One* Clear-Cut Idea

- Confusing Specific Purpose: To persuade my audience to exercise three times a week and pursue a college degree.

- Acceptable: To persuade my audience that they must exercise three times a week for a healthy lifestyle.

Or

- Acceptable: To persuade my audience to complete their college education to maximize their future incomes.

The Central Idea

- The **central idea** is your road map, as to *how* you will get to your end destination.

- The central idea may be defined as a one-sentence statement that sums up the main ideas of your speech.

  - The central idea may also be known as a subject sentence, a thesis statement, or a major thought.

- Using the term **residual message** is another way of conceptualizing the purpose of your central idea in your speech preparation.

  - The residual message is what a speaker wants the audience to remember after it has forgotten everything else in the speech.

Central Idea Example

- Topic: Computers
- General Purpose: To inform
- Specific Purpose: To inform my audience of the key criteria to consider when buying a laptop computer.
- Central Idea: When purchasing a laptop computer pay attention to the cost, speed and storage space, screen resolution, and the manufacturer's warranty.

The Central Idea Example

- Topic: Entrepreneurship
- General Purpose: To persuade
- Specific Purpose: To persuade my audience that they should start their own business.
- Central Idea: Starting a business will help your tap into your creativity, build wealth, and allow you flexibility in your schedule.

Rules for the Central Idea

- The central idea needs to be expressed in a full sentence
- Should not be in the form of a question
- Should avoid using figurative language
- Should not be overly general or vague

Chapter Five

Public Speaking is an Audience-Focused Activity, so who is your Audience?

The Audience Must Be First and Foremost in the Speaker's Mind

- Public speaking is an audience-focused activity, so as you prepare for your speeches, your audience must be first and foremost in your mind and in your preparation.
- Keep some of these questions in mind during your preparation process:
  - To whom am I speaking?
  - What do I need my audience to know, to do, or to believe as a result of my speech?
  - How can I best put together my speech to meet the needs of my given audience?

The Mindset of the Audience

- The successful public speaker is focused on delivering and adapting a message to the audience.
- **Egocentrism** may be defined as the tendency of people to be concerned above all with their own values, beliefs, and well-being.
- The audience does not process a speaker's message exactly as the speaker intends.
- The auditory perception is always selective; so if the information presented is significant to the listener then that information will stick, while other valuable information would slip by the wayside.
- Keep in mind that your listeners will hear and judge what you say based on what they know and already believe.

Demographics

- Webster's defines demographics as: "the statistical characteristics of human populations (as age or income) used especially to identify markets; or a market or segment of the population identified by demographics."
- Age
- Gender
- Race/Ethnicity
- Educational Level
- Religion
- Group Membership

Age

- By grasping the collective age groups of your audience it is easier to speculate on the range of life experiences they may have had.

Gender

- When thinking about gender relations, it is easy to come up with stereotypes and assumptions.
- However, in speechmaking you need to take your thinking a step further and question those assumptions and find them to be correct before presenting them.
- A well-prepared public speaker will be sure to avoid using sexist language.
  - Almost any audience you address will contain both men and women who will take offense at words and phrases that suggest gender stereotypes or put down people on the basis of their gender.

Race/Ethnicity

- Our world is getting smaller and smaller every day with the developments of technology and our global economy.
  - Therefore understanding the cultural dynamic of your audience is becoming more and more prominent.
- Public speakers who have honorable intentions can inadvertently use figures of speech, metaphors, language, or examples that members of your audience may find offensive.
  - When in doubt, run your speech by someone who can give you an accurate account of your presentation before delivering your speech to the class.

Educational Level

- A person's educational status may tell you very little about his or her intelligence, self-motivation, or personal refinement.
  - However, people with more formal education tend to read more, are more familiar with current events, have probably traveled extensively, and are likely to have higher incomes.
- With this in mind, how does this influence the way you approach your topic to meet the needs of your audience?

Religion

- Knowing the religious affiliations of your audience can give you some good clues about their values, beliefs, and attitudes.
  - However, you cannot assume that all members of a religious group follow the organization's official doctrines and declarations.

Group Membership

- The group affiliations of your audience may provide excellent clues about listener's interests and attitudes.
- Getting into the minds of the group's philosophy will help you customize your message to the particular group.

Gathering Audience Intelligence

- Gathering audience information is incredibly important because it takes the unknowns to knowns, and makes the invisible visible.
- In general, the higher the level of uncertainty that exists in a given situation, the higher the level of anxiety.
- Two ways to collect valuable information about your audience is through audience surveys and interviewing audience members.

The Audience Survey

- The keys with the audience survey are to be brief and to the point and to make replying to the survey user-friendly for the responders.
- There are three types of questions you want to ask when assembling an audience survey:
1. the fixed-alternative question,
2. the scale-question,
3. and the open-ended question.

The Fixed-Alternative Question

- The **fixed-alternative question** offers a fixed choice between two more alternatives.
- The purpose for asking the fixed-alternative question is to establish the listener's knowledge base and their amount of involvement with the topic.
- By asking the fixed-alternative you are limiting their responses to produce clear-cut answers.

Sample Fixed-Alternative Questions

- Do you drink at least one soda a day?
    Yes ___ No ___
- Did you vote in the last mayoral election?
    Yes ___ No ___ Not sure? ___
- Do you spend more than $50 a month on video games?
    - Yes ___ No ___ Not sure? ___

Scale Questions

- **Scale questions** are used to gain more accurate information about the audience members to gain an understanding of how they fit in a range of possible responses to a question.
- The range of possible responses is usually made into fixed intervals along a scale.
- The scale questions are similar to the fixed-alternative questions, but provide the respondent more options.
- Scale questions offer a glimpse into the *attitudes* of listeners towards a particular topic.

Sample Scale Questions

- The federal government should mandate a $250 annual tax that will be exclusively used to pay off the national debt.

  Strongly agree Somewhat agree Not sure
  Somewhat disagree Strongly disagree

- The legal driving age should be raised to 21 years old.

  Strongly agree Somewhat agree Not sure
  Somewhat disagree Strongly disagree

Open-Ended Questions

- The **open-ended question** allows the respondent to answer freely.
- Because you are giving the respondent the keys to the car, they may take you places you do not want to go, or provide information that is irrelevant to the purpose of your speech.
- On the flip side you may find that the respondent answered your questions and illustrated a new way of thinking about your topic, or an area of expertise you did not expect an audience member would have.

Sample Open-Ended Questions

- How do you feel about the proposal to ban alcohol on campus?

- Why do you think America is facing such an obesity problem?

- Do you feel video games contribute to the high absenteeism in our Speech class?

Interviewing Audience Members

- Interviewing your classmates on a one-on-one basis is the most thorough way to learn about each of your audience members.
- Interviewing your audience requires you to be very organized in devising your questions and coordinating the time to meet the individual audience members.
- The interviewing practice is by far the most meticulous, but is the least practical to implement.

Tips for Interviewing Audience Members

- First you need to define the purpose of your interview.
  - Ask yourself, "what do I hope to accomplish with this interview?"
  - By answering this question, you will be on your way.
- Next, you need to know whom to interview.
  - Ask yourself, "will this person provide me the information to fulfill my purpose?"
- The most important task when preparing for an interview is formulating your interview questions.
  - Write those questions out and spend time wording those questions appropriately so you sound credible.

Other Tips for Interviewing Audience Members

- During the interview be sure to be on time for your appointment.
  - In addition, being on time expresses the message of respect, and your interviewee will appreciate that gesture.
- Immediately after the interview review your notes while the dialogue is still prominently in your mind.
  - Write-out those notes clearly so you can implement the interview in your presentation.
- Make sure that you have written the person's name, title, and organization accurately.
  - Nothing hurts your credibility more than calling someone by the wrong name.
- Finally, send a thank you note to the person you interviewed.
  - This person took the time out of his or her busy schedule to help you with your presentation, give them the common courtesy to say thank you.
  - The interviewee will remember your thoughtfulness and will be more willing to be a resource at a future date.

Analysis and Audience Expectations of the Situation

- Size of the Audience
- The Environment
- The Occasion
- Time
- Importance

Size of the Audience

- The size of the audience is something to consider because the number of listeners may determine your level of formality, the amount of interaction you have with the audience, the use of a microphone, and your need to make adjustments to your visual aids.

- Speaking to a large audience reduces the speaker's capability to observe and respond to facial expressions, posture, and other nonverbal messages sent by the audience.

The Environment

- Where you deliver your speech may be less than desirable, but the show must go on.

- Mishaps with your environment may happen, it is your responsibility to build contingency plans so you are not caught off-guard in case something goes wrong.

The Environment (Continued)

- There will be times when your room will be less than optimal. This is *not* your time to announce to your audience that the room is small, or hot, or uncomfortable.
- At the very least you will want to inquire in advance about the room in which you are to speak.
- Visiting the room will help you get the look and feel of where you will be presenting, in addition, going the extra mile here will allow you to visualize your success in the preparation of your speech.

The Occasion

- Your disposition and demeanor need to match the mood of the occasion.
  - With the numerous occasions and interactions we have, there is an unwritten expectation of acceptable behavior.
- For the different environments you will be speaking, think ahead and make sure that the emotional tone of your speech matches the mood of the occasion.

Time

- The occasion that you will be speaking at will dictate the appropriate time of your speech.
- By violating the time rule of what is acceptable will turn-off an audience, and diminish your credibility.

Importance

- The last factor to consider when assessing the situation is the importance of the occasion, and the significance that is attached to the circumstances.

Adjusting to your Audience
Before Your Speech

- As part of your preparation you need to predict how your audience will respond to your message, and make adjustments to your message so the audience finds your speech clear, appropriate, and convincing.
- The findings from your audience survey will help you anticipate how your audience will react to your message.
- Stepping out of your frame of reference and into the perspective of the audience is a big step towards being an effective public speaker and on your pathway to success.

Audience Adaptation
During the Speech

- While delivering your speech, be on the lookout as to how your audience is receiving your message through their feedback.
- If your listeners are leaning forward in their chairs, looking at you fully engaged in your speech, and nodding their heads in approval, it is safe to assume you are on the right track.
- On the other hand if you find your audience disinterested, slouching in their chairs, or giving you quizzical looks, you need to make some adjustments to your presentation on the fly.

Chapter Six

Researching Your Sources for the
Ultimate Credibility

Gathering Your Materials

- By accessing information from your college or university library, you will put yourself in a stronger position to be more informative and persuasive.

- Using your college or university library and all of its resources will help establish your credibility, competence, and confidence as a public speaker.

- The three primary areas where your information for your speech will be coming from are: library research, Internet research, and field research.

Organizing Your Data Gathering Project

- Consider using file folders representing each of your potential main points as a place to hold your printed materials.

- For each of your printouts or photocopies be sure to have all bibliography information clearly written so you can track down the original source if necessary.

- In addition, when you document your bibliography on your outline, all of the needed information will be readily available.

Organizing Your
Data Gathering Project

- Another strategy that may be helpful is using note cards for key ideas.
- For each of your note cards a heading is needed, with the author's name, page number of the work that the information came from, and a summary of the line of reasoning you want to remember.

Primary and Secondary Sources

- Primary sources are first-hand accounts, much like your class audience survey, and your one-on-one individual interviews.
- Secondary sources are information coming from books, magazines, databases, and newspapers.

Develop a Timeline for the
Research Process

- That 3x5 card with your specific purpose will serve as your anchor when you get hit with information overload.
  - Understanding your purpose clarifies the data gathering decision making process.
- It is best to develop a timeline to schedule where you want to be and when, and stick to the schedule.
  - Other things to consider when putting together your plan is scheduling expert interviews, meeting with librarians, conducting surveys, and even deciding which libraries you will visit.
- If you wait too long, these valuable resources may not be available to you, so *start early*.

Finding Your Materials

- When using the many electronic databases at the library, it is to your advantage to use the database's built-in bibliography feature and create the bibliography as you go.

- By documenting those sources while you come across them in the first place, you will save time from backtracking and trying to relocate those sources.

Library Research Resources

- Your college or university invests a lot of money for paid subscriptions that are of higher caliber quality than an ordinary Internet search.

- In addition, you will have the opportunity to have highly qualified and devoted librarians help you gather your materials for your speech.

- Other alternatives you may have besides your college or university library are your local public library, or dedicated libraries operated by historical societies, museums, professional associations, or corporations.

Utilize Your Library's Orientation Workshop

- The best advice is to utilize the library's orientation workshops that will walk you through how to utilize all of the valuable information available at your fingertips.

- By participating in the workshop orientations you will learn the finer points of how to gather materials, saving you hours of time and needless frustration.

- Moreover, by participating in the workshop orientation, you will have the opportunity to meet the library staff, and build a relationship with the librarians that will help you in your researching needs during the duration of your college experience.

Make Use of Your Librarian

- A tip that should be abided by before talking to the librarian is to have your specific purpose clearly stated, along with any specific directions for the particular assignment, so the librarian can get the appropriate context of the assignment to better serve you.

- In short, you want to respect the time and effort of your librarian so be prepared ahead of time.

Locating Books

- In locating a specific book in your library, you will have to access your library's catalog, which allows you to compose a quick search using at least three categories, the author's name, the title, or the subject.

- Locating the call number of the book will inform you where this book is located in the library's stacks so that you can find the book in an organized and systematic fashion.

- Moreover, if you are using a computerized catalog, the computer may tell you whether the book is checked out, or on hold, maximizing your time as opposed to looking for a book that is already checked out.

Articles

- Articles that support your ideas may come in three different forms of periodicals at the library: newspapers, magazines, and academic journals.

- When accessing articles via electronic databases, the data are commonly provided in three different forms.

- First is the citation, in the simple bibliographical reference that includes the title of the article, the name(s) of the author(s), the name of the publication, publication date, and page numbers.

- Next is the abstract form, where a brief summary of an article is shown for you to decide whether the information presented is what you were looking for in your source. The abstract provides just enough information for you gauge whether you want to see the article in its entirety.

- Lastly, some databases offer a full-text view of the article you have retrieved.

Newspapers

- When researching newspapers to support your ideas the common papers to look for are prominent papers like: *The New York Times, The Los Angeles Times, The Chicago Tribune, The Washington Post, The Wall Street Journal,* and *USA Today*.

- However, the real hidden gem is the local coverage of an event.

Reference Works

- The reference area is composed of encyclopedias, dictionaries, yearbooks, quote books, and maps.
- These resources are carefully researched and verified for accuracy.
- Reference materials come in three different forms: print, CD-ROM, and the Internet.
- Other advantages to using reference works are that they can provide a synopsis of your topic, verify information gathered from other sources, or find a person's credentials.

Reference Works

- *The Statistical Abstract of the United States* is a standard summary of statistics on the social, political, and economic organization of the United States.

- *The Statistical Abstract of the United States* may also be accessed through the Internet at http://www.census.gov/compendia/statab/.

Documentation of Your Sources for Your Bibliography

- There are two major style guidelines that are used to document your sources for the bibliography of your speech.
- The first is the Modern Language Association style guide also referred to as "MLA" or the American Psychological Association style guide also referred to as "APA."
- Ask your instructor what his or her preference is when documenting sources for your speeches.
  - Refer to your textbook for formatting your sources.

Orally Citing Your Sources

- The appropriate oral citing of your sources is needed during your speech.
- Your audience does not have the luxury of reading your speech while you are delivering your message so it is essential to mention your sources during your speech.
- During the oral citation, the speaker shares with the audience what the source is, a date reference for the information presented, and the source's credentials.
- When orally citing a Web site, it is not customary to say the address during your presentation unless you specifically want your audience to visit the site.

Internet Research a Good Supplement

- It is recommended that the use of the Internet for gathering research materials should be a *supplement* to the library-based research avenue.
- Therefore the information may be very biased and erroneous, because no one is monitoring the content.
  - Web sites need to be incessantly updated and regrettably many are not regularly updated and maintained.

The Benefits of
Internet Research

- The Internet does have its benefits. First the Internet is easily accessible to almost everyone.

- Next the Internet provides numerous multimedia files for you to download, like videos, audio, pictures, and the like from reputable sites, that can add value to your material gathering for your speech.

- Another advantage of the Internet is the use of Really Simple Syndication (RSS). You can subscribe to an RSS feed, which allows you to receive and save up-to-date information from the participating site.

  - So, instead of having to repeatedly access the page to see if any updates have happened, you will be notified of any updates.

Evaluating Information
from the Internet

- After looking at the timeliness of the information you have gathered, ask yourself if the information presented is verifiable with other library-based sources such as those found in reference materials.

- Look for the qualifications of the people writing the material, does this person have the appropriate credentials to talk about the given topic?

- Also examine the relationship between the organization sponsoring the site and the article, from there you can examine any hidden agendas or biases in the information presented.

Access to
Government Publications

- One of the strengths of using the Internet is for its access to government documents.

- *FirstGov* is a good site that serves as a portal to government documents (federal, state, local, and tribal government levels) FirstGov is located at http://www.usa.gov/

Internet Communities

- The Internet offers like minded users of topics to form message boards, discussion forums, blogs, vlogs, and podcasts as options for you to gather information for your speech.
- Again when assessing the validity of blogs, vlogs, and podcasts, check the credentials of the people driving the content.

Field Research

- Field research is the process of gathering information first-hand by observing, surveying, interviewing, or being part of some activity.
- Under the field research arm of data gathering, interviewing experts or people who have first-hand experience (peer testimony) with your topic would fall under this category.

Chapter Seven

Supporting Your Ideas

Supporting Your Ideas Can Make or Break a Speech

- Supporting your ideas effectively requires you to take your abstract ideas and make them more tangible.

- The practiced art of supporting your ideas can make the difference between a poor speech and an outstanding speech.

Supporting Your Ideas With Sound Sources

- As you assemble the materials for your speech, extra care is needed in assessing that your supporting materials are precise, applicable, and dependable.

- Questions that you should be asking yourself are, "Am I quoting highly regarded, authorized sources?" "Am I using statistical measures properly?" "Are my examples typical?"

- In this chapter we will be focusing on the customary forms of supporting materials: examples, statistics, and testimony.

Examples

- A speech without examples may lead your audience to think that your thoughts are abstract, impersonal, and not real.
- Conversely, a speech filled with useful examples will help your audience interpret your ideas as specific, personal, lively, and believable.

Brief Examples

- A **brief example** is often noted as being a specific instance, and may be referred to in passing, to illustrate a point.
- A brief example that is verifiable means that the example can be supported by a source that the audience can check.

Narratives or Extended Examples

- **Narratives** are also called anecdotes, illustrations, and extended examples. The narrative is longer and more detailed than the brief example.
- However, make sure that your narrative directly relates to your speech topic and the specific point you are trying to make. It is easy to get off on an unrelated tangent.

Hypothetical Example

- A **hypothetical example** is speculative, imaginative, and fictional. The hypothetical example cannot be verified for its legitimacy, and can be either in the brief or narrative format.
- A speaker using the hypothetical example is painting a picture for the audience using an imaginary circumstance.

Examples Must be Representative and Concrete

- Be careful to use examples that are representative, and do not deal with uncommon or extraordinary cases. Your listeners are likely to feel deceived if they believe you have chosen an uncharacteristic example to prove a general point.
- People are fascinated with people. Whenever you talk to a general audience you can include examples that add human interest to your speech. The abstract idea becomes more meaningful when applied to a person.

Statistics

- Statistics are used to quantify the speaker's idea, and are mentioned in passing to simplify or bolster a speaker's points. The use of statistics makes the speaker's claim credible and clear.
    - One pitfall many public speakers fall into is to clutter their speech with statistics.
- When using statistics for your speeches, be sure to evaluate them using the following benchmarks: Are the statistics used representative? Are the statistics measured correctly? And are the statistics from a reliable source?

The Mean, The Median, and The Mode

- The mean, median, and mode are three kinds of "averages."
- The **mean** can be defined as the average value of a group of numbers. The mean of a group of numbers is found by adding the numbers and dividing that number by the number of numbers.
- The **median** may be defined as the "middle number" in a group of numbers arranged from highest to lowest.
- The **mode** is defined as the value that occurs most frequently in a group of numbers. If no number is repeated, then there is no mode for the list.

The Implementation of Your Statistics

- When using your statistics in a speech there is a three-point process to implement those statistics effectively.

  1. Identify the Source of your Statistic
  2. State Your Statistic
  3. Explain Your Statistic

Testimony

- Audience members tend to respect the opinions of people who have special knowledge or experience on the speech topic being delivered.
- There are two kinds of testimony, expert testimony and peer testimony.

Expert Testimony

- **Expert testimony**, is testimony from people who are recognized authorities in their field. Expert testimony is especially helpful for student speakers because citing the views of people who are experts is a good way to lend credibility to your speeches.
- Remember, however, when quoting an expert, to make sure that the person's name, organization, and title are correct. Having incorrect information about the "expert" will hurt your credibility as a public speaker.

Peer Testimony

- **Peer testimony** is the opinions of ordinary people who have first-hand experience on the topic.
- This kind of testimony is especially valuable because it gives a more personal viewpoint on issues than can be gained from expert testimony.
- It conveys the feelings, the knowledge, and the insight of people who speak with the voice of genuine experience.

Quoting versus Paraphrasing

- A direct **quotation** may be defined as a testimony that is presented word for word. In contrast, **paraphrasing** may be defined as restating or summarizing a source's ideas in one's own words.
- Paraphrasing surpasses a direct quotation in two situations: (1) when the wording of a quotation is confusing or awkward, as is often found with government documents; (2) when a quotation is longer than two or three sentences.
  - Audiences will tune out through a lengthy quotation.

Accuracy in Quoting

- When using testimony in your speech accuracy is needed with the quote and paraphrase.

- This means making sure that you do not misquote someone, do not violate the meaning of statements you are paraphrasing, and that you do not quote out of context.

- Also, verification is needed that the person you are quoting is qualified on the subject matter of your speech.

Chapter Eight

Organizing and Outlining your Speech

Organizing and Outlining your Speech

- Mark Twain said it best, "it usually takes more than three weeks to prepare a good impromptu speech."

- The process of organizing and outlining your speech will take much of the nervousness out of the public speaking experience, because planning and organizing your speech is an empowering process.

Organizing and Outlining your Speech

- On the other hand a disorganized speech makes it very difficult for the audience to follow along with your message, therefore the probability of your audience daydreaming and thinking of everything else besides your presentation is highly likely.

- Your listeners do not have the luxury of rereading a particular part of your speech; they need to hear your message the first time around.

The Three Parts of a Speech

- By having a strong grasp of the three parts of a speech, *the introduction, the body, and the conclusion*, you will be able to navigate your audience so they can capture your core message.

- So once the main points in your body are clearly established, supported, and written, from there it is much easier to write the introduction and conclusion.

Establishing Your Main Points

- Having your main points established clarifies your intended residual message that you want your audience to grasp.

- Often the main points will emerge as you research the topic of your speech followed by evaluating the soundness of your supporting materials.

Number of Main Points

- The usual rule of thumb is your speech should have between two and five main points.

- One factor to consider is how much time you have to present your speech. Some assignments may be for you to speak for two minutes or even forty-five minutes.

- It would be very difficult to adequately discuss three main points in two-minute speech or two main points in a forty-five minute speech.

Limiting the Number of Main Points

- By limiting the number of main points to between two and five your audience will have an easier time remembering your main points.

- The purpose of limiting the number of your main points is so that they stand out and are remembered by your audience.

Organizational Strategies for Your Main Points

- Clear organization is vital to effective public speaking. Your audience must be able to grasp the advancement of your ideas in your presentation from your introduction through the conclusion.

Chronological Order

- Speeches arranged in the **chronological order** follow a time pattern.
- The main points used in the chronological order may describe a series of events in the order in which they occurred.
- The chronological order is also used in speeches explaining a process or demonstrating how to do something.
- The chronological order is especially useful for informative speeches.

Spatial Order

- Speeches using the **spatial order** follow a directional pattern.
- Main points continue from top to bottom, left to right, east to west, front to back, inside to outside, or some other route.
- When preparing an informative speech, the spatial order might be an appropriate organizational choice.

Causal Order

- The **causal order** strategy is used to underline the cause-effect relationship.
- The causal order regularly contains two main points, one addressing the causes of an event, the other concentrating on the effects.
- Because of its adaptability the causal order can be used for both informative and persuasive speeches.

Problem-Solution Order

- The **problem-solution order** are divided into two key parts.
- The first explains the existence and seriousness of a problem.
- The second reveals a realistic solution to the problem.
- The problem-solution order is most appropriate for persuasive speeches.

Topical Order

- The **topical order** is derived when you divide the speech topics into subtopics, each of which becomes a main point in the speech.

- The topical order is the most commonly used organizational strategy in public speaking because it is applicable to almost any subject and any kind of speech.

- The topical order is an effective organizational strategy for both informative and persuasive speeches.
  - In a persuasive speech, each of your topical subdivisions are the reasons/arguments why a speaker has chosen to advocate for a certain point of view.

How Much Time Should I Allocate for Each of My Main Points?

- The amount of time spent on each main point depends on the quantity and complexity of the supporting materials for each theme.

- The average American speaks at approximately 125 to 150 words per minute. Use this numerical gauge a guide as to how many words you should have in your speech.

- Keep this in mind, when you are at the podium your rate of speech will be a lot faster due to adrenaline, so plan accordingly.

Supporting Materials

- There are three types of examples to support your main points, brief examples, narrative examples, and hypothetical examples.

- Further discussion about supporting your ideas for your presentation is discussed in more detail in Chapter 7.

Connectives

- **Connectives** are words or phrases that join one thought to another and reveal the relationship between them—much like going from first gear to second gear efficiently.
- There are four types of connectives that would be appropriate for a speech: *transitions, internal previews, internal summaries, and signposts.*
  - Connectives are like the fluid gear shifts that make the ride smooth for your passengers or, in our context, our audience.

Transitions

- **Transitions** are words or phrases that reveal when a speaker has just finished one thought, and is moving on to another.
- In theory, the transitions state both the idea the speaker is leaving and the idea she or he is coming up to.

Internal Previews

- **Internal previews** give the audience a "heads up" so they know what the speaker will discuss next; however, internal previews are more detailed than transitions.
- An internal preview works like the preview statement in a speech introduction, but it happens in the body of the speech, as the speaker is starting to discuss a main point.

Internal Summaries

- **Internal summaries** remind the audience of what was just stated.
- A speaker may have just completed a point that was particularly complex or complicated and the internal summary reviews what the speaker just talked about in a concise way.

Signposts

- **Signposts** are concise statements that show the audience where you are in the speech.
- A common signpost strategy is to use numbers as a way of letting your audience know where you are in your speech.

Outlining the Speech

- Your **speech outline** is your game plan during the preparation phase of your speech development and requires a good amount of thinking.
- The process of outlining requires you to consider if each part (introduction, body, and conclusion) of the speech is fully cultivated, if the supporting materials for your main points are appropriate, and if the main points are properly composed.

Two Types of Outlines

- There are two kinds of outlines you will use in preparing for a speech.
- First is the **preparation outline** that is a detailed roadmap of your speech.
- The second type of outline is the **speaker's outline** which is less detailed, but offers valuable delivery cues while you are at the podium.

Preparation Outline

- Your preparation outline includes the labeling of the parts of the speech (introduction, body, conclusion, and bibliography), which can be broken down into the specific purpose, central idea, introduction, main points, subpoints, sub-subpoints, sub-sub subpoints, connectives, conclusion, and the bibliography.

Preparation Outline

- From the example of a preparation outline your text, your specific purpose and central idea are documented at the top of the page, above the introduction.
- A title would go on top of the specific purpose and central idea, but that is optional for a speech, so ask your teacher if a title is needed with your preparation outline.

Preparation Outline

- Your speech will have three parts, the introduction, the body, and the conclusion.
- Each of these parts needs to be labeled and is usually centered on the page on your preparation outline.
- The labels distinguish the different parts of a speech and are *not* included in the procedure of symbolization used to classify main points and supporting materials.

Preparation Outline

- A challenging aspect in the outlining process is using a harmonious pattern of symbolization and indentation, also know as your **visual framework**.
- Main points are identified by Roman numerals and are on the left margin down the page.
- Your subpoints (components of the main point) are identified by capital letters and are indented to the right equally so as to be lined up with each other.
- Continuing the visual framework are your sub-subpoints and your sub-sub subpoints, which are also aligned with each other and indented to the right.

Preparation Outline

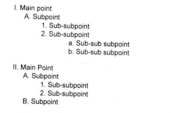

I. Main point
  A. Subpoint
    1. Sub-subpoint
    2. Sub-subpoint
       a. Sub-sub subpoint
       b. Sub-sub subpoint

II. Main Point
  A. Subpoint
    1. Sub-subpoint
    2. Sub-subpoint
  B. Subpoint

- Remember that all points at the same level should immediately support the point that is just above and one level to the left in your outline.

Your Bibliography and
Your Outline

- Finally, the preparation outline needs to include a bibliography attached at the end of your speech.
- The bibliography will confirm all the books, magazines, newspapers, and Internet sources you referred to, as well as any interviews or field research you performed.
- The two chief bibliographic formats are the Modern Language Association (MLA) and the American Psychological Association (APA).
  - These bibliographic formats are commonly used in your college courses, so ask your teacher his or her preference when documenting your consulted sources.
- Details of how to document your sources are explained in Chapter 6 on researching your sources.

The Speakers Outline

- The speaker's outline is used while you are delivering your extemporaneous speech in front of your audience.
- The purpose of the speaking outline is to serve as a memory aid while at the podium.
- The speaker's outline provides delivery cues for you to follow while delivering your speech.
- It is a more compact translation of your preparation outline that limits itself to key words or phrases so you can remember what you want to say.

The Speakers Outline

- Other guiding principles to follow for your speaker's outline are to go along with the framework used in your preparation outline, using the same symbols, and the same indentation pattern.
- As you speak you will look down at your outline periodically to make sure you are covering the right ideas in the right order.
  - It will be of little help if you have to hunt around to find where you are every time you look down.
  - Try finding your place if your notes consist of text—much like in an essay format.
- As you progress in your public speaking development you will create your own shorthand for your memory aids on your outline.

Chapter Nine

Introductions and Conclusions

Introductions and Conclusions

- An effective introduction should be structured so the speaker will: get the listeners' attention, express that the topic is something that will relate to the audience, set themselves up as trustworthy to speak on the topic, clarify their purpose, and preview the main points of the speech.

- In an introduction your speech must have the following four goals. First, you need to get the attention and interest of your audience. Next, you need to reveal the topic of your speech. Third, establish your credibility and goodwill towards your audience, and finally preview the body of speech.

Get the Attention and Interest of Your Audience

- Your audience will be asking themselves, "why is this topic relevant to me?" and it is your job to figure that question out before heading to the podium.

- So during the introduction of your speech, spend some time building bridges by connecting your topic to the audience.

- The following attention-getting strategies will help you capture and maintain the audience's interest level.

Relate the Topic to the Audience

- Your audience will listen to your speech as long as your content has something that directly relates to their interest.
- One strategy that will work in achieving this specific goal is to utilize your audience survey.
- Remember public speaking is an audience-focused activity.

Startle the Audience

- One strategy to get the attention of your audience is to startle your audience with an astonishing or captivating statement.
  - This strategy is easy to implement but you need to remember that the statement needs to directly relate to the audience.
- If for whatever reason you decide to make a shocking statement and proceed with your speech and your message does not relate to your statement, your audience will be confused and that will discredit your authenticity.

Stir-Up the Curiosity of the Audience

- One way to lure the audience into your speech is with a succession of statements that increasingly awakens the interest about the subject for the audience.
- Stirring-up the curiosity of the audience is a strong tactic to capture and hold the audience members' attention and interest.

Begin with a Quotation

- When using a quote make sure it is brief and catchy.
- If the quote is too long, your audience will lose its attention and begin to wonder when they get to listen to the speaker's ideas as opposed to someone else's ideas.

Tell a Story

- When telling a story not only is the content important, but also your delivery can make or break the success of the story.
- Extra time and care is needed in working with the delivery aspect to capture the true essence of your story.
- The story must directly reinforce the specific purpose of your speech.

Humor

- Using humor in your introduction requires you to use some caution and have a good sense as to what makes your audience tick.
- Remember that your stories and jokes need to illustrate a point that is reflective of your specific purpose and central idea.

Ask a Question

- Asking a question is a useful way to get the attention of the audience; however, there are some pitfalls to avoid.
- Let us say you ask a thought-provoking question and pause after asking the question.
- Ask yourself, will my audience be listening to me or will they still be reflecting on what was just said?
- Conversely, what if the question you asked is really weak, bordering on silly.
- Your audience may consider your topic, and you the speaker, as insignificant and questionable, and you will lose credibility with your audience.

Reveal the Topic

- In the process of crafting a strong introduction, you must reveal the topic of your speech to your audience.
- If you do not reveal your topic, your audience will not grasp what you are trying to accomplish and will likely be confused.

Establishing Your Credibility

- Your introduction is a critical time to establish yourself as a person who can talk about this topic so it makes sense to your audience.
- Another objective in establishing your credibility is to be perceived as qualified by your listeners.

Establishing Your Credibility

- Confirming your credibility in your introduction can either come from first-hand experience with your subject matter, or through studying applicable documentation about your topic, interviewing authorized people in the field, or taking a class relating to your speech topic.

Establishing Your Credibility with Goodwill

- Establishing your goodwill is another challenge you will face in your introduction.
- If you are facing a hostile environment you must make special efforts to consider the opposing views, which builds goodwill.

Preview the Body of the Speech

- The preview introduces your main ideas, so that your audience can follow you along the main points of your presentation.
- The preview statement is a signal that the speaker is transitioning from the introduction into the body of the speech.

Other Tips for the Introduction to your Speech

- The length of the introduction varies from speech to speech, but should be relatively brief.
- When preparing for your speech it is easier to develop your introduction only after the main points have been identified and developed.
- Another common error made by beginning public speakers is to apologize for one reason or another.
    - Just go to the podium and deliver your speech the best you can and leave the apologies to another time when you are truly sorry about something.

Other Tips for the Introduction to your Speech

- Keep your introduction relatively brief, but engaging, because the core of your message comes from the body of the speech.
- Spend a lot of time practicing the delivery of your introduction because it will give you good momentum you can carry throughout the remainder of your speech while building your confidence.
- Your goal should be able to deliver your introduction with minimal reference to your notes so you can maintain strong eye contact with your audience.
- Your audience will be more engaged with a speaker who is looking at them, and your audience prefers seeing your eyes as opposed to the top of your head.

The Conclusion

- Your audience may not remember every one of your points, but they will remember their overall impression of you and your speech.
- Your conclusion has two key purposes, to signal that you will be finishing your speech, and to reinforce your central idea.

Signal the End of the Speech

- One of the easiest and most obvious ways to let your audience know that you are ending your speech is to say: in conclusion, finally, one last thought, in closing, in short, in summation.
- A more subtle and indirect way to let your audience know that you are ending your speech is through your delivery.
- By using the voice's tone, pacing, intonation, and rhythm, a speaker can build the momentum of a speech so it is clear that the speech is ending.

Signal the End of the Speech (Continued)

- The **crescendo ending** strategy is when the speech builds to a high point of power and intensity in your delivery.
- Another strategy is to use the dissolved ending. The **dissolved ending** is a conclusion that generates an emotional appeal by fading step-by-step to a dramatic final statement.

Reinforce the Central Idea

- One of the most common techniques used to conclude a speech is to present a summary of your main points for your listeners.
  - Using a summary emphasizes the most important points and reminds the listeners of your key ideas.
- A good brief quote can reinforce the central idea of a speech.

Tips for Your Conclusion

- The conclusion is not the time to introduce new information.
- Do not drag out your speech.
- If you were to close your speech with a, "I think that is all I got" as you are walking back to your chair, your audience will think much less of your speech and that conclusion will leave a weak lasting impression of you as a public speaker.

Chapter Ten

Delivery

Delivery and Nonverbal Communication

- The nonverbal component of the message clearly demonstrates how important delivery impacts the message you are delivering to your audience.

- The text of your speech is valuable; however, the nonverbal message of how you deliver the content carries more weight with the audience.

Well-Prepared Delivery

- Unfortunately many beginning public speakers wait until the last minute to prepare their outlines and usually head to the podium cold, without rehearsing their speech, and that lack of preparation usually leaves the audience with a flat presentation.

- A well-prepared and practiced delivery communicates the speaker's ideas more clearly and interestingly than an unprepared delivered speech.

Delivery and Confidence

- When you head up to the podium and you know that you have not practiced your delivery as much as you believe you should have, that doubt is communicated nonverbally, and your audience will pick up on that lack of confidence.
- The lack of confidence is usually communicated by staring down at the podium instead of scanning the room, stuttering and stammering with lots of uhms and uhs, staring in the sky for divine intervention, or delivering your speech with a monotone voice because you are reading your speech.

Delivery and a Focused Message

- Remember this is public speaking and not public reading.
- The easiest way to ensure the most appropriate style of delivery is to focus on the message that you are trying to communicate to your audience.
- If your focal point is on delivering this message to this audience, your nonverbal messages will come naturally.

Methods of Delivery

1. Speaking from a Manuscript
2. Delivering your Speech from Memory
3. Impromptu Speaking
4. Extemporaneous Speaking

Speaking from a Manuscript

- Speeches that are of great importance are usually reserved for the manuscript delivery method.
- **Manuscript speeches** are delivered word for word, and are written and re-written numerous times for absolute accuracy in content and correct word choice.

- However, delivering a speech from a manuscript is challenging, because it is so easy to just read to the audience as oppose to speaking to the audience.
- The audience needs to get the sense that you are talking to them, and not a blank wall.

Delivering your Speech from Memory

- Except for the shortest of speeches, it is not expected that you memorize your speech.

- When a speech is memorized there is more effort on the speaker's behalf to remember their words as opposed to communicating with the audience.

Impromptu Speaking

- **Impromptu speaking** is a speech delivered with little or no advance preparation.
- When faced with this situation take a deep breath, compose yourself, and think of a few words to say, say them and then sit down.
- Make sure your speech is relatively brief, because the longer you babble, the probability of saying something ridiculous gets higher, and your credibility in the eyes of the other people in the room will evaporate into thin air.

Extemporaneous Speaking

- An **extemporaneous speech** is a carefully prepared speech that is practiced ahead of time.
- When using an extemporaneous delivery style, you will be referring to a brief set of notes (speaker's outline) as a memory aid while delivering your speech.
- **Conversational quality** means that no matter how many times you have practiced your speech, it still sounds natural to the audience.

The Speaker's Voice

- Volume
- Pitch
- Rate of Speech
- Pauses
- Vocal Variety
- Pronunciation
- Articulation
- Dialect

Volume

- If your audience cannot physically hear you, then even the most powerful messages will not be received by your audience.
- **Volume** is the loudness or quietness of the speaker's voice.
- On one end of the spectrum, if you speak too loudly your audience will perceive you to be unrefined or rough around the edges.
- Conversely if you speak so softly that no one can hear you, your audience may perceive you as not confident and not a credible person to speak on your topic.
- Your own voice will always sound louder to you than to your audience

Pitch

- The highness or lowness of the speaker's voice is also known as the **pitch** of the speaker's voice. Changes in the speaker's pitch are referred to as **inflections**.
  - Adjusting the pitch of your message allows you to match the mood of your speech with your voice.
- **Monotone** can be defined as a constant, unchanging pitch or tone of voice. Such a flat line range in your pitch is a sure way to disengage and tire the audience.
- Another pitch variation that will turn off an audience is a repetitious inflection pattern that does not change, regardless of the content.

Rate of Speech

- It has been documented that speakers in the United States speak between 125 to 150 words per minute, but that rate allows for some flexibility based on the speaker's own communication style. The term **rate of speech** refers to how fast a person speaks.
- When a speaker delivers a speech that is considerably slow the audience will be left with a lot of spare time, and their minds will begin to wander, as opposed to listening to your speech.

Pauses

- A **pause** may be defined as a momentary break in the vocal delivery of a speech. A pause can close a thought, while your audience reflects on what you have just said, or it can let a dramatic statement just sit there while the audience ponders its significance.
- **Vocalized pauses** are pauses that occur when a speaker fills the silence between words with vocalizations such as "uh," "er," and "um."
- These voiced pauses are distracting and create a perception from the audience that the speaker is not confident or competent.

Vocal Variety

- **Vocal variety** is the changes and variety in the speaker's rate of speech, volume, pitch, and how the speaker expresses his or her thoughts through the voice.
- Vocal variety enlivens a speech and makes it more relatable to an audience.

Pronunciation

- **Pronunciation** refers to the way a word or a language is usually spoken, or the manner in which someone utters a word.
- When in doubt about the proper pronunciation of a word, just look it up in a reputable dictionary.

Articulation

- **Articulation** is the physical production of particular speech sounds.
- So, poor articulation is the failure to form exact speech sounds crisply and clearly.

Dialect

- A speech **dialect** is a variety of language that is distinguished by variations of accent, grammar, or vocabulary.
- The United States contains four major regional dialects, Eastern, New England, Southern, and General American.
- Dialects are primarily based on regional or ethnic speech patterns.

The Speaker's Physical Characteristics

- **Kinesics** is the study of body motions as a systematic mode of communication.
- How you use your body at the podium— such as the position of your head, eyes, and torso—impact the speaker's message.

Personal Appearance

- Your personal appearance should reflect the time and place of the situation and occasion.
- The clothing you wear should not detract from you the public speaker.
- However, regardless of the speaking situation, you should do your best to keep the best impression you can with your audience.

Movement Behind the Podium

- A common distracting mannerism behind the podium is nervous movement.
  - Some speakers sway from left to right like a clock.
- Other distracting movements that need to be avoided are playing with the change in your pocket, fidgeting with your outline, shifting your weight from one leg to another, and leaning on the podium.
- As you concentrate on delivering your message to your audience, a natural movement will evolve with practice and public speaking experience behind the podium.

Gestures

- In your everyday conversation you use your hands to reinforce particular points you are trying to make.

- When using your hands to gesture to the audience the movements need to come across as genuine and sincere, and not forced and unnatural.

Eye Contact

- One of the strongest ways to develop a connection with your audience is through eye contact.
- On the flip side, the best way to lose your audience is to not look at them at all.
  - This usually happens when you read your speech, stare at the ground, or stare at the ceiling.

Practicing Delivery

- First spend some time going over your speaker's outline. Do your main points lead you to your specific purpose?
- Do your introduction, body, conclusion, and transitions fit together like a puzzle? Are your points supported well and are they accurate?
- Spend time going over your speech aloud. Does it sound right to the ear? Writing for the eye is different than writing for the ear, so does your speech sound as good as it looks?

Delivery and the Speakers Outline

- Next take a look at your speaker's outline. Will the speaker's outline help you while you are at the podium?
  - For example, is the font large enough for you to refer to while delivering your presentation?
- Should you incorporate different-colored fonts to highlight your delivery cues?

Grasping Your Main Ideas While Practicing Your Delivery

- Practice your speech aloud. Do not worry the first few times you practice that you will not sound like you are ready to deliver the State of the Union address—just keep at it.
- You must focus on gaining command of the ideas of your presentation, and not try to learn the speech word for word.
- If you try to memorize your speech, your message will come across as stiff and not engaging to the audience.
- After a few runs through your speech you will capture the main ideas, examples, and statistics of your presentation.

Recording Your Delivery During the Practice Phase

- The best thing to do here is to record your speech either on video or by audio for you to capture how an audience will see and hear your message.

- You want to evaluate your eye contact, rate of speech, volume, articulation, pronunciation, vocal variety, and pauses.

- Next, ask a few of your friends, family, co-workers, or classmates to listen to your speech.

- Remember public speaking is an audience-focused activity so it is best to practice in front of people.

Chapter Eleven

Using Language to Maximize
Your Message

Using Language to Maximize
Your Message to Your Audience

- A strong understanding of who you are speaking to should guide you in your word choice.

  – For example if you are speaking to an audience with little or no familiarity with your topic, you must use elementary terms and communicate the most fundamental issues regarding your topic.

- On the flip side if you used advanced terminology with this same audience, the audience would be lost and become disinterested in your presentation.

- Your word choice can make or break the success of your speech, so think critically about your word choice.

Language is Symbolic

- Words are random symbols that do not have any significance in and of themselves.

- Language uses a symbol system to arrange, classify, and communicate thought.

- Our words are symbolic and indicate concrete objects and abstract thoughts.

Use Simple Language to Get Your Point Across

- In short you want your message to be clear and understandable for your audience.

- You never want to talk down to your audience or they will be insulted; instead speak directly to the audience using words that put across a clear and concrete message.

The Gettysburg Address

- The Gettysburg Address is probably one of the most memorable speeches in American history.

- In a little over two minutes Abraham Lincoln's Gettysburg Address contained 268 words, and only 18 of those words were more than two syllables.

- Interestingly, of the 18 multi-syllable words in Lincoln address, he used the word dedicate or dedication six times.

- The point is that using simple language that an audience can easily understand and remember will impact the audience.

Restate Your Message

- By restating your essential messages throughout your speech, you will allow your audience to absorb the heart of the message that you want them to walk away with.

The Use of Power Language will Strengthen Your Command at the Podium

- You communicate power by spending time thinking about the right words for your particular audience, and delivering them with absolute conviction.

- Moreover the delivery of your message needs to be free of stammering, stuttering, and continuous voiced pauses, such as, "uhm" or "uh..," and "like" or "you know."

The Language of Responsibility

- Taking responsibility for your language helps make the content of your message unambiguous and shape the tone of the relationship you will have with the audience.

- "It" statements usually replace the personal pronoun "I." "It" statements usually avoid responsibility and ownership of the message.

"But," "I," and "You," Language

- A "but" statement sounds like, "You have done a great job for us here, *but* I'm going to have to fire you."
  - The word "but" cancels the thought that came before it.
- "I" language shows that the speaker is taking responsibility in relating his or her position in a speech.
- "You" language by and large communicates a judgment of another person, which can offend an audience.
  - "You" language implies that the speaker is qualified to make the judgment for another person, so let us hope you have established the necessary credibility and goodwill to speak on the particular topic.

Levels of Abstraction

- Abstract words tend to be very general, broad, and not specific, whereas concrete words are specific, particular, and based on something you can see.
- (Concrete)
- 2010 Chevrolet Corvette
- Chevrolet
- General Motors
- Automotive
- Industry
- Commerce
- (Abstract)

Denotative and Connotative Words

- The **denotative meaning** of a word may be defined as the direct or explicit meaning or reference.
  - When looking for the denotative meaning of a word, you may look at the *dictionary* definition of the word.
- The **connotative meaning** of a term is the suggested or the emotional tone of the word.

Descriptive, Evaluative, and the Etymology of Language

- **Descriptive language** depicts a specific behavior or action.
- Conversely, **evaluative language** witnesses a particular behavior or action, and then attaches a subjective interpretation of that behavior or action.
- Sharing the etymology or the origin of the word will help your audience get a stronger understanding of where and how the word was derived.
  - For example a speaker may say something like this: "The word commit comes from the Latin word committere or "to bring together."

Using Inclusive Language

- When addressing an audience it is important that you build the spirit of inclusion as opposed to division.
- **Inclusive language** is language that unites an entire audience into your message, and that does not leave portions of your audience out of the mix.

Bringing Life to Your Words

- Using **literal language** uses words as facts; conversely, **figurative language** compares one concept to another similar but different concept.

Similes

- When a public speaker uses a **simile**, the speaker is making a clear comparison of two things that uses the word "like" or "as."
- Here are some examples of similes:
  - I'm stiff as a board
  - Runs like a deer

Metaphor

- A **metaphor** is the comparison of two dissimilar things in order to imply a resemblance.
- So when you use a metaphor you are transferring the qualities from one thing to another while showing their similarities.
- Here are some examples of some metaphors:
  - Life is not a sprint it is a marathon.
  - The doctor inspected the rash like a hawk.

Mixed Metaphor

- A **mixed metaphor** makes irrational comparisons between two or more things. When a speaker applies a mix in their metaphors, they begin with one metaphor and then half way through switch to another.
  - Keep your eye on the ball, your ear to the ground.

Personification

- A public speaker uses **personification** when he or she attributes human qualities (sight, speech, hearing, thought, emotion, action, or sensation) to animals, object, or concepts.

Rhythm

- **Rhythm** is the arrangement of words into a relationship so the sounds of the words together enhance the meaning of a phrase.

Parallelism

- When a public speaker coordinates related words so they are balanced or arranges related sentences so that they are identical in structure, the speaker is using parallelism.
- **Parallel:** The hiring supervisor was told to write his speech accurate*ly*, quick*ly*, and thorough*ly*.

Repetition

- Using **repetition** in a speech is when the speaker repeats keywords or phrases at the beginnings or endings of sentences or clauses.
- "Mad world! Mad kings! Mad composition!" (*King John*, by William Shakespeare)

Alliteration

- **Alliteration** may be defined the repetition of an initial consonant.
- Here are some examples using alliteration:
  - The *b*asketball *b*ounced *b*eyond the court into the *b*arrel.

Antithesis

- Using **antithesis** in a speech is when you place words and phrases in contrast or in disagreement with one another.
- Jim Elliot, an evangelical Christian missionary, used this antithesis, "He is no fool who gives what he cannot keep to gain that which he cannot lose."

Imagery

- The **imagery** descriptions would describe a human's senses: sight, sound, taste, touch, and smell.
- Birds are chirping
- Fresh out of the oven bread
- SweetTarts candy
- Scraping your knee on the asphalt
- The mansion on the hill

Gender and Language

- **Gender-linked** words are words that directly or indirectly categorize males or females, such as, policeman, fireman, congresswoman, or chairwoman.

- A **gender-neutral** style of language would say: police officer, firefighter, congressperson, or chairperson.

Chapter Twelve

Visual Aids

Adding Visual Aids to Your Presentation

- Adding visual aids to your speech can improve the clarity of your message.

- A properly used visual aid will contribute to making the speaker's ideas come alive, and assist the audience in retaining the information presented.

- As you go through the process of putting together a speech, when you have completed your preparation outline and are absolutely sure of the content of your speech, you can now think about how to communicate your key ideas using visual aids.

Types of Visual Aids to Improve your Message

- Adding visual aids to your speech can come in many forms such as the speaker, objects, models, photos, drawings, charts and graphs, transparencies, audio, and video.

The Speaker as a Visual Aid

- Often times the speaker may use themselves to show a dance step, a yoga position, a message in sign language, a particular cultural attire, or a tae kwon do move.

- When using yourself as a visual aid, spend time coordinating between you and the speaker's outline so that your visual does not drag on as you meet your desired time requirement.

Objects

- Any physical object may be used as a visual aid.
  - However, one thing to keep in mind is that the object needs to be large enough for the audience members in the back of the room to see, and small enough for you to carry around.

- Objects that have been used as a visual aids have ranged from rocks, to tools, to jewelry, to computers, to clocks.
  - If the object you plan to use is small do not pass it around the room while you are speaking.

Models

- If you are delivering a presentation in which your item is either too big or too small to easily present, then using a model can help you visualize that item for your audience.

- One advantage of using a model is that it is mobile and something you can use to show your audience from one end of the room to another.
  - Examples would be planes, lady bugs, or boats.

Photos

- Photos take an abstract idea and make it real for the audience to comprehend.
- A few questions you want to ask yourself are:
  - Is the photo large enough for your audience to see?
  - Does it capture the point I'm trying to make?
  - Should I place it on a transparency or PowerPoint for my audience to adequately see?

Drawings

- If you are looking for a more "authentic" approach than photos, then drawings may be your best bet.
- By physically drawing your picture you can tailor the drawing to the specific point you are trying to make.
- One major drawback to drawing is that it is time consuming and that takes away from other more important aspects of the public speaking process.

Graphs

- Graphs come in handy when you are discussing statistics and numerical data in your speech.
- Reciting numbers to an audience is hard on the ears, but can be easy on the eyes.
  - Graphs clarify statistics and difficult series of numbers, so as a courtesy to your audience consider graphing your numerical data.
- There are three kinds of graphs that you can use to illustrate your points more clearly for your audience, the *pie graph, the bar graph, and the line graph.*
- The **pie graph** is often used to show a percentage of the whole.

Pie Graphs

- The **pie graph** is often used to show a percentage of the whole.

- A pie graph should have between two and five wedges and no more than eight.

- For a picture of a pie graph please see an example pie graph in chapter 12.

Bar Graphs

- The **bar graph** may be used to show comparisons between two or more items.

- It usually does not matter whether you display the bars horizontally or in a column chart that displays the bars vertically on the chart.

- For a picture of a bar graph please see an example bar graph in chapter 12.

Line Graphs

- The most common graph used in a presentation is a **line graph** that uses one or more lines to show changes in statistics over time or space.

- The line graph would work well in demonstrating changes in statistics over time.

- For a picture of a line graph please see an example line graph in chapter 12.

Charts

- Charts are particularly helpful if there is information that you think your audience may want to jot down such as key phone numbers, addresses, or Web sites.
- A flow chart is a diagram that represents a process or a hierarchical structure.
- For a picture of a chart please see an example line graph in chapter 12.

Transparencies

- Transparencies displaying graphs, photos, charts, and tables are easy to use and produce.
    - They can be made from any computer and printed onto the transparency film directly from your printer.
- In addition it is frowned upon to write on your slides while delivering your presentation.
- As part of your preparation process become familiar with the overhead projector ahead of time so when you are delivering your speech you are not trying to figure out how to use the machine in front of your audience.

Video

- Video can be an excellent way to help you illustrate your message in motion.
- Moreover video technical difficulties take attention away from the speaker which may hurt how the audience perceives the speaker.
- If you do decide to use video, your clips need to be brief, well edited, and really hit the point you are trying to make.
- Limit your video or audio clips to no longer than 20 or so seconds.

Guiding Principles for Using Visual Aids

- After you have your preparation outline complete and the foundation of your speech has been established, the thought process of using a visual aid must be developed.

- Your choice of visual aids must add value to your message, and not get in the way of your message.

Critically Think Ahead When Implementing Visual Aids

- Organizing your speech preparation timeline well will allow you to think creatively about presenting visual aids that are simple and highlight your ideas clearly and accurately.

- Moreover, not every point in your presentation needs a visual aid; so do not clutter your speech with visuals.

Your Visuals Need to be Seen By Everyone

- A guiding principle for using visual aids is that everyone needs to be able see and read your aid.
  - Therefore, knowing the size of the room and other distinct characteristics of the room is vital when creating your visual aids.

- The common and accepted practice is to use dark print or lettering on a light background especially if you are using poster boards or an overhead transparency.

- If you are using a multimedia presentation like PowerPoint you may find that light print on a dark background works better.

Font Use and Your Visuals

- Recognized experts in using visual aids recommend using a 36-point font for your headings, a 24-point font for subtitles, and 18-point font for other text.

- Moreover, it is not recommended to use the ALL CAPS for your fonts. ALL CAPS make it difficult to read for your audience, and dilutes the importance of the words you are ALL CAPPING.

Don't Distract Your Audience with Your Visuals

- A sure way to create a distracting environment for delivering your speech is to pass out handouts while delivering your speech.

- Your audience's attention will be turned to viewing and passing your visual aids instead of listening to your address.

Your Visuals Must Support What You are Presenting

- Another tip that gets overlooked is to display your visual aid only when it corresponds to what you are talking about in your presentation.

- If you are discussing an object, chart, or photo keep it out of sight until you are ready to discuss it. When you finish your discussion regarding the visual aid, move the visual aid out of sight of the audience.

Body Position and Your Visual Aids

- How your body is positioned is an important feature when you are utilizing a visual aid.

- It is okay to briefly look at your visual, but you are required to make eye contact with the audience to gather the necessary feedback from your audience.

- Also, make sure that the visual aid you are using is not being blocked by you or other objects like a podium; your audience needs to be able to see what you are referring to in your presentation.

- In addition, you never want to turn your back to the audience or talk to the visual aid.

Think Simplicity When Using Multimedia Software for Your Presentations

- After completing your preparation outline you will need to think about picking and choosing your spots to use multimedia software.

- A potential drawback of working with PowerPoint is that the creator of the presentation focuses on awing the audience with all of the razzle-dazzle features as opposed to using simple graphics to add value to the message.

  - Sometimes the creators of the slide presentation think more sizzle than steak.

Using PowerPoint Slides

- When working with PowerPoint you will be working with **slides**, the single frame in a PowerPoint presentation.

Font Styles for Slides

- There are two categories to choose from when selecting a font, serif or sans-serif.
- **Serif fonts** have the little tails on each of the letters, whereas **sans-serif fonts** do not have the tails.
  - When a slide has a large amount of text the serif font is the preferred style.
- Conversely, the sans-serif fonts are used in slide titles, headings, and brief bulleted text-points.
- Titles and major headings are usually in the 46 to 36-point type range, whereas the subheads and other text are in the 32 to 24-point range.
- Lastly copyright credits use a 10-point font.

Information Overload on Your Slides

- A common error when using PowerPoint is to put too much information on one slide.

- The overload of information leads to clutter and confusion for the audience viewing the messy slide.

- There should be no more than six or seven lines on a slide if it is text only.

Photos and Your Multimedia Presentation

- If you are looking online for photos to use in your presentation, one place to go is Pics4Learning that shows thousands of free photos with no copyright restrictions.

- **Clip art** encompasses pictures and symbols representing common objects and ideas and can be retrieved from PowerPoint itself.

Videos and Your Multimedia Presentation

- PowerPoint also has the capability to incorporate video and sound into your presentation.

- Keep in mind that you want to keep your clips brief so use no more than 30 seconds of music, video, or lyrics from an individual musical work without obtaining permission.

Color Consistency and Your PowerPoint Slides

- Consistency in color is important throughout your PowerPoint presentation.
- It is customary to have one color for your background, one for your title, and one color for other text throughout the presentation.
- The consistent color patterns unify your message into a harmonious theme both in context and aesthetics.
- When using a LCD projector using a light text against a dark background provides the best contrast for your visuals.

Using Animation to Communicate Your Message

- Animation may be defined by how objects or text enter or exit a slide while presenting your speech.
- If you did not use the animation feature on PowerPoint all of the information on the slide would appear at the same time once the slide was displayed.
- By using the animation feature you control what and when the audience sees the information on your slides as it correlates to where you are in your speech.

Chapter Thirteen

Speaking at a Special Occasion

The Special Occasion Speech

- The ancient Greeks labeled special occasion speeches an *epideictic*.
  - An **epideictic** is a speech that one would deliver when you pay tribute to someone, present or accept an award, or acknowledge some kind of special occasion or event.
- Through the special occasion speech we are reminded of our culture, traditions, individual champions, and shared social values while offering inspiration and strength.
- We will be exploring the following different special occasion speeches: welcome and farewell speeches, commemorative, speech of introduction, receiving or accepting an award, and the after dinner speech.

Welcome Speeches

- The welcome speech must be brief and concise because the audience will be focused on the main events or activities of the occasion's purpose.
- First, the presenter needs to recognize the honored guests and key people who are in attendance.
- Next, briefly share with the audience the purpose of the occasion.
- Again the presenter must be mindful of the mood he or she wants to set in the welcome address.

Farewell Speeches

- There are two different perspectives from which a farewell speech may be delivered.
- One, the farewell speech may be delivered from the group who are staying in a particular place.
  - If you are saying goodbye to someone, create a brief introduction and create the emotional tone of the event.
- Next express the contributions the person may have had in the organization.
  - Finally, wish the person well in their new life.
- The general theme in a farewell speech is to show gratitude for the person's contributions to the organization.

Farewell Speeches (Continued)

- Another perspective on a farewell speech will be delivered by the person who is leaving and that person would be addressing the people who will be remaining at the company or organization.
- That person should talk briefly about their time at the organization and perhaps share stories, and thank those people who made their stay a good one.

Commemorative Speeches

- A commemoration is a ceremonial speech that marks an important date or event, and is usually presented at an event like a graduation, holiday, or a special local occasion to a particular community.
- When commemorating, analysis needs to be done in evaluating which specific values need to be highlighted in the address.

Paying Tribute

- Tribute speeches are another type of commemorative speech that are intended to honor, commend, and observe a person, a movement, or an organization.
- Presentations of tributes are usually offered at retirement parties, funerals, weddings, anniversaries, or birthday celebrations.
- Anecdotes and narratives are terrific ways to pay homage to the group or person being celebrated.
  - In addition, it is appropriate to give some biographical information, but stories using thoughtful language that reveal the person or group's moral fiber and individuality carry a tenor that will stick with the audience.
- The speech that pays tribute must convey appreciation, value, or respect to the person, occasion, or organization.

Speech of Introduction

- The purpose of a speech of introduction is to have the presenter deliver a brief introduction of the main speaker to an audience.
- The focus must be on the main speaker and *not* on the presenter introducing the main speaker.
- The principle of the speech of introduction is to share the main speaker's credentials, give a brief description of what the main speaker will be talking about, and generate great enthusiasm for both the person and the event.
- Moreover, a welcoming theme for the main speaker needs to be established.

Speech of Introduction (Continued)

- When introducing the main speaker being brief is important, so your introduction should not last longer than two minutes.
  - It is also a good idea to introduce yourself and how you fit in the occasion.
- A critical point in the speech of introduction is to pronounce the main speaker's name correctly, so you do not embarrass yourself and the main speaker.
  - Moreover, absolute accuracy is needed when sharing the speaker's credentials and experience.

Speech of Introduction
(Continued)

- Following the establishment of the speaker's credibility to speak to this particular audience, you will briefly share the general theme that the speaker will be talking about and build a brief bridge between the theme and how that pertains to the audience and the occasion.

- Another point to remember when delivering a speech of introduction is to not embarrass the speaker, where the speaker will feel uncomfortable delivering his/her speech.

Acceptance of an Award or Some Other Form of Public Recognition

- If you are given an award, or a promotion, or some other form of public recognition, an acceptance speech may be in order.

- The goal of the acceptance speech is to give thanks to those who helped you earn the award, and thank the organization that is presenting the award.

- Another important point to remember when accepting an award is to be brief.

Speech of Presentation of an Award or Some Other Form of Public Recognition

- The speech of presentation needs to address the purpose of the award and information about the person receiving the award.

- First, the presentation of an award should embody any background information about the recipient that will help the audience understand the purpose or circumstances of the award so they have the appropriate context.

Speech of Presentation of an Award or Some Other Form of Public Recognition

- Next, the speaker would explain the criteria used to select the recipient of the award.

- Finally, share the achievements of the person receiving the award.

  - Moreover, it is common to save the speaker's name for last as a way to build up suspense as to who will be the recipient of the award.

Speeches to Entertain
(After Dinner Speeches)

- Speeches to entertain are used to make a serious point via humor, light-hearted and other thought provoking means.

- The after dinner speech is different than an informative or persuasive speech, because your goal is not to inform or persuade, but to facilitate a diversion and offer food for thought in an interesting manner.

- Practicing your delivery is essential here, because it is not only what you say, but how you say it, so maximize that opportunity to deliver a strong message.

Chapter Fourteen

Speech to Inform

The Purpose of the Speech to Inform

- The purpose of the informative speech is to convey information or knowledge so your audience understands your topic more comprehensively.

- In short the informative speech can raise awareness, awaken interest, and enlighten your audience.

Principles of the Speech to Inform

- However, an important guideline for the informative speech is that it does not persuade or advocate for a particular cause or purpose.

- The informative speech needs to be communicated clearly, accurately, and grippingly to your specific audience.

- The precision and accuracy of the information you are presenting must be top priorities when delivering an informative speech.

- There are four kinds of informative speeches that we will be discussing in this chapter: descriptions/objects, processes, events, and explanations/concepts.

Informative Speeches About Descriptions or Objects

- Many of your informative speech topics will be derived from some sort of object, which may be defined as something that is tangible and secure in form.

- Objects may be people, places, things, animals, building, structures, or cars—just to name a few.

Organizing Informative Speeches about Descriptions or Objects

- If you decide to explain the evolution of your object you may want to consider organizing your speech chronologically.

- If you decide to describe particular features of your object, consider using the spatial (directional pattern) order to organize your speech.

- Generally speaking, many of the informative speeches that fall under the object category will be organized using the topical order.

Informative Speeches About Processes

- When delivering a speech about a process you are expressing a chain of actions that lead to an outcome, result, or product.
  - The process speech clarifies how something is done, made, or how something works.
- There are two different directions you can take the process speech.
  - The first direction is to explain the steps of the process and how those steps relate to each other, and how that leads to a final output.
  - The second direction you can take a process speech would be to explain how to *perform* the respective steps of the process that lead to an end result.
- The strongest organizational strategy to use would be the chronological order, which starts at the beginning of the process and goes through each of the steps involved, until you reach the end of the process and the final output.

Informative Speeches
About Events

- An informative speech about an event may be defined as a happening.

- The key in informing your audience about an event is to emphasize the meaning of the event in language that helps your audience understand its true level of importance.

- Therefore the causal organizational strategy would be appropriate for this kind of speech.

Informative Speeches of
Explanations or Concepts

- Speeches about concepts embrace theories, ideas, principles, and philosophies- topics that are more abstract in form.

- If you are discussing an explanation/concept topic you must be able to define the concept's main points or parts, its significance, and concrete examples to make it more real for your audience to comprehend.

- Because the discussion about abstract ideas may be difficult for your audience to grasp, special consideration to use visual aids would help your audience understand your message easier.

Informative Speeches and
Your Audience

- A strong audience analysis will help you know the level of knowledge your audience may have about your topic, guiding you know what and how to present your information.

- Other findings you can learn from your audience survey will help you build a bridge between your topic and the relevance of your topic to the audience's interests and needs.

- The goal as a public speaker is to take the most complex ideas and simplify them for your audience by using understandable words.

Informative Speeches and Your Audience (Continued)

- Your audience will be thinking "what's in it for me?" and your job is to fill in those blanks and answer that question for them.

- If you are able to relate your speech specifically to the needs of your audience, you will be a very successful public speaker.

Message Overload and the Informative Speech

- A common error made by public speakers is delivering an informative speech that tries to pack in too much information that an audience member cannot realistically absorb.

- Limiting your main points to between two and five will allow you to not overwhelm your audience with too much information.

- The quality of your information in your speech needs to be accurate and timely.

- In addition, take extra care in citing your sources accurately and quote your material in its proper context.

Chapter Fifteen

Speech to Persuade

The Purpose of Persuasive Speaking

- When you are persuading an audience, your purpose is to have your audience agree with you and your position, and/or take action on behalf of your message.

- Persuading your audience obliges you the speaker to communicate information clearly, correctly, and convincingly to influence the listener's opinions, ethics, and actions.

Knowing All Sides to the Persuasive Argument

- In order to be a truly effective persuasive public speaker it is your responsibility to know all sides of the issue and not just the position you are advocating.

- By understanding the wide range of perspectives of the issue, you will be able to address the opposing points of view that may be shared by the audience, only to disprove them.

Credibility and the
Persuasive Speech

- Generating your "ethos" is a two-pronged approach:
- 1) establishing your expertise and knowledge base regarding the given topic and
- 2) developing your character or goodwill toward the audience with your speech.

Credibility and
First Hand Experience

- Your audience needs to know that you have some first-hand experience or have utilized reliable sources and/or are using highly regarded testimony for your given topic.
- Another concern that may arise is "how about if I don't have first-hand experience with my subject matter, how am I supposed to sound credible to my audience?"
- The quality of research sources you use to support your message becomes more important.
  - By using highly respected and well-known experts in the field as your expert testimony and including the views of others who have first-hand experience, you can boost your peer testimony which will serve you well as you advocate for a particular issue.

Looking Out for Your Audience
Helps Your Credibility

- Your audience needs to have that same feeling from you when you deliver your persuasive speech.
- When your audience believes and senses that you are looking out for *their* best interest, they are sure to follow along with your message.

Communicating Goodwill Towards Your Audience

- A sure way to build that strong relationship with your audience is to be honest in what you are presenting, and stay away from clever ways to deceive and misguide your audience.

- Moreover, you can communicate goodwill for your audience by presenting their thoughts, feelings, and concerns in your presentation from their feedback from their surveys.

- Once a person feels that they have been heard, the communication channels between the speaker and the audience are now open, and your audience will be more inclined to be receptive to your message.

Persuasion is More Demanding Than Informing an Audience

- Persuading your audience is much more demanding than informing an audience.

- The test comes in the area of audience analysis, which requires more scrutiny of what makes your audience tick.

- Understanding your audience's attitudes, values, and beliefs will give you the competitive edge when persuading your audience.

Handling Audience Skepticism in a Persuasive Speech

- Entering into your persuasive speech, have a realistic approach as to what you can achieve with your presentation.

- While listening to your presentation, your audience will be continuously judging you by the quality of your arguments, your evidence (examples, statistics, and testimony), your sources, your emotional appeals, and your delivery.

- In addition, the listeners are expecting you to answer their skepticism about you the speaker and your speech topic.

Three Categories of Audience Members

- The first camp will be in support of your position, the second camp will be those undecided to your position, and the third camp will be those who are adamantly against your position.
- By distinguishing the three sets of people in your audience you can now tailor your message to the group who is most persuadable, the undecided group.

Request Moderate Changes from Your Target Audience

- The undecided group is also known as your **target audience**. You never want to disregard any part of your audience, but special attention is needed in analyzing the group in the undecided camp.
- A familiar slip-up made by persuasive speakers is to ask for radical changes of their audience. A more prudent approach would be to request small, doable, and incremental changes to their actions, values, or beliefs.

Types of Persuasive Speeches

- There are three types of persuasive speeches, the question of fact, the question of value, and the question of policy.

Questions of Fact

- However, many questions of fact cannot be answered definitively, and are in the form of predictions.
  - For example: will the Dow Jones Industrial hit 15,000 by 2011?
- When delivering a question of fact type of persuasive speech you are presenting your speech from the place of a promoter and supporter of your specific purpose.

Organizing Questions of Fact

- A frequent organizational strategy for a question of fact is the topical strategy.
- Another organizational strategy that may be beneficial for the question of fact is to use the spatial order.

Goals for the Question of Fact

- The goal of the question of fact speech for these examples is to persuade the audience to accept a specific point of view regarding each of the topics.
- Whatever your specific purpose is for your question of fact presentation, relevant examples, trustworthy statistics, and believable testimony are needed to support your specific purpose.

Questions of Value

- The question of value is based on a value judgment, based on the speaker's belief about what is fair or unfair, right or wrong, correct or incorrect, good or bad, moral or immoral, just or unjust.
- It is important to remember that when addressing the question of value, you are not merely spouting your opinions with little or no supporting materials to strengthen your argument.
- Strong sources of information and a well-organized speech will enhance your status in the eyes of the audience.
- When delivering a question of value speech, specific thought must be considered towards the standards you have established in your value judgment.

Questions of Policy

- Unlike the question of value, the question of policy speech demands a specific course of action from the audience.
- However, what distinguishes the question of policy from the question of fact and the question of value is that something should or should not be done.
- There are two types of agreement that you will need to decide on for your question of policy, passive agreement or active agreement.
  - If your aim is to have your audience reach **passive agreement** with you, you want the audience to concur that the policy you have selected is desirable, but you will not have your audience do anything to realize the particular policy.

Immediate Action and the Question of Policy

- When crafting your specific purpose for the question of policy the word "should" is usually used in your statement.
- **Immediate action** prompts your audience to take a specific, doable action towards your specific purpose.
  - Once your audience takes an action toward your specific purpose, the audience will be more committed to the particular cause.

Requirements for the Questions of Policy: Need-Plan-Practicality

- The first area you need to address in a question of policy is the *need*. Your audience needs to get a sense that a change to an existing policy is needed and it is your job to illustrate that point.
  - The burden of proof will sit squarely on the shoulders of the speaker that there is a need to change. The **burden of proof** may be defined as "the responsibility of the persuasive speaker to establish that a change from an existing policy exists."

Requirements for the Questions of Policy: Need-Plan-Practicality

- The next area to address in a question of policy is the *plan* to change an existing policy. With most plans that are proposed there will be gaps from the audience's perspective that need to be addressed.
- The final piece to address in a question of policy will be the *practicality* of the plan for the speaker's new policy.
  - Your new plan is going to have to stand up to this question, "will this plan solve the problem, or will it create even more problems?"

Organizing the Question of Policy

- When delivering your question of policy speech, you have four options that will help you organize your speech effectively.
- Common organizational strategies used are: problem-solution, problem-cause-solution, comparative advantages order, and Monroe's motivated sequence.

Problem-Solution Order

- The problem-solution order has two main points.
- The first main point addresses the problem, or the need that a problem does exist.
- The second main point examines the plan for the solution to the problem and the practicality of your plan.

The Problem-Cause-Solution

- The problem-cause-solution order produces three main points to persuade the speaker's audience to take a specific course of action.
- The first main point speaks to the problem, the second main point accounts for the causes to the problem, and the third main point offers a solution to the problem in the specific purpose.

The Comparative Advantages Order

- The comparative advantages order occurs when your audience is in harmony that a problem exists and needs to be remedied.
- Since there is agreement that a problem exists, your efforts and speech development can be focused on the advantages and disadvantages to a particular plan of action to solve a specific problem.
- When using the comparative advantages order organizational strategy, each of your main points will be amplifying why your solution is favorable to other proposed solutions.

Monroe's Motivated Sequence

- Monroe's motivated sequence was developed by Alan Monroe from Purdue University in the 1930's. There are five points to cover in the Monroe's motivated sequence strategy.
1. Attention
2. Need
3. Satisfaction
4. Visualization
5. Action

Monroe's Motivated Sequence

Specific Purpose: To persuade my audience…
Central Idea:

		Introduction
(Attention)	I.	
		Body
(Need)	I.	
(Satisfaction)	II.	
(Visualization)	III.	
		Conclusion
(Action)	I.	

Chapter Sixteen

Techniques of Persuasion

Factors of Credibility

- Competence and character are two primary traits that are often evaluated when persuading another person.
- Character and competence are the cornerstones of the principle of *ethos* from the great Greek philosopher Aristotle.
- **Competence** is how an audience regards the speaker's intelligence, expertise, and knowledge of the subject matter.

Character and Credibility

- **Character** also demonstrates concern for the audience's best interest.
- The audience will continuously be assessing the speaker's honesty, trustworthiness, and believability, including whether the speaker has the audience's best interest at heart.
- Credibility must pass the audience's judgment of legitimacy and authenticity and not the speaker's belief in their own credibility.

Phases of Credibility

- **Initial credibility** is the credibility of the speaker *before* he or she starts to deliver their speech.
- **Derived credibility** is the credibility formed from the time the speaker starts his/her speech to the time the speech is completed.
  - The audience will scrutinize the speaker's message, strength of evidence and support, emotional appeals, organization, audience adaptation, quality of research, catchiness of the introduction and conclusion, and the fluidity of the speaker's delivery.

Phases of Credibility (Continued)

- Last but not least is **terminal credibility**, which occurs after the speech is complete and the entire presentation is marinating with the audience.

Building Common Ground with Your Audience

- Creating a common ground with your audience is essential in a speech to persuade setting.
  - If you are able to identify with your listeners, then your listeners will be more inclined to listen to your message.
- By stressing the common understanding of the predicament, the speaker will hit it off with the audience, and once that commonality is established, it is easier to move into more controversial points to your persuasive speech.

How Delivery Impacts Persuasion

- However, using vocal variety surely adds value to your persuasiveness as opposed to a monotonous tone of voice.

- The kiss of death in poor delivery is the speaker who consistently loses his/her place, hesitates, and masters the vocalized pauses such as "uhm, uh, er..." your audience will discredit you in a heartbeat.

- When you diligently practice your delivery, you will then be able to speak with conviction.

Improving Your Credibility Through the Use of Supporting Materials

- The supporting materials in your speech, such as the examples, statistics, and testimony, will be your tools to prove or disprove the ideas in your persuasive speech.

- When analyzing your supporting materials during the research phase of your preparation you must continuously ask yourself, "Do these examples, statistics, and testimony support my specific purpose?"

Emotions and the Persuasive Plea

- Tapping into the emotions of the audience, such as feelings of sadness, happiness, anger, or sympathy, will likely move the audience towards a specific course of action or a change in position or point of view.

- A way to generate the necessary emotional appeal is through your choice of language in your speech.

- However, using too many emotionally charged words in a short span of time can put off many listeners or weaken your message, so use them sparingly.

- The underlying purpose of emotional appeals is to complement your evidence and reasoning and not use emotional appeals as a substitute for persuasion.

Reasoning

- As a speaker it is your responsibility to walk your audience through your thoughts which led to the desired conclusion or outcome of your persuasive speech.

- **Reasoning** may be defined as the process of drawing a conclusion on the basis of evidence.

Reasoning from Specific Instances

- When you reason from a specific instance, you take a few particular instances, and then make a general conclusion based on those specific instances.
  - Reasoning from specific instances to general conclusions is also known as **inductive reasoning**.
- Gaining a strong grasp of representative samples is challenging since it forces the speaker to make a hypothesis about the distinctiveness that might be most significant to the generalization.

Reasoning from Principle

- Reasoning from principle progresses from the general to specific, just the opposite from reasoning from specific instances.
  - Reasoning from principle is also known as **deductive reasoning**.

Causal Reasoning

- **Causal reasoning** is when the speaker attempts to create a relationship between the causes and effects of a given situation.
- There are two common errors to avoid when using causal reasoning. The first is the fallacy of false cause which is often referred by its Latin name, *post hoc, ergo propter hoc*, translated as "after this, therefore because of this."
  - In other words, the fact that one episode happens after another does not mean that the first episode is the sole cause of the second episode.
- The second error to avoid in causal reasoning is assuming that events have only one singular cause.
  - An ordinary approach to causal reasoning is to assign an event to a single remote cause, yet the majority of events may have numerous causes.
  - The responsible advocate qualifies his/her statements and admits that there is not a single or exclusive cause to the complex problem.

Analogical Reasoning

- **Analogical reasoning** examines whether the two instances being compared are fundamentally the same.
  - If the two instances are fundamentally the same, the analogy is valid. On the other hand if the two instances are not fundamentally the same, the analogy is invalid.
- Your analogical reasoning will gain traction and be more persuasive the more clear-cut the analogy is to a comparable situation.

Fallacies

- A **fallacy** is an error in reasoning or evidence.
- Fallacies often occur when the speaker states unconnected conclusions, applies flawed reasoning, presents poor evidence, or succumbs to personal attacks.

Red Herring

- The **red herring fallacy** brings up an unrelated issue simply to divert attention from the argument or point that is being discussed.
- Often times using the red herring fallacy in a persuasive speech is an attempt to throw an audience off-target with an emotional matter that prevents the heart of the issue to be analyzed by the audience.

Ad Hominem

- The **ad hominem fallacy** refers to the fallacy of attacking the person rather than taking up the real issue in the debate.
  - In political elections, the integrity and character of a candidate is often addressed regardless of the issue being discussed.

Bandwagon

- The **bandwagon fallacy** assumes that because something is popular, it must be good, appropriate, or advantageous.

Slippery Slope

- A speaker who commits the **slippery slope fallacy** suggests that taking a first step will lead to a second step and so on all the way down the slope.

The Hasty Generalization

- The **fallacy of hasty generalization** occurs when a generalization of a claim is made based on too-little evidence.

Guilt by Association

- **Guilt by association** occurs when we judge a program, a proposal, or a person exclusively on their association with other programs, proposals, or persons.

The Final Word on Fallacies

- Fallacies generate conclusions that do not flow rationally from the evidence presented.
- Fallacies are merely a way to divert attention from the real issue at hand.

BROTHER AGAINST BROTHER
The War Begins

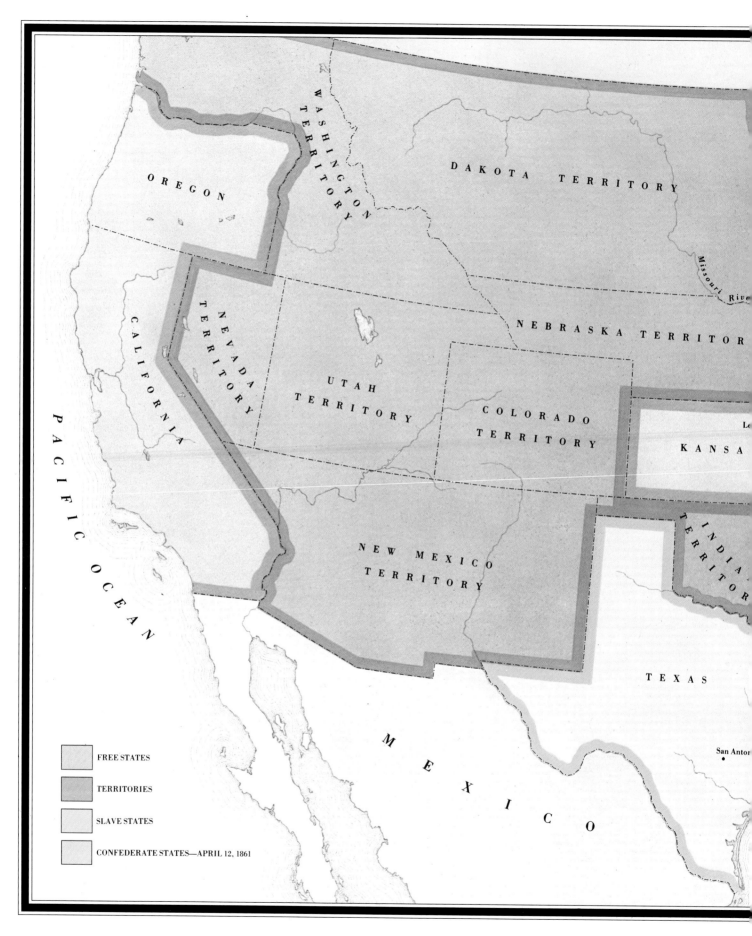

PACIFIC OCEAN

WASHINGTON TERRITORY

OREGON

DAKOTA TERRITORY

Missouri River

NEBRASKA TERRITORY

CALIFORNIA

NEVADA TERRITORY

UTAH TERRITORY

COLORADO TERRITORY

Le

KANSA

INDIA
TERRITOR

NEW MEXICO TERRITORY

TEXAS

MEXICO

San Anton

FREE STATES

TERRITORIES

SLAVE STATES

CONFEDERATE STATES—APRIL 12, 1861

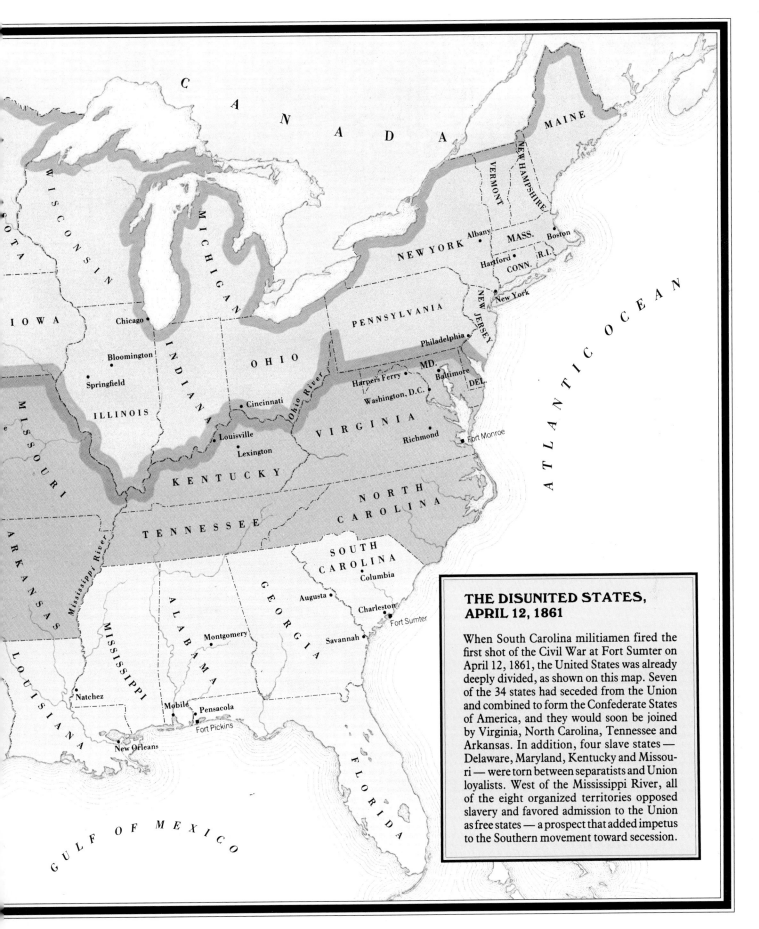

THE DISUNITED STATES, APRIL 12, 1861

When South Carolina militiamen fired the first shot of the Civil War at Fort Sumter on April 12, 1861, the United States was already deeply divided, as shown on this map. Seven of the 34 states had seceded from the Union and combined to form the Confederate States of America, and they would soon be joined by Virginia, North Carolina, Tennessee and Arkansas. In addition, four slave states — Delaware, Maryland, Kentucky and Missouri — were torn between separatists and Union loyalists. West of the Mississippi River, all of the eight organized territories opposed slavery and favored admission to the Union as free states — a prospect that added impetus to the Southern movement toward secession.

TIME® LIFE BOOKS

This volume is one of a series that chronicles in full the
events of the American Civil War, 1861-1865. Other books in
the series include:

The Cover: Two young Americans, now enemy
soldiers fighting for the Union *(left)* and the
Confederacy, stand stiffly for portraits taken early
in the Civil War. This was the first war to be
covered in detail by the camera, and soldiers sent
many pictures home as mementos.

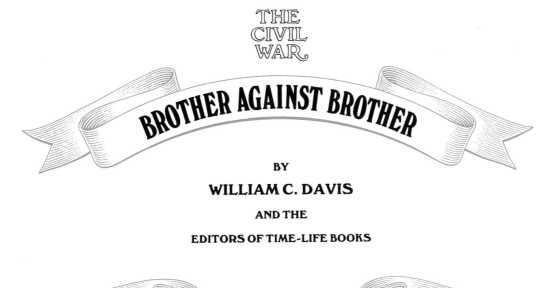

THE
CIVIL
WAR

BROTHER AGAINST BROTHER

BY

WILLIAM C. DAVIS

AND THE

EDITORS OF TIME-LIFE BOOKS

The War Begins

TIME-LIFE BOOKS, ALEXANDRIA, VIRGINIA

Time-Life Books Inc.
is a wholly owned subsidiary of

TIME INCORPORATED

FOUNDER: Henry R. Luce 1898-1967

Editor-in-Chief: Henry Anatole Grunwald
Chairman and Chief Executive Officer: J. Richard Munro
President and Chief Operating Officer: N. J. Nicholas Jr.
Chairman of the Executive Committee: Ralph P. Davidson
Corporate Editor: Ray Cave
Executive Vice President, Books: Kelso F. Sutton
Vice President, Books: George Artandi

TIME-LIFE BOOKS INC.

EDITOR: George Constable
Executive Editor: Ellen Phillips
Director of Design: Louis Klein
Director of Editorial Resources: Phyllis K. Wise
Editorial Board: Russell B. Adams Jr., Thomas H.
Flaherty, Lee Hassig, Donia Ann Steele, Rosalind
Stubenberg, Kit van Tulleken, Henry Woodhead
Director of Photography and Research:
John Conrad Weiser

PRESIDENT: Christopher T. Linen
Chief Operating Officer: John M. Fahey Jr.
Senior Vice Presidents: James L. Mercer,
Leopoldo Toralballa
Vice Presidents: Stephen L. Bair, Ralph J. Cuomo, Neal
Goff, Stephen L. Goldstein, Juanita T. James, Hallett
Johnson III, Carol Kaplan, Susan J. Maruyama, Robert
H. Smith, Paul R. Stewart, Joseph J. Ward
Director of Production Services: Robert J. Passantino

The Civil War

Editor: Gerald Simons
Designer: Herbert H. Quarmby
Chief Researcher: Jane Edwin

Editorial Staff for *Brother against Brother*
Associate Editors: Henry Woodhead (text);
Richard Kenin (pictures)
Staff Writers: Adrienne George, C. Tyler Mathisen,
John Newton, Kirk Y. Saunders
Researchers: Harris J. Andrews, Sara Schneidman
(principals); Betsy Friedberg, Brian C. Pohanka,
Alfreda Robertson, Jayne Wise
Assistant Designer: Jeanne Potter
Copy Coordinators: Allan Fallow, Victoria Lee,
Brian Miller
Picture Coordinators: Rebecca Christoffersen,
Eric Godwin
Editorial Assistant: Annette T. Wilkerson
Special Contributor: Peter Chaitin

Editorial Operations
Copy Chief: Diane Ullius
Editorial Operations Manager: Caroline A. Boubin
Production: Celia Beattie
Quality Control: James J. Cox (director)
Library: Louise D. Forstall

Correspondents: Elisabeth Kraemer-Singh
(Bonn); Maria Vincenza Aloisi (Paris); Ann Natanson
(Rome). Valuable assistance was also provided by: Gail
Cameron Wescott (Atlanta); Juliette Tomlinson
(Boston); Cheryl Crooks (Los Angeles); Cronin Buck
Sleeper (Manchester Center, Vermont); Lynne Bachleda
(Nashville); Carolyn Chubet (New York); Enid Farmer
(Trevett, Maine).

The editors also thank the following individuals who
gathered picture material for the Civil War series:
Marion F. Briggs, Esther Brumberg, Diane Cook,
Rosemary George, Catherine Gregory, Robin Raffer,
Mariana Tait.

Library of Congress Cataloguing in Publication Data
Davis, William C., 1946-
  Brother against brother.
  (Civil War series; v. 1)
  1. United States — History — Civil War, 1861-1865 —
Causes. I. Time-Life Books. II. Title. III. Series.
E459.D265 1983   973.7'11   82-17014
ISBN 0-8094-4700-2 (retail ed.)
ISBN 0-8094-4701-0 (lib. bdg.)
ISBN 0-8094-4702-9

The Author:
William C. Davis was for 13 years editor of the *Civil W[ar]
Times Illustrated* and is the author or editor of more than [a]
dozen books on the Civil War, among them *Battle at B[ull]
Run, The Orphan Brigade* and *The Deep Waters of th[e]
Proud,* the first in a three-volume narrative of the War. H[e]
is also editor of the six-volume photographic history of th[e]
conflict, *The Image of War: 1861-1865.*

The Consultants:
Colonel John R. Elting, USA (Ret.), a former Associat[e]
Professor at West Point, is the author of *Battles for Scand[i]
navia* in the Time-Life Books World War II series and *Th[e]
Battle of Bunker's Hill, The Battles of Saratoga, Militar[y]
History and Atlas of the Napoleonic Wars* and *America[n]
Army Life.* He is also editor of the three volumes of *Mil[i]
tary Uniforms in America, 1755-1867,* and associate edit[or]
of *The West Point Atlas of American Wars.*

James I. Robertson Jr. is C. P. Miles Professor of Histor[y]
at Virginia Tech. The recipient of the Nevins-Freema[n]
Award and other prizes in the field of Civil War history, h[e]
has written or edited some 20 books, which include *Th[e]
Stonewall Brigade, Civil War Books: A Critical Bibliogr[a]
phy* and *Civil War Sites in Virginia.*

William A. Frassanito, a Civil War historian and lecture[r]
specializing in photograph analysis, is the author of tw[o]
award-winning studies, *Gettysburg: A Journey in Time* an[d]
*Antietam: The Photographic Legacy of America's Bloodie[st]
Day.* He has also served as chief consultant to the phot[o]
graphic history series *The Image of War.*

Les Jensen, Curator of the U.S. Army Transportatio[n]
Museum at Fort Eustis, Virginia, specializes in Civil Wa[r]
artifacts and is a conservator of historic flags. He is [a]
contributor to *The Image of War* series, a freelance write[r]
and consultant for numerous Civil War publications an[d]
museums, and a member of the Company of Military His[
torians. He was formerly Curator of the Museum of th[e]
Confederacy in Richmond, Virginia.

Michael McAfee specializes in military uniforms and ha[s]
been Curator of Uniforms and History at the West Poin[t]
Museum since 1970. A fellow of the Company of Militar[y]
Historians, he coedited with Colonel John Elting *Lon[g]
Endure: The Civil War Years,* and he collaborated wit[h]
Frederick Todd on *American Military Equipage, 1851[-]
1872.* He has written numerous articles for *Military Im[
ages Magazine,* as well as *Artillery of the American Revolu[
tion, 1775-1783.*

James P. Shenton, Professor of History at Columbia Uni[
versity, is a specialist in 19th Century American politica[l]
and social history, with particular emphasis on the Civi[l]
War period. He is the author of *Robert John Walker* an[d]
Reconstruction South.

CONTENTS

Smoke-belching steamboats dock at the New Orleans levee at the mouth of the Mississippi. The mighty river bound North and South in mutually beneficial trade.

The Two Americas

"It is no more possible for this country to pause in its career than for the free and untrammeled eagle to cease to soar," exulted Florida Congressman Stephen R. Mallory in 1859. And he had plenty of reason for optimism.

The decade of the 1850s brought the United States exceptional growth and prosperity. The population increased by 35 per cent, to more than 31 million. Railroad trackage more than trebled, reaching 30,000 miles. The production of all kinds of foodstuffs and manufactured goods rose dramatically. And the country had enormous resources to sustain its phenomenal progress: vast unoccupied lands, a network of navigable rivers, incalculable riches in timber, iron, coal, copper, California gold.

It was true that the 1850s also exacerbated the political tensions between North and South. But in the cold light of economics, the sections were interdependent—perhaps inseparable. Southern plantations provided bountiful raw materials for the industrial North, and Northern factories made most of the finished goods consumed by the South. "In brief and in short," concluded Senator Thomas Hart Benton of Missouri, "the two halves of this Union were made for each other as much as Adam and Eve."

Boom Time in the Cotton Kingdom

The famed Southern boast that "Cotton is king!" became increasingly true in the 1850s. Though many plantations thrived on rice, tobacco and other cash crops, more and more land was planted in cotton to meet the demands of British and Yankee textile mills, and more and more slaves were put to work bringing in the harvests. The annual yield soared from two million bales in 1849 to 5.7 million bales in 1859. This amounted to seven eighths of the world's cotton and more than half of all American exports.

Slaves pick cotton while oth[er] process the harvest in a cotton gin[?] stacks exhaling smoke at rear. [?] cotton was planted in spring and e[?] summer; the picking, ginning, ba[?] and shipping lasted into early win[ter]

A workaday plantation comprises a big house *(center)* flanked by slave quarters, smokehouses, gardens and stockyards. Large plantations were virtually self-sufficient.

Laboring alongside hired whites, a gang of slaves harvests rice under a planter's direction. A planter would consider it a good year if each field slave produced a profit of $250.

The Lordly Life of the Landed Gentry

The popular notion of life in the South was set by a small minority, the well-to-do planters. They liked to think of themselves as heirs to the traditions of the knights and cavaliers, and they played the part stylishly, practicing chivalry toward women, kindness to inferiors and an elaborate code of honor among equals. The planters cultivated a taste for blooded horses, fine foxhounds, handmade firearms, and Southern belles of affluent families. And many studied the arts of war. A Mississippi planter, Jefferson Davis, said with pride that only in the South did "gentlemen go to a military academy who do not intend to follow the profession of arms."

Spectators head toward the Oakland House and Race Course in Louisville, Kentucky. Planters, by and large, were keen judges of horseflesh and inveterate bettors. Some brought surplus slaves to the races to back especially large bets.

Wealthy Virginians gather at a river for a mass baptism. Virginia's Tidewater planters tended to be Episcopalians. According to an old local saying, there were many ways to go to heaven, but a gentleman would choose the Episcopalian way.

A plantation owner on horseback holds his gun at the ready while his dogs attack a stag. Southern men, rich and poor alike, learned to ride and shoot in early boyhood.

Southern belles ascend a grand staircase while their beaux wait at the foot. Lavish house parties and balls were held frequently by wealthy planters. "The Northerner loves to make money," noted a Mississippian, "the Southerner to spend it."

Huntsville, Alabama, has a rural look in this view, painted around 1850. "From the quiet appearance of their towns," said a visiting Yankee, "the stranger would think business was taking a siesta."

A Realm of Sleepy Towns and Scattered Hamlets

"Every step one takes in the South," wrote a British visitor in 1856, "one is struck with the rough look of the whole civilization. Towns and villages are few and far between." Cities were scarcer still, and practically all of them were relatively small; Charleston, Richmond and Savannah each had populations of less than 40,000. Only New Orleans, with about 150,000 inhabitants, was comparable to Northern cities in size and diversity.

The bucolic landscape and the slow, agrarian life were just what most Southerners desired. Said an Alabama politician: "We want no manufactures; we desire no trading, no mechanical or manufacturing classes. As long as we have our rice, our sugar, our tobacco and our cotton, we can command wealth to purchase all we want."

In Athens, Georgia, the buildings of Franklin College (later the University of Georgia) stand atop a wooded hill (left) across the Oconee River from the terminus of the Georgia Railway. Though Athens was founded in 1801, it had only 3,848 inhabitants by 1860.

Melting Pots for New Americans

In marked contrast to their Southern counterparts, Northern cities were crowded, bustling, boisterous places, many expanding too fast to digest their growth. The population of New York soared from 515,000 to 814,000 in the 1850s. Chicago, incorporated as a city in 1837 with a population of 4,170, had 112,000 inhabitants in 1860.

Foreign voices were heard on all sides. Between 1850 and 1860, more than 2.8 million immigrants poured into port cities; nearly one half of the New York population was foreign-born. Most of the immigrants drudged long hours for meager pay and lived in squalor. But they adapted readily to their new country, embraced its egalitarian values and made great strides as Americans. By the 1850s, the Irish had become political powers in Boston, Philadelphia and New York, and the Germans were the dominant voting bloc in St. Louis and Milwaukee.

Many Americans resented the foreign influx, but others exulted in it. "We are not a narrow tribe of men whose blood has been debased by maintaining an exclusive succession among ourselves," wrote novelist Herman Melville. "No: our blood is as the flood of the Amazon, made up of a thousand noble currents all pouring into one."

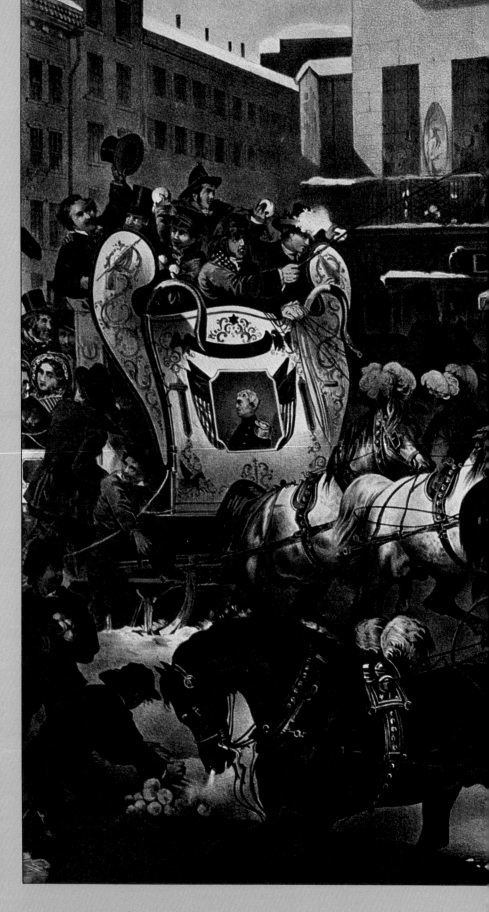

A wild snowball fight among rowdy New Yorkers disrupts traffic in front of P. T. Barnum's curiosity museum in lower Manhattan in 1855. Rivalries between neighborhoods, ethnic groups and political clubs often led to pitched battles in the streets.

BARNUM'S MUSEUM.

17

The North's "Great, Silent Revolution"

Throughout the 1850s, the North industrialized at almost breakneck speed. By the close of the decade, the Northern states contained four fifths of America's factories, two thirds of the nation's railroad mileage and practically all of its shipyards. The New York *Tribune* described the economic development of the North as "a great, silent revolution."

But the revolution was not really noiseless at all. It thrived on clattering, roaring phalanxes of new machines: circular saws, power looms, rotary presses, hydraulic turbines, shoe peggers, sewing machines, steam locomotives, corn planters, wheat drills, reapers, road scrapers, posthole augers. These inventions and countless others made "Yankee ingenuity" an international byword, and when Samuel Colt of Connecticut perfected the use of standardized, mass-produced, interchangeable components for his revolver, the British dubbed his method of manufacturing "the American system."

Workers fashion railroad forgings at rolling mill in New Jersey. In the railroad craze of the 1850s, a number of lines went broke by overbuilding or engaging in rate-cutting wars.

Factories in Pittsburgh spew clouds of smoke in this 1838 painting. Pittsburgh owed its success to an enormous vein of bituminous coal that ran beneath the city and to iron-ore deposits nearby.

Standing in the bow of a bobbing boat, a Yankee harpooner prepares to deliver the death blow to a foundering whale. In the 1850s, when whaling was at its peak, more than 700 New England-based ships ranged the globe, bringing home catches worth an average of eight million dollars a year.

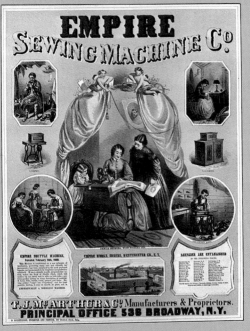

A sewing-machine advertisement features improved models for the home and workshop. By 1859, Northern factories were turning out 37,000 machines a year.

Yankee families socialize while making maple sugar *(top)* and apple cider *(detail, bottom)*. Such farm products were moved rapidly to urban markets on New England's extensive transportation system.

Living By a Gospel of Hard Work

Northern prosperity was deeply grounded in the Protestant work ethic. Ministers and itinerant evangelists preached a gospel of hard work, thrift and self-discipline. Worldly success was interpreted as a sign of God's favor, but labor was considered to be an end in itself rather than merely a means to an end.

Nowhere was this austere creed practiced more faithfully than on the many small farms of New England, where families produced a great variety of vegetables, fruit, poultry and dairy goods. Here the work ethic fostered excellence. "Fifty acres properly managed," wrote a progressive Yankee, "will produce more than 500 badly conducted."

An evangelist exhorts a swooning crowd at a revival meeting. Preachers at such gatherings painted grim word pictures of the evils of drink. Partly as a result, the per capita intake of alcohol dropped and the productivity of labor rose sharply.

Neighboring Yankee farmers join forces to harvest a crop of hay along the shores of the Acushnet River in southeastern Massachusetts.

Pride and Peril in the "Wisest System Ever Devised"

When Andrew Jackson described Americans as "guardians of freedom for the human race," and when James K. Polk spoke of American government as "this most admirable and wisest system ever devised," the Presidents' sentiments were not considered hyperbolic by the vast majority of their countrymen. To Northerners and Southerners alike, such statements represented the truth, pure and simple.

Besides their abiding faith in democratic ideals, Americans everywhere shared an avid interest in the political process that translated those ideals into practice. Patriotic celebrations on the Fourth of July and Washington's Birthday were built around political speeches, and during the rest of the year any candidate appealing for votes could count on drawing a fair-sized crowd. Indeed, electioneering appeared to be a great constant in American life. The visiting English novelist Charles Dickens remarked: "Directly that the acrimony of the last election is over, the acrimony of the next begins."

American politics was a fiercely partisan affair, and for decades, that had been all to the good, spurring the people's interest in national issues, putting new ideas and policies to the test of the ballot box. But as the 1850s drew to a close, thoughtful citizens wondered whether their shared ideals could sustain the nation through its mounting crises—or whether their political passions would split the Union.

Verdict of the People, painted by noted American artist George Caleb Bingham, shows a street scene in a Missouri town as the results of an election are announced. The facial expressions of the listeners clearly indicate whether their candidate was the winner or the loser.

One Nation, Divisible

1

Nothing could keep Edmund Ruffin away from the secession convention. Not his grief for his dear daughter Elizabeth, who had just died in childbirth. Not the heavy storm that had covered his plantation north of Richmond, Virginia, with nine inches of snow and was discommoding travelers in the region. Ruffin had long been agitating for Southern independence, and now that South Carolina was on the verge of quitting the United States, he was determined to be there, to witness with his own dimming eyes (he was 66) the dawn of the glorious new era. So on December 17, 1860, the old man packed his luggage, journeyed by carriage and river steamer to Richmond, and there caught a southbound train.

Ruffin's destination was the South Carolina capital, Columbia, where delegates from all over the state convened on the 17th for the declared purpose of terminating relations with the government "known as the United States of America." But during a stop along the way at Wilmington, North Carolina, Ruffin learned that the convention had been driven out of Columbia by an outbreak of smallpox and had reconvened in Charleston—an appropriate move, since that city had always been a hotbed of secessionist sentiment. He changed trains accordingly and arrived in Charleston on the morning of December 19. He was lucky to find accommodation in a tiny, unheated room in the Charleston Hotel.

The town was overflowing with enthusiastic Southern patriots—Southrons, they called themselves. In addition to the convention delegates, the entire South Carolina government was on hand, along with such visiting dignitaries as the Governor of Florida, official representatives of Alabama and Mississippi, four former United States senators and one former United States attorney general. Ruffin encountered scores of old friends and fellow "fire-eaters" who had been leaders in the fight to break up the Union. They were the gentry of the South: planters and newspaper publishers, judges and lawyers, clergymen and bankers—some of them wearing the bright uniforms and the gold braid of officers in the militia. David F. Jamison, a gentleman-scholar who lived quite graciously on the proceeds of a 2,000-acre, 70-slave plantation, was the presiding officer of the convention, and he saw to it that Ruffin would have a seat in the two jam-packed convention buildings.

Using a gavel incised with the word "Secession," President Jamison called the session of December 19 to order in St. Andrew's Hall, a small auditorium where speakers could make themselves heard more easily than in the big auditorium of Institute Hall. The exact language of the Ordinance of Secession was still being mooted in committee, and Jamison pointedly read a telegram from the Governor of Alabama urging the convention to brook no delay.

Many things remained to be settled. Concurrent with secession, the state of South

Cockades of South Carolina palmetto fronds were worn by Charlestonians to symbolize their defiance of the Union at the secession convention in December of 1860. Later, the cockades were worn throughout the South as emblems of sectional solidarity.

Carolina would cease to be bound by federal law, and a complete new code for the infant republic of South Carolina would have to be framed. Local patriots had to be appointed to take over the functions of United States officials. How best could the postal service be handled? What regulations would need to be adopted for collecting customs at the port of Charleston?

The delegates quickly addressed themselves to one matter that soon would become a critical problem. A committee was appointed to report on United States properties inside the territorial limits of South Carolina; most prominent of these were three federal military installations in Charleston Harbor —Fort Moultrie, Castle Pinckney and Fort Sumter. A resolution was then passed instructing the Committee on Foreign Relations to send three commissioners to Washington to negotiate with the United States government for the transfer of all such real estate to the new republic of South Carolina. Regarding this and other momentous issues, Edmund Ruffin made a laconic entry in his diary: "Heard several interesting discussions on subjects incidental and preliminary to the act of secession."

Everyone was disappointed when the day ended without a formal declaration of secession. But during the delay, the symbols of rebellion—the colors and devices of South Carolina—had time to come into full bloom throughout Charleston. Assistant Surgeon Samuel Crawford, attached to the small federal garrison at Fort Moultrie, reported that "blue cockades and cockades of palmetto appeared in every hat; flags of all description, except the National colors, were everywhere displayed. The enthusiasm spread to more practical walks of trade, and the busi-

ness streets were gay with bunting and flags, as the tradespeople, many of whom were Northern men, commended themselves to the popular clamor."

At noon the next day in St. Andrew's Hall, Ruffin attended a closed meeting of the Committee to Prepare an Ordinance of Secession. The product of the committeemen's anxious travail was read aloud:

We, the people of the State of South Carolina, in Convention assembled, do declare and ordain . . . that the union now subsisting between South Carolina and other States under the name of "The United States of America" is hereby dissolved.

At 1:15 p.m. all 169 delegates voted to adopt the ordinance as read. The document was then turned over to the attorney general of South Carolina to see that it was properly engrossed. The public signing ceremony was scheduled to take place in Institute Hall at 7 o'clock that evening.

The delegates—the founding fathers of the new nation—emerged from the hall and were immediately greeted by the start of a long, loud, citywide celebration. Church bells were rung, cannon were fired and joy was nearly universal. One of the few people to admit dissatisfaction was a cranky old judge named James Louis Petigru. Petigru was walking down Broad Street when the bell ringing began and, upon bumping into a friend at the city hall, he inquired sourly of the man, "Where's the fire?" Petigru's friend replied that there was no fire, just happy noise to celebrate secession. "I tell you there is a fire," the judge retorted. "They have this day set a blazing torch to the temple of Constitutional liberty and, please

A throng of cheering Southern separatists rallies in front of Charleston's Mills House during the South Carolina secession crisis of December 1860. Impassioned speakers on the hotel balcony kept whipping up the crowd's enthusiasm.

God, we shall have no more peace forever."

At 7 p.m., the delegates to the convention marched into Institute Hall through dense crowds of celebrants. The signing ceremony took two hours. Finally, President Jamison held up the completed document and declared, "I proclaim the State of South Carolina an independent commonwealth." An enormous roar of approval shook the hall. The deed had been done.

The convention adjourned, and old Edmund Ruffin—honored with the gift of a pen that had signed the Ordinance of Secession—made his way back to the Charleston Hotel. Once he had reached his room, he took out his diary and contentedly summed up the hectic scene: "Military companies paraded, salutes were fired, and as night came on, bonfires, made of barrels of rosin, were lighted in the principal streets, rockets discharged and innumerable crackers discharged by the boys. As I now write, after 10 p.m., I hear the distant sound of rejoicing, with music of a military band, as if there were no thought of ceasing."

Exactly what had happened in Charleston on December 20, 1860? The answer was by no means certain at the time.

According to Northerners with a Consti-

A special edition of the Charleston *Mercury* hails South Carolina's vote to secede. The extra hit the streets at 1:30 p.m. on December 20, 1860, just 15 minutes after the Ordinance of Secession was passed.

tutional turn of mind, nothing had happened; the United States was a sovereign nation, not a mere confederation of independent states; thus by its very nature the republic was indivisible, and secession was impossible. Other, more pragmatic Northerners regarded secession as a very real crime against the Constitution, a breach of popular contract so grave that force of arms would have to put it right. Most Southerners, for their part, were willing to take up arms to defend their action. And many people on both sides saw secession as the only peaceful way out of their quarrels.

In any case, the first of the Southern states had seceded. It was the beginning of the end of the early Union—an event that Southerners called the second American Revolution. Looked at another way, it marked the end of the beginning—an abrupt halt to the nation's first phase of helter-skelter growth. It would lead, after four months of increasing tension and hostility, to the start of the deadliest of American wars, a four-year struggle that would consume the lives of more than 620,000 young Americans, or roughly one out of every 50 citizens.

That the nation was so vigorous made its breakup and descent into war all the more tragic. Europeans were beginning to recognize the United States as a world power and the epitome of democratic ideals. Indications of prosperity and progress were abundant: Well-off families in large cities were beginning to have indoor privies; plans were in the works for a railroad to California; and a transatlantic cable—which had twice barely failed—seemed certain to succeed in the near future. Moreover, some gifted leaders had strode the political stage in recent decades—men who had fashioned careful com-

CHARLESTON MERCURY

EXTRA:

Passed unanimously at 1.15 o'clock, P. M. December 20th, 1860.

AN ORDINANCE

To dissolve the Union between the State of South Carolina and other States united with her under the compact entitled " The Constitution of the United States of America."

We, the People of the State of South Carolina, in Convention assembled, do declare and ordain, and it is hereby declared and ordained,

That the Ordinance adopted by us in Convention, on the twenty-third day of May, in the year of our Lord one thousand seven hundred and eighty-eight, whereby the Constitution of the United States of America was ratified, and also, all Acts and parts of Acts of the General Assembly of this State, ratifying amendments of the said Constitution, are hereby repealed; and that the union now subsisting between South Carolina and other States, under the name of " The United States of America," is hereby dissolved.

THE UNION IS DISSOLVED!

Southern patriots, filling Secession Hall, witness the ceremonial signing of the Ordinance of Secession on the night of December 20, 1860. "The signing occupied more than two hours," said one observer, "during which time there was nothing to entertain the spectators except their enthusiasm and joy."

promises to resolve sectional disputes. But the plain fact of the matter was that the North and the South had become so different—so damnably incompatible and antagonistic—that no amount of political ingenuity could avail.

The two sections had been following divergent paths ever since the start of settlement in America. Geography and climate at once began shaping radically different economic and social patterns in the North and in the South. In the upper Atlantic regions, the terrain was hilly and rocky, with the interior heavily forested and difficult of access. These conditions tended to keep farms small and to build up large pools of population along the coast; many Northern settlers became seamen, fishermen, shipbuilders and merchants. When the Industrial Revolution began late in the 18th Century, entrepre-

neurs moved steadily inland along the rivers, building mills and factories to exploit the ample water power. They were followed by plenty of surplus workers from the coastal cities. By the early years of the 19th Century, the North was becoming a region of large-scale industry, big cities and long-distance commerce, with a great deal of small-scale farming of varied food crops.

In the South, the terrain and climate favored an agrarian way of life. Good land was plentiful and accessible, for the coastal plain extended well inland, and the rivers were navigable to the fall line far to the west. The warm weather, the long growing seasons and the great stretches of level, unbroken terrain were just right for the plantation system—a method of large-scale, intensive farming in which gangs of unskilled laborers worked to cultivate a single cash crop: tobacco or rice, sugar cane or long-staple cotton. The South's most important crop, short-staple cotton, became profitable in the 1790s, when Eli Whitney's cotton gin solved the problem of separating the tough seeds from the fleecy white fiber.

At first, workers were everywhere in short supply in the Southern colonies, with white indentured servants doing much of the menial labor. But the real plantation work forces were gradually provided by the slave trade with Africa and the West Indies. In the 17th Century, slavery was still widely regarded as a legitimate means of maintaining the subservience of conquered enemies or analphabetic inferiors. More than a century later, slaves were recognized as a form of property in the United States Constitution. Being mere chattel, the slaves were not citizens and had no vote. But in an effort to redress the imbalance of national representation between the thinly settled South and the populous North, the Southern states were allowed to count each slave as three fifths of a person for their Congressional apportionment. Thus an added indignity for slaves: Votes conferred by the head count of blacks were cast by whites to keep the slaves servile.

As black slavery spread in the South during the 18th Century, opposition to it spread in the North. The first important protests came from austere Protestant groups, primarily the Quakers, who objected to the ownership of people on moral grounds. Oth-er Northerners, however, considered such protests academic, for slavery was fading out in their states; manufacturers and businessmen preferred self-sufficient employees who could be hired and fired to suit economic conditions. Thus, since the Northern states did not need or want slaves, they outlawed slavery one by one.

There were enlightened Southern planters who agreed that slavery—they referred to it as "our peculiar domestic institution"—was distasteful. Some liberals among them began freeing their slaves. Other planters pointed

out correctly that they were far more humane than their South American counterparts, who tended to work their slaves to death. Still, the Southern planters profited handsomely by whatever degree of humane treatment they practiced. By 1808, when the United States became the last democratic nation to ban international slave trade, Southern slaves were living long enough, and reproducing fast enough, to provide their masters with a lucrative side line of salable human chattel.

It turned out that slavery and the plantation system were self-perpetuating. In a pattern set early in the tobacco plantations of Virginia, intensive one-crop farming quickly exhausted even the best of soils. The big planters, who lived like feudal lords on very small amounts of cash, declined to sacrifice profits by rotating crops, letting fields lie fallow, or fertilizing to any substantial degree. Instead, the planters purchased more and more land—and so they needed more and more slaves to work the new holdings. Latecomers established plantations farther to the west and south, practicing the same one-crop

iting shipment to mills in New land and Great Britain, bales of on line a street near the New ans docks in the 1850s. Although Southern states produced most e world's cotton, they possessed 6 per cent of the nation's cotton-ufacturing capability.

Tall-masted merchant ships crowd the South Street docks in New York City, the North's busiest port. In the 1850s, America's merchant marine replaced England's as the leader in world commerce.

style of agriculture, usually with cotton.

By the early 18th Century, the great Virginia families with plantations dotting the Tidewater were expanding inland, driving the South's small yeoman farmers ahead of them into less favorable lands in the piedmont areas and the Appalachians beyond. By the 1820s, cotton culture was spreading rapidly southward into the Gulf Coast regions, and during the next decade it overleaped the Mississippi into Texas.

Production of cotton rose steeply—from $15 million in 1810 to $63 million in 1840. The value of slaves also increased sharply, from $600 each in 1810 to $1,000 in 1840 to $1,200 and even $1,800 for a prime field hand on the eve of secession. But the lot of the planters did not improve. Lacking middlemen and credit arrangements of their own, planters were victimized by Northern factors, who would pay only the prices set by the English market. Planters suffered cruelly from the volatile American economy, with its quick succession of booms and busts, flush times and depressions.

From time to time, constructive Southerners attempted to diversify their economy—to industrialize, if only to the extent of building mills to process their own cotton. But the Southern planters, slave-poor and land-poor in their struggle to expand apace with demand, had very little to invest; the entire South could not muster as much capital as the single state of New York. Moreover, Southern efforts to raise Yankee capital for building mills and factories generally failed; Northern bankers and financiers were unwilling to invest in a region that lacked both a free labor supply and an adequate transportation system.

In the view of many Southerners, the

South had become a hapless colonial region that was exploited by the industrialized North. "Financially we are more enslaved than our Negroes," complained an Alabamian. In 1851 a newspaper in Alabama published a long and bitter inventory of the ways in which the South was a vassal to the North:

"We purchase all our luxuries and necessities from the North. Our slaves are clothed with Northern manufactured goods, have Northern hats and shoes, work with Northern hoes, plows and other implements. The slaveholder dresses in Northern goods, rides in a Northern saddle, sports his Northern carriage, reads Northern books. In Northern vessels his products are carried to market, his cotton is ginned with Northern gins, his sugar is crushed and preserved with Northern machinery, his rivers are navigated by Northern steamboats. His son is educated at a Northern college, his daughter receives the finishing polish at a Northern seminary; his doctor graduates at a Northern medical college, his schools are furnished with Northern teachers, and he is furnished with Northern inventions."

Against this backdrop of economic troubles, a succession of great political crises beset the nation in the first half of the 19th Century. All of them were brought to seemingly viable resolutions. But each one raised the level of sectional hostility to new heights, and each one left behind a legacy of deepening rancor and frustration. By the beginning of the decade of the 1850s, there was precious little left of the sense of common interest and mutual sympathy that had bound the North and the South together during the American Revolution.

It was the country's great good fortune in this period to be served by three giants—political leaders who represented different interests with power, clarity, honest conviction and unfailing responsibility. Daniel Webster of New Hampshire and later Massachusetts spoke for mercantile, antislavery New England. Henry Clay of Kentucky, representing both slaveowners and a strong antislavery element in his border state, became the mediator for the nation. John C. Calhoun of South Carolina captured in his changing political outlook the course of the country and the trend of the times: He began his career as an ardent nationalist and ended it as a passionate sectionalist.

Lawyer Calhoun cut an impressive figure when he arrived in Washington in 1811 as a newly elected Congressman from South Carolina. At the age of 29 he was tall and square-shouldered, a man with the burning eyes of a visionary. His seriousness of purpose and his Calvinist piety allowed little room for humor; logic and law were what consumed his thoughts. He was said to have sent his wife-to-be a love poem consisting of 12 lines, each of which started with the word "Whereas"—except for the last, which began with "Therefore."

In his calm, crisp courtroom manner, Calhoun swayed men and won votes with his own particular brand of radical patriotism. Declaring that "the honor of a nation is its life," he successfully pushed for war against British aggression in 1812. Later he joined with Henry Clay to promote what came to be called the "American system," a master plan for national strength and growth that included proposals for national defense, a national protective import tariff, a national bank for a uniform currency and a nationwide transportation system.

Calhoun's opponents, chiefly conservative

New Englanders, argued that the Constitution did not delegate such sweeping powers to the federal government, that the American system would usurp authority belonging to the individual states. But the notion of states' rights was anathema to young Calhoun. "We are under the most imperious obligation to counteract every tendency to disunion," he declared. "Let us, then, bind the Republic together with a perfect system of roads and canals. Let us conquer space."

On February 13, 1819, the first of the period's great struggles was joined. James Tallmadge, an obscure one-term Representative from New York, introduced a resolution that electrified the United States Congress. The debate that it provoked came, the aging Thomas Jefferson wrote, "like a firebell in the night," which "awakened me and filled me with terror. I considered it at once the knell of the union." To another former President, John Quincy Adams, it seemed to be "a title page to a great tragic volume."

Tallmadge's measure sought to prohibit slavery in the Missouri Territory, a section of the Louisiana Purchase that was petitioning to enter the Union as a slave state. The proposed restriction reflected a growing anti-slavery sentiment on the part of Northern legislators and represented a challenge that the South could ill afford to ignore, for it had implications that extended far beyond the status of Missouri. It was cotton that produced the lion's share of the South's income, and planters were fearful that unless the cultivation of cotton continued to expand, their whole economy would wither and die as cultivated areas were exhausted. And, just as frightening to Southerners, it threatened to shift the balance of power in Washington in favor of the North.

Daniel Webster of Massachusetts, whose noncommittal attitude toward slavery often prompted criticism, outraged abolitionists with his speech in favor of the 1850 Compromise condoning slavery. Poet Ralph Waldo Emerson accused him of venality in a bitter couplet: "Why did all manly gifts in Webster fail? / He wrote on Nature's grandest brow, *For Sale*."

Kentucky's Henry Clay, whose Compromise of 1850 reconciled North and South for a decade, presented himself as a presidential candidate five times and was five times rebuffed. Out of his disappointments came his famous declaration that he "would rather be right than be President."

South Carolina's John C. Calhoun (*right*) was so unyielding and passionate in his defense of South rights that a visiting Englishman called him both "the cast-iron man" and "a volcano in full force."

Southerners had already lost control of the House of Representatives to the Northern states, whose populations were swelling as immigration increased. The Senate was controlled by neither section: Of 22 states in the nation in 1819, exactly half were free and half were slave. But if Missouri entered the Union as a free state, the Senatorial balance would tip against slavery. The South would then be helpless to prevent the passage of ruinous legislation: tariffs that crippled the Southern cotton trade with Europe; huge funds allocated to the development of ports, canals and turnpikes beneficial to the North; eventually, the abolition of slavery, even in the slave states.

The volatile issue of the extension of slavery to Missouri touched off an acrimonious debate that spanned two sessions of Congress. The Northerners were seething with moral outrage. "How long will the desire for wealth render us blind to the sin of holding both the bodies and souls of our fellow men in chains?" demanded Representative Arthur Livermore of New Hampshire. "Do not, for the sake of cotton and tobacco, let it be told to future ages that, while pretending to love liberty, we have purchased an extensive country to disgrace it with the foulest reproach to nations!"

The Southern planters, trapped in their dependence on slavery, accused Northerners of exaggerating the evils of the institution and challenged the right of the North to meddle in the affairs of the South. "The slaveholding states," declared the Lexington, Kentucky, *Western Monitor*, "will not brook an invasion of their rights. They will not be driven by compulsion to the emancipation, even gradually, of their states."

Not until 1820 was the debate over the

admission of Missouri finally calmed by moderates. Henry Clay had stepped forward with a compromise that seemingly settled the slavery issue. To preserve the tenuous balance in the Senate, Missouri was to be admitted as a slave state and Maine would come into the Union as a free state. Further, a demarcation line would be drawn from east to west at latitude 36° 30'. Henceforth, all new states that might be fashioned from Louisiana Purchase territories north of that line would be free, whereas all of those below it would be slave.

The Missouri Compromise papered over the problem of the extension of slavery, but it was satisfactory to no one. For the first time in the short history of the nation, an action by Congress had aligned the states against each other on a sectional basis. Suspicions grew on both sides. Northerners suspected that a Southern cabal they called "the Slave Power" was conspiring to circumvent the principle of rule by the majority. Southerners, in turn, suspected that Northerners were plotting to destroy them. Said James M. Garnett of Virginia, "It would seem as if all the devils incarnate, both in the Eastern and Northern states, are in league against us."

Calhoun did his best to allay Southern fears of a Northern conspiracy against slavery. But cries for help from the planters of South Carolina were pulling him to their side. Tariffs that protected the profits of Northern manufacturers caused increasing hardship in the South, raising the prices that Southerners had to pay for imported manufactures. And then, in the 1820s, the Southern predicament was further exacerbated by a recession.

More and more Southerners, Calhoun in-

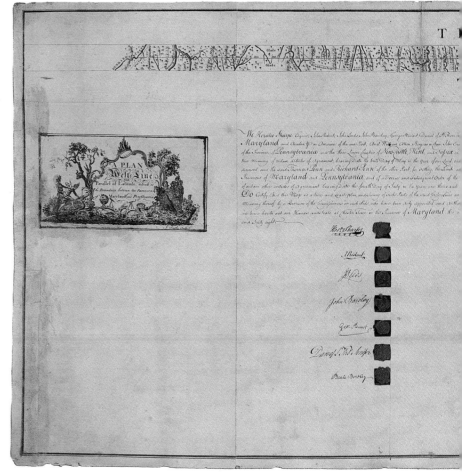

cluded, turned against nationalism. In 1827, while serving as Vice President in the administration of John Quincy Adams, he made his first break with his past. On the Senate floor, with the vote tied on a new tariff bill, Calhoun cast the decisive ballot against it. But the next year, rival politicians managed to force through Congress another, higher tariff on a variety of manufactured goods. Angry Southerners labeled it the Tariff of Abominations, and soon they were blaming it for all their economic ills.

In Calhoun's South Carolina, those troubles were acute. As plantation profits declined during the recession, planters aban-

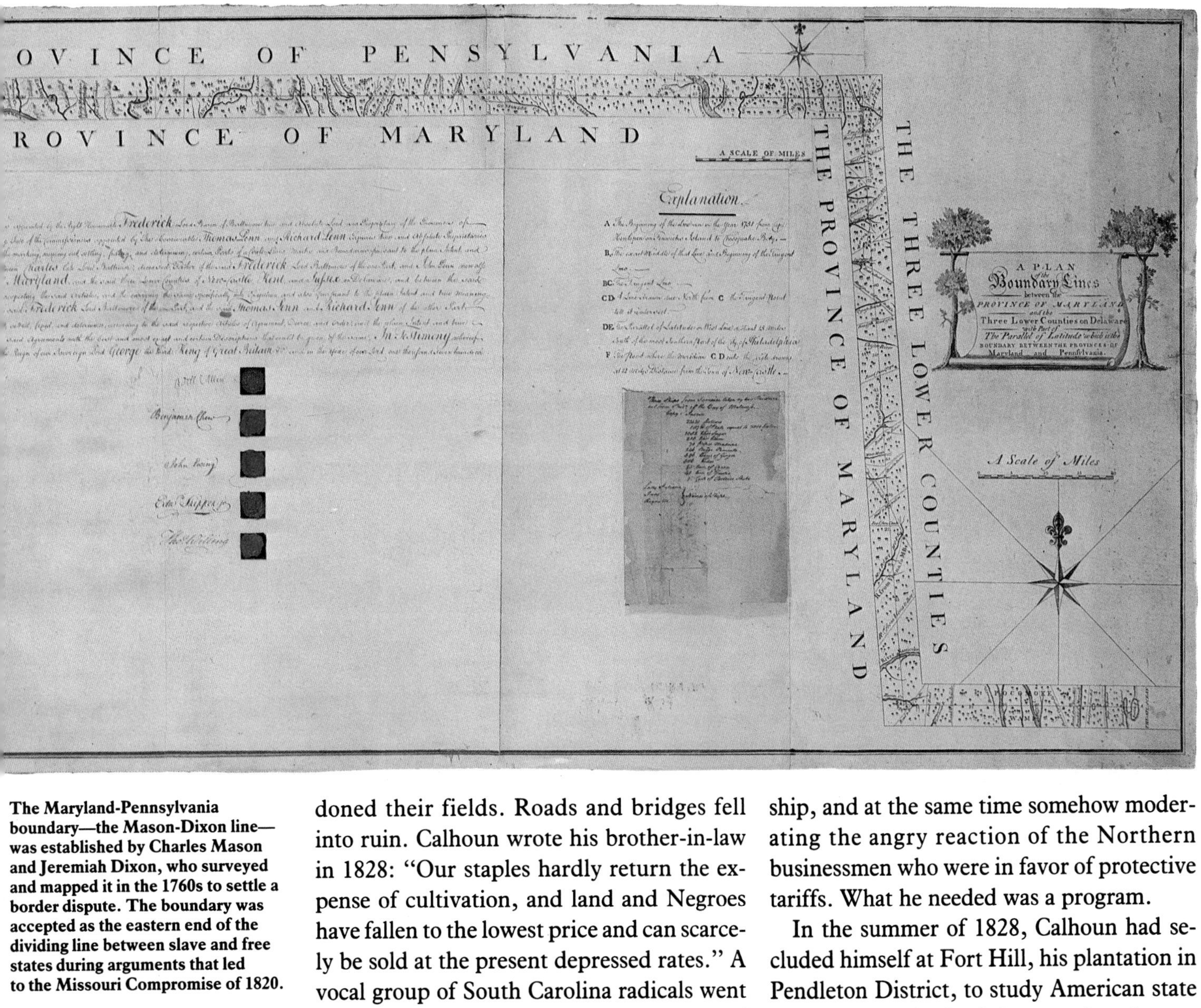

OVINCE OF PENSYLVANIA
ROVINCE OF MARYLAND
A SCALE OF MILES
Explanation
THE PROVINCE OF MARYLAND
THE THREE LOWER COUNTIES
A PLAN of the Boundary Lines between the PROVINCE OF MARYLAND and the Three Lower Counties on Delaware with Part of The Parallel of Latitude which is the BOUNDARY BETWEEN THE PROVINCES OF Maryland and Pennsylvania
A Scale of Miles

The Maryland-Pennsylvania boundary—the Mason-Dixon line—was established by Charles Mason and Jeremiah Dixon, who surveyed and mapped it in the 1760s to settle a border dispute. The boundary was accepted as the eastern end of the dividing line between slave and free states during arguments that led to the Missouri Compromise of 1820.

doned their fields. Roads and bridges fell into ruin. Calhoun wrote his brother-in-law in 1828: "Our staples hardly return the expense of cultivation, and land and Negroes have fallen to the lowest price and can scarcely be sold at the present depressed rates." A vocal group of South Carolina radicals went so far as to speak of secession as a means of eradicating the intolerable tax.

Calhoun now faced a dilemma. Elected to serve as Vice President under Andrew Jackson, he wanted to succeed to the presidency. But to stand any chance he would have to tread a precarious path, satisfying the radicals at home, maintaining Jackson's friendship, and at the same time somehow moderating the angry reaction of the Northern businessmen who were in favor of protective tariffs. What he needed was a program.

In the summer of 1828, Calhoun had secluded himself at Fort Hill, his plantation in Pendleton District, to study American state papers in search of a defense against the tariff. He paid particular attention to the 1781 Articles of Confederation, which recognized the "sovereignty, freedom, and independence" of each state, and to the Kentucky and Virginia Resolutions of 1798 and 1799, which stated the controversial opinion that the Constitution was a "compact" between the states, each of which had the right to pass on the constitutionality of the federal government's acts. In the case of federal laws that were unfair or unfavorable to particular states, the Kentucky Resolution declared: "It is the right and duty of the several states to nullify those acts, and to protect their citizens from their operations."

By summer's end, Calhoun had developed the doctrine of nullification, which he published in a pamphlet. In it, he proclaimed the right of any state to overrule or modify not only the tariff but also any federal law deemed unconstitutional. Nullification was a complete theory of government that placed the greatest powers on the state level rather than the national. With this proclamation of states' rights, Calhoun had come full circle in his political philosophy.

Calhoun's doctrine failed to produce the results he had anticipated. It alarmed the North and antagonized President Jackson, who saw nullification as a knife poised over the Union's vitals. Jackson made his sympathies clear with a toast at a gathering just after nullification was unveiled on the Senate floor. "Our Federal Union!" said Old Hickory. "It *must* and *shall be* preserved!" Calhoun, forced to hoist his own standard, could only respond: "The Federal Union—next to our liberty, the most dear."

The showdown over the nullification issue came in 1832, when a South Carolina convention formally disallowed two federal tariff acts. President Jackson labeled that action treasonous and immediately called South Carolina's bluff by threatening to use force to ensure obedience to the tariff law. Calhoun and his fellow nullifiers were unable to muster support from the other Southern states, and they finally accepted a compromise tariff

of lower rates. Calhoun had learned a lesson—that it would take a group of states to make the doctrine of states' rights stick. He began at once to recruit followers and to spread the gospel of Southern solidarity.

Even as Calhoun campaigned for Southern unity, opposition to slavery came of age in the 1830s, winning acceptance in a period of reform and religious revivalism. The various antislavery factions still adhered to different principles and goals, which prevented cooperation, not to mention consolidation. Nevertheless, all the groups were backed by a sympathetic press and separately made many converts in their furious efforts to rid the nation of slavery.

The most important antislavery factions were groups of abolitionists; they wanted slavery outlawed and the freed blacks absorbed into society on an equal footing with whites. Besides these social idealists, a group of political pragmatists plumped for abolition only in the new territories, thinking slavery would eventually perish in the Southern states. And there were numerous emancipationists. Like the abolitionists, they demanded that the slaves be freed. But they wanted no part of the freed slaves as fellow citizens; far better, they said, to ship all blacks to Africa. One emancipationist organization, the American Colonization Society, raised large sums of money to ship freed blacks to Liberia. An African nation was set up in 1847 to receive more freed slaves.

Of all the antislavery groups, the abolitionists were the most vigorous and vociferous promoters of their cause. Angry and eloquent, they damned slavery as a sin and slaveowners as criminals. The fiercest of them all was New Englander William Lloyd

John Calhoun, ascending a pedestal of Southern affronts to the Union, reaches for a despot's crown in this Northern cartoon from 1833. At right, President Andrew Jackson warns Calhoun and his fellow separatists to reverse their perilous course.

Garrison, founder of the abolitionist newspaper *The Liberator*. Garrison insisted that opposition to slavery was more vital than the preservation of the Union, and because the Constitution protected slavery, he burned a copy in public, calling the document "a covenant with death and an agreement with hell." Garrison made no apology for his extreme views. "I do not wish to think or speak or write, with moderation," he raged. "I will be as harsh as truth, and as uncompromising as justice. And I will be heard."

Some abolitionists were so daring as to take their crusade into the camp of the enemy. James G. Birney, a wealthy man who had owned slaves himself, boldly attacked the institution in the slave state of Kentucky. So did emancipationist publisher Cassius M. Clay. Protected somewhat by his fearsome reputation as a duelist and by the two cannon that guarded his office, Clay railed against slavery in his Lexington newspaper. Finally, irate Kentuckians put him out of business by dismantling his press in his absence and shipping it to Cincinnati.

A few abolitionists risked their lives to

help slaves flee north to freedom on the so-called Underground Railroad. The fugitives were smuggled in wagons and led through woods to the farmsteads and city houses of sympathizers; they followed many escape routes, most of them ending in Ohio and Indiana. Workers on the Railroad claimed to have rescued or assisted as many as 100,000 escapees in three decades—undoubtedly a considerable exaggeration, since the South reported only 1,000 escapes a year. Yet the Railroad was invaluable as an inspiration for those who opposed slavery as well as for those who plotted to escape it.

Naturally, the abolitionist campaign enraged the Southerners. And it also frightened them, conjuring the nightmarish possibility of an immense uprising among their more than two million slaves. A small version of such an insurrection occurred in the summer of 1831, when a Virginia slave by the name of Nat Turner led about 70 fellows on a bloody rampage that left 55 whites dead. Turner and 16 of his followers were tried and quickly hanged, and soon afterward the slave states acted to prevent abolitionist rhetoric from sparking much worse disasters. Stiff laws were passed restricting freedom of speech and the press; abolitionist tracts were actually burned in the United States Post Office in Charleston.

Faced with increasing pressures both from without and from within, Southerners closed ranks. It ceased to be safe to whisper even a word against the "peculiar institution," and any stranger suspected of antislavery agitation was likely to be hustled out of town in a coat of tar and feathers. Those humane planters who once had thought of slavery as a temporary aberration now claimed defensively that the institution was a positive

An 1857 poster advertises a speech given in Eaton, Ohio, by a clergyman wanted in Kentucky for helping runaway slaves. Many fugitive blacks passed through Kentucky on their way into Ohio and thence to Canada.

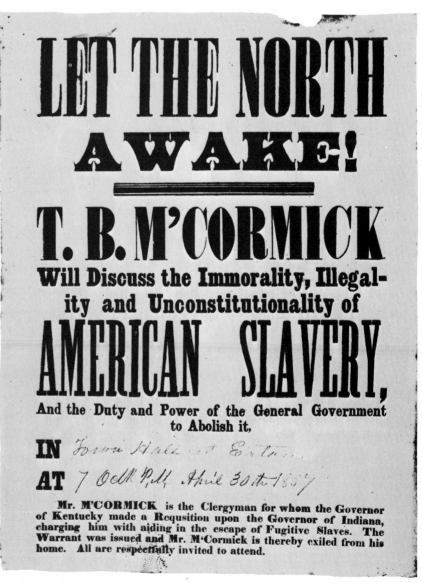

good, that it benefited the slave with food, clothing and housing, that it uplifted him with Christian tutelage.

In 1838 John Calhoun endorsed the new Southern attitude: "Many in the South once believed that slavery was a moral and political evil. That folly and delusion are gone. We see it now in its true light, and regard it as the most safe and stable basis for free institutions in the world."

A new political crisis threatened with the beginning of the Mexican War in 1846. Americans from every state rushed to join the Army and to fight in behalf of a jingoistic credo with a newly coined name, Manifest Destiny. The credo excused any and all conquest by declaring that it was the God-given right of Americans to inherit the continent from sea to sea. Although Manifest Destiny was popular nationwide, it was made to order for Southern interests. Some Southern firebrands openly discussed annexing Mexico once the government of Santa Anna surrendered. The country could be broken up into dozens of new slave states. The horizons of the more ardent cotton imperialists extended even to the Spanish colony of Cuba, where slavery conveniently existed. The acquisition of just a few new states for slavery would give the South control of the Senate, where the count presently stood at 15 slave states and 15 free states.

John Calhoun did not share the Southerners' enthusiasm for war with Mexico. He foresaw a bitter dispute over the enticing Mexican spoils, which he called "forbidden fruit." And he was right: Even before the brief conflict with Mexico came to an end, a move was made in Congress that sent Northerners and Southerners to their political ram-

An angry Southern handbill, hastily produced with a misprinted date, announces a rally in Augusta, Georgia, to protest the torrent of antislavery tracts from the North. Southern reaction to the abolitionist movement grew so violent that local people who opposed slavery went underground or moved north.

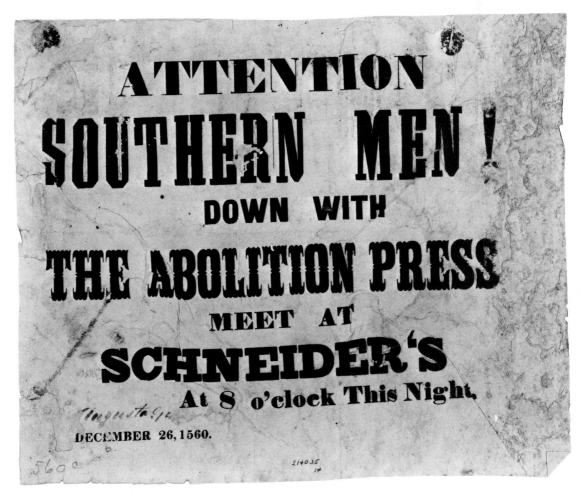

ATTENTION
SOUTHERN MEN!
DOWN WITH
THE ABOLITION PRESS
MEET AT
SCHNEIDER'S
At 8 o'clock This Night.
Augusta Ga.
DECEMBER 26, 1560.

parts for the third time in as many decades.

The provocation came from David Wilmot, a slovenly, profane, tobacco-chewing country lawyer from Pennsylvania. He introduced a measure proposing that "neither slavery or involuntary servitude shall ever exist" in any territory that might be acquired as a result of the Mexican War. The Wilmot Proviso never made its way into law: Over a span of six months it passed the House twice, but it failed in the Senate. Nevertheless, its impact was staggering. It split Congress along sectional lines, with nearly all members voting on the measure not as Democrats or Whigs—the two major parties of the day—but as Northerners or Southerners. An unsuccessful Southern attempt to quash the proviso in the House demonstrated the extent of the rift: 74 Southerners and four Northerners voted to table Wilmot's measure, 91 Northerners and three Southerners voted to keep it alive. "As if by magic," a Boston journalist wrote of the proviso, "it brought to a head the great question which is about to divide the American people."

Calhoun, his health now failing, was shaken by the Wilmot Proviso and its naked effort to limit the extension of slavery. But he was well enough to enunciate the Southern view when, with the signing of the Treaty of Guadalupe Hidalgo in 1848, Mexico ceded to the United States an immense domain of nearly one million square miles, including all the territory between Texas and the Pacific. Calhoun argued that the territories were not federal property but the joint possession of the individual states, and that Congress therefore had no authority to intervene on the question of slavery. And since slaves were no more than chattel, the Southerners should be as free to transport them to new

territories as others were to move with their mules and oxen. He declared: "I am a Southern man and a slaveholder. I say, for one, I would rather meet any extremity upon earth than give up one inch of our equality—one inch of what belongs to us as members of this great republic!"

The controversy hung like a black cloud over Congress. In both houses, routine was often shattered by invective and threats of disunion. Calhoun warned his sectional rivals, "The North must give way, or there will be a rupture." Congressman Robert Toombs of Georgia, a large-hearted bull of a man, proclaimed his attachment to the Union but then warned, "I do not hesitate to avow before this House and the country, and in the presence of the living God, that if by your legislation you seek to drive us from the territories of California and New Mexico and to abolish slavery in this District, thereby attempting to fix a national degradation upon half the states of this Confederacy, I am for disunion."

Northerners in Congress answered quickly in kind. Senator Salmon P. Chase of Ohio declared, "No menace of disunion will move us from the path which in our judgment it is due to ourselves and the people whom we represent to pursue." Congressman John P. Hale of New Hampshire refused to consider any further compromise. He cried, "If this Union, with all its advantages, has no other cement than the blood of human slavery, let it perish!"

In the meantime, the issue of the extension of slavery caught the eye of recently elected President Zachary Taylor, the hero of the Mexican War. Taylor was a Louisianian and a slaveowner, but he was first and foremost an old general who wanted to serve his coun-

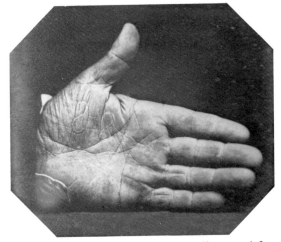

The brand *SS* for "slave stealer" disfigures the palm of Captain Jonathan Walker. The mariner, arrested in 1844 while trying to smuggle seven slaves from Florida to liberty in the West Indies, was held in solitary confinement for a year.

try. And with a soldier's naïve disregard for political protocol, he sought and found a simple solution to the problem.

In 1849, California and New Mexico were still being administered by military officers. Neither had been authorized to organize a territorial government, under whose aegis each region would prepare for statehood. It was during this fledgling stage before statehood that the issue of slavery was most volatile; because a territory was still a ward of the federal government, the U.S. Congress could meddle in any decision made by the territorial government.

As it happened, California, thanks to the gold rush, already had far more than the 60,000 people required for statehood. Since every established state had an unchallenged right to decide for itself the status of slavery, Taylor decided to get California, and later New Mexico, to apply for statehood without going through the territorial phase, thus removing the federal government from the troublesome slavery decision.

Taylor sent agents to California and New Mexico to persuade the settlers there to make application for statehood. California, very much in need of civil government to estab-

lish order in the unruly gold camps, complied gladly with the President's proposal. By November of 1849 a constitution had been drawn up and California had opted to enter the Union as a free state. New Mexico made a start on a similar procedure.

When the proslavery Southerners woke up to Taylor's maneuverings, they could scarcely believe what was taking place. They saw a betrayal by one of their own, a President whom they had expected to protect their sectional interests. They accused Taylor of pressuring California into applying for statehood before the citizens really wanted it. They voiced a suspicion that the President was conspiring with Northern zealots to deny the South any rights in the new territories. They threatened secession. Northerners tried to pacify them with the argument that the Mexican lands were unfavorable for slavery anyway. But Alexander H. Stephens of Georgia retorted that a principle was involved. "Principles, sir, are not only outposts, but the bulwarks of all Constitutional liberty; and if these be yielded, or taken by superior force, the citadel will soon follow."

All the angry Southern voices only provoked familiar rhetoric from the Northerners. "The North is determined that slavery shall not pollute the soil of lands now free, even if it should come to a dissolution of the Union," an Ohio newspaper proclaimed. Slavery, said Senator William Upham of Vermont, was "a crime against humanity, and a sore evil in the body politic."

It seemed that the country would surely break apart. From Mississippi came a summons to Southern states to meet in Nashville in June 1850 to draw up a plan for dealing with the "gross injustice" of the North. But then men of moderation on both sides turned

Margaret Garner, a runaway slave cornered in a room in Cincinnati, shows her captors the bodies of two of her children. It was said that she killed the pair rather than see them returned to bondage; presumably she was interrupted before she could slay her two other children.

for a solution to Henry Clay, the so-called Great Pacificator. Clay was aged and ailing, but his stature and oratory still could sway intransigent partisans.

In January of 1850, Clay presented his solution to the gravest crisis of the half century. He proposed that California should be allowed to enter the Union as a free state, just as it wished, but that Congress should refrain from intervening in the slavery question in any other new territories carved from the Mexican cession. Clay also offered resolutions on three side issues that had cropped up during the debate: that Texas be compensated for yielding certain western tracts to New Mexico, that the sale of slaves be abolished in the District of Columbia, and that Congress enact stiff new laws to assist slaveowners in the capture and return of runaway slaves.

Clay defended his compromise plan in a series of speeches in the Senate; for each address, the gallery was packed with citizens who sensed that the occasion would be Clay's swan song. The old Kentuckian was nothing less than magnificent. In his rich voice he called for reason. He urged Southerners not to complain if the state of California rejected slavery. And he demanded of Northerners: "What do you want, you who reside in the free states? Have you not your desire in California? And in all human probability you will have it in New Mexico also. What more do you want? You have got what is worth more than a thousand Wilmot Provisos." Clay pointed out that Northerners had nature on their side and facts on their side—that the territories in question had no slavery and were unsuited to slavery. He ended by warning Southern extremists that secession would mean nothing less than war, and he begged them "to pause at the edge of the precipice, before the fearful and disastrous leap is taken into the yawning abyss below."

Clay's plea for moderation was countered on March 4 by John Calhoun, now dying of tuberculosis. (He had less than a month to live.) He was so weak that a colleague had to read his speech. In it Calhoun never mentioned Clay or the compromise measures; instead, he called on the North, as the stronger section of the country, to make concessions to preserve the Union. The North, he said, should grant slaveowners equal rights in the territories of the new West, quiet the abolitionist agitation against slavery and guarantee the return of fugitive slaves. Barring those concessions, Calhoun proposed that the North and the South separate and each section govern itself in peace. If that were not possible, he warned the North, "We shall know what to do, when you reduce the question to submission or resistance."

Calhoun's challenge was met by the magisterial Daniel Webster, in what was perhaps his finest speech. He began, "I wish to speak today, not as a Massachusetts man, nor as a Northern man, but as an American, and a member of the Senate of the United States. I speak today for the preservation of the Union. Hear me for my cause." Webster implored the Northern radicals to soften their position. The Wilmot Proviso, that "taunt or reproach" to the South, was unnecessary because conditions in the West were unfavorable to slavery. "I would not take pains to reaffirm an ordinance of nature," he stated, "nor to reenact the will of God."

Webster's speech was considered a betrayal by the abolitionists, but its message of moderation received high praise elsewhere. Even the fiery Charleston *Mercury* lauded his effort: "With such a spirit as Mr. Webster has shown, it no longer seems impossible to bring this sectional contest to a close." Under the able direction of Senator Stephen A. Douglas of Illinois, Clay's proposals ran the legislative gantlet and were enacted into law by September.

Clay's Compromise of 1850 was hailed as the Union's salvation. A schism had been averted, and Americans, now breathing a bit more easily, looked ahead hopefully to a future free of sectional rancor. Indeed, the compromise strengthened the Southern moderates and thereby helped thwart the plans of belligerent Southern agitators to forge a bloc of separatist Southern states.

But far from curing the nation's ills, the compromise contained a minor measure that would do major damage to the chances for a lasting settlement. That measure was the Fugitive Slave Law.

Runaway slaves were not a serious problem for planters; not many more than a thousand escaped each year, even with the help of the Underground Railroad, and relatively few of them were able to reach sanctuary in the North. Even so, the Fugitive Slave Law was designed to mollify the South, and it did so with some of the harshest national regulations yet instituted by Congress. It placed the full power of the federal government behind efforts to recapture escaped slaves. It created federal police power: A cadre of U.S. commissioners was authorized to issue warrants for the arrest and return of runaways. And it empowered the commissioners to dragoon citizens into slave-catching posses.

The intervention of the federal government in the plight of escaped slaves infuriated even moderate Northerners. Ralph Waldo Emerson called the fugitive measure a "filthy law," and many Northerners vowed to resist it. Not even the U.S. Army could enforce the law, predicted Ohio Congressman Joshua Giddings: "Let the President drench our land of freedom in blood; but he will never make us obey that law."

Once the Fugitive Slave Law was on the books, it was no longer enough for a runaway to reach the North. Professional slave hunters, armed with affidavits from Southern courts, scoured Northern cities, not only ferreting out runaways but sometimes kidnapping free blacks, of whom almost 200,000 lived in Northern communities. Runaways who had felt secure in New York and Philadelphia and Boston were frightened enough to take flight across the Canadian border.

Others fought back. Blacks and whites in Northern cities formed vigilance committees to protect fugitives from the slave catchers. Boston was virtually in a state of insurrection, with abolitionist mobs roaming the streets and influential abolitionist clergymen advocating civil disobedience to the slave-catching municipal police. A Boston slave couple named William and Ellen Craft were whisked from the reach of a Georgia lawman who had come to get them. Fred Wilkins, a black waiter who was being held in a federal courthouse in Boston, was spirited away by a crowd of blacks who burst through the doors of the courthouse.

Then came the wrenching case of Anthony Burns, a Virginia escapee who had been working in a Boston clothing store. When Burns was arrested by a federal marshal,

Escaped slave Josiah Henson, famous as the model for Harriet Beecher Stowe's character Uncle Tom, lectured to abolitionist audiences on his life in bondage.

The Webb family (*below*) toured the Northern states giving dramatic readings of *Uncle Tom's Cabin*. Mary Webb (*center*) took her act to England, where the novel had sold one million copies within a year of its publication in 1852.

abolitionists held a mass meeting at Faneuil Hall and were whipped into action by fiery oratory. "I want that man set free in the streets of Boston," shouted Wendell Phillips, the well-born reform lecturer. "If that man leaves the city of Boston, Massachusetts is a conquered state."

The crowd stormed the federal courthouse where Burns was being held. In the melee a special deputy was killed, and the federal marshals and deputies were hard put to restrain the mob. Finally, the federal government sent in Regular Army troops to take Burns out. With flags flying at half-mast and bells tolling a dirge, Burns was marched through crepe-hung streets to the harbor and put aboard a Virginia-bound ship.

"When it was all over," a Boston attorney wrote, "and I was left alone in my office, I put my face in my hands and wept. I could do nothing less." Countless Northerners were galvanized by Burns's fate. "We went to bed one night old-fashioned, conservative, Compromise Union Whigs," wrote one, "and waked up stark mad abolitionists." Popular outrage stirred the North to legal action. Nine states passed personal-liberty laws designed to frustrate the Fugitive Slave Law and protect blacks in their domain. Southern slave hunters found it so difficult to prove their case and to get cooperation from Northern authorities that most gave up the chase.

The plight of the runaways inspired and brought to publication in 1852 the ultimate piece of abolitionist propaganda. This work, a novel by a meek and pious New Englander named Harriet Beecher Stowe, was *Uncle Tom's Cabin, or Life among the Lowly.*

As literature, the book suffered from a contrived plot and stereotyped characters.

Yet it personalized the evils of slavery, and the suffering of Uncle Tom and Eliza and Little Eva tugged at the heartstrings of readers who had been unmoved by abolitionist rhetoric. The book became a bestseller almost overnight; within a year 300,000 copies were sold, and the story reached an even wider audience in the form of a drama, which dozens of touring troupes performed in lyceums and in meeting halls all over the country. Meanwhile, Southern readers ground their teeth over Mrs. Stowe's claims that their society was evil; their rage and frustration strengthened the garrison mentality that had gripped the South.

So it was that the United States at midcentury stood in grave peril. Opposition to slavery had permeated and pervaded the North; few Northerners knew of or cared about the Southern planters' plight. In the South, the commitment to slavery was now inalterable. It did not matter that only about 350,000 people—one family out of four—actually owned slaves. Most Southern whites firmly believed that their livelihood, their dear institutions and traditions, and indeed their personal safety amid almost four million blacks all depended on preserving and extending the use of slave labor.

The meager chances for a rapprochement between the North and the South were further dimmed in 1852. Henry Clay and Daniel Webster followed John Calhoun to the grave, leaving their constituencies in the hands of less seasoned, less wise, less patient leaders. At the same time a new ingredient was added to the North-South quarrels—an ingredient that gave Americans everywhere a preview of their future. It was organized violence, and it erupted in Kansas.

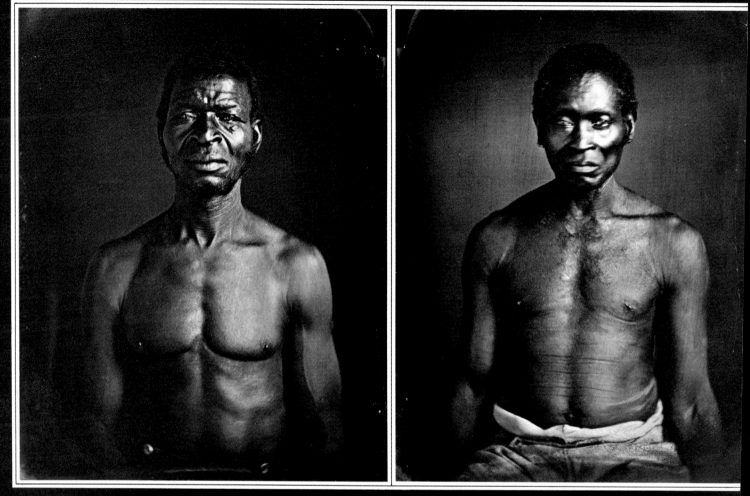

JACK, A SLAVE DRIVER

FASSENA, A CARPENTER

To Be a Slave

"I'd ruther be dead than be a nigger on one of these big plantations," a white Mississippian told a Northern visitor. For those who were slaves, the plantation life often did lead prematurely to the grave.

Born into bondage, very likely sold at least once during the course of his or her lifetime, a slave normally began to work in the fields by the age of 12. From that point on, overwork was his daily portion. One former slave said of his servitude on a Louisiana plantation: "The hands are required to be in the cotton field as soon as it is light in the morning, and, with the exception of 10 or 15 minutes, which is given them at noon, they are not permitted to be a moment idle until it is too dark to see, and when the moon is full, they often labor till the middle of the night."

The majority of slaves were fed poorly; many subsisted chiefly on a "hog and hominy" diet, which consisted of a peck of corn and about three pounds of fatty salted meat a week. They were generally clothed in shabby homespun or in cheap fabrics known as "Negro cloth," which were man-

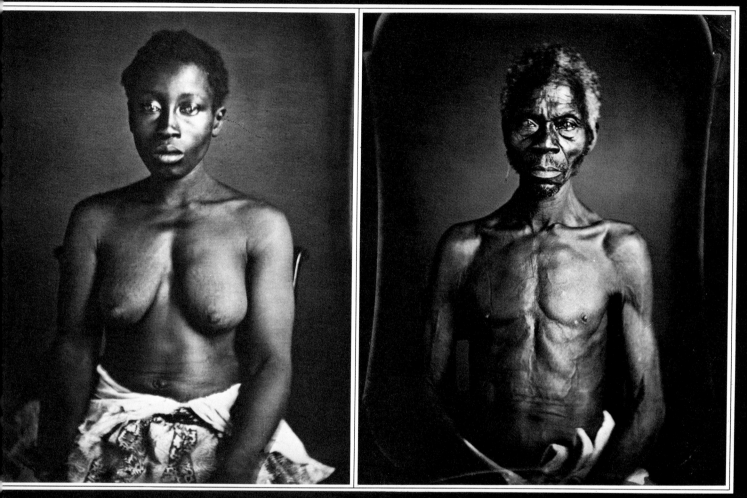

DELIA, OCCUPATION UNKNOWN

RENTY, A FIELD SLAVE

ufactured in Northern or English spinning mills. Children wore only shirts and went shoeless even in winter.

From six to 12 slaves were quartered in each leaky, drafty, dirt-floored one-room shack. "Their houses," wrote an Alabama physician, "can be but laboratories of disease." What medical care slaves received was primitive at best. Malaria, yellow fever, cholera, tuberculosis, typhoid, typhus, tetanus and pneumonia took terrible tolls. Many slaves were afflicted with worms, dysentery and rotten teeth. Fewer than

four out of 100 lived to be 60 years of age. Slaves were kept in a state of fear by punishment and the threat of punishment. They were required to show abject humility when they addressed whites: They had to bow their heads and lower their gaze. No wonder that slaves—even those who received relatively good treatment—yearned for freedom. "O, that I were free!" wrote a slave who finally managed to escape. "O, God, save me! I will run away. Get caught or get clear. I had as well be killed running as die standing."

Four slaves gaze impassively from daguerreotypes taken in South Carolina in 1850. The pictures, among the earliest known photographs of slaves, were part of a study on racial characteristics conducted by scientist Louis Agassiz.

49

Stripped, Prodded and Paraded

Slaves approached the auction block in dreadful uncertainty, fearing the worst. Nothing in their dreary lives was quite so frightening, or so degrading.

The slaves, freshly scrubbed and dressed in clean clothes, were paraded in front of the white shoppers, who sometimes made them jump or dance to show their liveliness. Young men and women were often stripped, partly to show that they had never been whipped. "The customers would feel our bodies," recalled a former slave, "and make us show our teeth, precisely as a jockey examines a horse."

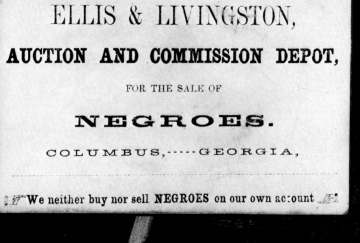

ELLIS & LIVINGSTON,

Davenport Ellis.   Lewis Livingston.

AUCTION AND COMMISSION DEPOT,

FOR THE SALE OF

NEGROES.

COLUMBUS,----GEORGIA,

We neither buy nor sell NEGROES on our own account

one, advertising the services of professional slave auctioneers, were widely displayed in Southern towns.

626

1829

A numbered identification tag, attached to the slave by the auctioneer, was keyed to a full description that was presented with the bill.

At a slave sale in Richmond, the auctioneer (*left*) accepts a bid for a female slave while prospective buyers examine other blacks awaiting sale. A few traders had special rooms for displaying "choice stock"— pretty quadroons and octoroons who fetched up to $2,500 or more from New Orleans brothel owners.

The Breakup
of a Slave Family

Slave families are broken up at a railroad station in Richmond. In most cases, slaves were sold between October and May so that they could become accustomed to their new plantations in time for the next growing season.

A dealer's broadside announces his willingness to purchase slaves for cash. Many a slave was sold without warning to pay the debts of his owner.

A prosperous planter (*below, right*) sells a young mulatto— his own illegitimate son.

A slave family sent to auction was seldom sold to a single buyer. And so followed the breakup every slave expected: a child taken from its mother, a couple separated.

The slave family was a tenuous unit to begin with; from the master's viewpoint, couples existed to produce more slaves to be put to work or sold for profit. A man and woman might be matched for breeding purposes against their will. With the master's permission, the couple might have a wedding ceremony, though slave marriage had no status in law. Since the union might soon be broken up by one partner's sale, a preacher changed the marital vow to say, "Until death or distance do you part."

CASH!

All persons that have SLAVES to dispose of, will do well by giving me a call, as I will give the

HIGHEST PRICE FOR

Men, Women, &
CHILDREN.

Any person that wishes to sell, will call at Hill's tavern, or at Shannon Hill for me, and any information they want will be promptly attended to.

Thomas Griggs.

Charlestown, May 7, 1835.

PRINTED AT THE FREE PRESS OFFICE, CHARLESTOWN.

A Slave's Sense of Caste

"Go along, half-priced nigger!" one slave joshed another. "You wouldn't fetch $50, and I'm worth $1,000." The gibe was good-natured but had a sharp edge. "Everybody," explained a former slave, "wants the privilege of whipping somebody else."

The division of plantation labor fostered a slave caste system. The slave aristocrats were the skilled craftsmen, the house servants who served the master and his family, and the so-called drivers—field foremen. At the bottom of the social ladder were the unskilled field hands. And even the lowly field hands felt superior to slaves who worked in coal mines.

Some slaves used another criterion of status, ancestry, to claim a modicum of respect or a better job. One Georgia slave of mixed blood asked her owner to relieve her of field labor "on account of her color."

A house slave prepares a meal amid the clutter of a plantation kitchen. Kitchen workers, who had access to extra food, were popular and important among the slaves.

In an 1840s daguerreotype (*left*) from Louisiana, a nurse holds her master's child. The planters' children often depended on their "mammy" for affection and deferred to her even as adults.

A groom feeds his mistress's horse in a painted collage known as a "pastie." This pastie and the one below were made in the 1840s for the children of a Mississippi family; their mother was the horsewoman shown above.

A collage entitled *Hauling the Whole Week's Picking* depicts field slaves of various ages. Most masters used a fraction system to rate the slaves' work capacity. Children began as "quarter hands" and worked their way up to "half hands" and "full hands." Elderly slaves started sliding back down the scale.

Precious Hours of Free Time

Slaves were usually granted time off on Sundays, and sometimes on Saturday afternoons. Most of them spent these precious hours cleaning their own houses, tending their gardens, or working on other plantations for a little money. The remainder of their time was devoted to simple pleasures.

They went fishing, fashioned baskets or brooms, danced to the music of a banjo or fiddle. Some slaves were satisfied to go to prayer meetings or simply to savor the luxury of having nothing to do. Said a free black of a slave he had known: "Her idea of the joy of heaven was simply rest."

Slave children pass time by their cabins. They grew up on black folktales such as the Br'er Rabbit stories, in which the weak use cunning to overcome the strong.

Slaves enjoy a holiday dance in this idealized painting. Although many planters sponsored festivities at Christmas time, few of their slaves were as well dressed as these.

Slaves gather around a coffin to mourn the death of a fellow. Burials were frequently held at night because of work requirements; weeks later, on a rest day, joyous funeral celebrations were held to sing, drink and dance the dead to heaven.

Tools of Punishment and Intimidation

A slave collar hung with bells (*left*) revealed a miscreant's every move. A pronged neck ring (*above*) prevented the slave from lying down.

"He has been gelded, and is not yet well," wrote a Louisiana jailer after capturing a runaway slave. Although this barbaric punishment was used to control only the most unruly blacks, nearly all slaves endured some form of brutal coercion at some time.

Almost all the large plantations were equipped with various instruments of punishment, and masters who were squeamish hired "slave breakers" to apply them forcefully. The most common implement was a long rawhide whip. Blows from this whip took the skin off the back of a stripped and spread-eagled offender. Standard punishment was 15 to 20 lashes, but the number for serious offenses often ran into the hundreds. To prevent infection, whip wounds were sluiced with salt water, and the resulting pain was excruciating. At the mere recollection of it, a former slave wrote, "The flesh crawls upon my bones."

Iron fetters, such as the two sets of shackles shown here, were used to restrain rebellious slaves and prevent them from running away.

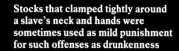

Stocks that clamped tightly around a slave's neck and hands were sometimes used as mild punishment for such offenses as drunkenness and disobedience. A wrongdoer might spend a full 24 hours standing in the stocks with nothing for sustenance except bread and water.

(*left*) for administering clublike blows. A canvas paddle coated with rubber (*below*) did the work of a whip without tearing up a slave's back.

Stripped naked, a slave receives a brutal whipping in front of other slaves. After several blows, the lash usually became wet with blood; as the beating continued, the victim's cries of pain turned into low moans.

A statement signed by a Kentucky official certifies that a professional slave breaker is owed four dollars for whipping eight slaves.

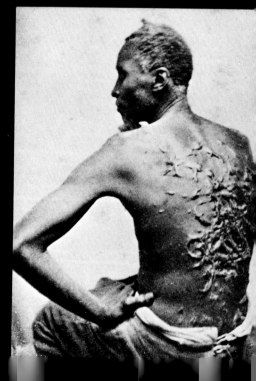

The Urge to Escape: a Troublesome "Disease of the Mind"

According to a Louisiana doctor, blacks suffered from a peculiar "disease of the mind" that caused them to run away from their masters, and the proper cure was "whipping the devil out of them." Whippings, along with curfews and antifugitive patrols, did keep down the number of runaways. But slaves continued to run away.

Often, the fugitive had been recently sold to another plantation and was trying to return to his family. Others fled grueling labor or a cruel overseer. Some runaways sought freedom in the distant North. Whatever drove them, only small numbers made good their escape, often with the help of the Underground Railroad. Most fugitives were captured after a few days at large.

Some runaways chose death over recapture. A Louisiana fugitive caught on a raft on the Mississippi refused to surrender, and so he was shot. "He fell at the third fire," a white reported. "So determined was he not to be captured that when an effort was made to rescue him from drowning, he made battle with his club and sunk waving his weapon in angry defiance."

Exhausted fugitives reach a farm in Newport, Indiana, a way station on the Underground Railroad to Canada. "I feel lighter," said one slave. "The dread is gone."

Crusaders for Freedom

A shackled slave begging for freedom was the poignant emblem of the abolitionist cause. This lithograph appeared on a broadside with a poem by John Greenleaf Whittier, "Our Countrymen in Chains."

Abolitionism, the militant movement that turned most Northerners against slavery, was born in a jail in 1830. At that time, more than a hundred antislavery groups were already at work—but with more high-mindedness than heat: Their members, like generations of moralists and humanitarians before them, patiently called for improvement in the slaves' lot in preparation for emancipation at some later date. Antislavery efforts began changing fast, however, when William Lloyd Garrison, a 24-year-old editor from Massachusetts, was released from jail in Baltimore in June of 1830, after serving seven weeks for libeling a merchant who was legally ferrying slaves up and down the coast.

During his imprisonment Garrison made an angry resolve to end slavery—not later, but now. Returning to Boston, he started publishing *The Liberator* on New Year's Day, 1831. Though the newspaper would never exceed a circulation of 3,000, it enlisted hundreds of gifted followers in the abolitionist crusade and infused them with Garrison's tireless, fearless, selfless zeal. With several friends, Garrison in 1833 founded the American Anti-Slavery Society, whose membership rose to nearly 250,000 in 1838. This was the first American organization in which women as well as men, and blacks as well as whites, played an active role.

The organization operated on a shoe-string; its main asset—often its only one—was the time members gave to making speeches, distributing literature and collecting signatures on petitions to Congress. The leading crusaders, 12 of whom are vignetted on the following pages, were not content merely to demand freedom and equality for blacks. Many espoused other radical causes: women's rights, prison reform, amelioration of the harsh debtors' laws, temperance, pacifism.

Risk and adversity were standard fare for society members. They ran safe houses on the Underground Railroad and defied mobs of workers who feared that emancipation would bring hordes of freed slaves to take their jobs. The members' strident campaigning made them distasteful to polite Northerners, even those who shared their two basic beliefs—that slavery was a sin and that everyone was his brother's keeper. Garrison and a few extremists alienated reverent, patriotic folk by attacking organized religion and advocating civil disobedience.

The Anti-Slavery Society thrived on opposition, but internal dissension was another story: The society was fragmented by clashes among its aggressive leaders and their multiple causes. For example, when Garrison insisted on electing a woman to the executive board, three cofounders went off in a huff to start a rival organization. Others left to promote abolition through the Liberty Party, which ran James G. Birney for President in 1840 (and polled only 7,000 votes). But by then the drive for abolition had built up irreversible momentum.

Garrison enjoyed the first taste of victory years before emancipation became the law of the land. In 1855, after decades of arguing that true equality was impossible as long as the races were kept separate by law, he and several colleagues persuaded the state of Massachusetts to open its public schools and public transportation to all races.

Members of the American Anti-Slavery Society rally outdoors in Syracuse, New York, in this rare early photo from the 1840s. The speaker, at center, is believed to be philanthropist Gerrit Smith; seated in front of him is Frederick Douglass, the fugitive slave turned abolitionist orator.

Leaders in the War against Slavery

Frederick Douglass

"I appear this evening as a thief and a robber," announced Frederick Douglass, a self-taught fugitive slave, at an anti-slavery meeting in 1842. "I stole this head, these limbs, this body from my master, and ran off with them." With just such pathos and outrage Douglass evoked the suffering of slaves in uncounted speeches, in his autobiography and in *The North Star*, a weekly newspaper he founded and edited for 17 years in Rochester, New York. Originally convinced that abolition should be achieved by "moral suasion" alone, without political action, Douglass eventually joined the Liberty Party. He never stopped campaigning for complete black equality. At the end of his long life, when asked for a word of advice for a young man just starting out, he replied: "Agitate!"

Theodore Parker

Theodore Parker, a scholarly Congregational minister, attacked the Fugitive Slave Law from his Boston pulpit, urging his parishioners to aid runaways in any way they could. And Parker did more than preach. Serving as a leader of the Boston Vigilance Committee, he concealed scores of fugitives from the federal agents deputized to recapture them, and he engineered their escapes to Canada. Parker justified his criminal conduct on purely religious grounds. "The Fugitive Slave Law contradicts the acknowledged precepts of the Christian religion," he declared in 1851. "It violates the noblest instincts of humanity; it asks us to trample on the law of God. It commands what nature, religion, and God alike forbid; it forbids what nature, religion, and God alike command."

Sojourner Truth

An illiterate slave who ran away from her New York master in the 1820s, Isabella Baumfree began calling herself Sojourner Truth in the 1840s because, as she later told Harriet Beecher Stowe, God intended her to "travel up an' down de land, showin' de people der sins, an' bein' a sign unto dem." Tall, gaunt and dynamic, she became a popular speaker at abolitionist rallies. Her plain speaking about the evils of slavery moved many audiences, and her wit silenced those who dared challenge her. After one speech, a listener demanded, "Old woman, do you think that your talk about slavery does any good? Why, I don't care any more for your talk than I do for the bite of a flea."

"Perhaps not," replied Sojourner Truth, "but, de Lord willin', I'll keep you scratchin'."

William Lloyd Garrison

The radical genius of the movement, William Lloyd Garrison was arrogant and relentless in preaching against slavery and inequality. Conviction alone, not status or wealth, made him so self-assured; he had been abandoned by his drunken immigrant father and had eked out a living as an apprentice cobbler, carpenter and printer. He went on to become a newspaper editor and dabble in politics, backing the commercial interests he later attacked with such virulence. After his conversion to abolitionism, he borrowed some type and, in the autumn of 1830, published the manifesto to which he devoted the rest of his life:

"The liberty of a people is the gift of God and nature."

"That which is not just is not law."

"He who oppugns public liberty overthrows his own."

Harriet Beecher Stowe

The author of *Uncle Tom's Cabin* was the pious daughter, wife, sister and mother of ministers, and she could not help preaching herself, even though she was self-effacing to a fault. She advocated abolition in the belief that slavery jeopardized Christian souls. "Such peril and shame as now hangs over this country is worse than Roman slavery," she wrote in 1851, adding mildly, "I hope every woman who can write will not be silent." Her modesty was unshaken by the enormous success of her novel. If anything made her vulnerable to the sin of pride, it was praise from arch-abolitionist William Lloyd Garrison. "I estimate the value of anti-slavery writing by the abuse it brings," he wrote her after reading her book. "Now all the defenders of slavery have let me alone and are abusing you."

Charles Calistus Burleigh

At 24, lawyer Charles Burleigh became an agent and influential lecturer for Massachusetts' Middlesex Anti-Slavery Society. In answer to those who feared that newly freed slaves would inundate the North and undercut the wages of white workers, Burleigh argued that blacks would stop coming north once they were freed, and that wage-earning blacks would increase the market for Northern products. Further, he argued that with education a free black would work far harder than any slave and prove more valuable to society: "As much as brain and muscle are worth more than muscle only; as much as moral joined to mental power is a better wealth than mere brute force; so much will the emancipation of a nation's slaves enrich the nation. Why, then, should not our slaves go free?"

Lucretia Mott

Quaker minister Lucretia Mott helped found the Philadelphia Female Anti-Slavery Society in 1833. With her abolitionist husband, she supported the work of the Underground Railroad, harboring runaways in her Philadelphia home. In her lectures she called for boycotting the agricultural products of slavery, and she dared to take her anti-slavery message into Virginia. In 1840, she attended London's World Anti-Slavery Convention, and when women were denied an active part in the proceedings, she became an ardent feminist. In keeping with her Quaker heritage, Mrs. Mott was a confirmed pacifist; she would use any tactic but outright violence to oppose injustice to slaves. She declared, "I am no advocate of passivity. Quakerism does not mean quietism."

Charles Lenox Remond

Born free in Salem, Massachusetts, Charles Remond was the first black to address public meetings on behalf of abolition. As an agent of the Massachusetts chapter of the American Anti-Slavery Society, he canvassed New England and in 1840 represented the parent organization at the first World Anti-Slavery Convention in London. Back home after a 19-month lecture tour of Great Britain and Ireland, Remond became famous for his powerful speeches. Not content with emancipation, Remond demanded that blacks be rewarded in proportion to their contributions to society. To do anything less, he told Massachusetts legislators in 1842, was an "unkind and unchristian policy calculated to make every man disregardful of his conduct, and every woman unmindful of her reputation."

Wendell Phillips

The scion of one of Boston's wealthiest and most influential families, Wendell Phillips was converted to the cause of abolitionism by his future wife in 1836. He abandoned the practice of law, which he considered boring, and quickly became one of the outstanding orators of the anti-slavery movement. Following in the radical footsteps of William Lloyd Garrison, Phillips cursed the Constitution for permitting the existence of slavery and refused to support it by running for public office—or even voting. He stopped short of advocating violence but did call for the Northern states to secede from the Union rather than put up with Southern slavery any longer, declaring, "If lawful and peaceful efforts for the abolition of slavery in our land will dissolve it, let the Union go."

Harriet Tubman

A Maryland slave who ran away in 1849, tiny, fearless Harriet Tubman earned the *nom de guerre* "Moses" for leading more than 300 slaves to freedom on the Underground Railroad. She was so skillful at disguise and evasion that she was never caught, nor were any of the fugitives in her charge. In the War she served the Union Army as cook, laundress, nurse and spy. Because she worked in secrecy, praise for her successes came first from those who shared her labors. "I have had the applause of the crowd," Frederick Douglass wrote her, "while the most that you have done has been witnessed by a few trembling, scarred and foot-sore bondmen and women, whom you have led out of the house of bondage, and whose heartfelt 'God bless you' has been your only reward."

Maria Weston Chapman

Maria Chapman, a well-to-do matron of Pilgrim stock, was one of the 12 founders of the Boston Female Anti-Slavery Society. She became a disciple of William Lloyd Garrison and edited *The Liberator* when he was away from Boston on lecture tours. Mrs. Chapman showed her courage in 1835, when a mob surrounded the society's meeting place. Since the black members were in particular danger, she told the whites each to take the arm of a black companion; then, two by two, the women marched from the hall. "When we emerged into the open daylight," she recalled, "there went up a roar of rage and contempt, which increased when they saw that we did not intend to separate." Mrs. Chapman calmly led her friends through the mob to her home, where she reconvened the meeting.

John Greenleaf Whittier

The son of a Massachusetts Quaker farmer, John Greenleaf Whittier was an inveterate campaigner for liberal causes. Hundreds of antislavery poems, written between 1833 and 1865, made him the poet laureate of abolition. In his stirring "Stanzas for the Times," Whittier used rhetorical questions to imply that slavery sullied the freedom American patriots had died for: "Is this the land our fathers loved? / The freedom which they toil'd to win?" He warned his readers that they must continue their ancestors' war against tyranny by working to free the slaves or they would eventually sacrifice their own freedom to Southern slaveholders. Shall we, demanded the poet, fairly insisting on "no" as the answer, "Yoke in with marked and branded slaves, / And tremble at the driver's whip?"

The Avenging Angel

> *"Better that a whole generation of men, women and children should pass away by a violent death than that a word of either [the Bible or the Declaration of Independence] should be violated in this country."*

JOHN BROWN

Shortly before midnight on May 24, 1856, James Doyle heard a knock at the door of his cabin near Dutch Henry's Crossing on Pottawatomie Creek in eastern Kansas. Minutes earlier, the settler might have heard his two bulldogs barking, but they were silent now, cut to pieces by the visitors' swords or put to flight. Doyle apparently feared nothing as he opened the door.

Five armed men forced their way into Doyle's house. They demanded that he surrender to their "Army of the North." They took Doyle outside and very likely questioned him about his politics; he was well known locally as a proslavery man. Then a visitor reentered the house and ordered Doyle's two oldest sons, William and Drury, to come outside. Doyle's wife, Mahala, begged that no harm come to her youngest son, 14-year-old John, and he was allowed to remain behind.

Out on the prairie, the visitors cut down and killed James Doyle with their swords. They split his sons' skulls like melons. They sliced the arms off one of the corpses. They kept on hacking at the bloody bodies for a while, and then they departed, to a litany of wails from Mrs. Doyle. John Brown of Osawatomie had come to call.

"Old Man" Brown, as he was called, did not start the violence that was tearing Kansas apart. Others before him had killed to win the new territory for slavery, or to keep slavery out. A few were even avowed terrorists like Brown, men for whom killing was not just a means to an end but an end in itself. But only Brown, starting on that dark night on the Kansas prairie, murdered in the name of the Lord and managed to convince others that killing over the issue of slavery was acceptable and in some wise justified. Indeed, Brown, more clearly than anyone else, argued that slavery was a just cause for war.

Brown's fanatic zeal grew naturally from his troubled origins. His family background was notably unstable. Certain relatives on his mother's side were said to have died mad. His father was a frontiersman, always pulling up stakes and moving on. As a child, John had had little schooling, little love. As a man, he was a chronic failure. He failed at farming, tanning, land speculation and stock breeding. In all, he suffered 15 business failures in four states and weathered numerous lawsuits and accusations of dishonesty.

It was from his stern Calvinist father that Brown inherited his devout hatred of slavery. He yearned to harm slaveowners greatly, to smite them hip and thigh for God. He styled himself the Angel of the Lord, and he meant to be an avenging angel; he openly advocated the use of violence against God's slaveholding enemies and against the bounty hunters enforcing the Fugitive Slave Law. His fire-and-brimstone exhortations won admirers all through the East. "Whenever he spoke," wrote Frederick Douglass, an escaped slave turned abolitionist preacher, "his words commanded earnest attention. His arguments seemed to convince all; his appeals touched all, and his will impressed all."

To those who fell under his spell, John Brown was quite simply intimidating. At 56, he was lean, sinewy and ramrod straight. His associates invariably described him as being six feet tall, though he actually was just five feet nine inches. An awed disciple compared his thin, grim, leathery face to an eagle's—to which one of Brown's sons reportedly added, "or another carnivorous bird." A second son said he looked like a meat ax. And when Brown declared that God had ordered him to "break the jaws of the wicked," his fol-

John Brown, a driven abolitionist, owned this revolver in May 1856, when he and his companions killed five proslavery Kansans in cold blood along Pottawatomie Creek.

lowers believed him and were ready to obey.

Brown's first venture into ritual murder did not end with the butchery at the home of James Doyle. The Old Man and his companions—including four of his seven sons—rode on for half a mile or so to the sod house of Allen Wilkinson, a member of the proslavery territorial legislature. Again there was discussion of where the householder stood on the slavery question, and Brown ordered the man outside. Again a wife pleaded and then waited helplessly while her husband was murdered, a blade run through his side and his skull laid open.

Brown had just one more stop to make now, the James Harris house. He was looking not for Harris himself but for Harris' boss, "Dutch" Henry Sherman, a thuggish saloonkeeper and a known proslavery man. By chance, Dutch Henry was out on the prairie searching for some missing cattle, but his

brother, "Dutch" Bill, was staying overnight at the Harris home. Brown's men split Dutch Bill's skull, ran him through the side and then, in the inexplicable final act of their night of terror, severed one of his hands.

These five killings became known as the Pottawatomie Massacre. Of course, the success did not sate John Brown's sense of murderous mission. He must go on, for—as he was fond of saying—"without the shedding of blood there is no remission of sins." There were sins aplenty to be remitted in Kansas and everywhere in the slave-owning South.

The chain of events that had brought John Brown to Kansas had begun two and a half years earlier. On January 4, 1854, Senator Stephen A. Douglas of Illinois reported out of his Committee on Territories a bill to organize the so-called Nebraska Territory, which included Kansas, in preparation for statehood. Douglas saw Kansas as a thoroughfare for a railroad line to the West Coast, with its eastern terminus in his native state. But as always, slavery was a stumbling block.

The new territory was north of the Missouri Compromise line, which meant that slavery was automatically prohibited. Precisely because of this, Southern Senators had opposed previous attempts to organize the territory and could be expected to do so again. One of them, Senator David R. Atchison of Missouri, vowed that he would rather "sink in hell" than see Kansas enter the Union as a free state.

There seemed to be no way around the problem—no way, that is, until Douglas' bill incorporated the idea of popular sovereignty. In the terms of the bill, the Nebraska and Kansas lands would be admitted to the Union "as their constitution may prescribe at the time of their admission." In other words, it would be left up to the settlers of the territories to choose by their own vote whether or not they wanted slavery.

Douglas was an ambitious man, given rather too much to drink and boast, but he was a great statesman. A firm believer in Manifest Destiny, he knew that the admission of more states to the Union would remain deadlocked so long as the slavery issue divided the North and the South. Indeed, the whole settlement of the Great Plains and the West could be stalled by the sectional controversy—and so could his own drive for the presidency. But if he could unite the country behind the idea of popular sovereignty, then he would stand an excellent chance of winning the White House.

Southern Democrats and other assorted proslavery men were indignant to note a serious flaw in the Douglas bill. It made no mention of the Missouri Compromise, whose terms had not been abrogated. Thus the legislation created an obvious contradiction: The ban on slaves effectively kept out of the territory the slaveowners who would vote for a proslavery constitution at the time Kansas was up for admission to statehood.

The solution was simple enough: In exchange for crucial Southern support for his bill, Douglas accepted an amendment repealing the part of the Missouri Compromise that prohibited slavery north of the 36° 30′ line. "By God, sir, you are right," he reportedly remarked to a Southern Senator. "I will incorporate it into my bill, though I know it will raise a hell of a storm."

The Congressional debate was perhaps the fiercest in American history. In a letter to a Washington newspaper, Senator Salmon P. Chase of Ohio and five of his antislav-ery colleagues denounced Douglas' Kansas-Nebraska bill as "a gross violation of a sacred pledge"; as "a criminal betrayal of precious rights; as part and parcel of an atrocious plot to exclude from the vast unoccupied region immigrants from the Old World and free laborers from our own States, and convert it into a dreary region of despotism, inhabited by masters and slaves." Tempers flared in debate and insults were traded that nearly led to a duel between Congressmen John C. Breckinridge of Kentucky and Francis Cutting of New York. Newspapers fanned the flames. In one satirical poem Douglas was lampooned as a puppet of the South:

> *The Dropsied Dwarf of Illinois*
> *By brother sneaks called, 'Little Giant'*
> *He who has made so great a noise*
> *By being to the slave power pliant.*

The Kansas-Nebraska bill passed the Senate in March and the House two months later. The vote was resolutely sectional. Most Southern members of Congress, whatever their party affiliation, voted "Yea," while nearly all Northerners said "Nay." With passage of the Act, the last vestiges of the truce of 1850 were struck down. Serious trouble was now a certainty, and radicals on both sides rejoiced at the prospect of a showdown. Senator Charles S. Sumner of Massachusetts called the new law "the best bill on which Congress ever acted" because it "makes all future compromises impossible."

The showdown was swift in coming, for whichever side rushed more of its own to the new land would win the upper hand, gaining control of the territorial legislature and with it the authority to write the final word on slavery. Senator William H. Seward of New

Youthful and beardless, John Brown pledges allegiance to an unidentified flag—possibly an abolitionist banner. The photograph, the earliest known picture of Brown, was most likely taken in 1846 in Springfield, Massachusetts. At the time, Brown made a living grading wool for New England textile manufacturers. On the side, he aided runaway slaves, attended abolitionist meetings and formulated grandiose plans for freeing the South's slave population.

Proslavery Missourians trek to Kansas to cast illegal votes and harass Free Staters. These outlanders were known pejoratively as "Border Ruffians" in the North, but the term became so popular in Missouri that businessmen added it to their company names.

York had made clear the issue and the goal. "Come on then, Gentlemen of the Slave States," he said. "Since there is no escaping your challenge, I accept it in behalf of the cause of freedom. We will engage in competition for the virgin soil of Kansas, and God give the victory to the side which is stronger in numbers as it is in right." Even before the Act passed Congress, Massachusetts had chartered an Emigrant Aid Company to encourage antislavery people to go to Kansas.

The other side was at least as determined to capture Kansas. "When you reside within one day's journey of the territory," roared Senator Atchison to an audience of fellow Missourians, "and when your peace, your quiet and your property depend on your action, you can, without an exertion, send five hundred of your young men who will vote in favor of your institutions." Nor did Atchison expect to stop at mere voting. He confided in a letter to Senator Jefferson Davis of Mississippi, "We will be compelled to shoot, burn and hang, but the thing will soon be over."

In the months following passage of the Act, more and more men made their way to the plains. One of them was Andrew Reeder of Pennsylvania, sent by President Franklin Pierce to be governor of the territory. When Reeder called for the election of a territorial legislature, the situation began to unravel.

A census taken before the voting showed only 2,905 eligible voters. But when the polls closed in March 1855, the tally revealed 6,307 ballots cast, most of them for proslavery candidates. Clearly, Senator Atchison had succeeded in his campaign to flood Kansas with proslavery Missourians; hundreds of the interlopers, called Border Ruffians by the abolitionist press, had come over the line en masse to stuff the ballot boxes. Actually, the trip was unnecessary, for bona fide proslavery settlers far outnumbered their opponents, and the Free State men had further limited their own influence by flocking together around the town of Lawrence.

Reeder was thoroughly intimidated by the Border Ruffians, and so, despite fevered protests from Free Staters, he let the election stand. So did his chief in Washington, President Pierce. Then salt was rubbed in the Free Staters' wounds: The new Kansas legislature, meeting at Shawnee Mission during the summer and autumn, enacted a series of draconian laws designed to protect slavery. Harboring a fugitive slave became a hanging offense; merely expressing doubts about slavery could lead to jail. Capping it all, the proslavery legislators expelled the few Free State members who had been elected.

The Free Staters left in a rage to form their own government. They proceeded to elect a governor, draft a constitution outlawing slavery and apply to Washington for admission to the Union as a free state. This sorry episode cost Governor Reeder his job

Six Kansas Free Staters stand ready to fire their outdated cannon at proslavery troublemakers. Some of the artillery pieces employed in the Kansas conflict were trophies from the Mexican War. Others were even older relics used to fire salutes during Fourth of July celebrations.

for failing to keep order and all but ensured a violent collision between the rival factions.

The collision came in November 1855, when a Free Stater was killed in a land-claim dispute with a slavery advocate. The known killer was not arrested, and the slain man's friends vented their wrath by burning the murderer's home. Action followed reaction until the proslavery sheriff of Douglas County—a man named Samuel Jones—enlisted the aid of a small army of Border Ruffians to help him arrest the Free State men. By early December several hundred raiders had mustered along the Wakarusa River near the Free Staters' town of Lawrence.

The enemies of the Border Ruffians hastily sent out the call to arms. "We want every true Free State man in Kansas at Lawrence immediately," said James Lane, a prominent antislavery partisan who was to be elected a United States Senator. One of those who turned out was John Brown, who had just joined five of his sons in Kansas. Seeing the exciting possibilities for violence, he volunteered for the fight against the Border Ruffians. His son John Jr. was given command of a small company of Free Staters.

The newly appointed Governor, Wilson Shannon of Cincinnati, managed to pacify the hotheads and prevent any shooting. But the bloodshed was not postponed for long. In the spring of 1856 Sheriff Jones twice went to Lawrence to enforce arrest warrants, and both times he was forcibly rebuffed. Shortly after the second attempt, he was shot and wounded in an ambush by Free State men. Soon thereafter, the Douglas County grand jury returned indictments against several Free Staters, two newspapers, and the Free State Hotel—all in Lawrence, and all charged with treason.

A federal marshal made a few arrests, but the Border Ruffians were unsatisfied. Bent on bringing the whole settlement to heel, if not to justice, they rode into Lawrence on May 21 and sacked the town. They wrecked the offending presses, bombarded the seemingly impregnable Free State Hotel with cannon and set it afire along with the Free State Governor's house. By chance, the only casualty of the drunken spree was a proslavery man killed by the collapsing hotel.

These goings-on had immediate and angry repercussions in Washington. Charles Sumner, the sonorous Senator from Massachusetts, delivered a speech he called "The Crime against Kansas," and it was one of the most violent antislavery harangues of a career noted for oratorical intemperance. The crime against Kansas, Sumner thundered, was "the rape of a virgin territory, compelling it to the hateful embrace of slavery." He reserved his harshest remarks for an aging proslavery Senator from South Carolina, Andrew P. Butler, who was absent from the Senate at the time. He ridiculed Butler's manner of speech and lambasted him for having "chosen a mistress who, though ugly to others, is always lovely to him; though polluted in the sight of the world is chaste in his sight—I mean the harlot, Slavery."

Sumner's remarks offended Southerners in general and even some of his abolitionist friends, but the angriest response came from Senator Butler's cousin, Representative Preston Brooks of South Carolina. Entering the Senate on May 22, Brooks strode up to Sumner, who was seated comfortably at his desk. Denouncing the abolitionist, Brooks brought a gutta-percha cane down on Sumner's head and continued to rain blows upon him even as the cane broke into smaller

Angry Free Staters survey the ruins of the elegant Free State Hotel, defense headquarters for the abolitionist town of Lawrence, Kansas. On May 21, 1856, proslavery Border Ruffians fired their cannon point-blank at the fortified structure, then completed their destructive handiwork by setting the hotel on fire.

and smaller pieces. It would take more than two years for the severely injured Sumner to resume his Senate seat, and until then his empty chair would remind Northerners of Southern irrationality and violence in defense of slavery. What Southerners thought of Brooks became a matter of record. He resigned his seat to permit his district to voice its opinion and was reelected almost unanimously in November 1856.

When the news of Brooks's attack on Sumner reached Kansas, John Brown was already in a dangerous mood. He had just heard of the sack of Lawrence and reportedly said to his companions, "Something must be done to show these barbarians." Sumner's caning was entirely too much for Brown; the Old Man "went crazy—*crazy*," his son Salmon reported. At Brown's command, his

sons sharpened the swords that his party was to use on May 24 at the homes of James Doyle, Allen Wilkinson and James Harris. One of Brown's neighbors urged caution. "Caution? Caution, sir?" replied Brown. "I am eternally tired of hearing that word 'caution.' It is nothing but a word of cowardice."

In choosing his victims, Brown almost certainly was thinking of more than a bloody statement of moral principle. He had some personal scores to settle as well. All of his victims, save one of Doyle's sons, were connected with the Osawatomie territorial district court—the district where John Brown lived. A month earlier, Brown's son John Jr. had been rebuffed by that court for asking incredulously whether the territory's proslavery laws would be enforced, and his subsequent declaration of resistance to the court's edicts made him guilty of contempt, an offense described as treason by the proslavery legislature. The murders of May 24 effectively removed several witnesses who could have testified against John Brown Jr.

As for the killers, there was never a question in Kansas of their identity. James Harris recognized Brown, and the widowed Mrs. Wilkinson and young John Doyle provided matching descriptions of the chief murderer. Just four days after the slaughter, enough evidence had been gathered for the sheriff to issue a warrant for Brown's arrest. Indeed, the murders so outraged frontiersmen of every stripe that even some staunch abolitionists joined with proslavery friends of the dead men to condemn the atrocity and demand that the killers be brought to justice.

But the truth about the massacre did not travel well. Within a few weeks, exaggerated and falsified reports of the killings began appearing in the Eastern press. There had been no murders at all, said one paper. Another claimed that the mutilation of the corpses proved the murders to be the work of Comanches. Some articles implied that the killings were done during a fair battle between Brown's party and proslavery men—a simple matter of self-defense. The New York *Tribune* even printed a story claiming that Brown had happened upon a band of rowdies about to do violence to a Free Stater, and that he killed the villains in the act of saving the poor antislavery man. None of those who rushed to Brown's defense seemed to notice the fact that the dead men were unarmed and murdered at their homes.

There was whitewash enough to cover Congress as well. When a Congressional committee investigated the massacre and its first witness, James Harris, began to tell

SOUTHERN CHIVALRY — ARGUMENT VERSUS CLUB'S.

A Northern cartoon condemning South Carolina Representative Preston S. Brooks for his caning of Massachusetts Senator Charles Sumner shows Southern Senators enjoying the sight and preventing intervention by Sumner's friends. "Every Southern man sustains me," Brooks boasted in a letter to his brother. "The fragments of the stick are begged for as *sacred relics.*"

what really happened, the antislavery majority immediately cut him off and later omitted all adverse testimony from the majority report. For years, the known facts about the killings were submerged in abolitionist rhetoric. In the popular imagination of the North, the cold-blooded act became exactly what Brown had intended it to be—a righteous strike for the freedom of slaves.

In the aftermath of the Pottawatomie Massacre, John Brown lay low in his camp in the Kansas brush. For weeks the antislavery forces and the Border Ruffians postured and threatened but managed to avoid a pitched battle. A few skirmishes did take place. The largest was an attack by 250 proslavery men on Osawatomie, near where Brown and his followers were camped. One of Brown's sons was killed in the clash.

In the autumn of 1856, a newly appointed federal Governor, John W. Geary, arrived in Kansas and quickly dominated events. His policy was unprecedented in the territory: He treated Free Stater and proslavery man with the same rough justice. In the end, both factions backed down from him—and from a force of U.S. Army troops who brooked no nonsense from either side. At last, a troubled quiet settled on the plains. Both sides returned to the business of gobbling up and profiting from the land. Old opponents often were seen working together. The New York press soon commented that "the love of the almighty dollar had melted away the iron of bitterness and Anti-Slavery and Pro-Slavery men were standing together as a unit on their rights as squatters."

The whole nation seemed to heave a great sigh of relief as the crisis in Kansas cooled. The disunion talk—or at least most of it—had subsided. Yet the quiet was bound to be short-lived, for in March of 1857 the Supreme Court was to announce its verdict in a case that supposedly would settle the precise legal status of slavery in the territories.

The case in question went back almost two decades—to a time when the Missouri Compromise, with its ban of slavery in territories north of 36° 30', was still the law of the land. At stake was the status of an elderly black man named Dred Scott. In 1834 Scott's owner—an Army surgeon named John Emerson—took his slave from Missouri to a military post in Illinois, though slavery was outlawed in that state. Two years later, transferred to another post, Emerson took Scott to the Wisconsin Territory, where slavery was also outlawed. Emerson eventually brought Scott back to Missouri, where the surgeon died in 1843.

Three years later Scott, with the help of local antislavery lawyers, sued Emerson's heirs for his freedom, contending that his years in Illinois and Wisconsin had made him free. Scott lost his case, then won on appeal in 1850, only to see the Missouri state supreme court reverse the appeal and once again consign him to slavery. Scott thereupon took his case to the federal courts, where he lost again in 1854. After another two years the U.S. Supreme Court agreed to hear the case.

The two key questions posed by the case were prickly. First, was Scott a citizen with the right to sue in the federal courts? Second, was he free as a result of having lived in the Wisconsin Territory, where slavery was outlawed by the Missouri Compromise? Moreover, the second question patently involved the constitutionality of the Missouri Compromise's prohibition of slavery. Did Con-

Chief Justice Roger Taney, the wealthy Marylander who handed down the Supreme Court's proslavery decision in the Dred Scott case, personally deplored slavery and had even freed his own bondsmen.

gress really have the power to regulate slavery in the territories?

Chief Justice Roger B. Taney, the 79-year-old scion of a wealthy, slave-owning Maryland family, announced the Court's decision on March 6. As to Scott's right to sue, Taney held that he had none: Slaves and freed descendants of slaves were not citizens, said Taney, because at the time the Constitution was written, blacks "had for more than a century been regarded as beings of an inferior order . . . so far inferior that they had no rights which the white man was bound to respect." As to Scott's freedom, Taney held that he had none of that either: Slaves were property, and slaveholders had an absolute right to take their property with them into the territories. The Fifth Amendment guaranteed that no person should "be deprived of life, liberty or property without due process

of law." Any law, said Taney, that abridged such a constitutionally protected right was in itself a violation of due process. In other words, Congress had violated the Constitution in enacting the Missouri Compromise. Dred Scott had lost on all counts.

The reaction was immediate. Proslavery people hailed the decision as the final vindication of their rights. From the antislavery states came cries of outrage. The Dred Scott ruling had come from a Supreme Court dominated by Southerners, rekindling fears of a "slave power" conspiracy in the federal government—a plot by a wealthy, cruel minority to thwart democratic rule by the majority. The attack on the Court was venomous. Chief Justice Taney was vilified for his "wicked and false judgment," for his "gross historical falsehoods," and for his "jesuitical decision"—a slurring reference to his Roman Catholic faith. "If epithets and denunciations could sink a judicial-body," said one observer, "the Supreme Court of the United States would never be heard from again."

And so the South had gained another victory. Yet the Southern triumphs in the controversy over the Fugitive Slave Law, the Missouri Compromise repeal, the crooked Kansas legislature and now the Dred Scott decision brought the South closer and closer to defeat, for each victory made old enemies stronger and added new enemies to the ranks of hard-line abolitionists and emancipationists. And by 1857, more pyrrhic victories were in the offing for the South and more enemies were about to be made. For Kansas was ready to bleed again.

Shortly before Democrat James Buchanan became President in 1857, the proslavery Kansas legislature started a drive for state-

Dred Scott, the slave who sue his freedom on the ground his master had transported h a territory where slavery prohibited, was the subject of f page stories like this one for mc after the Supreme Court against him in March 1857. But won out in spite of the court deci He, his wife and their two daug were freed by a new ma

FRANK LESLIE'S ILLUSTRATED NEWSPAPER

Entered according to Act of Congress, in the year 1857, by FRANK LESLIE, in the Clerk's Office of the District Court for the Southern District of New York. (Copyrighted June 22, 1857.)

No. 82.—VOL. IV.]   NEW YORK, SATURDAY, JUNE 27, 1857.   [PRICE 6 CENTS.

TO TOURISTS AND TRAVELLERS.

We shall be happy to receive personal narratives, of land or sea, including adventures and incidents, from every person who pleases to correspond with our paper.

We take this opportunity of returning our thanks to our numerous artistic correspondents throughout the country, for the many sketches we are constantly receiving from them of the news of the day. We trust they will spare no pains to furnish us with drawings of events as they may occur. We would also remind them that it is necessary to send all sketches, if possible, by the earliest conveyance.

VISIT TO DRED SCOTT—HIS FAMILY—INCIDENTS OF HIS LIFE —DECISION OF THE SUPREME COURT.

WHILE standing in the Fair grounds at St. Louis, and engaged in conversation with a prominent citizen of that enterprising city, he suddenly asked us if we would not like to be introduced to Dred Scott. Upon expressing a desire to be thus honored, the gentleman called to an old negro who was standing near by, and our wish was gratified. Dred made a rude obeisance to our recognition, and seemed to enjoy the notice we expended upon him. We found him on examination to be a pure-blooded African, perhaps fifty years of age, with a shrewd, intelligent, good-natured face, of rather light frame, being not more than five feet six inches high. After some general remarks we expressed a wish to get his portrait (we had made

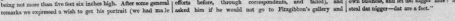

ELIZA AND LIZZIE, CHILDREN OF DRED SCOTT.

efforts before, through correspondents, and failed), and asked him if he would not go to Fitzgibbon's gallery and

have it taken. The gentleman present explained to Dred that it was proper he should have his likeness in the "great illustrated paper of the country," overruled his many objections, which seemed to grow out of a superstitious feeling, and he promised to be at the gallery the next day. This appointment Dred did not keep. Determined not to be foiled, we sought an interview with Mr. Crane, Dred's lawyer, who promptly gave us a letter of introduction, explaining to Dred that it was to his advantage to have his picture taken to be engraved for our paper, and also directions where we could find his domicile. We found the place with difficulty, the streets in Dred's neighborhood being more clearly defined in the plan of the city than on the mother earth; we finally reached a wooden house, however, protected by a balcony that answered the description. Approaching the door, we saw a smart, tidy-looking negress, perhaps thirty years of age, who, with two female assistants, was busy ironing. To our question, "Is this where Dred Scott lives?" we received, rather hesitatingly, the answer, "Yes." Upon our asking if he was home, she said,

"What white man arter dad nigger for?—why don't white man 'tend to his own business, and let dat nigger 'lone? Some of dese days dey'll steal dat nigger—dat are a fact."

DRED SCOTT. PHOTOGRAPHED BY FITZGIBBON, OF ST. LOUIS.   HIS WIFE, HARRIET. PHOTOGRAPHED BY FITZGIBBON, OF ST. LOUIS.

hood. As President, Buchanan encouraged the movement, hoping to sweep Kansas into the Union as a Democratic state. His hand-picked new Governor, a 110-pound bantam rooster named Robert J. Walker, tried his best to get a hold on the situation. But both Walker and the President misjudged the depth and bitterness of the divisions that racked the territory.

Further, Buchanan underestimated the chances for error in the normal process by which a territory became a state. A census of the territory had to be taken so that district lines could be laid out and delegates elected to a constitutional convention. The convention, in turn, would determine how slavery would be handled in the constitution of the new state. And as usual in Kansas, everything that could go wrong would go wrong.

Quite reasonably, the Kansas Free Staters assumed that the census and the ensuing election of convention delegates would be fraudulent, like everything else that had been administered by Kansas' proslavery forces. Their assumption was on the mark. Proslavery officials gerrymandered the election districts so that proslavery counties were certain to control the constitutional convention. Consequently, Free State voters boycotted the election, and when convention delegates met in the autumn of 1857 at Lecompton, the territorial capital, they were an all-proslavery fraternity.

Meanwhile, the regularly scheduled election for a new Kansas legislature had taken place. Free Staters had recently been pouring into the territory, and assurances by the territorial governor that the election would be fair brought them to the polls. Outnumbering proslavery settlers by almost 2 to 1, they won control of the legislature. Kansas

now had a legally chosen antislavery legislature and a legally chosen proslavery constitutional convention. Of course the two were bound to clash.

The convention quickly passed a constitution that was essentially proslavery. However, knowing that the document would have to stand the test of a general referendum, the delegates adopted an alternate strategy. They drafted an article that guaranteed a slaveholder's right to retain title to slaves then living in the territory and to their direct descendants, but that outlawed the importation of any more slaves. Taking remarkable liberties with the English language, they called their new document the constitution "without slavery." Voters were to be given a choice between the new document and the original provision—the constitution "with slavery"—which allowed the future importation of slaves.

Free State men, recognizing the referendum as a farce, boycotted it, and on December 21 the Lecompton Constitution passed "with slavery." Thereupon the antislavery legislature pushed through a law that would put the entire Lecompton Constitution, not just the slavery question, to a popular vote. On January 4, 1858, only 14 days after it had passed "with slavery," the constitution was roundly defeated in a vote that the proslavery men now boycotted. For the third time, Kansas saw an election in which one side or the other declined to participate.

And now President Buchanan stepped in with his customary lack of sagacity. He saw himself as a "pacificator," a man who would settle these annoying problems once and for all. He declared the rejection of the constitution invalid, and recommended that Congress admit Kansas as a state on the basis of

A Republican cartoon, published during the presidential campaign of 1856, attacks the Democrats for favoring a popular vote to decide the status of slavery in Kansas, implying (correctly, as it turned out) that stuffed ballot boxes would force the Free Staters to swallow slavery. Even though Kansas remained open to slavery, the territory was so poorly suited to slave-grown crops that in 1860 it had only two slaves.

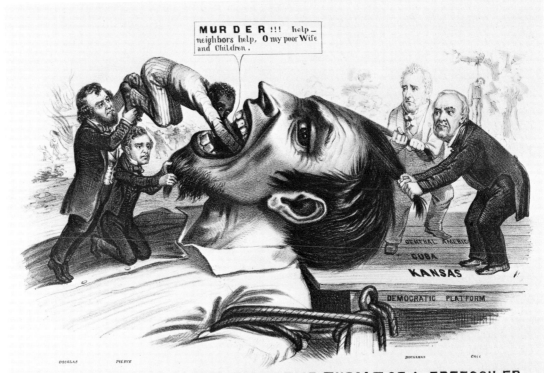

MURDER !!! help_ neighbors help, O my poor Wife and Children .

FORCING SLAVERY DOWN THE THROAT OF A FREESOILER

the Lecompton Constitution "with slavery." If Congress accepted his wishes, he avowed, the Union would at last have "domestic peace" on the Kansas question.

Instead of bringing peace, Buchanan's proposals raised hob. His fellow Democrat Stephen Douglas broke with him over the Lecompton mess, as did many others in the party. Some Northern and most Western Democrats sided with Douglas; Southerners went down the line with Buchanan. Despite the breaches of party loyalty, Buchanan still could marshal a majority in the Senate, where he got a victory in late March. The House was another matter, however, and Buchanan made matters worse by rejecting compromise. The bill must go through "naked," he said.

Buchanan's obstinance doomed the mea-

sure, and it was defeated in the House on April 1. Yet finally a compromise of sorts was worked out. Congress would resubmit the constitution to the voters of Kansas along with a thinly veiled threat. They could vote on the whole constitution. If they accepted it, Kansas would be a slave state. If they rejected it, then Kansas could not reapply for statehood for several years, until the population rose to the 90,000 mark.

Kansas did reject it overwhelmingly. That was the end of the Lecompton Constitution. And, since the Free Staters were increasingly in control, that was the end of nearly five years of strife in and over Kansas.

In that time the Democratic Party had been fatally split and the Republican Party was born. In the deepening crisis the nation had been left with a single, bitter political alignment—North against South. Statesmanship had disappeared. The press in both the North and the South carried inflammatory rhetoric to new heights of passion, new depths of unreasoned partisanship. The North feared a conspiracy by the slaveholders. The South feared an increasingly enraged North and an ever more powerful antislavery force in Congress.

The reaction to these fears was dramatic. In the streets of every big city in the North, in the park lands and parade grounds of the South, fraternal and recreational militia companies were being mustered and drilled. There was no hostile intent, the organizers claimed. But there was a martial spirit in the air. Everyone loved the gay uniforms, the fancy precision marching, the ideal of competition exemplified in contests between drill teams.

But in the hills of Western Maryland a private citizen was raising his own special kind of militia with intentions that were intensely and undisguisedly hostile. John Brown had come there to pay a call on Harpers Ferry, a town just across the Maryland line, in Virginia (later West Virginia).

Although Brown had controlled his thirst for blood in the months after the Pottawatomie Massacre, he was anything but inactive. He was now a full-time worker for emancipation, and he nurtured a grandiose plan for a death blow against slavery. To realize his dream he would need money to equip a small army. For that he first procured letters of recommendation from the current Free State "governor" of Kansas, Charles Robinson, and then launched himself on an ambitious fund-raising tour.

For two and a half years, between January 1857 and July 1859, Brown shuttled back and forth between Kansas and the Northeast, principally Boston, where he was welcomed into the salons of the country's most prominent abolitionists. Among those who contributed small sums of money were Gerrit Smith, Thomas Wentworth Higginson, Theodore Parker and Amos Lawrence, the man for whom Lawrence, Kansas, was named—four of the most influential antislavery men in the Northeast. Brown visited Senator Charles Sumner, who was still recuperating from his caning by South Carolina's Preston Brooks. The Old Man asked to see the bloodstained coat Sumner had worn the day of the attack. Handed the sanctified garment, Brown fell silent and, recalled Sumner, "his lips compressed and his eyes shone like polished steel."

The money Brown raised in the Northeast turned out to be a mere pittance; it bought equipment and supplies for a tiny band of soldiers—barely more than a dozen followers, among them four of his sons. He also hired an English mercenary, Hugh Forbes, to act as military adviser and drillmaster for his minuscule legion. Then he commissioned the manufacture of 1,000 long pikes, for what purpose he did not reveal. Indeed, Brown revealed little of his vague plans to anyone.

By the beginning of 1858, however, his strategy had jelled somewhat. Kansas was no longer a satisfactory arena for the Lord's revenge against slaveowners; the Free Staters were clearly winning command. He and his men must take their crusade elsewhere. So he dismissed them for a while and told them to rendezvous in Tabor, Iowa, where they would drill and he would reveal to them his wondrous plans for the future. Only nine recruits showed up in Tabor. Undismayed by the poor turnout, Brown announced, "Our ultimate destination is Virginia."

Brown had long harbored the notion of setting up a base in the Alleghenies from which he could invade Virginia, liberate many slaves and bring them back into the mountain fastnesses. There he would train the freed blacks and lead them on a larger raid that would, he thought, foment a general slave insurrection in Virginia. Eventually he and his army of rebels would take over a substantial piece of territory in the South, forming a kind of black state in which he would confiscate the land of slaveholders, proclaim martial law and exercise his own form of government.

All this Brown made clear in a "constitution" that he drew up in January 1858. He discussed his wild plan with some backers in the East, and some of them tried to discourage him. But a few—the men who would come to be known to Brown and to one another as the Secret Six—agreed to provide him with funds. Besides Smith, Higginson and Parker, the six included George L. Stearns, Franklin B. Sanborn and Samuel Gridley Howe—all well-connected leaders of their Northeastern communities.

At first, Brown was apparently reluctant to inform the Secret Six of the precise time and place of his initial strike. He did tell the mercenary Hugh Forbes that his intention was to stage an arms-stealing raid on the U.S. arsenal at Harpers Ferry. And in May of 1858, Forbes, angry because Brown had failed to pay him, disclosed the plan to two abolitionist Senators—Henry Wilson of Massachusetts and William H. Seward of New York. The legislators kept the secret, but they berated the Secret Six for their in-

volvement in such a harebrained scheme. Thereupon, the six told Brown to stop, urged him to go back to Kansas to cover his tracks, and further declared that henceforth Brown was not to reveal any of his intentions to them. What they really meant was quite simple: They still wanted him to strike a blow, but they did not want to know anything that might be damaging to them. Brown lamented that his backers "were not men of action."

Ostensibly chastened but fundamentally undeterred, Brown went back to Kansas in mid-1858 and, adopting the pseudonym Shubel Morgan, soon led a successful foray into Missouri and freed 11 slaves, two of whom joined his band. For months he was constantly on the go. Then, in July 1859, he journeyed to Maryland and rented a farm just to the north of Harpers Ferry. There he made his final plans and passed the summer trying to raise more men and money.

By October the pikes had arrived, several hundred guns were ready, and friends assured Brown that the slaves in Virginia were eager to join him. His 21 men grew restless; they worried about being betrayed, for dozens of people now knew of their intentions. In fact, John B. Floyd, Buchanan's pro-Southern Secretary of War, had been warned of the guerrilla raid, but he dismissed the story as ludicrous.

Yet Brown, for all his grand plans, had overlooked the details on which the attack would hinge. He made no careful reconnaissance of Harpers Ferry, no effort to alert the Virginia slaves, no plans for emergencies in case his attack went awry. All would go flawlessly, he believed, because God was on his side. And so he would wait no more. Late on October 16, 1859, John Brown and his army

of 16 whites, four free blacks and one escaped slave were primed for their great mission. "Men, get on your arms," he said to them. "We will proceed to the Ferry."

Brown led the party through a cold drizzle—he in a wagon, his men hiking behind him, their rifles hidden under gray woolen shawls. Soon they were crossing the Potomac River on a covered bridge that took them directly into Harpers Ferry. Brown posted two guards on that bridge and sent sentries to the other bridge leading into town. Then the party moved toward the U.S. arsenal on Potomac Street.

It all went with remarkable ease. The watchman at the arsenal was taken by surprise. Brown told him: "I came here from Kansas, and this is a slave State; I want to free all the Negroes in this State; I have possession now of the United States armory, and if the citizens interfere with me I must only burn the town and have blood."

Soon afterward the raiders captured the nearby Hall's Rifle Works. Next, Brown sent a few of his men to seize some prominent hostages, particularly Colonel Lewis Washington, a prosperous slaveowner and a great-grandnephew of the first President. Following explicit instructions from Brown, the contingent brought back not only Colonel Washington but also a sword belonging to him that tradition said had been presented to George Washington by Frederick the Great. Brown strapped the weapon around his waist and waited, expecting slaves by the thousands to rally to him. Once he had armed them from the arsenal, they would march on in his campaign of liberation.

The slaves did not come, and Brown's plan began to fall apart. An eastbound train was stopped at the bridge and the engineer was warned to back away. One of Brown's men shot and mortally wounded a railroad baggageman near the bridge. The victim was a free black.

The town was thoroughly aroused by now, and before long, telegraph wires all over the East hummed with exaggerated reports of "Negro insurrection at Harper's Ferry! Fire and Rapine on the Virginia Border!" In the nearby Virginia countryside, several militia companies formed up and headed for the town. They arrived on October 17 and found the townsmen and Brown's raiders in a blistering exchange of fire.

The raiders were pinned down in the armory buildings and in Hall's Rifle Works, under a constant fire from positions in the town. John Brown was paralyzed by indecision; not knowing what to do next, he did nothing. After four hours of battle the raiders suffered their first casualty. Dangerfield Newby, a black, was killed. Townspeople dragged his body to a gutter and cut off his ears and let hogs chew on the corpse. Clearly, the raiders could expect no mercy from the townsmen, whose heavy drinking only added to their savagery.

Faced with a siege, Brown withdrew most of his men to the fire-engine house adjacent to the armory and there barricaded himself with his hostages. Soon after 1 p.m. he sent two men out to negotiate under a truce flag. They were shot down. One of them, his son Watson, struggled back to the engine house in agony.

The battle went on all afternoon. When a raider tried to flee, townsmen shot him to death and for hours used his body for target practice. Three of Brown's men were driven out of Hall's Rifle Works. One was killed outright, one mortally wounded in a cross

fire, and the third was taken prisoner and nearly lynched before a local physician rescued him. In the melee the mayor of Harpers Ferry was shot dead. Drunken townsmen took revenge at about 4 p.m. They hauled out a raider whom they had captured that morning, killed him in cold blood and used his body, too, for target practice.

Brown tried yet again to parley, offering to release his hostages if he and his 14 remaining men were allowed to leave. No deal could be made. The raiders spent a cold, hungry night in the engine house, listening to desultory gunfire and a drunken ruckus in the town. By then, Brown's son Oliver had been wounded, and he lay beside brother Watson, both of them dying in vivid pain. Oliver begged his father to kill him and end his misery. "If you must die, die like a man," Brown replied in cold anger. Some time later he called to Oliver and got no reply. "I guess he is dead," said John Brown.

The next morning Brown looked out of his "fort" at 2,000 hostile people, including a company of Marines newly arrived from Washington. The Marines were armed with muskets, fixed bayonets and sledge hammers, and were preparing to storm the engine house. Their commander was Lieutenant Colonel Robert E. Lee of the 2nd United States Cavalry. Lee sent Lieutenant James Ewell Brown (Jeb) Stuart forward under a white flag to demand surrender and promise protection for the raiders.

Brown met Stuart at the door and made impossible counterproposals to the surrender ultimatum. Thereupon Stuart jumped aside and waved his hat as a signal for the Marines to charge. They battered through a door and killed two raiders with the bayonets. A hostage pointed out Brown to the

Lieutenant Colonel Robert E. Lee was home on leave in Arlington, Virginia, when he was called to put down an insurrection at Harpers Ferry—actually, John Brown's raid. Lee hurried off without donning a uniform; he commanded the Marine assault force in civilian dress.

Lieutenant James Ewell Brown (Jeb) Stuart of the 1st U.S. Cavalry journeyed to Harpers Ferry as Lee's aide. There, he distinguished himself by carrying Lee's surrender demand to John Brown—an act that foreshadowed his gallantry as a Confederate cavalry commander.

troops, and a lieutenant bludgeoned him to the ground with his blunt sword.

With that, the Marine assault ended abruptly. Of the 21 raiders who had come to Harpers Ferry with Brown, only he and four others remained. Ten were dead or dying, and the rest had fled, though two would be captured later. Four civilians and one Marine also were dead, along with two slaves who had answered Brown's call to arms.

News of the raid electrified the nation. Almost without exception, Southern whites were frightened. Many of them accused the North in general and the Republicans in particular of a plot to subdue the South with a gigantic slave rebellion. "Yea, a servile war with all its untold horror," a South Carolina legislator declaimed, and a South Carolina militiaman harped on the South's constant racist fear of "mongrel tyrants who mean to reduce you and your wives and your daughters on a level with the very slaves you buy and sell." Confronted with this sort of poisonous invective, the Republicans tried to dissociate themselves from Brown, and some even hoped that the Old Man would be tried and hanged quickly to spare them further embarrassment.

The trial of Brown and his fellow captives, conducted by the state of Virginia, did begin quickly, just 10 days after the raid. The injured Old Man was carried into the courtroom at Charles Town, Virginia; he lay on a cot through the week-long trial. He was skillfully defended, and spoke eloquently in his own behalf, but the verdict was never in doubt: John Brown and his raiders must hang for murder and treason.

During the trial and the wait for execution, Brown won no little admiration for his dignity, his iron will, his implacable commitment to his ideals. Archsecessionist Edmund Ruffin said, as one fanatic of another: "It is impossible for me not to respect his thorough devotion to his bad cause, and the undaunted courage with which he has sustained it, through all losses and hazards."

Another agitator, the noted abolitionist Reverend Henry Ward Beecher, understood that John Brown would soon render his greatest service to his cause. "Let Virginia make him a martyr!" he cried. "Now, he has only blundered. His soul was noble; his work miserable. But a cord and a gibbet would redeem all that, and round up Brown's failure with a heroic success."

Brown himself wanted martyrdom and claimed it, delivering, on the occasion of his sentencing, a speech that instantly became a revered classic in the North. Said he: "I believe that to have interfered as I have done, as I have always freely admitted I have done, in behalf of His despised poor, is no wrong, but right. Now, if it is deemed necessary that I should forfeit my life for the furtherance of the ends of justice, and mingle my blood further with the blood of my children and with the blood of millions in this slave country whose rights are disregarded by wicked, cruel, and unjust enactments, I say, let it be done."

John Brown uttered no last words on the scaffold. But on the way to his execution on a December day in 1859 he handed a guard a final note that exactly predicted the national calamity he had done so much to make inevitable. "I John Brown," the message said, "am now quite certain that the crimes of this guilty land will never be purged away but with blood."

John Brown's Body

John Brown was a dead man. So Brown himself realized on October 18, 1859, even as federal troops crushed his 22-man raid on Harpers Ferry; his attempt to start a great slave revolution in Virginia had ended with 17 people killed, and it would lead to his execution for conspiracy, treason and murder. In fact, the bloodstained fanatic was to be hurried to his death just 45 days hence.

The rush to hang him was not vindictive. Local officials felt that if the law moved too slowly, Brown might be lynched by outraged Southerners. So on the 19th of October, the "Old Man," weakened by injuries he had suffered during his capture, was whisked off to stand trial in Charles Town, Virginia (later West Virginia). He was carried into the courtroom and deposited on a cot. Despite his lawyers' urging, he refused to demean himself by pleading insanity. "Not guilty," said Brown, which was exactly how he felt.

It took three days for the lawyers to have their say. Then it took barely 45 minutes for the jury to hand down the verdict. Brown showed not a flicker of emotion as Judge Richard Parker sentenced him to hang.

During his last month, Brown was allowed to receive visitors in his cell and to write farewell letters to supporters. In a note to his brother, he accurately appraised his fate: "I am worth inconceivably more to hang than for any other purpose."

Such was his victory. On December 2, John Brown mounted the gallows and went calmly to his death, inspiring countless others to press his crusade to free the slaves. Not long afterward, as Yankee soldiers marched off to fight the Confederates, they would sing: "John Brown's body lies a'mouldering in the grave. . . ."

Rifle in hand, old John Brown holds a hostage at bay shortly before U.S. Marines broke into the Harpers Ferry arsenal and clubbed him down. Two of Brown's raiders keep up their musket fire; another lies wounded at his feet.

Lying injured after the battle, Brown tells his captors, "I acknowledge no master in human form." Among his visitors was Virginia Governor Henry A. Wise.

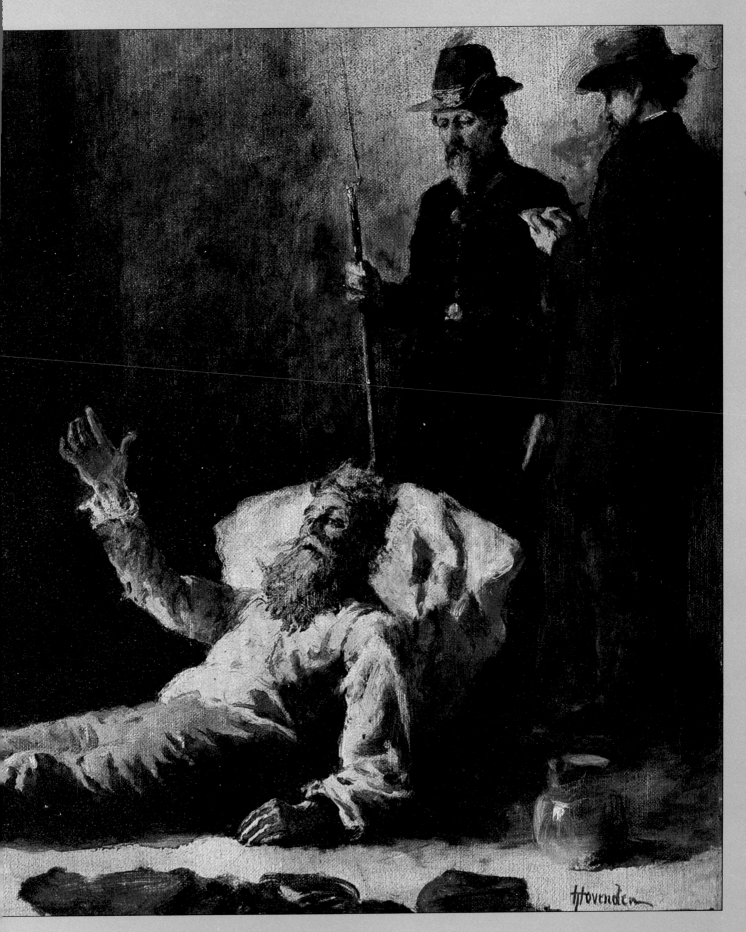

Lifted from his cot and supported by deputies, John Brown makes a statement shortly before Judge Richard Parker (*left*) sentences him to hang. Brown informed the hushed courtroom, "I feel no consciousness of guilt."

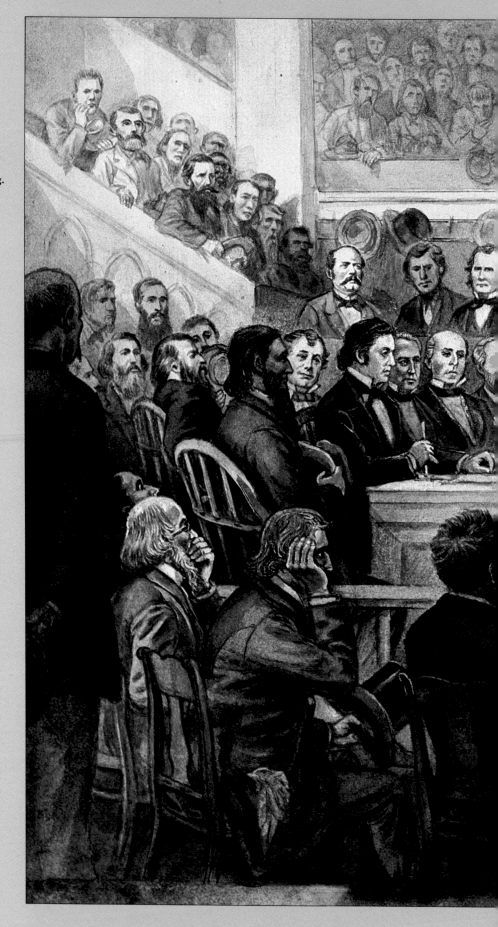

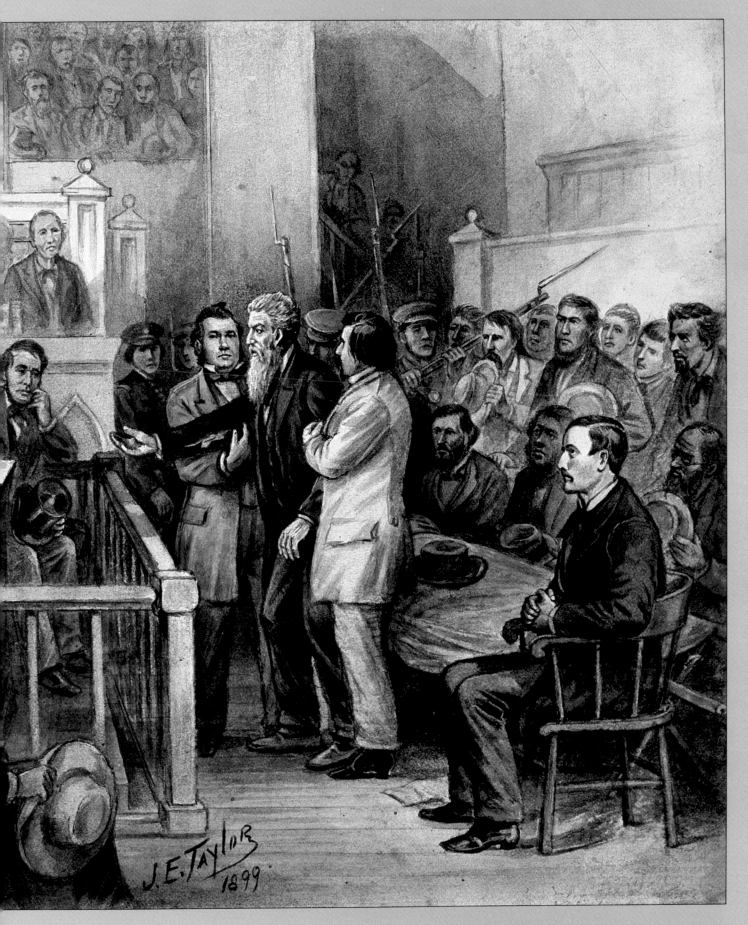

J.E. Taylor
1899

A guard of 1,500 troops looks on as John Brown's body swings from a gallows outside Charles Town. The witnesses included actor John Wilkes Booth

...rofessor at the Virginia Military Institute in Lexington—Thomas J. Jackson (later called Stonewall).

Lincoln of Illinois

"I most earnestly and anxiously desire Lincoln to be elected—because I have hope that at least one state, South Carolina, will secede, and that others will follow."

EDMUND RUFFIN

On the evening of February 27, 1860, some 1,500 New Yorkers braved a snowstorm to hear Abraham Lincoln, a little-known Illinois politician, speak at Cooper Union, an institution of free instruction in the arts and applied sciences. Lincoln was to discuss the cruel problems facing the nation, and inevitably the central issue would be slavery and its future in America.

The tall Westerner would be addressing the cream of New York's intellectual and political society, leaders and opinion makers who surely would influence, for good or for ill, Lincoln's chances for the Republican presidential nomination. This was not the sort of group that a partisan stump speech could rouse to fever pitch; closely reasoned arguments rather than passion were clearly called for. If the outlander could move the gathering merely to judicious applause, then he would have gone some distance toward the prize he ardently sought.

Lincoln had his doubts about whether he was up to the task. These well-to-do sophisticates might snicker at his rude, rural twang, at the ill-fitting suit stretched over his lanky frame. They might follow their Eastern prejudices against men of the West and refuse to hearken to his words. But Lincoln had suffered snobbery before and he had not been stopped by it.

As his topic, Lincoln chose to discuss the question of whether the federal government had the Constitutional right to control the extension of black servitude to the territories. Three years before, the Supreme Court had ruled in the Dred Scott decision that Congress lacked that power, setting off a tumult of protest in the Northern states and rallying to the antislavery cause countless people who had previously been content to ignore the issue. Now, at Cooper Union, Lincoln argued that the Supreme Court decision was wrong.

If Lincoln was nervous when he began his speech, his unease quickly vanished; he warmed to his subject and the audience warmed to him. Citing the voting records of the Founding Fathers in Congress and in various pre-Constitutional conventions, he established that they had voted routinely on proposals to extend slavery to the old Northwest Territory and, later, the Louisiana Territory. Lincoln declared that even though the Constitution did not specifically forbid or endorse the extension of slavery, the framers of the Constitution had always acted on the assumption that Congress would rule on the slavery question on a case-by-case basis. The Supreme Court, in sum, had failed to take into account the obvious intent of the framers of the Constitution. Having drawn this conclusion, Lincoln used it to rebut the Southern charge that the Republicans were wild-eyed radicals. They were no more radical, he said, than the Founding Fathers.

Then Lincoln turned his attention to slavery as a moral issue. Here he found himself caught in a contradiction. On the one hand, he said, neither he nor the Republican Party

98

Wooden statuettes carved by contemporary folk artists represent Stephen A. Douglas (*top*) and Abraham Lincoln, political archrivals whose spirited contests for the Senate and the Presidency riveted the nation in the years before the War.

sought to interfere with slavery in those states where it then existed. On the other, slavery was, in his view, a dreadful wrong, a denial of the American principle that all men are created equal. The South, he declared, would be satisfied only when the free states recognized slavery as being right. "Can we," Lincoln asked, "cast our votes with their view, and against our own? . . . If our sense of duty forbids this, then let us stand by our duty fearlessly and effectively. . . . Let us have faith that right makes might, and in that faith, let us, to the end, dare to do our duty as we understand it."

Thus, Abraham Lincoln was challenging not only the South but his own political party as well. When he ended, his listeners rose as one; many cheered immoderately. The man from Illinois had deeply impressed this powerful group. He was not yet their choice as candidate, but that night he had emerged as a major contender for the honor and the travail. Later, after his election, Lincoln remarked that this speech more than any other had brought him the Republican presidential nomination.

Perhaps only in an overheated political climate could a man like Lincoln have vaulted to prominence. True, he was little known in the East before the Cooper Union speech, but he was hardly obscure. Two years before, he had startled the nation when his attempt to unseat Stephen A. Douglas, the powerful Democratic Senator from Illinois, had come within a hairbreadth of success. In his home state, he was already something of a legend. Tales of his obscure Kentucky birth in 1809, his hardscrabble childhood on the Indiana and Illinois frontiers, and his young manhood splitting rails and studying

for the bar had circulated widely. His own summation of his youthful years was a line from Thomas Gray's "Elegy Written in a Country Churchyard": "The short and simple annals of the poor."

Yet there was nothing simple about Abraham Lincoln. Wit, drive, intelligence and years of experience as a country lawyer had made him a masterly politician. He had gone on to serve four terms in the state legislature and one in Congress. From his office in Springfield, Lincoln had become one of the state's chief political wire pullers, first in the service of the Whigs, then for the Republicans. He enjoyed a perception more acute than most men and an unequaled power to express it. He could speak compellingly in the idioms of coarse country humor or a rolling rhetoric he had learned from reading Shakespeare and the Bible.

His antislavery sentiments reflected the complicated yet practical cast of his mind. Though he loathed slavery unequivocally, he was not a doctrinaire abolitionist. As a lawyer, he had no difficulty representing a slaveholder seeking the return of a fugitive slave. And in the 1850s he refused to join the clamor for the early emancipation of blacks. For the short run, he was willing to tolerate slavery in those states where the institution already existed. But he staunchly opposed its extension to new territories, believing that this would saddle the Union with a system that was both evil and economically retrograde. If contained, slavery might be eradicated in time through peaceful means; if allowed to spread, it would undermine free labor, retard economic development and, inevitably, destroy the democratic basis on which the nation was built. Now, in early 1860, Lincoln—though neither he nor any-

AN AMALGAMATION POLKA.

Blacks and whites dance together in an 1845 cartoon lambasting a Boston clergyman who declared that the "blending of the two races by amalgamation is just what is needed for the perfection of both." Proponents of race-mixing were few, but Southerners called the abolitionists "amalgamators" for urging that blacks be absorbed into white society on an equal footing.

one else knew it—stood atop the shambles of a political-party system that had been falling apart for at least eight years. A new America waited to be born, and Abraham Lincoln would be its progenitor.

The disintegration of the old regime had begun in 1852, when Young America—a faction of the Democratic Party that wanted to pry control from the hands of the "old fogies" who had been running things for years—failed to gain the presidential nomination for its candidate, Stephen Douglas. Instead, the Democrats' nod went to a former general and undistinguished Congressman named Franklin Pierce, a Northerner with Southern views. After Pierce's nomination and election, the Young America organization withered, and its exuberant nationalism was replaced by the sinister forces of nativism and resurgent sectionalism.

In spite of the stated American ideals of religious and social tolerance, the country had always displayed a strain of prejudice. During the early 1850s it grew more pronounced, with many native-born Americans turning against foreigners and many Protestants turning against Catholics. The cause or excuse was, quite simply, the great increase in the number of people arriving from famine-stricken Ireland and from the German states, where liberal revolutions had been crushed in the 1840s. Hundreds of thousands of German and Irish immigrants swelled the populations of East Coast cities and moved west into the Mississippi Valley and the states and territories around the Great Lakes. They vied with the native-born for jobs and land. Moreover, if they were Catholics, their loyalty to the United States was feared to be secondary to their obedience to the Pope in Rome. The members of the aristocratic, puritanical Whig Party, which was slowly breaking up into contentious splinter groups, discerned yet another detestable quality in the immigrants: Almost invariably, they joined the Democratic Party, which traditionally campaigned for the welfare of the ordinary citizen.

In reaction, a new party evolved. Under the banner of the American Party, thousands of disillusioned Whigs and Democrats turned to nativism, convened in secret, developed all manner of clandestine signals and signs, and dedicated themselves to restricting the political power of immigrants. When questioned by outsiders, the nativists denied all knowledge of the new movement or anything related to it, prompting New York *Tribune* editor Horace Greeley to label them the "Know-Nothings."

In the four years following the election of Franklin Pierce, the Know-Nothing movement seemed irresistible, with its candidates in local and statewide elections capturing much of New England, New York and Pennsylvania and making inroads into the Upper South. Yet most old-line Whigs resisted the xenophobic tide. In Illinois, Abraham Lincoln, then still a Whig, loathed the Know-Nothings and wrote that if they came to power, the Declaration of Independence would have to be changed to read, " 'All men are created equal,' except negroes, and foreigners and catholics."

By 1856, the Know-Nothing madness had begun to recede: The Kansas issue had once again brought the sectional controversy to the fore. In the meantime, thousands of Northern Whigs were joining the burgeoning Republican Party.

Tradition has it that the Republican Party was born on February 28, 1854, in the small Wisconsin town of Ripon, when a group of Whigs, Free Soilers (members of a splinter party opposed to the extension of slavery) and Democrats met to express their outrage over Stephen Douglas' recently introduced Kansas-Nebraska bill. Actually, many such groups sprang up independently at the time, all of them eager to establish a new party capable of uniting the various antislavery factions under a single banner. The Ripon meeting adopted a motion that this movement call itself Republican. The name was a logical choice, harking back to two mainstreams in the American political legacy: Thomas Jefferson's Democratic-Republican Party, the institutional expression of the equality of man; and John Quincy Adams' and Henry Clay's National Republicans, the precursors of the Whigs and proponents of a strong central government.

From the outset, the Republicans were a sectional party—but theirs was a mighty section. They drew their support entirely from the North and the West, which possessed much of the nation's food supply, most of its population, most of its industry, most of its commerce and most of its railroads. The Republicans could afford to lose the entire South and all of the border states and still win national power. The time was approaching when it would be possible to bind the North and West together in a grand coalition of disappointed Whigs, frustrated Free Soilers, disaffected Democrats and reformed Know-Nothings to oppose the extension of slavery—and, ultimately, slavery's very existence.

Still, it was no easy matter for an active partisan to cast off loyalty to an old party, even if it was moribund. Lincoln, who was then engaged in the private practice of law in Springfield, shunned the new Republicans at first, fearing that he would be associated with the radical abolitionists. As late as August of 1855, he confessed that he was uncertain where his loyalties lay, but "I think I am a Whig," he wrote. By the end of that year, Lincoln had moved closer to the Republicans, seeking a working relationship with those he had once considered radicals. He finally joined the new party by allowing his name to be placed in nomination as a delegate to an antislavery convention that was scheduled to meet in Bloomington, Illinois, on the 29th of May, 1856. In Bloomington, he was soon in the thick of debate over the Republican state platform.

There remained a formidable opposition. The Democratic Party, although wounded by sectional strife and increasingly at odds with itself over the extension of slavery, retained the loyalty of millions. Like the Republican Party, it was composed of factions that had joined together in a mutually beneficial association; its objectives were generally to oppose industrialization and modernization, to further states' rights and territorial expansion. Unlike its rival, it was truly national in character, drawing strength from every section of the Union. Despite defections, the Democrats in 1856 succeeded in papering over their disputes and presenting a unified front.

At the national convention that year, the party turned away from lackluster Franklin Pierce, rejected controversial Stephen Douglas and selected Pennsylvanian James Buchanan. This "doughface" (a Northerner with Southern sympathies) was acceptable to both the North and the South and had a unique advantage over his party rivals: He

Presidential candidate Millard Fillmore gained the endorsement of the proslavery wing of the Know-Nothings (*banner below*) in the 1856 campaign, but his loyalty to Know-Nothing tenets was suspect. During his single year of membership in the nativist, anti-Catholic organization, he attended none of its secret meetings. Furthermore, his daughter was educated by nuns.

alone had made no enemies during the debate over Kansas, for he had been off in England serving as U.S. minister. To make their ticket even more attractive, the Democrats chose John C. Breckinridge of the key state of Kentucky as their candidate for vice president. Southern yet not too Southern, Breck-

John C. Frémont, the Republican presidential candidate in 1856, had to carry Pennsylvania to win the election against Pennsylvania Democrat James Buchanan. Frémont wanted as his running mate a moderate from the Keystone State, Senator Simon Cameron, but the Republican convention saddled him with William L. Dayton of New Jersey, who failed to carry even his own state.

inridge had a sizable following in all sections of the Union.

When the Republicans journeyed to Philadelphia for their own national convention in mid-June, they realized that they were not likely to win the election against the strong Buchanan-Breckinridge ticket. Their acknowledged leader was Senator William H. Seward of New York, who was backed by a most able political manipulator named Thurlow Weed. Seward, ambitious for the presidency, conceded that 1860 would probably be a more propitious year and put up little resistance when the party leaders decided on a figurehead candidate. He was a national hero but a political newcomer—John C. Frémont, called "The Pathfinder" for his Western explorations.

There was a third candidate in the race, former President Millard Fillmore, nominated by the Southern faction of the Know-Nothings and supported by the remnants of Southern Whiggery and some conservative Whigs in the North as well. Though Fillmore had no chance of winning an electoral majority, he could hope to garner votes in the border states and possibly throw the election into the House of Representatives, where he might win as a compromise candidate.

In the North, the Republicans showed astounding strength. Thousands marched in torchlight parades shouting, "Free speech, free press, free soil, free men, Frémont and victory." Republican speakers flayed the Democrats as lackeys of the "slavocracy" and accomplices in the rape of Kansas. The Democrats answered with smear campaigns against Frémont, who was, they charged without a shred of evidence, a secret Catholic and a hypocrite who once owned slaves himself. A far more effective argument against the Republican cause was voiced by Senator Robert Toombs of Georgia, who maintained that the party's close association with abolitionism made it totally unacceptable to the South. He declared, "The election of Frémont would be the end of the Union, and ought to be."

The threat of secession had its effect. Fearing economic chaos should Frémont win, bankers and financiers in New York opened their purses to the Democrats. One financier, August Belmont, contributed the then-fantastic sum of $50,000. Editor Horace Greeley admitted that "we Frémonters have not one dollar, where the Fillmoreans and Buchanans have 10 each."

When the electoral ballots were counted, Buchanan had won by 174 votes to Frémont's 114. Though 11 Northern states had gone Republican and the combined popular vote for Frémont and Fillmore exceeded Buchanan's by 10 per cent, the Democrats had been granted a final opportunity to solve the slavery issue. Should Buchanan and his party fail, the Republicans would surely be ready to assume power and impose their own solution. A prophetic poet put it succinctly: "If months have well-nigh won the field / What may not four years do?"

The whole nation seemed to heave a great sigh of relief after the election. For the moment, Kansas was pacified and talk of disunion was muted. But the partisans were not to be distracted for long. In December, outgoing President Pierce delivered a diatribe against the Republicans, sparking anew the bitter debate between the two parties and the two sections, and incoming President Buchanan added fuel to the fire in his inaugural address on March 4, 1857. Although he had been given advance word of the Supreme

Court's Dred Scott decision, Buchanan pretended ignorance. In a devious effort to conciliate the North, he declared in his address that the future of slavery in the territories rested with their populations. Two days later the Court issued its decision and, as Buchanan had known full well, thereby undercut popular sovereignty as a meaningful ideal, at least if the Court's interpretation of the Constitution was enforced.

The South responded to the Dred Scott

Democrat James Buchanan, "Old Buck," won the presidency in 1856 with a shrewd and subtle campaign that used partisan newspapers to full advantage. Scores of small-town editors were recruited to promote him as "the people's choice" even before he announced his candidacy, and Buchanan emerged as a formidable contender seemingly without the aid of politicians.

In this Republican lampoon of the Buchanan-Breckinridge platform, a slave chained hand and foot sits astride a ram, a symbol of the Missouri Border Ruffians' violent defense of slavery in Kansas. The Democrats' sympathetic attitude toward the extension of slavery won Buchanan 14 of the 15 slave states in the 1856 presidential election.

first and only choice of Illinois for the United States Senate." In accepting the nomination, Lincoln delivered what would become one of his most famous addresses. " 'A house divided against itself cannot stand,' " he told the assembled party delegates. "I believe this government cannot endure, permanently half slave and half free. I do not expect the Union to be dissolved—I do not expect the house to fall—but I do expect it will cease to be divided. It will become all one thing or all the other."

Lincoln went on to imply a conspiracy, with Douglas a prime mover, to promote the extension of slavery, and warned that the next logical move of the Supreme Court would be to declare slavery legal not just in the territories but in the Northern states as well. Lincoln's intention was to cut the middle ground from under Douglas. He would try to hang the albatross of slavery around his opponent's neck; this would weaken the benefit Douglas derived from his break with the Buchanan administration and his repudiation of the proslavery Lecompton Constitution in Kansas.

The campaign following Lincoln's nomination lacked nothing in the way of drama. Douglas, recognizing his opponent's oratorical talents, ran hard from the beginning. "I shall have my hands full," he said of Lincoln. "He is the strong man of his party—full of wit, facts, dates—and he is the best stump speaker in the West. He is as honest as he is shrewd, and if I beat him my victory will be hardly won." In July, Douglas embarked on a speaking tour of the state. Everywhere, he was accompanied by partisans who waved banners, carried torches and played martial music to announce the arrival of the Little Giant. Hard on his heels came

decision with jubilation, the North with fury. More Democrats, more Whigs and more Know-Nothings prepared to cast their lot with the Republicans as that party gathered strength to contest the midterm Congressional elections of 1858. Nowhere would the issue be more dramatically fought out than in Illinois, where Abraham Lincoln, seeking a national platform, challenged the "Little Giant," Stephen Douglas, for his seat in the Senate.

United States senators were still elected, in those days, by state legislatures, with the party in control of the legislature making the selection. Public nomination of a candidate was unknown. In Illinois in 1858, the Republicans broke the mold.

Meeting in their state convention on the 16th of June, 1858, the Republicans of Illinois declared that "Abraham Lincoln is the

Abraham Lincoln. If Douglas spoke in front of a small-town courthouse one night, Lincoln would appear there the next day to attack his opponent, employing irony and logic with equal effect.

Lincoln was accused of following Douglas because he could not get a crowd otherwise. In response, he asked for face-to-face debates. Douglas hesitated—quite reasonably, from his viewpoint. Why enhance the candidacy of a lesser-known politician by sharing a platform with him? Besides, it might be dangerous to let audiences compare Lincoln with him as a speaker. But in the end, Douglas' pugnacity got the better of him, and he agreed to a series of seven debates.

The two rivals met in seven prominent country towns in as many Congressional districts: Alton, Charleston, Galesburg, Ottawa, Freeport, Jonesboro, Quincy. Yet so great was their pulling power and so momentous were the issues they discussed, that many people—and of course the press—came from far and wide to hear their arguments. To a degree unprecedented in a statewide canvass, the entire country was caught up in this contest.

In speech after speech, Douglas never weakened in defense of his favorite doctrine, popular sovereignty. Yet he aired more than political theory. Believing that blacks were inherently inferior to whites, Douglas declared that Lincoln's views would inevitably lead to granting blacks full political and social equality. He played frankly upon the prejudices of the voters. Knowing that many whites were opposed to slavery and biased against blacks, he appealed to racists by stating that the government "was established upon the white basis. It was made by white men, for the benefit of white men."

Douglas did not feel that the Negroes should necessarily be slaves, but in his opinion they should not necessarily be free either. That was a decision for whites. He declared that moral arguments had no place in the discussion and that he was fighting for the great principle of self-government. To his opponent's assertion that the nation could not endure half slave and half free, Douglas rejoined that diversity in local and domestic institutions was "the great safeguard of our liberties." These representations confirmed Lincoln's earlier opinion that Douglas seemed to have "no very vivid impression that the Negro is human."

A similar charge might well have been leveled at Lincoln. Stung by Douglas' attacks that his program would bring black equality, Lincoln associated himself with views that were both antislavery and antiblack—at least when he spoke in southern Illinois, where Democratic sentiment was strong. In Charleston, for example, Lincoln remarked: "I am not . . . in favor of bringing about . . . the social and political equality of the white and black races—I am not . . . in favor of making voters or jurors of Negroes, nor of qualifying them to hold office, nor to intermarry with white people. And inasmuch as they [blacks and whites] cannot so live, while they do remain together there must be the position of superior and inferior, and I as much as any other man am in favor of having the superior position assigned to the white race." At other times, and when addressing more liberal audiences, Lincoln would take a high-minded tack. In one speech he urged his audience to stop arguing about race and unite as one people, "declaring that all men are created equal."

Over all, the contest was about even, but

Wearing a stovepipe hat, Stephen Douglas
campaigns from an open carriage *(center)* in Chicago
on the 9th of July, 1858. That night, a dramatic
fireworks display, cannonades and rocket barrages
set the stage for the Little Giant's opening
speech in the Senatorial race against Lincoln.

at Freeport, Douglas committed a tactical error. Replying to the charge that the Dred Scott decision had jeopardized popular sovereignty, denying territorial voters the right to decide whether to enter the Union as a free state or as a slave state, Douglas suggested that the Court's ruling was itself a nullity. Slavery, he insisted, could only exist in those territories where a majority of the people desired it and protected it with police power. In territories where there was no liking for slavery, it could not survive, because the populace would deny it protection. "Hence, no matter what the decision of the Supreme Court," he stated, "the right of the people to make a slave Territory or a free Territory is perfect and complete." In the South, where Douglas' defection on the Lecompton Constitution had already cost him wide support, he was anathematized for this Freeport Doctrine, which suggested that the proslavery Dred Scott decision could be ignored with impunity.

When the voters of Illinois finally went to the polls, the Republicans outvoted the pro-Douglas Democrats by a margin of 125,000 to 121,000. However, the legislative districts had been realigned, which gave Douglas a majority in the state house and one more term in the Senate.

Lincoln, in defeat, had gained more than he lost: The debates with Douglas had elevated him to national stature. With 1860 a mere two years distant, men like Horace Greeley could now look to Lincoln as a compromise presidential candidate. The path to the White House that led through the great auditorium at Cooper Union had begun in the tiny Illinois townships where Lincoln found his platform.

Naturally enough, Lincoln was dejected

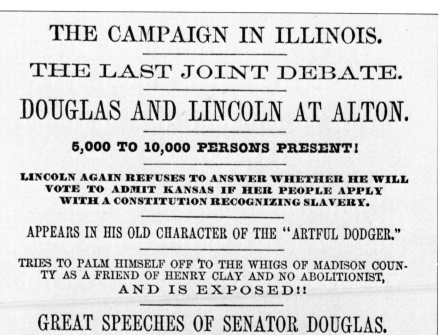

THE CAMPAIGN IN ILLINOIS.

THE LAST JOINT DEBATE.

DOUGLAS AND LINCOLN AT ALTON.

5,000 TO 10,000 PERSONS PRESENT!

LINCOLN AGAIN REFUSES TO ANSWER WHETHER HE WILL VOTE TO ADMIT KANSAS IF HER PEOPLE APPLY WITH A CONSTITUTION RECOGNIZING SLAVERY.

APPEARS IN HIS OLD CHARACTER OF THE "ARTFUL DODGER."

TRIES TO PALM HIMSELF OFF TO THE WHIGS OF MADISON COUNTY AS A FRIEND OF HENRY CLAY AND NO ABOLITIONIST, AND IS EXPOSED!!

GREAT SPEECHES OF SENATOR DOUGLAS.

by his defeat. As the election returns drifted in and Douglas' victory became obvious, Lincoln left his law office to walk home. It was dark, the path was worn slick, and he lost his footing. He caught himself on his hands just before he hit the ground, then got up and walked on home. Years later, he remembered saying to himself, "It's a slip and not a fall."

No sooner had Congress convened in December 1859 than the sectional controversy found a new focus: the Speakership of the House of Representatives, where the Republicans held a plurality but not a majority. Their candidate for Speaker was John Sherman of Ohio, and normally, as the leading party's choice, his election would have been assured. But not this time. The Republicans had only a 10-vote plurality, and Sherman made his election difficult by endorsing a digest of a book entitled *The Impending Crisis of*

An article in the frankly partisan *Chicago Daily Times* portrays Lincoln as a slippery character who behaved in an "improper and ungentlemanly" fashion in his debate with Douglas in Alton, Illinois.

routine manner. True or not, the protest did nothing to soothe his opponents.

Behind the arguments that raged over the Speakership lay an increasing sense of Southern impotence. As the Republicans gained strength in Washington, Southern members of the House fell back on tactics of deadlock and delay. Tempers went wild as the debate heated up. "The only persons who do not have a revolver and knife," bemoaned Senator James H. Hammond from across the rotunda, "are those who have two revolvers." On the floor of the House, O. R. Singleton of Mississippi called for disunion and war, while Illinois Representative John A. Logan waved a pistol and shouted at the gallery, "By God, if I can't talk, I can do something else!" Eventually Sherman withdrew, and on the 44th ballot a compromise candidate, Republican William Pennington of New Jersey, was selected.

Throughout the contest for the Speakership, the Southern Representatives had been much less concerned about Sherman's views than about the Northern attitude toward the death of John Brown. On December 2, 1859, when the old fanatic had gone to the gallows, church bells in Northern towns tolled a mournful tribute. To many Southerners, this was an endorsement of the atrocity and meant that they had better prepare to fight.

So a new decade began with the issue truly joined—Union or disunion, war or peace. One hope remained, albeit a forlorn hope, and that lay with the Democrats in the upcoming presidential election. If the Democrats could settle on a candidate who appealed to all factions, they might well defeat the Republicans. If the party chose a candidate who alienated any significant segment of the party, it was abundantly clear that a

the South. The author, a 27-year-old poor white named Hinton Helper, attacked slavery not out of sympathy for the slaves but because he believed that the institution was creating a permanent class of impoverished whites. In any case, wealthy and influential Southerners feared that the Helper tract would foment rebellion among the region's lower classes.

Congressman John B. Clark of Missouri introduced a resolution saying that no member of the House who endorsed the Helper doctrine was fit to be Speaker. Though the resolution never passed, it started a battle royal. Realizing that he had caused more trouble than he could handle, Sherman declared that he had not even read the offending volume and had endorsed it in a purely

Republican, perhaps an out-and-out abolitionist, would be elected President, with civil war a likelihood.

Everything went wrong for the Democrats from the first. In an ill-advised selection of convention site, intended to reassure the South, the Democrats decided to meet in Charleston, South Carolina, the very heart of secessionist sentiment, where the fire-eaters of Dixie would be playing to a home audience. Most Northern Democrats arrived for the opening gavel on April 23 determined to reject the Southerners' demand for a pro-slavery plank and backing a candidate repugnant to the South, Stephen Douglas. The South would have neither. Addressing the gathering, the veteran Alabama radical William L. Yancey laid down his terms before his Northern colleagues: unconditional surrender. In a blunt warning that Northern Democrats must adopt a platform calling for a federal slave code that would protect the rights of slaveholders anywhere in the Union, he declared, "We are in a position to ask you to yield." The Northerners refused, and Yancey headed a walkout of 50 Southern delegates.

When voting for the presidential nomination got under way, it soon became painfully clear that, with 50 fewer delegates on hand, neither the front-runner Douglas nor anyone else had the necessary two thirds of the full convention needed for the nomination. After 57 ballots, the delegates were so exhausted and depressed that they voted to adjourn until June 18 and then try again in a less partisan place, Baltimore. "The proceedings at Charleston," wrote John Breckinridge, "threaten great calamities, unless there is wisdom and forbearance enough to redeem errors, at Baltimore."

But wisdom and forbearance were still in short supply when the Democrats reconvened. Failing once more to get a tolerable platform, Southerners again walked out, and 110 delegates set up their own rump convention nearby. With so many opposition delegates gone and a simple majority rule instituted, Stephen Douglas had two thirds of the remaining votes; he easily won the nomination—and with it a hopeless cause.

The Southern Democrats, for their part, wanted Breckinridge to run for President. He refused to let his name be used at a seceders' convention. Despite his disavowals, Breckinridge was nominated on a platform that called for the federal government to "protect the rights of persons and property in the Territories and wherever else its Constitutional authority extended." This was a platform on which the South could stand but not win. Upon being informed of his selection, Breckinridge was appalled and decided to decline the honor.

Opposition to the Republicans was further fragmented by a faction of Whigs who had reconstituted themselves as the Constitutional Union Party and had chosen as their standard-bearer John Bell of Tennessee. Bell was expected to run not on a platform but on a platitude: "The Constitution of the Country, the Union of the States, and the enforcement of the laws."

Then came the last attempts at compromise and statesmanship that the country would see for some time. Mississippi Senator Jefferson Davis realized that the split in the Democratic Party virtually guaranteed a victory for the hated Republicans. He proposed that Breckinridge accept the nomination, for he assumed Douglas would then realize that his own candidacy was futile. At that point a deal would be struck: Douglas, Breckinridge and Bell would all withdraw in favor of some compromise nominee who could unify the various anti-Republican elements under one umbrella. Bell agreed early to the scheme, and now Breckinridge did so too. He accepted his nomination and waited for Douglas to withdraw, so that he too could make a graceful exit.

But Douglas declined his prescribed part. After years of effort he had a presidential nomination, and he was not going to give it up. His refusal wiped out Davis' compromise. Three candidates were left in the field to oppose the Republicans.

Between the two Democratic meetings in Charleston and Baltimore, the Republicans held their own convention in Chicago, where an enormous frame building called the Wigwam was hastily thrown up to accommodate them. Despite the party's seriousness of purpose, the Republicans came to Chicago in a raucous mood. The delegations were accompanied by 900 reporters and thousands of hangers-on who came in claques to flood the Wigwam and stampede the convention for one candidate or another. Lincoln's Illinois supporters were among the most numerous, since they had the shortest distance to go. And Lincoln's astute managers printed up hundreds of tickets to hand out to Honest Abe's enthusiasts, so that the followers of Lincoln's archrival, William Seward of New York, could not dominate the crowds.

The sectional nature of the Republican Party could hardly escape notice. There were few representatives from the border states, and those who did come represented constituencies of dubious size and commitment. The Deep South sent not a single representative, though a group from Michigan proclaimed itself the Texas delegation. Another example of geographic prestidigitation was supplied by Horace Greeley. An anti-Seward New Yorker, he had been barred from his home state's delegation by its pro-Seward party boss, Thurlow Weed. Politically following his own advice to "Go West, young man," Greeley wangled an appointment to the Oregon delegation.

In contrast to their contentious Democratic rivals, the Republicans were most obliging in carpentering their platform. Hoping to gain support from moderates, anti-Douglas Democrats and Whigs—and at the same time to lay to rest its radical reputation—the party adopted a mildly worded platform. A protective-tariff plank appealed to businessmen and a homestead plank expressed the yearnings of thousands of Americans for cheap land beyond the Mississippi. There was something for just about everyone in the Republican platform; even Southern slaveholders were vaguely assured the sanctity of their property rights.

The desire of the party to appear moderate had a powerful effect on its choice of presidential candidate. Seward, the front runner at first, did not come across as a moderate, though his prediction several years earlier of an "irrepressible conflict" between North and South made him appear far more radical and intransigent than he actually was. Besides, his long years in high political office had made him almost as many powerful enemies as friends. His support outside his home state and New England was shallow.

Still, other candidates had similar problems. Edward Bates of Missouri, having flirted with the Know-Nothings, had earned the enmity of the many German-Americans, and Simon Cameron of Pennsylvania suf-

fered from a reputation as a political fixer and ideological wanderer whose travels had carried him into the Democratic, Whig and Know-Nothing Parties before he finally settled down as a Republican. Cameron could not count on the wholehearted support of even his home-state delegation.

There were other candidates with the credentials to compete for the Republican Party nomination. Among them were Salmon P. Chase of Ohio and U.S. Supreme Court Justice John McLean. There was also Lincoln, considered moderate on the slavery issue, properly conservative on the tariff and on the construction of transportation facilities, free of the Know-Nothing taint, and just prominent enough to have made his mark without acquiring too many enemies. As Lincoln himself realized, few delegates aside from his Illinois friends were committed to his candidacy, but he had become the second choice of many and would be in a good position should front-runner Seward falter. Just before the convention opened, he wrote to a friend: "My name is new in the field; and I suppose I am not the first choice of a very great many. Our policy, then, is to give no offence to others—leave them in a mood to come to us, if they shall be impelled to give up their first love."

From the beginning, Lincoln's managers took to the floor, buttonholing delegates, cajoling waverers, promising jobs great and small in the Lincoln administration. Back home in Springfield, where he was awaiting the vote, Lincoln dispatched a telegram to his supporters: "I authorize no bargains and will be bound by none." Whether Lincoln really hoped to disavow deals or merely wished to show clean hands, he well knew that patronage was the grease of politics, and

David Davis, his convention manager, paid no heed to his message except to remark perfunctorily, "Lincoln ain't here and don't know what we have to meet, so we will go ahead as if we hadn't heard from him, and he must ratify it."

Davis' deals paid off. On the first ballot Seward led, as expected, but drew only 173½ votes, while Lincoln was stronger than expected with 102. On the second ballot, Cameron and Bates began to falter. Lincoln's tally increased to 181 while Seward inched forward to just 184½, an ominous sign for the New Yorker. The third ballot confirmed the trend: Seward dropped back to 180 and Lincoln surged to 231½, just a vote and a half short of the nomination. Before that roll call ended, a delegate from Ohio leaped to his feet and shouted: "I arise, Mr. Chairman, to announce the change of four votes of Ohio from Mr. Chase to Mr. Lincoln."

Abraham Lincoln was over the top, and the convention broke into a roar of approbation. Outside the Wigwam someone fired a cannon, and boat whistles shrieked on Lake Michigan.

Thus there would be four candidates of as many political outlooks. Breckinridge represented protection of slavery in the territories; Douglas held fast to popular sovereignty; Lincoln stood for containing slavery in the states where it then existed and looked forward to a time when the practice would perish, presumably of natural causes; and Bell studiously wished away the present strife and looked backward to a time when the slave question hardly ruffled the surface of domestic tranquillity.

In the campaign that followed, the complex slave issue became secondary to the threat of disunion. Breckinridge, supported

In full regalia, the Wide-Awake sported a hat and a cape and carried a rail (a reference to Lincoln the Railsplitter) topped by a tin lamp for nocturnal marches. The group's name came from the hat members wore: Made of a fabric that had no nap, it was punningly referred to as a wide-awake.

The Wide-Awakes: Lighting a Path for "Old Abe"

"Broadway was one river of fire, as though Vesuvius had poured forth a torrent of molten lava." The reporter who wrote those lines was describing one of the many torchlight parades of the Wide-Awakes—in this case, through New York City on the night of October 3, 1860. Wide-Awakes were young Republicans, zealous and downright tireless in their campaigning to get Abraham Lincoln elected President.

The phenomenon began in Hartford, Connecticut, in March of 1860, when about 50 young men formed a club and adopted bizarre uniforms. Amid the overheated politics of the time, the idea proved contagious: Wide-Awake groups sprang up everywhere; East Chatham, New York, even had a club of daring young women. When Lincoln rode to victory on Election Day, November 6, his loudest boosters were no fewer than 400,000 Wide-Awakes.

up of Wide-Awakes from Mohawk, New York, assembles for a demonstration. Their marching song was "Ain't You Glad You Joined the Republicans?"

115

by avowed secessionists though deeply attached to the Union, found himself on the defensive in the North and the border regions. Lincoln was attacked not as a disunionist but as one whose election would assuredly bring about that result. For his part, Douglas saw himself as the realistic compromise, the only candidate with support in every section, the one man who could cool passions and bring a new unity to the nation. Recognizing that the odds favored Lincoln, he alone among the four broke with tradition and personally took to the hustings. Wherever he could gain a platform, whether in Massachusetts, Illinois or North Carolina, the stocky little Senator deplored with equal vigor the secessionists of the South and the abolitionists of the North.

The campaign was tumultuous throughout the North, South and West. In every town, partisans held parades, threw picnics and bellowed speeches. Liberty and Union were the watchwords of Republican orators in abolitionist New England; Union and economic growth were their themes in the Middle Atlantic States, where slavery was less compelling. In the South, the local press, bracing for the anticipated victory of Lincoln, sounded the secessionist battle cry. An Atlanta journal went so far as to say, "We regard every man an enemy to the institutions of the South who does not boldly declare that he believes African slavery to be a social, moral and political blessing." The Charleston *Mercury* was particularly vitriolic, branding Lincoln "the beau ideal of a relentless, dogged, free-soil Border Ruffian, a vulgar mobocrat and a Southern hater." And rather than "submit to such humiliation and degradation as the inauguration of Abraham Lincoln," proclaimed another South-

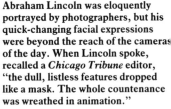

Abraham Lincoln was eloquently portrayed by photographers, but his quick-changing facial expressions were beyond the reach of the cameras of the day. When Lincoln spoke, recalled a *Chicago Tribune* editor, "the dull, listless features dropped like a mask. The whole countenance was wreathed in animation."

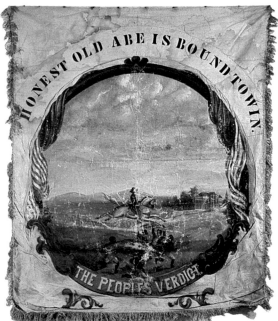

"Honest Abe" Lincoln gallops toward the White House as a quartet of jubilant blacks carry off the body of John C. Breckinridge, the Southern Democrats' candidate for President. Though such campaign symbolism succeeded in the North, it backfired in the South, where Lincoln was looked upon as a rabid abolitionist and archenemy of whites.

Greeting local Republicans, Abraham Lincoln towers above supporters at the front door of his house in Springfield, Illinois, during a rally in August of 1860.

ern newspaper, the South would see "the Potomac crimsoned in human gore, and Pennsylvania Avenue paved ten fathoms deep with mangled bodies."

Northern and Republican newspapers answered in kind, but for the most part refused to take Southern talk of secession seriously. They declared the threats of disunion to be "the idlest gossip imaginable," intended "to bully the people out of their choice," and with blind optimism they announced that Lincoln's election, far from bringing disunion, would inaugurate "a time of actual repose and peace quite unheard of for the last 10 years."

Lincoln himself looked upon the secession talk as essentially bluff and bluster. He pointed to the fact that all the candidates, even Breckinridge, opposed secession, and he placed his faith in the South's underlying attachment to the Union. When asked to issue a statement reassuring the South that slavery would be protected in those states where it existed, Lincoln refused, stating that he had already made his stand on that point abundantly clear.

The first significant portents of a Republican victory came in October, when state elections were held in Pennsylvania and Indiana, where Northern Democrats thought they stood a chance. In both states, Republicans swept the field. Douglas read these signs clearly. "Mr. Lincoln is the next President," he said. "We must try to save the Union. I will go South." Submerging his personal ambition, disregarding his failing health, Douglas plunged into Dixie, imploring and demanding that, whatever the outcome in November, the Union be preserved. But the South had read the same portents and agreed that all of them pointed to disunion. Many

baseless rumors stiffened Southern resolve. Abolitionists, it was said, had invaded Texas and were poisoning wells. Tales of slave rebellions, reported as fact in the press, added fear to the impulses galvanizing the South. The few Southern voices of moderation went unheeded. During his tour of Dixie, Douglas occasionally met with courtesy, occasionally met with boos, but always his save-the-Union preachments were wasted on the soft Southern air.

Election Day (the 6th of November, 1860) found Douglas on the road in Mobile, Alabama, and Lincoln at home in Springfield. At nightfall in Illinois, the telegraph reported that the state had gone Republican. Indiana soon followed suit. Then came a flood of Republican returns from the other states of the Northwest. Before midnight, Pennsylvania—home state of President Buchanan—fell into the Republican column. When heavily Republican returns began to flow in from New York, the state with the largest electoral vote in the nation, the election of Lincoln was certain.

The citizens of Springfield went wild. The President-elect walked over to a reception where refreshments were available. He was serenaded by the crowd. Among his well-wishers were people who had undoubtedly voted for Douglas; Lincoln had failed to carry his home county.

When the final returns were at last recorded, the electoral vote reflected with appalling accuracy the sectional split within the country. Lincoln had carried every free state except New Jersey, which divided its electors between the two Illinois candidates. South of the Mason-Dixon line, Lincoln carried nothing—indeed, many Southern states had not even placed his name on the ballot. Bell, the

THE QUESTION

IF LINCOLN

will be elected or not, is one which interests all parties North and South. Whether he

IS ELECTED

or not, the people of

SOUTH CAROLINA

(whose rights have been for a number of years trampled upon) have the advantage of supplying themselves with CLOTHING, at the well-known CAROLINA CLOTHING DEPOT, 261 King-street, at such prices as

WILL LEAD

them to be satisfied that the reputation of this Establishment has been

BOLDLY

and fearlessly maintained

FOR A

number of years, supplying its

SOUTHERN

Customers with all the Latest Styles, and at as low prices as any Clothing House in *the present*

CONFEDERACY

of all the States.

Thankful for the liberal patronage extended, the Proprietors desire merely to inform their customers and the public generally, that their present STOCK OF CLOTHING IS COMPLETE in all its departments, and are now prepared to offer Goods on the most reasonable and satisfactory terms. A call is therefore solicited by

OTTOLENGUIS, WILLIS & BARRETT,
November 5   261 King-street.

Anti-Lincoln headlines, vowing to form a Southern nation, lure readers to a mundane clothing advertisement published in the Charleston *Courier*. In fact, the South Carolinians were so rebellious that a local college president wrote: "You might as well attempt to control a tornado as to attempt to stop them from secession."

Constitutional Union candidate, captured Virginia, Kentucky and Tennessee. The rest of the South went solidly for Breckinridge. Douglas ended up with three of New Jersey's seven votes and all of Missouri's nine. Lincoln, with 180 electoral votes, had won a majority and was the next President.

The popular vote, however, told a more equivocal story. The combined opposition outpolled Lincoln by almost a million votes. Even in the free states, Lincoln's total majority was under 300,000; he would assume office with only a tenuous hold on the people of his own region. Arrayed against him were the seven states of the Deep South and undoubtedly, once they had time to adjust to realities, the four states of the Upper South. However the border states had voted, no one could foretell which side they would take in case of Southern secession.

In spite of the terrific momentum toward secession, a final effort was made to reconcile the South and salvage the Union. A committee of 13 Senators, led by John J. Crittenden of Kentucky, put forth a proposal to reestablish the Missouri Compromise line and extend it to California, permitting slavery in the territories south of latitude 36° 30'. The committee members also attempted to strengthen the Fugitive Slave Law and to make their amendments unrepealable and unamendable for all time.

Crittenden hoped to have the plan adopted by Congress and then put to a referendum. If he had succeeded, there is little doubt that the referendum would have been approved. But the Republicans were opposed, so the proposal was killed on the Senate floor. Crittenden would have a special reason for regretting the failure of his compromise: His sons Thomas and George would serve as generals on opposite sides in the fratricidal conflict ahead.

Yet even after the Crittenden Compromise failed, it did not quite die. It was resurrected in the form of seven Constitutional amendments and presented in Washington in a last-ditch peace assemblage that some observers called the "old men's convention." Elderly, shopworn politicians—the likes of former President John Tyler and David Wilmot, the author of the Wilmot Proviso—droned on for days. The Senate rejected their proposals and the House refused to consider the results of the convention, and that, at last, was the end of it.

Meanwhile, the South was reacting vigorously to the election of its bête noire, Lincoln. The agitators for secession were in control; their years of whipping up Southern passions and Southern patriotism had borne fruit at last. The aged provocator Edmund Ruffin had actually prayed for Lincoln's election because he hoped that South Carolina would secede from the Union, and that other states would do the same. Ruffin traveled to Charleston to watch his hope turn to prophecy. The breakup of the Union began on December 20, when delegates from all over South Carolina met in Charleston and voted unanimously to pull the state out of the Union. Charleston rejoiced. Mary Boykin Chesnut, the vivacious wife of a South Carolina aristocrat who owned several plantations and as many as 500 slaves, wrote in her diary, "We are divorced, North and South, because we have hated each other so."

Charleston had become a tinderbox, needing only one spark to explode into war—one spark in a city full of firebrands.

Storm over Sumter

The man who decided where the Civil War would begin arrived in Charleston in late November of 1860, about two weeks after Lincoln's election and four weeks before the secession of South Carolina. He was Major Robert Anderson, the new commander of the three Federal forts in Charleston Harbor: Moultrie, Sumter and Castle Pinckney.

Anderson had been appointed to his post by President Buchanan's subversive Secretary of War, John B. Floyd, because he came from good Kentucky stock, was married to a Georgia woman, had owned slaves and would presumably act with Southern bias in the looming crisis. Floyd, whose loyalty was to his native Virginia, was busily sending guns south to Federal installations where secessionist militia units could easily supply themselves when hostilities broke out.

Anderson's appointment suited another Virginian, General in Chief of the United States Army Winfield Scott, for the opposite reason. Scott, the greatest and, at 74, oldest American military hero, never wavered in his loyalty to the national government, and he was convinced that Anderson would not waver either. Anderson had served as Scott's aide during the Mexican War, and though he had shown no signs of outstanding talent, his determination and devotion to duty had driven him so hard that it took three bullets to knock him out of action.

Anderson viewed his Charleston assignment with healthy trepidation. He realized that his slightest misstep or miscalculation could touch off general warfare—a chilling responsibility. Besides, he was haunted by the past. By an odd coincidence, his father, Captain Richard Anderson, had defended Fort Moultrie in Charleston Harbor during the American Revolution, and had been forced to surrender to the British. The major feared he might repeat family history.

Above all, Anderson worried about his defensive posture. His main base, Fort Moultrie, on big Sullivan's Island, commanding the northern entrance to Charleston Harbor (*map, page 150*), was terribly vulnerable to land attack from the rear; in fact, Moultrie, with its 1,500 feet of works, was much too much fort to be held by Anderson's meager force of 60 Regular Army soldiers.

Castle Pinckney, lying less than a mile off the coast of Charleston, was unmanned and poorly armed, but it could be an effective counterthreat if only Anderson had enough troops and guns to garrison it properly; cannon in position here could do so much damage to the city that Confederate troublemakers might leave Moultrie alone.

But if worst came to worst, the most advantageous place for Anderson to make a stand was clearly Fort Sumter, on a tiny island 3.3 miles from Charleston. Although hasty efforts to strengthen this installation were still incomplete, Anderson's predecessor had laid in enough supplies to last for several months, and Sumter's guns could answer any attack by closing the harbor to Southern shipping to and from the city.

Anderson fully expected South Carolina to secede and to attack his fort. So he quickly began pelting the War Department in Washington with urgent reports of his shortages and requests for firm orders. Was he to surrender his forts if and when South Carolina so demanded? If not, when could he count on reinforcements? He must have troops to garrison Castle Pinckney, and to man the guns at Fort Sumter, where only an engineer and some workmen were stationed. As for Fort Moultrie, he told Secretary of War Floyd that South Carolina's intention "to obtain possession of this work, is apparent to all," and that Floyd must help him thwart that design at once. "The clouds are threatening," Anderson warned, "and the storm may break at any moment."

Floyd did nothing to help. He even declined to mention Anderson's appeals to General Scott, who could have offered his former colleague sound advice. On December 1 the Secretary informed Anderson that no reinforcements would be sent, since there would be no attack on the forts. But he finally gave Anderson a little maneuvering room.

On orders from Floyd, Major Don Carlos Buell traveled to Charleston on December 9 and spent two days inspecting the forts. In private discussion with Anderson, Buell relayed Floyd's permission for the major to defend any fort of his choice if attacked. Anderson could also move his command to the most defensible fort if he acquired evidence of hostile plans by the South Carolinians.

Evidence of hostility abounded. As early as November 12, South Carolina authorities had stationed 20 militiamen to "protect" the Federal arsenal in Charleston—that is, to deny its arms and munitions to the rightful owners. And more evidence poured in. On December 20, South Carolina seceded as expected. Henceforth, bands of armed secessionists from Moultrieville, a small town outside Moultrie's walls, patrolled the boundary of the fort day and night, and the Federal officers there were soon so exhausted by their tense hours on duty that two of them let their wives take their shift. Casual exchanges between soldiers and local people were virtually cut off. Militia companies from all over South Carolina kept pouring into Charleston, and rumors of Rebel attack plans grew ever more numerous and intimidating.

For a while, Anderson felt that his duty was crystal clear. He was to avoid a clash if honor permitted; if not, he would defend his Federal enclave by strength of arms. But then on December 23 he received a note from Secretary Floyd that threw him into uncertainty again. The message seemed to suggest that if he was attacked, he should surrender rather than suffer pointless casualties. Suspecting Floyd's political motives and feeling abandoned by Washington, the major decided that the time had come to act. He would shift all his men to Fort Sumter on Christmas night and brace to face any emergency.

Anderson kept his plans quiet. On his unexplained orders, his soldiers and civilian workers spent all Christmas Day packing Moultrie's movable goods. Rain postponed the transfer that night. But the next night the men ferried their gear to Sumter so furtively that the crowds in Charleston suspected nothing until the following day, the 27th.

That morning they saw—across the water at Moultrie—smoke rising from the wooden gun carriages that the Federals had set afire to deny the secessionists use of the cannon. But it was not until noon that the Charlestonians and all the secessionists, gazing toward

The dapper young officers of a Charleston militia company assemble with their men at nearby Castle Pinckney, an undefended Federal fort they took over on December 27, 1860. The South Carolinians had found a single Union officer supervising workmen in the fort, and they courteously permitted him to join his command on Fort Sumter.

Sumter, realized that the fort was now fully garrisoned: The Stars and Stripes was being raised on the mast atop the ramparts. The secessionists reacted quickly, seizing Moultrie, the Federal arsenal in Charleston, the post office and the customs house.

Naturally, Anderson's move to Sumter was damned throughout the South as aggression. Naturally, too, Northerners praised the major for defying the disloyal Southerners. Anderson received a fair amount of fan mail, which the secessionists dutifully delivered. One admirer wrote: "The Lord bless your noble soul! Oh, my dear sir, the whole country will triumphantly sustain you."

Of course, Anderson had not intended his move to be aggressive or defiant. On the contrary, he hoped that by occupying a stronger position he would prevent or at least delay an outbreak of hostilities. Perhaps he did manage to postpone the war.

But with passing time, Sumter swelled in symbolic importance to the North and South, becoming an issue in itself. The fort was a Federal installation from which the United States could not retreat, and it was also a piece of South Carolina property that that self-declared sovereign state refused to leave in the hands of a so-called foreign power. Unwittingly, Anderson had made Fort Sumter the final cause and first objective of the unavoidable war.

The conflicting orders that so dismayed Anderson were a natural product of the utter confusion that reigned in Washington. The trouble began at the top. President Buchanan, always a weak executive, was now a lame duck to boot. Ill-informed and largely ignored, depressed by events beyond his control, believing it was Congress' responsibility to act, he vacillated, hoping that critical decisions could be deferred until he left office in March 1861. Buchanan apparently did not learn of Anderson's move to Fort Sumter until the day after the event, and then he was told not by his staff but by three Southern callers, among them Senator Jefferson Davis. "My God," the President groaned, "are calamities never to come singly?"

Another misfortune arrived at the White House on December 28 in the form of three commissioners from the state of South Carolina, appointed by the secession convention to negotiate with Buchanan for Anderson's removal, or for possession of Fort Sumter by purchase if need be. The President received them, which amounted to diplomatic recognition of South Carolina. Then he put off a decision until he could consult with his Cabinet. And he consulted as long as possible.

The Cabinet was now in the throes of therapeutic change. Floyd was under a dark cloud for financial corruption as well as for his political disloyalty, and so was Secretary of the Interior Jacob Thompson of Louisiana. Indeed, the cloud over Floyd was so black that Buchanan had already asked for his resignation—not face to face, at the risk of unpleasantries, but by sending Vice President Breckinridge. Floyd had agreed to resign but declined to hurry, and Buchanan did nothing to force the issue. But, in any case, the Southerners who had dominated the Cabinet were on their way out.

When the Cabinet met, Floyd undid himself completely by claiming that Anderson had disobeyed his orders in moving to Sumter. That allegation was proved false when someone produced a memorandum of the instructions Floyd had given Major Buell to deliver verbally to Anderson. Now, the Union men in the Cabinet—Attorney General Edwin M. Stanton, Postmaster General Joseph Holt and the newly appointed Secretary of State Jeremiah Black—gained the

Furtively evacuating Fort Moultrie, the Union garrison sets out for Fort Sumter on the evening of December 26, 1860. The first boat was intercepted by a secessionist patrol craft, but the officer in charge ordered his 30 men to cover their muskets with their coats and, he said, "The guard ship concluded we were all right and passed on."

Kneeling in newly occupied Fort Sumter, Union Major Robert Anderson *(left)* joins his men in a prayer of thanksgiving for their safe passage from Fort Moultrie. The Stars and Stripes was then raised, the band played "Hail Columbia" and the troops presented arms.

upper hand. Though this meeting and the next failed to wring a decision from the President, his resistance to his former Southern friends was itself a victory for the Union men. And the next day Buchanan continued to put off the Carolina commissioners: "You don't give me time to consider," he complained, "you don't give me time to say my prayers. I always say my prayers when required to act upon any great State affair."

It took several more Cabinet meetings before Buchanan made up his mind. In the midst of it all, Floyd finally resigned and Thompson prepared to do so. When the President's answer came, it was no. Anderson would not be ordered to leave Sumter. On December 30, Buchanan gave that word to the South Carolina commissioners and, more remarkable still, added that Sumter would be defended "against hostile attacks from whatever quarter they may come."

At last Buchanan was trying to get a grip on events. And the effort turned up some distressing news. After listening to blunt talk concerning the political situation from Robert Toombs, another once-influential Southerner, the President exclaimed, "Good God, Mr. Toombs, do you mean that I am in the midst of a revolution?"

"Yes, sir," Toombs replied. "More than that, you have been there for a year and have not yet found it out."

Unfortunately for Buchanan, his decision to offend South Carolina and keep Fort Sumter gave rise to a new problem: the need, called to his attention in a letter from General Scott, for an expedition to bolster Sumter with men and supplies. Buchanan had no choice but to agree, and thereby almost started the war three months early.

Buchanan left the enterprise in Scott's

usually capable hands. The general ordered four companies of Regulars at Fort Monroe in Virginia to prepare for embarkation on the U.S.S. *Brooklyn* and to take three months' supplies. But then Scott fell into Buchanan's habit of temporizing. He thought it only courteous to wait until the commissioners could study the President's reply. He worried that the deep-draft warship might run aground on the shoals outside Charleston Harbor. Further, he abandoned his own idea of using troops from Fort Monroe: It was unwise to weaken that garrison, for Virginia might at any time secede as well. No doubt it would be safer to use troops from New York.

After all of his cogitation, Scott decided against a simple, overt relief expedition and ordered a tricky, clandestine operation. He had his Assistant Adjutant General Lorenzo Thomas engage a merchant vessel, the *Star of the West*, at the exorbitant sum of $1,250 per day. The idea was that the *Star*, which regularly traveled between New York and New Orleans, could depart unnoticed with a secret cargo of 200 troops. Thomas made all arrangements privately so that no intelligence of his doings would go through normal government channels. The soldiers chosen for the expedition were told to stay below-decks as they approached Charleston Harbor, so that the South Carolinians would see only the ship's crew and would assume that another plain merchantman was arriving.

Well after dark on January 5, 1861, the *Star of the West* quietly left her berth in New York and started on her way. For all the earnest attempts at secrecy, word of the expedition quickly became public knowledge. Two days after the ship sailed, rumors of her mission began to appear in the New York press, and in Washington both Interior Secretary

Thompson and Senator Louis T. Wigfall of Texas learned more than enough about the plan. Thompson on January 8 notified South Carolina of the relief expedition and then, at last, resigned his Cabinet post. At the same time, Wigfall telegraphed to Governor Francis Pickens of South Carolina that the ship could be expected in Charleston Harbor at any hour. Unlike Thompson, who hurried home to Mississippi, Wigfall remained in Washington for two months, ferreting out news to send south.

While the *Star* was en route, Joseph Holt, who had shifted from postmaster general to replace Floyd as Secretary of War, was alarmed by a delayed dispatch from Anderson. The major said that he now felt quite secure, that he did not need reinforcement for the moment, and that the secessionists were building gun emplacements along the shore commanding the main ship channel to Sumter. At once Holt concluded that the *Star* was risking destruction, and possibly war, for no worthwhile purpose. He tried to call the ship back, but it was too late.

The worst of it was that Anderson did not know a relief ship was coming his way. Holt had sent him detailed information of the plan, along with permission to open fire should the *Star* be shelled. But the letter, on which war might hinge, was sent through the regular mails instead of by courier, and it would not arrive until after the event. The only advance warning Anderson received came on January 8, when a copy of the Charleston *Mercury* was brought to the fort by a workman. It carried the news that the Union relief ship *Star of the West* was expected to arrive that night or the following morning. Lacking any official notification to that effect, Anderson dismissed the report.

OUR NATIONAL BIRD AS IT APPEARED WHEN HANDED TO JAMES BUCHANAN MARCH 4 1857.

THE IDENTICAL BIRD AS IT APPEARED A.D. 1861.
"I was murdered i'the Capitol" Shakespere

A slashing 1860 attack on the Democrats alleges that four years of the Buchanan administration have transformed the once-proud American eagle into a plucked bird.

At 6 a.m. on January 9, the Sumter garrison heard cannon fire out in the harbor. The troops raced to their guns. Major Anderson, peering out to the harbor mouth, saw the *Star of the West* approaching, flying Old Glory. The ship was also spotted on Morris Island, where sat a South Carolina battery. One of the cannon, entrusted to gunner George E. Haynsworth, a cadet at The Citadel, fired two rounds. Haynsworth's aim was abominable, but arguably, those were the first shots of the Civil War.

Poor Anderson could not decide what to do. He merely stood on the parapet, excited and puzzled, watching the ship steam in. Then he and his officers saw the *Star* lower her flag and raise it again—obviously some sort of signal. But for what?

Fort Moultrie, manned by secessionists since the day after Anderson left, joined the shelling with its remounted guns. Anderson still took no action in support of the *Star;* he dithered about on the parapet, unable to commit the nation to war under circumstances he did not understand. Within minutes the *Star of the West* turned about, unable to stand the shelling. She suffered two minor hits while passing Morris Island but made her way safely back to the open sea.

It was a frustrating and humiliating experience for the Sumter garrison. Anderson angrily sent Governor Pickens a note demanding an explanation and threatening to use his guns to close the harbor unless Pickens apologized for the shelling of the *Star*. Of course the Governor declined; he said that his batteries had merely acted in defense, but if Anderson opened fire, then that would be an act of aggression. In the end, the two lapsed into something resembling a truce.

But passions in Charleston and elsewhere were too inflamed by the episode to accept a truce. Robert Barnwell Rhett, the fire-eating editor of the Charleston *Mercury*, wrote that "powder has been burnt over the decree of our State, timber has been crashed, perhaps blood spilled." The firing on the *Star of the West* was "the opening ball of the Revolution," and South Carolina was honored to be the first thus to resist the Yankee tyranny. "She has not hesitated to strike the first blow, full in the face of her insulter," Rhett exclaimed. "We would not exchange or recall that blow for millions! It has wiped out a half century of scorn and outrage."

The North entertained opinions hardly less vehement. "The authority and dignity of the Government must be vindicated at every hazard," declared the Albany, New York, *Atlas and Argus*. "The issue thus having been made, it must be met and sustained, if necessary, by the whole power of the navy and army." Private citizens called for arms to put down this obnoxious insurrection. A New

Yorker found it intolerable that "the nation pockets this insult to the national flag, a calm, dishonorable, vile submission." In turn, the talk of reprisal from the North played into the hands of the Southern fire-eaters, who urged the recalcitrant slave states to secede and close ranks for mutual defense.

Almost at once, a Mississippi convention voted 84 to 15 in favor of secession. "In an instant the hall was a scene of wild tumult," and amid deafening applause someone brought out an immense blue banner with a single white star, probably the inspiration of one of the South's most beloved patriotic songs, "The Bonnie Blue Flag." The next day, January 10, Florida joined Mississippi and South Carolina in secession, and a day later Alabama left the Union.

In addition to recording its grievances in its secession ordinance, Alabama became the first state formally to call for an affiliation of seceded states. "In order to frame a revisional as a permanent Government," the Alabama delegation declared, "the people of the States of Delaware, Maryland, Virginia, North Carolina, South Carolina, Florida, Georgia, Mississippi, Louisiana, Texas, Arkansas, Tennessee, Kentucky and Missouri, be and they are hereby invited to meet the people of the State of Alabama, by their delegates in convention, on the 4th day of February next in Montgomery." It was time to form a new nation.

On January 19, the state of Georgia joined the secession movement. Louisiana did the same a week later, and on February 1, Texas brought the number to seven. The United States was in chaos.

In Washington, on January 21, several congressmen and senators from the seceded states made farewell speeches and left their seats. Some used the occasion for a final stab at the Union, but others were obviously sorrowful. Mississippian Jefferson Davis declared in a voice quavering with emotion, "Whatever of offense there has been to me, I leave here. I carry with me no hostile remembrance. Whatever offense I have given, . . . I have, Senators, in this hour of our parting, to offer you my apology." Some wept as he spoke. There will be peace "if you so will it," he went on, but the North "may bring disaster on every part of the country, if you will have it thus." Should war come, "we will invoke the God of our fathers, who delivered them from the power of the lion, to protect us from the ravages of the bear." That night in his room as he prepared to travel home, Davis prayed for peace.

But the meager chances for peace were diminished steadily by Southern states in a bridge-burning mood. As each state passed its secession ordinance, it occupied or demanded the surrender of Federal arsenals and forts within its borders. On January 20, Mississippi forces seized Fort Massachusetts on Ship Island, controlling the mouth of the Mississippi River. Georgia state troops took the Augusta arsenal on January 24, and two days later occupied the Federal works in Savannah. Even before seceding, the state had taken possession of strategic Fort Pulaski at the mouth of the Savannah River. Similarly, Louisiana had taken possession of Federal installations below New Orleans.

Only in Florida did the secessionists meet resistance. In command of Fort Barrancas, near Pensacola, was a young Union lieutenant, Adam Slemmer. Expecting to be attacked as soon as Florida seceded, Slemmer withdrew his tiny command of 46 men to Fort Pickens, situated on Santa Rosa Island

A huge crowd in Savannah, Georgia, cheers the unveiling of an adoptive secessionist banner—the rattlesnake and "Don't tread on me" emblem of the American Revolution. The scene took place in early November of 1860, as the tide of anti-Union sentiment was cresting in the South.

at the mouth of Pensacola Bay. There he later received some two dozen reinforcements from a Navy ship, and when Florida demanded his surrender on January 12, he refused. And when the Governors of both Florida and Alabama demanded that he turn over the fort, he impudently replied that "a governor is nobody here." Slemmer would again be supplied and reinforced without a shot being fired by either side; the Union flag would fly over his fort throughout the War. Meanwhile, Fort Taylor on Key West was also garrisoned by Federals, providing the Union with another valuable base that served well in the years ahead.

Slemmer and brave Fort Pickens, however, brought the North only passing cheer in a secession winter that produced more and worse news every day. In February came a particularly galling affront: Brevet Major General David E. Twiggs—one of the four highest officers in the U.S. Army—eagerly surrendered military posts in Texas to the secessionists. Within days he was dismissed

from the service as a traitor, and he took such offense at the appellation that he wrote to Buchanan threatening to visit him "for the sole purpose of a personal interview"—the usual euphemism for a duel. It was an empty threat; Twiggs was 71 years old. Nevertheless, the incident gave ample warning that the Union must expect defections from the very army that would have to contest the growing insurrection.

For all practical purposes North and South passed the point of no return that February, when secessionist delegates meeting in Montgomery, Alabama, set up their Southern nation. From South Carolina came Robert Barnwell Rhett and former U.S. Senator James Chesnut, among others, and Georgia's delegation included its three foremost statesmen, Robert Toombs, Howell Cobb and Alexander H. Stephens. Most of the rest were Southern patriots little known outside their home states.

The delegates elected Cobb president of the convention. "The separation is perfect, complete, and perpetual," he told them. "The great duty is now imposed upon us of providing for these States a government for their future security and protection." Rarely had a revolutionary assembly acted with such speed and unanimity. On February 5, Christopher Memminger of South Carolina moved that the states form a new "confederacy," and was appointed head of a committee of 12 to begin working on a constitution. The committee reported back two days later, and on February 8 the Provisional Constitution of the Confederate States of America was adopted without dissent.

Predictably, the new charter did not differ greatly from that of the old Union; although these seceders tried to simplify the Constitution, they considered themselves the true constructionists and the Yankees the violators of the Constitution. Their temporary charter guaranteed the right to own slaves in any new territory but prohibited a resumption of the foreign slave trade. States were declared sovereign and independent; by implication, any state might even secede from the new nation. The President and Vice President would serve for six years and become ineligible for a second term.

With the easy adoption of this constitution, the delegates were faced with the critical task of choosing a leader. There was no time to arrange for a general election; that would come a year later when a permanent constitution was framed. The President had to be chosen here and now.

Who should lead them? The delegates of two states wanted Howell Cobb, though he did not seek the post. Among others considered for the post were blustery, hard-drinking Robert Toombs and quiet, somber Jefferson Davis. Both Toombs and Cobb suffered because they had made many enemies in their long careers. The decision was further simplified by a mistake Toombs made two days before the final vote. Alexander Stephens of Georgia, who was to become Vice President, wrote that Toombs "got quite tight at dinner and went to a party in town tighter than I ever saw him—too tight for his character and reputation by far. I think that evening's exhibition settled the Presidency where it fell."

With support for Toombs evaporating, the convention quickly voted for the man most acceptable to all factions, the man who had been neither too conservative nor too radical in the sectional crisis, the man who

Confederate cavalrymen of Texas Colonel Ben McCulloch swarm into the main plaza of San Antonio on February 18, 1861, to await the arrival of renegade Union General David Twiggs, who was to meet with Texas officials and surrender his forces.

could immediately present a unified front to the unseceded Southern states and the angry Northern states. Jefferson Davis was the man, and he would do.

While the convention discussed designs for a Confederate flag, word went out informing Davis of his selection. When the message reached him, he was helping his wife in the garden of Brierfield, their plantation near Vicksburg, Mississippi. Varina Davis saw his face pale as he read of his election. He said then, and would often repeat, that he had not wanted the office; rather, he had hoped for command of the Confederacy's army. Yet Davis, for all the faults that the coming years would reveal in him, was on balance the best available man for the job.

And thus at first, the Confederacy spoke

to the world in a moderate voice. On February 18, when Jefferson Davis took the oath of office as President of the Confederacy, he delivered a temperate inaugural address that sought to reassure both contentious sections. All the Southerners wanted, he told the North, was to be left alone. But if attacked, they would defend themselves, "and the suffering of millions will bear testimony to the folly and wickedness of our aggressors." Radicals like William L. Yancey began to feel better about this moderate when they heard those strong words. Many Northerners agreed with Davis' appeal for a peaceable separation and said of the seceded states, "Let the erring sisters go in peace."

Two weeks later another inaugural address was heard from a man even more committed to moderation. On March 4, 1861, Abraham Lincoln took his oath of office as the 16th President of the United States and addressed the South in conciliatory tones. He vowed to avoid war and at the same time to maintain the Union. He held that the Union was still whole, for it was by its nature indissoluble. He would enforce its laws and "hold, occupy, and possess" Federal property—meaning particularly Fort Sumter—but he would not initiate violent or aggressive action. "In your hands, my dissatisfied fellow-countrymen, and not in mine, is the momentous issue of civil war," he told them. "You can have no conflict without being yourselves the aggressors." He had sworn to defend the Union, and he would if he must, but surely the Southerners would not force his hand if they took time for reflection.

"I am loath to close," Lincoln said in a moving coda. "We are not enemies, but friends. We must not be enemies." Memories of the patriot days of the Revolution still bound them together. These fond sentiments would "swell the chorus of the Union, when again touched, as surely they will be, by the better angels of our nature."

But nothing President Lincoln could say made friends in the South. Emma Holmes of Charleston said that the speech was "just what was expected of him, stupid, ambiguous, vulgar and insolent," by virtue of which it "is everywhere considered as a virtual declaration of war."

Lincoln had been in office just one day when the simmering Sumter crisis boiled up again. With the U.S. mail and railroad service continuing to function more or less normally, a letter arrived from Major Anderson declaring that his position was nearly hopeless; that he needed 20,000 more troops to

hold position in Charleston Harbor; that even if Sumter were not attacked, his dwindling food supply would soon force him to choose between starvation and surrender. In fact, the major's only hope had failed. He had bought plenty of time for reinforcements to be sent, but since none had arrived, the hiatus had worked out to the great advantage of the South Carolinians. They had sunk several old hulks in the harbor's main channel to impede any Federal attempt to relieve Sumter. And they had brought in many cannon seized from Federal arsenals and emplaced batteries to fire on Sumter from three sides.

It was not hard to detect in Anderson's woe-filled letter an unstated hope that he would be permitted to evacuate his garrison. But Lincoln, mindful of his public pledge to defend Federal property, solicited advice on the feasibility of reinforcing or resupplying Sumter. The counsel he received was more alarming than informative.

Lincoln's aggressive postmaster general, Montgomery Blair, was the only Cabinet member who shared the President's resolve to help Anderson hold Sumter. The opposition was led by William Seward, the disappointed presidential aspirant, whom Lincoln had appointed Secretary of State as a fence-mending gesture to the radical Eastern Republicans. The imperious New Yorker had decided that, with a little appeasement, the seceded Southern states would return peaceably to the Union fold, and he was deliberately creating the impression among associates that he, not the President, would set policy toward the secessionists—and, indeed, run the government. It did not help Lincoln that General Scott declared that Sumter could not be reinforced in time.

Lincoln acted first to prevent another

Sumter, approving an order that supplies be sent forthwith to Florida's Fort Pickens. And then, unwilling to accept Scott's adverse opinion, he told the general to send agents to Charleston to judge whether—and how—an expedition could relieve Sumter. Lincoln was sure to get the decision he wanted; Scott chose an agent known to be prejudiced in favor of a relief expedition. The man was Gustavus V. Fox, a former Navy captain, who for weeks had been telling everyone, including the press, that Fort Sumter could be and should be reinforced.

It boded ill for the Federals that the secessionists, too, knew exactly what Fox stood for. When the agent reached Charleston, he applied to the Confederates for permission to visit Sumter and report on its condition. Suspecting Fox but unwilling to send him packing, Confederates escorted him to the fort and tried to prevent his speaking privately with Major Anderson. With great difficulty Fox hinted to Anderson that a relief expedition was under discussion in Washington. But Anderson learned none of the details.

As Lincoln awaited word from Fox, a new batch of three commissioners from the Confederate States arrived in Washington to discuss foreign relations with Seward. The Secretary of State was too discreet to make Buchanan's mistake of meeting with the emissaries, but he agreed to advise them through an intermediary, Supreme Court Justice John A. Campbell, a Confederate collaborator, who was about to resign from the bench and head south. On March 15, without confiding his plans to anyone, Seward told Campbell that Sumter would be evacuated soon—in fact, within three days.

Campbell and the Confederate diplomats were ecstatic; it seemed they had won with-

133

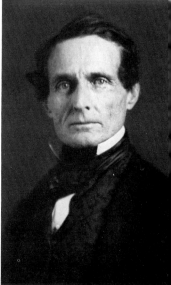

Jefferson Davis (*above*) is sworn in as President of the Confederate States of America on the capitol steps at Montgomery, Alabama, on February 18, 1861. "The audience was large and brilliant," he wrote to his wife. "Upon my weary heart was showered smiles, plaudits and flowers, but beyond them, I saw trouble and thorns innumerable."

out firing a shot. But six days went by and brought no word that Sumter had been abandoned. Seward, still cocky on March 21, reassured Campbell, and again the Confederates were mollified. Then came March 29 and a decision. Lincoln held a Cabinet meeting. Reports from his agents in Charleston, especially Gustavus Fox, advised that Sumter could be resupplied. And by then most of the Cabinet members had changed their views, goaded by Northern Republicans who were furious that nothing was being done. Seward found that he was suddenly all alone on the side of evacuation. Lincoln ordered that an expedition be assembled to relieve Sumter as soon as possible.

Now Seward, squirming to avoid the consequences of his folly, made matters worse by sending Lincoln a letter full of wild proposals. He suggested that the United States provoke war with either Spain or France in the expectation that the South would reunite with the North against the common foe, and he advised the President to let him take over the onerous chore of running the government. Lincoln had ample cause for dismissing Seward out of hand. But he admired Seward's abilities and expected to win his loyalty. He ignored Seward's letter.

On April 4, Lincoln informed Major Anderson by ordinary mail that the expedition was coming, but not when. Captain Fox,

A crowd of 30,000 watches the inauguration of Abraham Lincoln as the 16th President of the United States on the 4th of March, 1861. Sharpshooters were posted in the windows of the Capitol to guard against assassination attempts by Southern sympathizers.

who was to lead the mission as an unofficial representative of the President, had planned for an eight-ship fleet, but he was forced to compete for the few available vessels with officers arranging a relief expedition to Fort Pickens. Since Lincoln still hoped to avert a clash over Sumter, he ordered Fox to send ashore supplies only, no reinforcements—unless the Confederates attacked him or interfered with his mission. The President then sent a messenger with a letter to Governor Pickens, telling him of this strictly limited mission and stressing its peaceful intent.

The Governor, suspecting perfidy, rushed the letter to President Davis in Montgomery and alerted the Confederate commander at Charleston, a handsome, dapper Louisiana Frenchman named Pierre Gustave Toutant Beauregard. The brigadier general needed no special urging. But he was undoubtedly bemused by one of those poignant ironies that often crop up in wartime. While Beauregard was at West Point in the late 1830s, he had studied artillery under an instructor who became his friend and was now his adversary, Major Anderson. It appeared that he would have to recite his lessons to Anderson from the mouths of his cannon.

Beauregard had worked feverishly to complete his artillery build-up around the harbor. By early April he already had brought overwhelming strength to bear on Fort Sumter. Fort Moultrie on Sullivan's Island had three 8-inch, long-range cannon called columbiads, two 8-inch high-trajectory howitzers, five smoothbores that fired 32-pound shot and four 24-pounders. Deployed outside Moultrie's walls were five squat, wide-mouthed 10-inch mortars, designed expressly to reduce fortifications, and also two 32-pounders, two 24-pounders and a 9-inch

Brigadier General Pierre G. T. Beauregard, commander of Confederate forces confronting Fort Sumter, was a handsome man— and allegedly vain about it. When his black hair began turning white in 1861, friends blamed the burden of command, but cynics had another explanation: The Union sea blockade had cut off the import of hair dyes.

Dahlgren smoothbore, a lightweight gun that could fire a heavy charge. Soon to be moored off the west end of Sullivan's Island was an ungainly construction called the Floating Battery—two 42-pounders and two 32-pounders mounted on a raft and protected by iron shielding.

On James Island west of Sumter, Fort Johnson had a 24-pounder and four 10-inch mortars. And at the tip of Morris Island, immediately south of Sumter, stood seven 10-inch mortars, two 42-pounders, an English Blakely rifled cannon and the Ironclad Battery, so called because its three 8-inch columbiads were protected front and top by a wooden shield faced with heavy iron bars.

To man these guns and to storm Sumter if necessary, Beauregard had roughly 6,000 men of all ages and degrees of training. Established militia companies had been called out and marched into Charleston to welcom-

ing cannon salutes. Fuzz-cheeked boys had run away from home to bear arms against Sumter. A few old men, most notably the veteran crusader for secession Edmund Ruffin, came to take a hand in the great event.

Augustus Dickert, a 15-year-old militiaman who had hurried to Charleston fearing that the war would be over before he could get into it, wrote that "everyone was in a high glee—palmetto cockades, brass buttons, uniforms, and gaudy epaulettes were seen in every direction." The town was "ablaze with excitement, flags waved from the house tops, the heavy tread of the embryo soldiers could be heard in the streets, the corridors of hotels, and in all the public places." Southern patriots, even those "who were as ignorant and as much strangers to manual labor as though they had been infants," moved guns and dug emplacements until their hands were blistered and bloodied. By the end of the first week of April, Beauregard was ready and more than ready.

So was the Confederate government in Montgomery. Well before Lincoln's April 6 message arrived in the Alabama capital, the secessionists were tired of waiting and bitter over Seward's apparent duplicity—and therefore, presumably, Lincoln's. With Lincoln's message in hand, Jefferson Davis convened his Cabinet on April 9. Lincoln had maneuvered the Confederates into the position he had promised in his inaugural: There would be no first shot unless they fired it. Davis did not want that shot fired any more than Lincoln did. Yet after all the months of anxiety and indecision, the firing of that shot seemed less dreadful than before, a release and a climax that many Confederates demanded. A friend of Davis' warned him, "Unless you sprinkle blood in the face of the

Southern people they will be back in the old Union in less than ten days."

There was a likelier eventuality—that if the Confederate government did not act, South Carolina might do so on its own, undermining the new and untested authority of the Confederate States. All but one of the Cabinet members favored ordering Beauregard to go ahead and open fire. The exception was Secretary of State Robert Toombs. He counseled caution and warned that "the firing upon that fort will inaugurate a civil war greater than any the world has yet seen."

That was a risk that the Cabinet was prepared to take. On April 10, Secretary of War Leroy Pope Walker telegraphed Beauregard that he was to demand Sumter's immediate evacuation; if he was refused for any reason, he was to "proceed in such manner as you may determine, to reduce it."

That night in Charleston, the excitement and patriotic passions that had been building up since secession last December reached fever pitch. All night long parades snaked through the streets, drums rolled and horses' hooves clattered, great bonfires cast leaping shadows. Those Southerners who still treasured the Union did not dare to speak their minds. Even Southern patriots who were satisfied by the current peaceable progress of the Confederate States were swept aside in the hysteria of the moment.

This was no place for moderation, no time for trepidation. Charleston was in the hands of the fire-eaters; former Unionist Michael P. O'Connor called the Union "a dead carcass stinking in the nostrils of the Southern people." The night belonged to Roger Pryor who, from the balcony of his hotel, spoke as a Virginian to the seething crowd of South Carolinians in the street below.

"I thank you especially," Pryor shouted, "that you have at last annihilated this accursed Union, reeking with corruption and insolent with excess of tyranny. Not only is it gone, but gone forever.

"As sure as tomorrow's sun will rise upon us, just so sure will old Virginia be a member of the Southern Confederacy; and I will tell your Governor what will put her in the Southern Confederacy in less than an hour by a Shrewsbury clock.

"Strike a blow!" Pryor cried. "The very moment that blood is shed, old Virginia will make common cause with her sisters of the South."

The final day of peace, April 11, 1861, dawned warm and overcast in Charleston. Many people sensed that the long Sumter crisis would end this day, and their giddy expectancy increased hour by hour. Mary Boykin Chesnut, whose husband, James, now served as a colonel on Beauregard's staff, was as much a Southern patriot as anyone; but she did not share the radicals' passion for war, and she feared that war was just an inch away. "And so we fool on," she wrote in her diary, "into the black cloud ahead of us."

Putting aside her fears, Mrs. Chesnut that noon enjoyed "the merriest, maddest dinner we have had yet." By tacit agreement there was no talk of war at her table, but thoughts of war stirred the men's blood and loosened their tongues. Mary Chesnut noted that the men were "more audaciously wise and witty" than usual, and "for once in my life I listened." Then came a signal development.

Before noon, James Chesnut was summoned by General Beauregard. The colonel was given a written surrender ultimatum to

Confederate forces at Cummings Point on Morris Island prepare to bombard Fort Sumter in these on-the-spot sketches by William Waud, an artist for Frank Leslie's *Illustrated Newspaper*. At left, slaves mount a heavy gun. At bottom, soldiers unload supplies from rafts while engineers use palmetto logs to erect earthworks and emplace guns behind protective iron rails.

deliver to Major Anderson. Accompanied by Colonel James A. Chisholm and Captain Stephen D. Lee, Chesnut was rowed out to Fort Sumter, and there he presented his message to the Federal commander.

Anderson withdrew to discuss the ultimatum with his officers. They all agreed to reject it. Anderson wrote out his response and handed the note to Chesnut. Then as he strolled to the wharf to see the Confederates off, the major asked Chesnut, "Will General Beauregard open his batteries without further notice to me?"

"I think not," replied Chesnut. "No, I can say to you that he will not, without further notice."

"I shall await the first shot," Anderson said, then added quietly, "and if you do not batter us to pieces, we shall be starved out in a few days."

Returning to Charleston, Chesnut reported Anderson's hint to Beauregard. At once the general told Secretary Walker that they might get the prize without a shot simply by waiting until Sumter's provisions ran out. Walker replied that he did not "desire needlessly to bombard Fort Sumter," and if Anderson would state the date when he would evacuate, Beauregard could hold his fire. Beauregard composed a last message to Anderson and summoned Chesnut to deliver it. Chesnut was empowered to act on the spot according to Anderson's response.

Just before 1 a.m. on April 12, Chesnut and his party, this time accompanied by Roger Pryor, again approached Fort Sumter. Pryor stayed in the boat while the others delivered the message.

Again Anderson withdrew with his officers to discuss their response. They debated for three hours—so long that Chesnut concluded that they were deliberately stalling and interrupted them to hasten their answer.

Finally, shortly after 3 a.m. on April 12,

The opening shot of the Civil War, a shell fired from Fort Johnson (*far left*), explodes over Fort Sumter at 4:30 a.m. on April 12, 1861, signaling Confederate batteries to start their bombardment. Tracking the shell by its burning fuse, a South Carolina gunner on Morris Island (*foreground*) said it looked "like a firefly."

Anderson handed the envoys his response. He would evacuate on April 15, he said, holding his fire in the meantime unless fired upon, or unless he detected some act of hostile intent that would endanger the fort. Further, his agreement to hold fire might be altered if he received other instructions from his government, "or additional supplies."

Chesnut decided that Anderson was allowing himself too many ways out, offering terms that were "manifestly futile." So Chesnut wrote out a formal declaration. By Beauregard's authority, it read, "we have the honor to notify you that he will open the fire of his batteries on Fort Sumter in one hour."

It was 3:30 a.m. Anderson escorted the Confederates back to their boat and shook hands with each one. "If we never meet in this world again," he said in farewell, "God grant that we may meet in the next."

The bells of St. Michael's in Charleston were pealing 4 a.m. as Chesnut's party rowed up to Fort Johnson. Chesnut ordered Captain George S. James to fire the signal shell that would open the bombardment at 4:30.

Everyone was waiting. Roger Pryor was offered the honor of firing the signal gun. But he had dire second thoughts: "I could not fire the first gun of the war," he said. When Captain James gave the order to fire, it was Lieutenant Henry S. Farley who jerked the lanyard that sent the signal shell arcing high into the sky over Fort Sumter.

Mary Chesnut was lying awake in her Charleston hotel room when that first shell burst. "I sprang out of bed," she wrote. "And on my knees—prostrate—I prayed as I never prayed before."

It was too late. Now no one could stem the tide of events—not Anderson or Beauregard, not Lincoln or Davis. America had gone out of control.

West Pointers at the Crossroads

In the autumn of 1860, the 1,108 officers of the United States Army were scattered across the nation on garrison duty in forts along the coast or in the new Western territories. The news in November of Abraham Lincoln's election sent a shock wave through the ranks. Secession now loomed, and the officers from the South faced a wrenching decision: to remain loyal to the Union or to resign their commissions and defect to the Southern cause.

A good index of how the officer corps chose sides can be found in the West Point class of 1857. Thirty-six of the 38 graduates of this class—the first class to pose for graduation photographs—appear below and on the following pages according to their allegiance and academic ranking. The missing pair were John T. Magruder, who died in 1859, and Marcus A. Reno (later important in the Indian wars), who failed to show up for the picture-taking session. For most of these men, the choice was clear: They went the way of their home states. In fact, about 40 per cent of the class "went South," in the vernacular of the day.

The U.S. Army brass, fearing mass defection by Southern officers, tried to bribe the Southerners to remain loyal.

Defenders of the Confederacy

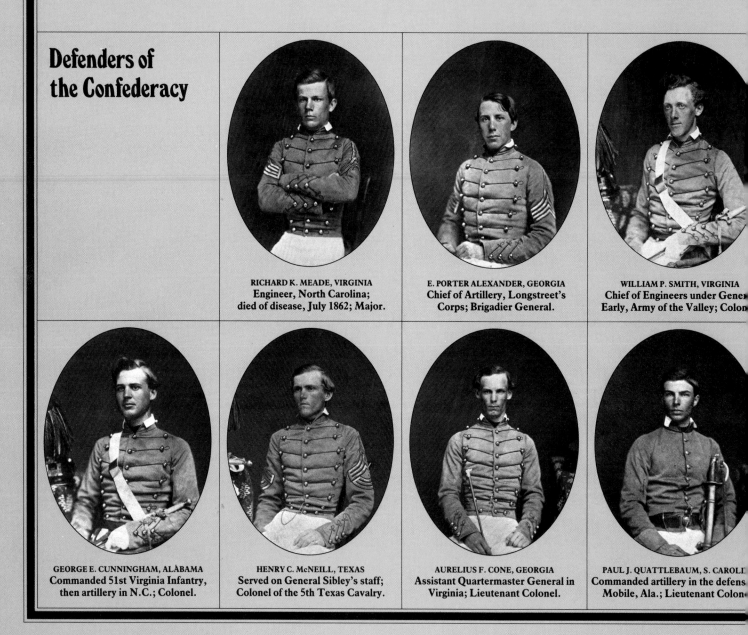

RICHARD K. MEADE, VIRGINIA
Engineer, North Carolina;
died of disease, July 1862; Major.

E. PORTER ALEXANDER, GEORGIA
Chief of Artillery, Longstreet's
Corps; Brigadier General.

WILLIAM P. SMITH, VIRGINIA
Chief of Engineers under Gene▸
Early, Army of the Valley; Colon▸

GEORGE E. CUNNINGHAM, ALABAMA
Commanded 51st Virginia Infantry,
then artillery in N.C.; Colonel.

HENRY C. McNEILL, TEXAS
Served on General Sibley's staff;
Colonel of the 5th Texas Cavalry.

AURELIUS F. CONE, GEORGIA
Assistant Quartermaster General in
Virginia; Lieutenant Colonel.

PAUL J. QUATTLEBAUM, S. CAROLI▸
Commanded artillery in the defens▸
Mobile, Ala.; Lieutenant Colon▸

E. Porter Alexander (*below*) was offered a tour of duty on the West Coast, far from the likely theaters of war. This, he was told, would spare him the anguish of raising his sword against his native state of Georgia, his family and his friends.

Alexander refused and became one of four cadets in the class of 1857 to resign upon learning that his home state had seceded from the Union. Eleven other Southerners in the class defected to the Confederate officer corps after hostilities commenced at Fort Sumter on April 12, 1861. Three of these men—Richard K. Meade, Manning M. Kimmel and Lafayette Peck—did not join the Confederate Army until they had seen service against the South. Meade, a second lieutenant from Virginia, was in the Fort Sumter garrison during the bombardment and later surrendered to Confederate forces under General P.G.T. Beauregard. One of Meade's West Point classmates, Samuel W. Ferguson, was the Confederate lieutenant who hoisted the Rebel flag over the fort.

During the War, the classmates of '57 served with distinction on both sides; highlights of their service records and their highest career ranks appear here below their pictures. Four Confederate and six Union officers rose to the rank of general or its honorary equivalent, brevet general. By the end of the War, seven of the classmates would be dead, killed in battle or victims of wounds or illness.

THOMAS J. BERRY, GEORGIA
Commanded the 60th Georgia Infantry; Lieutenant Colonel.

OLIVER H. FISH, KENTUCKY
Instructor; died New Liberty, Ky., February 1865; Second Lieutenant.

SAMUEL W. FERGUSON, S. CAROLINA
Commanded a cavalry brigade, W. H. Jackson's Division; Brig. General.

MANNING M. KIMMEL, MISSOURI
Union officer at First Bull Run; joined the Confederacy; Major.

JOHN S. MARMADUKE, MISSOURI
ommanded cavalry under General ce; captured 1864; Major General.

GEORGE W. HOLT, ALABAMA
Staff officer to Generals Stephen D. Lee and Nathan B. Forrest; Major.

ROBERT H. ANDERSON, GEORGIA
Brigade commander, Wheeler's Cavalry Corps; Brigadier General.

LAFAYETTE PECK, TENNESSEE
Instructor; died of disease in Alabama, 1864; Lieutenant.

Loyalists for the Union

JOHN C. PALFREY, MASSACHUSETTS
Chief Engineer, 13th Corps; Brevet Brigadier General.

HENRY M. ROBERT, OHIO
Chief Engineer of the defenses of Philadelphia; Captain.

GEORGE C. STRONG, MASSACHUSET
Mortally wounded at Fort Wagne S.C., July 1863; Major General

CHARLES H. MORGAN, NEW YORK
Chief of Artillery and Chief of Staff, 2nd Corps; Brigadier General.

ABRAM C. WILDRICK, NEW JERSEY
Colonel, 39th New Jersey Infantry; Brevet Brigadier General.

CHARLES J. WALKER, KENTUCKY
Commanded 10th Ky. Cavalry; C of Cavalry, 23rd Corps; Colone

GEORGE H. WEEKS, MAINE
Chief Quartermaster, 3rd Corps; Brevet Lieutenant Colonel.

IRA W. CLAFLIN, IOWA
Captain, 6th U.S. Cavalry; wounded at Funkstown, Md.; Brevet Major.

JOSEPH S. CONRAD, NEW YORK
Wounded at Wilson's Creek, Missouri; Lieutenant Colonel, Sta

J. L. KIRBY SMITH, NEW YORK
43rd Ohio Infantry; mortally
wounded, October 1862; Colonel.

THOMAS G. BAYLOR, VIRGINIA
On staff of General Sherman in
Atlanta Campaign; Brevet Colonel.

HALDIMAND PUTNAM, NEW HAMPSHIRE
7th N.H. Infantry; killed at Fort
Wagner, S.C., July 1863; Colonel.

GEORGE A. KENSEL, KENTUCKY
Artillery Chief of Department of the
Gulf; Brevet Colonel.

FRANCIS BEACH, CONNECTICUT
16th Conn. Infantry; captured at
Plymouth, N.C., April 1864; Colonel.

WILLIAM SINCLAIR, OHIO
Commanded 6th Pennsylvania
Reserves; twice wounded; Colonel.

AUGUSTUS G. ROBINSON, MAINE
Captain in Quartermaster General's
Office, Washington; Brevet Major.

EDWARD R. WARNER, PENNSYLVANIA
Inspector of Artillery, Army of the
Potomac; Brevet Brigadier General.

EDWARD J. CONNER, NEW HAMPSHIRE
8th U.S. Infantry; retired because of
illness, December 1863; Captain.

GEORGE RYAN, CONNECTICUT
140th N.Y.; killed at Spotsylvania,
Virginia, May 1864; Colonel.

CHARLES E. FARRAND, NEW YORK
11th U.S. Infantry; captured
at Corinth, Miss., 1862; Captain.

THOMAS J. LEE, INDIANA
Resigned commission, 1859; served
as private, 1863-1865.

The Guns Have Spoken

"Civil War is actually upon us, and strange to say, it brings a feeling of relief: the suspense is over."

SENATOR JOHN SHERMAN OF OHIO

Sergeant James Chester and several Federal soldiers were standing in the dark on the ramparts of Fort Sumter when, at 4:30 a.m. or soon thereafter, the Confederate signal shot came from Morris Island. Chester later wrote: "The eyes of the watchers easily detected and followed the burning fuse which marked the course of the shell as it mounted among the stars."

Almost at once the Confederate batteries all around Fort Sumter commenced firing, "and shot and shell went screaming over Sumter as if an army of devils were swooping around it." For a while the Union soldiers coolly stood in place making professional remarks on how the Confederate fire was too high. But "in a few minutes the novelty disappeared," and so did the Federals, who continued their discussions in the safety of the fort's interior.

Thus began a fight that bore practically no resemblance to the cruel headlong battles that came later. It was a strange, tentative, melodramatic fight. Both sides would make absurd mistakes—the natural result of inexperience. Both sides would sweat and strain to follow the rules of war, to prove themselves responsible and honorable men. Yet this sense of decorum went deeper than mere Victorian punctilio. Men who had hotly demanded war now drew back, shaken to find themselves facing an American enemy. It was as if the start of hostilities renewed, however briefly, the affection countrymen felt for one another.

Where did the first Confederate shot hit Fort Sumter? The men of the garrison later debated that question with great vehemence. Captain Abner Doubleday swore that it "struck the wall of the magazine where I was lying, penetrated the masonry, and burst very near my head." Smoke poured into the room through the magazine's ventilation shafts, and for an instant Doubleday thought that the magazine had caught fire. But he soon satisfied himself that there was no fire and stubbornly remained in bed, refusing to be disturbed by the mere commencement of war.

When the first sounds of firing reached Charleston, every bed emptied. Wrote Mary Chesnut in her hotel room: "There was a sound of stir all over the house, pattering of feet in the corridor—all seemed hurrying one way." In the darkness before dawn, the citizens raced to their rooftops or the Battery waterfront and watched the shells exploding. From her own vantage point on the roof of the hotel, Mrs. Chesnut reported that "the women were wild, there on the housetop"; they cried or prayed while the men stood yelling their encouragement to the Confederate gunners. The tension was oppressive for many. "I knew my husband was rowing about in a boat somewhere in that dark bay," wrote Mary Chesnut. "And who could tell what each volley accomplished of death and destruction?" So distressed was she that she sat down for a moment on something that looked like a black

In a banked headline for April 13, 1861, the St. Paul, Minnesota, *Pioneer and Democrat* tells a terse story of the bombardment of Fort Sumter and the start of the War.

stool. "Get up, you foolish woman—your dress is on fire!" shouted a man. She had sat on a chimney.

For more than two hours, the men of Fort Sumter made no effort to answer the bombardment. At 6 a.m. the enlisted men assembled for reveille in the bombproofs inside the walls. After the roll call, the men went to breakfast; most of them considered the meal a grim joke, for there was nothing left to eat except salt pork, which Sergeant Chester and others found "very rusty indeed." Their officers fared a bit better, swallowing a little farina and some rice.

Only after his men had finished their spartan meal did Major Anderson turn his attention to the bombardment. He had to decide whether to return fire and, if so, how. His biggest and most effective guns were mounted on the top level of the fort, the barbette tier. Chief among the 26 cannon up there were eight heavy columbiads of various sizes and four 8-inch howitzers. These weapons could do important damage to the Confederate batteries now assailing him. The trouble was that the big guns were out in the open, and they afforded no protection for the crews manning them.

Anderson decided that it was too risky to use the barbette guns. That left the 21 working guns sheltered in the vaulted masonry casemates on the fort's lower level. These cannon, 32- and 42-pounders, could be deadly against approaching ships, but they were much less effective against masonry and earthworks. For yet another problem, the Federals had no fuses for their explosive shells and would be able to fire nothing but solid shot.

So Anderson concluded that he could fight only a defensive battle. He would open a counterfire, of course. But he would be judicious about it; he would conserve his munitions and his manpower and defend the flag until Captain Gustavus Fox's relief expedition arrived. If the fort received enough men and supplies, he could continue to hold out no matter how much iron the Confederates threw at him.

At about 6:30, the drummer beat assembly and the garrison lined up once more in the bombproofs. Heading the force with Anderson were nine other officers, five of whom would become generals in the course of the War. In this first clash, they commanded 68 soldiers, eight musicians and 43 civilian workmen who were under no obligation to fight. Anderson's orders to the garrison were brief and explicit. "Be careful of your lives," he advised his troops. "Do your duty coolly, determinedly and cautiously. Indiscretion is not valor."

Anderson had decided that the gun crews would man the cannon in four-hour shifts. Commanding the first relief team was Abner Doubleday, the senior captain; he assigned his detail to a battery of 32-pounders that bore directly on Cummings Point, where the Ironclad Battery and other Confederate units were firing away furiously. On Doubleday's left, a lieutenant named Jefferson C. Davis led his crews to guns aimed at the Confederate batteries on James Island. And surgeon Samuel Crawford, who was also a competent artilleryman, joined a third party on the opposite side of the fort and manned the guns that aimed toward Fort Moultrie and the Floating Battery.

It was Doubleday who, at about 7 o'clock, delightedly fired the first Union shot. "In aiming the first gun fired against the rebellion," he declared later, "I had no feeling of

147

Nine Union officers in command of the Fort Sumter garrison were photographed before the Confederate bombardment. Seated left to right are Captain Abner Doubleday, Major Robert Anderson, Assistant Surgeon Samuel W. Crawford and Captain J. G. Foster. Those standing are (*from left*) Captain Truman Seymour, Lieutenant George W. Snyder, Lieutenant Jefferson C. Davis, Second Lieutenant Richard K. Meade and Lieutenant Theodore Talbot. Six of the officers eventually rose to the rank of general.

self-reproach, for I fully believed that the contest was inevitable, and was not of our seeking." It was simply a matter of good and evil, he believed, "a contest, politically speaking, as to whether virtue or vice should rule." This was the great moment in Doubleday's career. Though he rose to the rank of major general, he was never a distinguished general, and his latter-day fame as the man who "invented" the game of baseball rested on pure fabrication; he never had a thing to do with developing the sport.

Doubleday's shot was a miss. According to Captain George Cuthbert, whose Palmetto Guard was manning the Ironclad Battery, "The ball passed a few feet above the upper bolts of the shed." The Confederates were enormously relieved by that first shot. Ex-

plained old Edmund Ruffin, who was busily firing his own cannon: "I was fearful that Major Anderson did not intend to fire at all. It would have cheapened our conquest of the fort, if effected, if no hostile defense had been made—and still more increased the disgrace of failure."

Ruffin was pleased to note that the inexperienced Confederate gunners were rapidly learning their trade: "The proportion of effective balls and shells increased with the practice." After a while the white-haired Virginian wandered among the several batteries on Cummings Point and occasionally accepted the honor of jerking a lanyard. There Ruffin saw eight or 10 men running at full speed along the shore, and he thought at first that they were fleeing from a position that was taking Yankee hits. On the contrary, as he later observed, "they were running after spent balls, to secure them as memorials or trophies."

In fact, those cannonballs were but a few of the many misses by Doubleday's guns. In the full four hours of his first shift, only seven of his shots hit the works of the Ironclad Battery, and all of them bounced off the iron sheathing without doing much damage. Doubleday was happy to turn the guns over to Captain Truman Seymour and his relief party when the shift ended.

"Doubleday, what in the world is the matter here, and what is all this uproar about?" asked Seymour facetiously.

In the same vein Doubleday responded, "There is a trifling difference of opinion between us and our neighbors opposite, and we are trying to settle it."

Lieutenant Davis' guns fared no better than Doubleday's against the batteries on James Island; the cannonballs buried themselves in the sand in front of the palmetto-log Confederate breastworks. And surgeon Crawford became thoroughly frustrated in his attempts to damage the Floating Battery off Sullivan's Island. The shots that his gunners aimed at the roof of the battery bounced off harmlessly, and the shots that they tried to scale across the water and into the battery's vulnerable water line were blocked by

Union soldier John Carmody, a lone daredevil who ignored orders against firing the dangerously exposed cannon atop Fort Sumter, watches a shot hit home before dashing along the rampart to fire the next gun.

a sea wall. Yet Crawford also discovered that the Floating Battery, so much feared in the previous weeks, was not very effective either. As a result, the surgeon received Anderson's permission to shift his gun crews to three other cannon that bore directly on Fort Moultrie. In this assignment Crawford finally tasted success. Although his men failed to silence a single Moultrie gun, they did manage to inflict considerable damage on the wooden structures in and around the fort, pelting the Confederate forces there with flying splinters of wood.

Noontime found Sumter withstanding the bombardment fairly well. The outer walls of the fort were virtually impervious to the enemy round shot, and only the mortar shells lobbed into the enclosed parade ground did any real damage. Explosions here had severely damaged the adjacent barracks, and there was danger of a fire near the main powder magazine.

The men were holding up better than the fort. They had been penned in here for three and a half months, undernourished, inactive and depressed by their confinement. But under fire they performed with vigor and alacrity. So did the civilian workmen; some vol-

A map of Charleston Harbor pinpoints Fort Sumter's strategic location, shows the position and range of the surrounding Confederate batteries, and lists the cannon available to both sides.

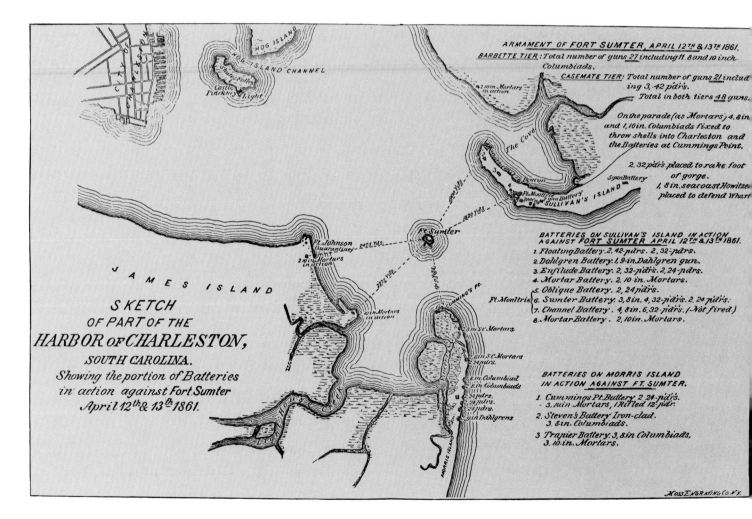

untarily carried ammunition, while others began sewing rags and clothing into additional cartridge bags for gunpowder charges. Anderson had every reason to be pleased with his command.

A few spirited soldiers did disobey the major's injunction against taking needless risks. The big columbiads that could do such interesting damage to the Confederates were sitting loaded and unmanned on the barbette tier. Although Anderson had declared that level to be off-limits, a soldier by the name of John Carmody could not put temptation behind him. After hours of the shelling,

he furtively made his way to the barbette, found the guns aimed at Fort Moultrie and fired them one after another. "The contest," wrote Sergeant Chester, "was merely Carmody against the Confederate States." But by himself Carmody was unable to reload the giant guns with 65-pound and 100-pound balls, and once he had fired them all he was forced to retire.

On the other side of the fort, two sergeants imitated Carmody's escapade. They manned one of the 10-inch columbiads facing Morris Island and fired a massive shot that barely missed the Ironclad Battery. Then, with

Wreathed in the smoke of battle, Fort Sumter exchanges fire with Confederate guns in an engraving from *Le Monde Illustré* of Paris. The long apex of Sumter's pentagon points toward Fort Moultrie on Sullivan's Island; Charleston is barely visible at upper left.

enormous effort, they managed to reload the gun with its 100-pound projectile. Their feat, together with Carmody's, persuaded the Confederates that the barbette guns were henceforth going to be used, so their gunners started to concentrate on Fort Sumter's upper level. Their fire soon became, according to Sergeant Chester, "a perfect hurricane of shot."

Anderson could scarcely have failed to notice the disobedience of Carmody and friends, but the major had more important matters to worry about. When the bombardment began, Fort Sumter had only 700 cloth gunpowder cartridges. The gunplay of the morning had severely reduced that supply, and the workmen sewing more bags were falling steadily behind. So, to avoid running out of cartridges even temporarily, Anderson shut down all but two guns firing on Cummings Point, two on Fort Moultrie and another two on the Sullivan's Island batteries. This way he could sustain at least a show of resistance.

An added problem was the constant danger of fire. The Sumter barracks had been faced with brick, supposedly to make them fireproof, but the Confederates made use of a proven countertactic. Some of the batteries placed cannonballs in a heavy-duty oven and heated them red-hot before firing them. These "hot shot" lodged inside the barracks and set the wood aflame. At midmorning, a fire started on one of the upper floors. It had hardly been extinguished when another one broke out. Three times that day flames spread through the barracks. Oddly enough, one of the fires was put out by a Confederate shot; it ruptured a water tank and drowned the blaze.

And always on the major's mind was the relief expedition. Would it arrive in time? He kept a lookout stationed at a seaward embrasure, but the hours slipped by and there was no sign of the ships. It was not until about 1 o'clock in the afternoon that the first vessels of Fox's relief expedition were sighted beyond the bar at the harbor mouth. The garrison cheered and Anderson delightedly dipped Sumter's flag to signal the ships that the fort was all right.

Fox, aboard the steamer *Baltic*, had arrived at his specified rendezvous at about 3 a.m. that morning. Though he expected to meet seven other vessels there, he found that only the cutter *Harriet Lane* had beaten him to the rendezvous, and three hours passed before the sloop *Pawnee* appeared. Two other sloops, the *Powhatan* and the *Pocahontas*, as well as three tugs for landing supplies, still had not shown up by 6 a.m. Though Fox did not know it, the *Powhatan* would never arrive; she had been diverted to Florida to hold Fort Pickens. And none of the tugs would show up in time.

Not long after 6 o'clock, Fox decided against waiting any longer for the two sloops. He could not see or hear from the distance that the fort was under attack, and so, obedient to his orders to land only supplies unless he was opposed, Fox took just the *Baltic* and the *Harriet Lane* in toward Sumter. But as soon as he saw and heard the intense bombardment, he put back out to inform the Naval officers on board the *Pawnee*. The officers worked out a plan to wait until nightfall and then send in a few boatloads of supplies in the darkness. Fox opposed the plan at first. But, considering the continued absence of the two warships, he was persuaded to wait for the *Powhatan* to arrive. Then the *Pawnee* and the *Harriet*

Lane would defy the shore batteries and accompany the *Baltic* in to Sumter.

The rest of the afternoon passed without change: The Confederates maintained their fire, Anderson kept up his token resistance and Fox lurked expectantly out beyond the harbor. Around 7 p.m. a sudden rainstorm came up and extinguished the last sparks of Sumter's barracks fire, and at the same time Anderson ordered his command to cease firing for the night. The Confederates reduced their fire, too; only the 10-inch mortars were left in action, and each one lobbed only four shells an hour into Sumter.

That evening Anderson ordered Lieutenant George W. Snyder to survey the damage to the fort. Snyder completed his tour of inspection with Crawford, and what they discovered was not particularly pretty. An 8-inch cannonball fired 1,250 yards at relatively low velocity from an unrifled cannon would penetrate brick masonry no more than 11 inches. But the masonry walls on all five sides of Sumter, especially the wall facing Moultrie, were deeply cratered. In one place, repeated shots striking a small area had carved out a cavity some 20 inches deep, and Crawford concluded that sooner or later the bombardment would breach the wall. The main gate, too, was damaged, and the parapet had been heavily battered, with its chimneys knocked down, its stair towers de-

From the Battery at Charleston Harbor, 5,000 soldiers and civilians watch the bombardment of Fort Sumter on the morning of April 13, 1861. As flame and smoke engulfed the Federal bastion, many women spectators wept for its defenders.

stroyed and its guns dismounted. Crawford reported that the fort "presented a picture of havoc and ruin." But Sumter could easily continue fighting.

The exhausted Federals slept as best they could that night. But the men on guard kept up a sharp watch for the relief boats and also for a Confederate attempt to storm the fort in the darkness. They suddenly realized that the possibility of confusion was dreadful in a war between Americans. An attack force as well as reinforcements would come by boat and would answer any challenge in English. "It would be horrible to fire upon friends," said Sergeant Chester, yet "it would be fatal not to fire upon enemies."

On the morning of April 13, Anderson's men breakfasted on a little salt pork and some rice, and then, grumbling because Captain Fox had failed to arrive, went back to their guns to answer Beauregard's bombardment. Anderson decided to concentrate his fire on Fort Moultrie, the only target he was damaging. But once again the arsenal's dwindling supply of cartridges forced him to cut back his rate of fire to only one round every 10 minutes.

Now, more Confederate gunners were firing hot shot. Time and time again the barracks caught fire and the men doused the flames. But by 10 a.m. the fire was raging nearly out of control, and the mortar shells exploding in the parade ground made any attempts at fire fighting extremely hazardous. Anderson ordered the men to let the blaze run its course.

By noon the fort was burning wherever there was wood to catch fire. The entire officers' section was aflame. The fire spread to the wooden main gate and devoured most of it. And all the while, the flames crept clos-

er to the 300 barrels of powder stored in the magazine, unwisely established near a wooden barracks.

Anderson put every available man to work removing the powder. It was perilous work, for much powder had been spilled in ribbons the day before, and if the loose stuff ignited, fire might race to the magazine. And of course, the Confederate shells plunging into the parade ground could just as easily dispatch the exposed men as they rolled the barrels to safety in the masonry casemate.

One officer said the men moved 96 barrels. Others thought only 50 or so were removed. In any case, the fire got so close that Anderson stopped the barrel-moving operation and ordered that the coppper-sheathed door be closed. He could only hope that the magazine would not blow.

By this time, the smoke billowing from the blaze had penetrated to every part of the fort. "We came very near being stifled with the dense livid smoke from the burning buildings," an officer later remembered. "The men lay prostrate on the ground, with wet handkerchiefs over their mouths and eyes, gasping for breath." Some of the soldiers clambered outside the gun embrasures, braving the Confederate cannon fire just to breathe clear air.

Flying cinders presented another threat. At any moment they might ignite the loose gunpowder and explode the moved barrels or the 9-inch shells that Anderson had hidden up on the parapet and in the stair towers, to be used as grenades in the event of an assault. Indeed, the flying sparks did detonate a pile of grenades just as Crawford started up to the parapet to search for the fleet. The whole stair tower exploded. The surgeon had to fight his way through rubble to

Union gunners in a Fort Sumter casemate work their cannon under the watchful eye of Major Robert Anderson, the garrison commander. Some of the gunners peer through the embrasure to determine where their last shot has landed.

In this contemporary engraving, a Confederate battery pounds away at a flaming Fort Sumter. The Rebel gunner felled by Union fire (*center foreground*) was a figment of the artist's imagination; in reality, no one on either side was killed or seriously wounded during the siege.

reach the top, and from there he could see the ships riding the wind-whipped waves exactly where they had been the evening before. They were not coming.

Things were going as badly for Fox as for Anderson. The seas were running so high that the sailors could not load provisions from the *Baltic* into small boats that would ferry them to Sumter. By noon, the *Pawnee* had captured a little schooner, which, Fox believed, could make a delivery run under cover of darkness. By 2 p.m. the *Pocahontas* had at last arrived and also a message that the *Powhatan* was not coming at all. Fox would have to make do without the *Powhatan's* guns and 300 fighting men and numerous assault boats. He could only hope that Anderson would somehow be able to hold out until nightfall.

That hope now appeared meager. The danger of fire spreading to the powder barrels in the casemate became so pressing that Anderson decided to throw all but five barrels into the harbor rather than risk an enormous explosion. Once more the exhausted soldiers rolled barrels by the score, this time to the open embrasures and into the sea. Yet once the barrels landed in the water, the waves kept them bunched dangerously against the base of the fort. Finally, a Confederate shell found them, touching off a loud explosion that did no damage except to fling an unmanned gun off its mounting inside the casemate. The men used sopping-wet blankets to shield what little powder remained from the sparks.

Nearly all the guns of Sumter were silent now, their crews barely able to breathe in the smoky air. Wrote Captain Doubleday, "The crashing of the shot, the bursting of the shells, the falling of walls, and the roar of the

Edmund Ruffin, the secessionist agitator who took part in the siege of Fort Sumter at the age of 67, sits for a victory photograph as a member of the Palmetto Guard—a South Carolina militia unit—six days after Sumter's surrender. A fervent rebel to the end, Ruffin committed suicide when the Confederacy fell.

flames, made a pandemonium of the fort." In the midst of all this, the thick mastlike flagstaff, already nicked several times during the bombardment, was hit once again and fell. Lieutenant Norman J. Hall raced out into the parade ground and recovered the flag, losing his eyebrows to the flames. He and Sergeant Peter Hart hastily improvised a flagpole, and then Captain Seymour led them in a dash to the parapet, where they affixed the staff to a gun carriage. The Stars and Stripes waved once more.

At last a breeze thinned the smoke, and Anderson ordered the men to increase their rate of fire. With the powder supply dwindling and no more cloth to make new cartridges, the workmen began sewing powder into socks donated by Anderson.

The Confederate gun crews, now sensing triumph at hand, redoubled their efforts, firing hot shot almost exclusively. Yet they admired the bravery of Anderson and his contingent, and when a shot came from Sumter after a prolonged silence, they sent up cheers and applause. Occasionally, the Confederates hurled epithets at the Yankee ships anchored out beyond the bar for failing to come to Sumter's aid.

When the flagpole on Sumter was knocked down, several Confederate officers concluded that the Sumter garrison was ready to capitulate. Beauregard ordered three aides to row out to Sumter and offer help in fighting the fire—his tactful way of telling Anderson it was high time to surrender. But someone else beat them there—with results that were nothing short of comic.

Former U.S. Senator Louis Wigfall, the Texan who had sent so much intelligence out of Washington, had arrived in Charleston and was serving on Morris Island as a volunteer assistant on Beauregard's staff. When Wigfall saw the Union flag topple, he decided that the fort had taken enough punishment. Moved by that sentiment and a chance for glory, he commandeered a small boat, drafted a South Carolina private and two slaves as oarsmen and started off for Fort Sumter holding a white handkerchief aloft tied to a sword.

It proved to be an exciting voyage. The little boat crossed the line of fire from Morris Island, passing just beneath the storm of Confederate shot and shell. It was almost hit by stray shots from guns on the other side of the harbor, where gun crews at and near Fort Moultrie could not see the boat. And it barely escaped errant shots from the smoke-blinded Federals on Sumter.

Incredibly, Wigfall reached Sumter without being detected by anyone in the garri-son. He landed, strolled around to an open embrasure and showed his bearded face beside the mouth of the cannon—just as the gunners were preparing to touch off another round. Waving his handkerchief, Wigfall climbed in and politely asked to meet with Major Anderson.

While someone set off to fetch the major, Wigfall conversed with Lieutenant Davis. "Your flag is down," he stated, "you are on fire. Let us stop this firing." Wigfall offered Davis his white handkerchief. "Will you hoist this?"

Davis declined to do it himself but said that Wigfall could wave his handkerchief if he wished. He began waving it. Then a Federal soldier took his place and continued waving the handkerchief until a ball from Moultrie nearly hit him. By that time, Anderson had approached.

"I am Colonel Wigfall," the visitor announced. Then, having awarded himself a rank he did not hold, Wigfall opened wholly unauthorized negotiations: "Major Anderson, you have defended your flag nobly, sir. You have done all that is possible for men to do, and General Beauregard wishes to stop the fight. On what terms, Major Anderson, will you evacuate this fort?"

Anderson knew his answer. He was down to just four kegs of powder and three cartridges. Captain Fox's fleet showed no sign of attempting to come to his aid. The fire in the fort was still out of control, and his men were exhausted and hungry. He had done his duty and miraculously had not lost a single man. It was time to yield.

"I have already stated to General Beauregard the terms upon which I will evacuate this work," he said, referring to his last communication with Colonel Chesnut at 3 a.m.

The fiery trails of projectiles light up the night sky around Charleston as Fort Sumter, shrouded in smoke, duels Confederate gun batteries on the 12th of April, 1861.

the day before. "Instead of noon on the 15th, I will go now."

A little more talk settled the matter. Anderson's men could evacuate, saluting their flag and taking their side arms with them. Delighted with himself, Wigfall departed the island to report the surrender. At approximately 1:30 p.m., Anderson hauled down his flag and ran up a white cloth that somehow had escaped the attention of the cartridge seamsters.

All this byplay with flags was mystifying to Beauregard's three legitimate envoys, who were still en route from Moultrie to Sumter. They had started rowing when the fort's Union flag was shot down. They were halfway to Sumter when Seymour raised the Stars and Stripes over the parapet. Observing this, they turned back toward Moultrie, but then at 1:30 they saw the U.S. flag come down again and a white flag go up. Weary and confused, they pulled once more for Sumter and arrived shortly after Wigfall departed the scene.

The envoys—Captain Stephen D. Lee and aides William Porcher Miles and Roger Pryor—dutifully made their diplomatic offer to help Anderson.

Puzzled and annoyed by this second visitation, the major answered stiffly, "Present my compliments to General Beauregard, and say to him I thank him for his kindness, but need no assistance." Then he asked whether the envoys had come direct from Beauregard. Yes, they said. Anderson informed them that Colonel Wigfall had just been there "by authority of General Beauregard" and terms had been agreed upon.

The aides had no choice but to admit that Wigfall had no authority and had not even seen the general for two days. Indeed, they themselves were not authorized to give Anderson permission, as he now insisted, to fire a salute as he lowered his flag.

Anderson was enraged; having swallowed the indignity of surrender, he now gagged on the news that it did not count. "Very well, gentlemen," he said, "you can return to your batteries. There is a misunderstanding on my part, and I will at once run up my flag and open fire again."

Sensing that an opportunity was slipping away from them, the Confederates urged Anderson not to be hasty. They drew him aside to a casemate where they could speak privately and managed to persuade him to defer any action until they had explained the mix-up to Beauregard. At their request, the major wrote down the substance of his agreement with Wigfall.

Meanwhile, Beauregard, having seen the white flag go up, had dispatched a second set of aides with instructions to complete the surrender arrangements. These envoys arrived just as Lee's group was making ready to depart, and they offered essentially the same terms that Anderson had already accepted. And, at seven that evening, a settlement was reached that was as honorable as a surrender could be.

The Union garrison would evacuate the next day. The troops could fire a 100-gun salute to their tattered flag, and then they would be transported out to Fox's fleet for the trip home. Until then, the Federals would retain full possession of their fort—whatever was left of it. The Confederates had fired 3,341 projectiles during 33 hours of bombardment. All the barracks were in ruins. The main gate was gone. The outer walls had been pocked by hundreds of shells. Incredibly, only four men of the garrison had been injured, each of them hit by flying bits of brick or mortar. The Confederates, too, had suffered only four men injured, all of them at Fort Moultrie.

That was all there was to it. "The men, released now from all responsibility, seemed to change in feeling," surgeon Crawford observed. "The enthusiasm that had so long inspired them seemed to have gone." There was nothing left for the troops to do but pack up their meager belongings and get ready to leave.

The Confederates rejoiced. The celebration started early in Charleston and the batteries all around the city. "A shout of triumph rent the air from the thousands of spectators on the islands and the mainland," wrote the 15-year-old Confederate Augustus Dickert. "Flags and handkerchiefs waved from the hands of excited throngs in the city. Soldiers mount the ramparts and shout in exultation, throwing their caps in the air." Beauregard sent a telegram to the Confederate government announcing the surrender, and copies were hurriedly broadcast through the Southern states. Cannon salutes were fired in the Confederate capital and 100 other Southern towns.

The Sumter garrison was ready to depart the next morning, April 14, 1861. Somehow the workmen had managed to sew together enough cartridge bags for the 100-gun salute. Major Anderson was seen in tears that morning, but he was grateful to his old friend Beauregard for allowing the salute. Grateful, too, no doubt, that the Confederate general had the consideration to refrain from setting foot on Sumter until after Anderson and his men were gone.

The salute began at about 2 o'clock that

afternoon. Thousands watched from boats in the harbor, among them Governor Pickens and Beauregard. Slowly the United States flag was lowered as the guns thundered on. Then Private Daniel Hough rammed another cartridge into his gun, apparently before sparks from the previous round were thoroughly swabbed out. A spark prematurely ignited the cartridge and the explosion tore Hough's right arm from his body. He died instantly.

The wind carried sizzling bits of cloth to the nearby stack of cartridge bags, and a second explosion mortally wounded another gunner and injured four others. Shocked by the double tragedy, Anderson cut short the salute at 50 guns.

Two hours later, with drummers beating time and musicians playing "Yankee Doodle," the men of Sumter marched out of the battered fort. Anderson tenderly carried the shot-torn flag, little suspecting that one day four years hence he would return as a general and once more raise that very flag over Fort Sumter.

The men of Sumter spent that night on board a steamer, the *Isabel*. Next morning the vessel ferried them out to Fox's U.S. fleet, and they were soon homeward bound aboard the *Baltic*. "Many an eye turned toward the disappearing fort," wrote surgeon Crawford, "and as it sunk at last upon the horizon the smoke-cloud still hung heavily over its parapet."

The guns had spoken. Like the sword that cut the Gordian knot, the Confederate cannon had sliced through the tangle of issues that reasonable men had failed to unsnarl for a half century and more. No longer would Northerners and Southerners have to grapple with the agonizing issues of slavery and states' rights, or with the rough-cut attempts to reconcile those issues. To the immense relief of many, the men of the North and the South were finally free to settle their complex differences in the simplest way— by force of arms.

"We are not enemies, but friends," Abraham Lincoln had told his countrymen, imploring them to listen to "the better angels of our nature" and remain friends. But those angels could no longer be of help, for now the Confederates and the Yankees were mortal enemies.

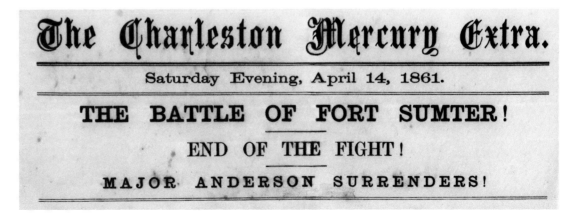

The Charleston Mercury Extra.

Saturday Evening, April 14, 1861.

THE BATTLE OF FORT SUMTER!

END OF THE FIGHT!

MAJOR ANDERSON SURRENDERS!

A special edition of the Charleston newspaper regales secessionists with stories of the surrender of Fort Sumter.

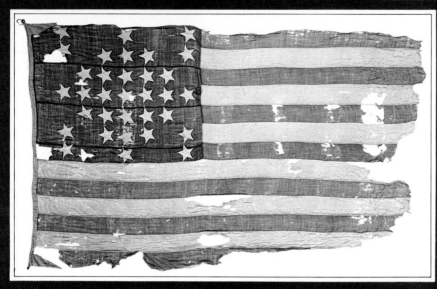

This United States flag flew over Fort Sumter
through most of General Beauregard's 33-hour
bombardment—until a Rebel shell shattered
its pole. Within 15 minutes, Federal troops had
raised the flag again by nailing it to a spar.
The nail holes appear along the left-hand margin.

Victorious Southerners stroll upon the esplanade fronting Fort Sumter in this composite photograph taken just after the Federal surrender. The walls of the fo

A Change of Flags

Hundreds of jubilant Southern patriots, many of whom had paid as much as 50 cents each for the pleasure, were watching from small boats in the waters off Fort Sumter as Union Major Robert Anderson struck his battle-torn flag (*left*) and fired his cannon in solemn salute. The withdrawal of the weary Federal garrison went on at a funereal pace through the early afternoon of Sunday, April 14, 1861. Finally, after waiting chivalrously for two hours for the last of the Union soldiers to depart, a group of important Southerners led by victorious General P.G.T. Beauregard put ashore at Sumter a little after 4 p.m. and took possession of the fort in the name of the Confederate States of America.

The exterior of the fort was chipped and pitted by Confederate cannon balls. But the damage to the façade was light compared with what the officers and politicians found when they entered the enclosed parade ground through the sally port. Confederate shells and shot, lobbed in by mortars and cannon firing at high angles, had exploded in the interior, setting fires in the officers' quarters and the enlisted men's barracks, strewing the parade ground with great jumbles of brick and masonry. The fires were still smoldering, and fire companies from Charleston would pump water into the ruins before the last embers died. Still, the wreckage inside Sumter looked much worse than it really was. Work parties began clearing away the rubble, and the fort would soon be ready to face far more ruinous bombardment by Federal warships.

For now, the Southerners were intent on enjoying their triumph. It had been an easy, almost painless victory, costing them only a few men slightly wounded, and when the Confederate flag and the palmetto-and-crescent flag of South Carolina were raised simultaneously above the fort, the celebrations that ensued were carefree and wild. Aboard all the sightseeing boats circling Sumter, men and boys cheered, women wept, horns and whistles blew. The victory scene and the condition of the fort were recorded by photographers, who were kept busy by officials and soldiers demanding pictures of themselves for their memory books. Eager visitors poked about in the ruins looking for shell fragments to send as souvenirs to friends and relatives.

In Charleston, some three miles across the harbor, churches celebrated the victory with thanksgiving services. In St. Michael's Church, the Reverend J. H. Elliott recalled a Biblical battle in which the captains of Israel "fully achieved their object, and were now returned in safety to their tents without the loss of a single comrade." The pastor ended his sermon with expressions of gratitude for the Lord's mercy and bounty: "His Providence is fast uniting the whole South in a common brotherhood of sympathy and action, and our first essay in arms has been crowned with perfect success."

re sides were pocked and cratered by more than 600 hits from Confederate gun batteries ringing the fort.

A cleanup crew gathers rubble at the damaged sally port inside Fort Sumter's main entrance. Behind the blackened brick wall at left are the burned-out officers' quarte

Confederate dignitaries in top hats and frock coats inspect five columbiads mounted on the parade ground. These guns were under fire throughout the siege.

Jaunty Confederate militiamen strike poses beside the captured guns on the parade ground. In the background, at one of the corners of the fort, a stairway tower leads to the rampart.

From the barbette tier of Fort Sumter, Southern sightseers survey Charleston Harbor. The gun at lower left was bowled over by the recoil of the neighboring cannon, whose upended carriage lies at lower right.

Confederate soldiers man three guns on the parade
ground as the Stars and Bars of the Confederacy
(*above*) snaps in the breeze atop a derrick used to
hoist guns to the fort's upper tier. The seven stars
in the flag represented the Southern states that
had seceded from the Union by the time Sumter fell.

ACKNOWLEDGMENTS

The editors thank the following individuals and institutions for their help in the preparation of the Civil War series:

Alabama: Birmingham—Birmingham Museum of Art. Mobile—Jay P. Altmayer; The First National Bank of Mobile; Caldwell Delaney, The Museum of the City of Mobile; R. Erwin Neville. Montgomery—Alabama Department of Archives and History; First White House of the Confederacy. Northport—Mrs. Ellis F. Cannon. Tuscaloosa—William Stanley Hoole Special Collections, University of Alabama Library; Jack Warner.

Arkansas: Jonesboro—Arkansas State University Museum. Little Rock—Robert Serio, The Old State House.

California: Los Angeles—Mamie Clayton, Western States Black Research Center. Redlands—Larry Burgess, Lincoln Shrine. San Marino—Carey Bliss, Alan Jetsie, Brita Mack, Harriet McLoone, Virginia Reuner, Huntington Library. Santa Barbara—Chris Brun, University of California, Special Collections.

Connecticut: Bridgeport—Bridgeport Public Library. Fairfield—Tom Lopiano Jr. Hartford—Connecticut State Library; Roberta Bradford, Stowe-Day Foundation; Edmund Sullivan, University of Hartford Dewitt Collection; Wadsworth Athenaeum; The Watkinson Library, Trinity College. Mystic—Mystic Seaport Museum. New Haven—Yale University Library. New London—U.S. Coast Guard Museum. New Milford—Norm Flayderman. Storrs—Mansfield Historical Society Museum. Wallingford—Wallingford Historical Society. Westport—William Gladstone, Ed Vebell.

Delaware: Wilmington—Delaware National Guard; Eleutherian Mills Historical Library; Historical Society of Delaware. Winterthur—Henry Francis du Pont Winterthur Library and Museum.

Florida: Bradenton—South Florida Museum. Ellenton—Judah P. Benjamin Confederate Memorial, Gamble Plantation State Historic Site. Fernandina Beach—Fort Clinch State Park. Fort George Island—Kingsley Plantation State Historic Site. Gulf Breeze—Gulf Islands National Seashore. Largo—Pinellis County Historical Museum-Heritage Park. Olustee—Olustee Battlefield State Historic Site. Pensacola—John C. Pace Library, University of West Florida; Pensacola Historical Museum; T. T. Wentworth Jr. Museum; West Florida Museum of History. St. Petersburg—Museum of Fine Arts; St. Petersburg Historical Museum. Tallahassee—Florida State Archives; Florida State Photo Archives; Florida State University Library; Museum of Florida History. Tampa—Hillsborough County Historical Commission Museum.

Georgia: Athens—Robert M. Willingham Jr., University of Georgia Libraries, Special Collections; Charles East, University of Georgia Press. Atlanta—Atlanta Historical Society; Tom Dickey; Beverly M. DuBose Jr.; William Erquitt; Georgia Department of Archives and History; The High Museum; Richard Kennedy; Richard Nee; Robert W. Woodruff Library, Special Collections, Emory University. Augusta—Augusta-Richmond County Museum. Columbus—Confederate Naval Museum. Crawfordsville—The Confederate Museum, Alexander H. Stephens Memorial. Fort Benning—Dick D. Grube, National Infantry Museum. Fort Oglethorpe—Chickamauga and Chattanooga National Military Park. Macon—Cannonball House. Marietta—Robert P. Coggins; Kennesaw Mountain National Battlefield Park. Richmond Hill—Fort McAllister. St. Simons Island—Museum of Coastal History. Savannah—Anthony R. Dees, Georgia Historical Society; United Daughters of the Confederacy Collection. Stone Mountain—Civil War Museum, Stone Mountain Park; Ralph Righton. Tybee Island—Fort

Pulaski. Villa Rica—Steve Mullinax. Washington—Washington-Wilkes Historical Museum.

Illinois: Cairo—Cairo Public Library. Chicago—Chicago Historical Society. Fort Sheridan—Nina Smith, Fort Sheridan Museum. Galena—Galena Historical Museum; Grant Home. Peoria—Peoria Historical Society, Bradley University Library. Rock Island—Dorrell E. Garrison, John M. Browning Memorial Museum. Springfield—Camp Lincoln; Rodger D. Bridges, James Hickey, Mariana James Munyer, Illinois State Historical Library, Old State Capitol. Wheaton—Du Page County Historical Museum.

Indiana: Bloomington — The Lilly Library, Indiana University. Fort Wayne — Mark E. Neely Jr., Louis A. Warren Lincoln Library and Museum. Indianapolis — The Children's Museum; Indiana Historical Society; Indiana State Library; Indiana War Memorials Commission. La Porte — La Porte County Historical Society. Notre Dame — The Snite Museum of Art, The University of Notre Dame; The University of Notre Dame Archives. Rensselaer — Jasper County Public Library. Vincennes — Jim Osborne.

Iowa: Des Moines—Iowa State Historical Society, Museum and Archives Division.

Kansas: Topeka—Kansas State Historical Society.

Kentucky: Frankfort—Linda Anderson, Kentucky Historical Society; Nicky Hughes, Kentucky Military History Museum. Lexington—Kent Masterson Brown; Hunt Morgan House; Frances Trivett, Waveland State Shrine. Louisville—The Filson Club; Frank Rankin. Perryville—Perryville Battlefield State Park. Radcliffe—Dr. Thomas Wheat. Richmond—Jane Hogg, Jonathan Truman Dorris Museum, Eastern Kentucky University.

Louisiana: Baton Rouge—H. Parrott Bacot, Anglo-American Art Museum, Louisiana State University; Beth Benton; Fred G. Benton Jr.; Dr. Edward Boagni; Shelby Gilley; M. Stone Miller, Main Library, Louisiana State University; Bill Moore; John E. Dutton, Rural Life Museum, Louisiana State University. Glenmora—Mrs. Francis Irvine. Mansfield—Greg Potts, Mansfield State Battle Park Museum. Natchitoches—Dr. John Price, Dr. Carol Wells, Louisiana Archives, Northwestern University. New Orleans—Barnard Eble, Pat Eymard, Confederate Memorial Hall; Charles Dufour; W. E. Groves; Patricia McWhorter, Kenneth T. Urquhart, The Historic New Orleans Collection; Mary B. Oalmann, Colonel Francis E. Thomas, Jackson Barracks; George E. Jordan; Vaughn Glasgow, Louisiana State Museum; Wilbur E. Meneray, Tulane University Library.

Maine: Augusta—Sylvia Sherman, Maine State Archives; Jane Radcliffe, Maine State Museum. Brunswick—The Hawthorne Longfellow Library; Elizabeth Copeland, Pejepscot Historical Society. Portland—Elizabeth Hamill, Maine Historical Society.

Maryland: Annapolis—Sigrid H. Trumpy, Alexandra H. Welsh, The Beverley R. Robinson Collection, The United States Naval Academy Museum; James W. Cheevers, The United States Naval Academy Museum. Baltimore—Donna Ellis, Paula Velthuys, Maryland Historical Society. Bethesda—Lucy Keister, National Library of Medicine. Boonsboro—Douglas Bast, Scoper House Museum. Clarysville—Clarysville Inn. Cumberland—Allegany Historical Society, Inc. Fort George G. Meade—David C. Cole, Fort Meade Museum. Hagerstown—Washington County Historical Museum. Sharpsburg—Antietam National Battlefield Center.

Massachusetts: Boston—Boston Public Library, Print Department and Rare Book Room; Commonwealth of Massachusetts, State Library; Francis A. Countway Library, Har-

vard Medical School; Craig W. C. Brown, First Corps of Cadets Military Museum; Massachusetts State House; Cynthia English, Sally Pearce, Library of the Boston Athenaeum; Massachusetts Historical Society; Museum of Fine Arts; Society for the Preservation of New England Antiquities; James Stamatelos. Cambridge—Houghton Library, Harvard University; The Arthur and Elizabeth Schlesinger Library, Radcliffe College. Ipswich—Lewis Joslyn. Marblehead—Marblehead Historical Society. Newburyport—Historical Society of Old Newbury. Northampton—The Sophia Smith Collection, Smith College. Salem—Essex Institute; Peabody Museum. Springfield—Springfield Armory National Historic Site. Worcester—Higgins Armory; Worcester Art Museum; Worcester Historical Society.

Michigan: Ann Arbor—Mary Jo Pugh, Bentley Historical Library; John Dann, The William L. Clements Library, The University of Michigan. Detroit—Thomas Featherstone, Archives of Labor and Urban Affairs, Walter P. Reuther Library, Wayne State University; Alice Cook Dalligan, Burton Historical Collection, Detroit Public Library; Anita D. McCandless, Detroit Historical Museum; William P. Phenix, Historic Fort Wayne. East Lansing—Frederick L. Honhart, University Archives, Historical Collections, Michigan State University; William J. Prince. Kalamazoo—James Brady Jr., Paul DeHaan; Patricia Gordon Michael, Mary Lou Stewart, Kalamazoo Public Library. Lansing—Ruby Rogers, Michigan Historical Museum, Michigan Department of State; John C. Curry State Archives, Michigan Department of State; Karl Rommel. Monroe—Matthew C. Switlik, Monroe County Historical Museum. Plymouth—Barbara Saunders, Plymouth Historical Museum.

Minnesota: St. Paul—Minnesota Historical Society.

Mississippi: Biloxi—Beauvoir. Clinton—Bill Wright. Jackson—Department of Archives and History; Patricia Carr Black, State Historical Museum. Natchez—The Historic Natchez Foundation; William Stewart. Vicksburg—Gordon A. Cotton, Old Courthouse Museum; Vicksburg National Military Park. Woodville—Rosemont Plantation.

Missouri: Blue Springs—Lone Jack Museum. Columbia—State of Missouri Historical Society; Western Manuscript Collection, University of Missouri. Independence—1859 Jail Museum; Jackson County Department of Parks and Recreation; Jackson County Historical Society Archives. Jefferson City—Missouri Department of Natural Resources; Missouri State Museum. Kearney—James Farm. Lexington—Battle of Lexington State Historic Site. Liberty—Clay County Department of Parks, Recreation and Historic Sites. St. Joseph—St. Joseph Museum. St. Louis—Missouri Historical Society.

New Hampshire: Concord—Mary Rose Boswell, New Hampshire Historical Society.

New Jersey: Camden—Margaret B. Weatherly, Camden County Historical Society. East Orange—Steven J. Selenfriend. Merchantville—C. Paul Loane. Newark—Alan Frazer, The New Jersey Historical Society. Pittstown—John Kuhl. Ridgefield—Val J. Forgett. Trenton—Daniel P. George; Trenton Fire Department. Woodbury—Edith Hoelle, Gloucester County Historical Society.

New York: Albany—Gene Deaton, The Military Museum, State of New York Division of Military and Naval Affairs; Joseph Meany, Robert Mulligan, New York State Museum. Fishers—J. Sheldon Fisher, Valentown Museum. Hudson—American Museum of Firefighting; D.A.R. Museum. New York—The New-York Historical Society. Pattersonville—Montgomery County Historical Society. Peekskill—Memoril Museum of the Field Library. Rochester—Janice Wass, Rochester Museum and Science Center. Troy—The Rensselaer County Historical Society. West Point—Marie Capps, U.S. Military Academy Library; Michael E. Moss, West Point Museum.

North Carolina: Carolina Beach—Chris Fonvielle, The Blockade Runners Museum. Durham—Robert Byrd, William Erwin, Ellen Gartell, Dr. Mattie Russell, William Perkins Library, Duke University. Kinston—Eugene Brown, Caswell-Neuse Historic Site. Kure Beach—Gehrig Spencer, Fort Fisher Historic Site. Raleigh—Dick Lankford, Division of Archives and Records; Keith Strawn, North Carolina Department of Cultural Resources. Southport—Colonel William G. Faulk, Ray Jackson, Fort Anderson Historic Site. Wilmington—Susan A. Krause, Bill Reaves, Janet Seapker, New Hanover County Museum.

Ohio: Cincinnati—Cincinnati Historical Society; First National Bank. Cleveland—Western Reserve Historical Society. Columbus—Ohio Historical Society. Coolville—Larry M. Strayer. Fremont—Rutherford B. Hayes Presidential Center. Hudson—Price Gibson; Thomas L. Vince, Hudson Library and Historical Society. Massillon—Margy Vogt, Massillon Museum. Mechanicsburg—Champaign County Historical Society. Sandusky—Follett House Museum. Sheffield Lake—William C. Stark, 103rd Ohio Volunteer Infantry Memorial Foundation. South Charleston—Jerry Rinker. Toledo—David Taylor.

Pennsylvania: Allentown—Lehigh County Historical Society. Carlisle—Randy Hackenburg, Dr. Richard Sommers, Michael S. Winey, Military History Institute. Enola—G. Craig Caba, Civil War Antiquities. Gettysburg—Gettysburg College; Gettysburg National Military Park. Gladwyne—Terry O'Leary. Harrisburg—Bruce Bazelon, William Penn Memorial Museum. Kittanning—Ronn Palm. Milford—Pike County Historical Society. North East—Irwin Rider. Philadelphia—Atwater Kent Museum; Free Library of Philadelphia; The Historical Society of Pennsylvania; Manuel Kean, Kean Archives; The Library Company of Philadelphia; Craig Nannos, First Regiment, Pennsylvania National Guard Armory and Museum; Philadelphia Maritime Museum; Russ A. Pritchard; The War Library and Museum of the Military Order of the Loyal Legion of the United States.

Rhode Island: Newport—Colonel James V. Coleman, Newport Artillery Company Armory. Providence—Richard B. Harrington, Anne S. K. Brown Military Collection; Jennifer B. Lee, John Hay Library, Brown University; Brigadier General John W. Kiely, Office of the Adjutant General; Providence Public Library; Joyce M. Botelho, Tom G. Brennan, The Rhode Island Historical Society Library and Museum.

South Carolina: Beaufort—June Berry, Beaufort Museum; Joel Martin. Charleston—Charleston Museum; Archives, The Citadel; Confederate Museum; Warren Ripley, *The Evening Post;* Martha Severns, Gibbes Art Gallery; Harlan Greene, South Carolina Historical Society; Julian V. Brandt III, Washington Light Infantry. Columbia—Fort Jackson Museum; Dr. Francis Lord; Laverne Watson, South Carolina Confederate Relic Room and Museum; Charles Gay, Alan Stokes, South Caroliniana Library, University of South Carolina; University of South Carolina McKissick Museums. Spartanburg—Robert M. Hicklin Jr. Sullivan's Island—David Ruth, Forts Moultrie and Sumter. Union—Dr. Lloyd Sutherland; Union County Museum.

Tennessee: Chattanooga—Chattanooga Museum of Regional History. Dover—Fort Donelson National Military Park. Franklin—Carter House. Greeneville—Andrew Johnson Historic Site. Harrogate—Edgar G. Archer, Abraham Lincoln Library and Museum, Lincoln Memorial University. Knoxville—Confederate Memorial Hall "Bleak House." Memphis—Eleanor McKay, Mississippi Valley Collection of Memphis State University; Jan Clement, Mud Island Mississippi River Museum; Pink Palace Museum; John L. Ryan. Murfreesboro—Stones River National Battlefield and Cemetery. Nashville—Belmont Mansion; Fisk University Library, Special Collections; Sarah and C. William Green-Devon Farm; Nashville Room, Public Library of Nashville and Davidson County; Tennessee Historical Society; Tennessee State Library and Archives; Tennessee State Museum. Sewanee—Jessie Ball duPont Library, The University of the South. Shiloh—Shiloh National Military Park and Cemetery. Smyrna—Sam Davis Home.

Texas: Austin—Eugene Barker Library, University of Texas; Confederate Museum; Texas State Archives. Mineral Wells—Mrs. Marjorie Cowan. San Antonio—William Green, Cecelia Steinfeldt, San Antonio Witte Museum.

Vermont: Bennington—Ruth Levin, Bennington Museum. Montpelier—Mary Pat Johnson, Vermont Historical Society; Philip Elwart, Vermont Museum.

Virginia: Alexandria—Wanda Dowell, Fort Ward Park; Boyhood Home of Robert E. Lee; Lee-Fendall House; Lloyd House, Alexandria Library. Arlington—Agnes Mullix, Arlington House, The Robert E. Lee Memorial. Fort Belvoir—John M. Dervan, U.S. Army Engineer Museum. Fort Monroe—R. Cody Phillips, The Casemate Museum, Department of the Army. Fredericksburg—Robert Krick, Fredericksburg/Spotsylvania National Military Park. Harrisonburg—Scott Zeiss, Harrisonburg-Rockingham Society Museum. Lexington—Robert C. Peniston, Lee Chapel Museum, Washington and Lee University; Barbara Crawford, Stonewall Jackson House; Virginia Military Institute Library; June F. Cunningham, Virginia Military Institute Museum; Washington and Lee University Library. Manassas—James Burgess, Manassas National Battlefield Park. Marion—Marion-Smyth County Historical and Museum Society, Inc. New Market—James G. Geary, New Market Battlefield Park. Newport News—Lois Oglesby, Charlotte Valentine, The Mariners Museum; John V. Quarstein, The War Memorial Museum of Virginia. Petersburg—Christopher M. Calkins, Petersburg National Battlefield Park. Portsmouth—Alice C. Hanes, Portsmouth Naval Shipyard Museum. Quantico—Marine Corps Historical Center. Richmond—Dr. Edward Campbell Jr., Cathy Carlson, Museum of the Confederacy; Valentine Museum. Williamsburg—Margaret Cook, Earl Gregg Swem Library, The College of William and Mary.

Washington, D.C.: Oliver Jenson, Jerry L. Kearns, Bernard F. Riley, Library of Congress, Prints and Photographs Division; James H. Trimble, Audio-Visual Archives, Still Pictures Branch, National Archives and Record Service; National Portrait Gallery; Smithsonian Institution.

West Virginia: Weston—Jackson's Mill Museum.

Wisconsin: Appleton—William G. Phillip. Madison—Dr. Richard Zeitlin, G.A.R. Memorial Hall Museum; State Historical Society of Wisconsin. Menomonee Falls—Theodore S. Myers. Milwaukee—Howard Madaus, Milwaukee Public Museum; Gary S. Pagel.

Great Britain: Bath—Kay Bond, American Museum in Britain; James E. Ayres, C. A. Bell Knight, John Judkyn Memorial. Bury—Andrew Ashton, Bury Art Gallery. Kingston Upon Hull—Iain Rutherford, Wilberforce House. Liverpool—Janet Smith, Liverpool Record Office. London—Maureen Alexander-Sinclair, Anti-Slavery Society; Elizabeth Moore, *Illustrated London News;* Caird Library, Roger Quarm, National Maritime Museum.

The editors also thank the following individuals: Sacie H. Lambertson, Katie Hooper McGregor, Nancy C. Scott.

The index for this book was prepared by Nicholas J. Anthony.

PICTURE CREDITS

Credits from left to right are separated by semicolons, from top to bottom by dashes.

Cover: Library of Congress; courtesy W. S. Hoole Special Collections, University of Alabama Library. 2, 3: Map by Peter McGinn. 8, 9: Tulane University Art Collection. 10, 11: In private collection; courtesy Jay P. Altmayer, photographed by George E. Jordan—photographed by John Miller. 12, 13: Courtesy Jay P. Altmayer, photographed by Larry Cantrell; from *Our Home and Country,* illustrated by W. L. Taylor, published by Moffat-Yard & Company, 1908, courtesy Frederic Ray—the J. B. Speed Art Museum, Louisville, Kentucky; Coggins Collection of Southern Art. 14, 15: Courtesy Harry M. Rhett Jr., Huntsville, Alabama, photographed by George Flemming; University of Georgia Libraries, photographed by Michael W. Thomas. 16, 17: Library of Congress. 18, 19: Courtesy Virginia E. Lewis, photographed by Harold Corsini; Library of Congress—Old Dartmouth Historical Society—courtesy of The New-York Historical Society. 20, 21: The Arts Museums of San Francisco, Gift of Mr. and Mrs. John D. Rockefeller III—the Metropolitan Museum of Art, purchase, Charles Allen Munn Bequest, 1966; Old Dartmouth Historical Society (2). 22, 23: Collection of The Boatmen's National Bank of St. Louis. 25: The Museum of the Confederacy. 26: Courtesy of The New-York Historical Society. 27, 28: Library of Congress. 29: The Museum of the Confederacy. 30: © The Historic New Orleans Collection, 533 Royal Street. 31: Lightfoot Collection. 32: Minnesota Historical Society. 34: Dartmouth College Library—The New-York Historical Society. 35: The Beinecke Rare Book and Manuscript Library, Yale University. 36, 37: Courtesy Benjamin Coates, Philadelphia, photographed by Henry Groskinsky. 39: Prints Division, New York Public Library, Astor, Lenox and Tilden Foundations. 40: Ohio Historical Society. 41: Library of Congress. 43: The Massachusetts Historical Society, copied by Kern Kovacik. 44: Courtesy Grand Central Art Galleries, Inc. 46: The Western Reserve Historical Society—Stowe-Day Foundation, Hartford, Connecticut. 48, 49: Copyright © President & Fellows of Harvard College, 1982, all rights reserved, courtesy Peabody Museum, Harvard University, daguerreotype by J. T. Zealy, copied by Hillel Burger. 50, 51: Courtesy Jay P. Altmayer, photographed by Larry Cantrell; courtesy of The New-York Historical Society; Chicago Historical Society, neg. no. 1920.7. 52, 53: Chicago Historical Society; Library of Congress—

BIBLIOGRAPHY

Angle, Paul M., ed., *Created Equal? The Complete Lincoln-Douglas Debates.* University of Chicago Press, 1958.

Annals of the War. Philadelphia *Weekly Times,* 1879.

Bartlett, Irving H., *Wendell Phillips: Brahmin Radical.* Greenwood Press, 1973.

Basler, Roy P., ed.:
Abraham Lincoln: His Speeches and Writings. Gosset and Dunlap, 1946.★
The Collected Works of Abraham Lincoln. Rutgers University Press, 1955.

Bennett, Whitman, *Whittier: Bard of Freedom.* University of North Carolina Press, 1941.

Berger, Max, *The British Traveller in America, 1836-1860.* Columbia University Press, 1943.

Blassingame, John W., *The Slave Community: Plantation Life in the Antebellum South.* Oxford University Press, 1972.

Blue, Frederick J., *The Free Soilers: Third Party Politics, 1848-1854.* University of Illinois Press, 1973.

Boatner, Mark M., *The Civil War Dictionary.* David McKen Company, 1959.★

Bradford, Sarah H., *Harriet: The Moses of Her People.* Corinth Books, 1961.

Bragdon, Henry W., and Samuel P. McCutchen, *History of a Free People.* Macmillan, 1954.

Brewerton, J. Douglas, *The War in Kansas: A Rough Trip to the Border.* New York, 1856.

Buel, C. C., and Robert U. Johnson, eds., *Battles and Leaders of the Civil War,* Vols. 1-4. Castle Books, 1956 (reprint of 1888 edition).★

Burns, James MacGregor, *The Vineyard of Liberty.* Alfred A. Knopf, 1982.

Catton, Bruce, *The Coming Fury (The Centennial History of the Civil War,* Vol. 1). Pocket Books, 1963.★

Chadwick, John White, *Theodore Parker: Preacher and Reformer.* Scholarly Press, 1971.

Cole, Arthur C., *The Irrepressible Conflict, 1850-1865 (A History of American Life,* Vol. 7). Quadrangle Books, 1934.

Commager, Henry Steele, ed.:
Documents of American History. Appleton-Century-Crofts, 1958.
Illustrated History of the Civil War. Promontory Press, 1976.

Conrad, Earl, *Harriet Tubman.* Eriksson, 1970.

Cooper, William J., Jr., *The South and the Politics of Slavery, 1828-1856.* Louisiana State University Press, 1978.

Craven, Avery O., *The Coming of the Civil War.* University of Chicago Press, 1959.

Crawford, Samuel W., *The Genesis of the Civil War: The Story of Fort Sumter, 1860-1861.* Charles L. Webster and Company, 1887.

Cromwell, Otelia, *Lucretia Mott.* Russell and Russell Publishers, 1971.

Current, Richard N., *John C. Calhoun.* Washington Square Press, 1966.

Davis, William C.:
Breckinridge: Statesman, Soldier, Symbol. Louisiana State University Press, 1970.
The Deep Waters of the Proud. Doubleday and Company, 1982.
Shadows of the Storm (The Image of War: 1861-1865, Vol. 1). Doubleday and Company, 1981.

Dickert, D. Augustus, *History of Kershaw's Brigade.* Elbert H. Aull Company, 1899.

Donald, David:
Charles Sumner and the Civil War. Alfred A. Knopf, 1960.
Lincoln Reconsidered: Essays on the Civil War Era. Vintage Books, 1961.

Doubleday, Abner, *Reminiscences of Forts Sumter and Moultrie in 1860-1861.* Harper and Brothers Publishers, 1876.

Douglass, Frederick, *My Bondage and My Freedom.* Arno Press, 1968.

Duberman, Martin, ed., *The Anti-Slavery Vanguard: New Essays on the Abolitionists.* Princeton University Press, 1965.

Dumond, Dwight Lowell, *Southern Editorials on Secession.* Peter Smith, 1964.

Eaton, Clement:
A History of the Old South. Macmillan, 1975.
Jefferson Davis. The Free Press, 1977.

Edward, C., "Marats, Dantons and Robespierres," *American History Illustrated,* July 1977.

Elliot, Charles W., *Winfield Scott: The Soldier and the Man.* Macmillan, 1937.

Fehrenbacher, Don E.:
The Dred Scott Case. Oxford University Press, 1978.
Slavery, Law, and Politics: The Dred Scott Case in Historical Perspective. Oxford University Press, 1981.

Fite, Emerson D., *The Presidential Campaign of 1860.* New York, 1911.

Freeman, Douglas Southall, *R. E. Lee: A Biography.* Charles Scribner's Sons, 1934.

Gara, Larry, *The Liberty Line: The Legend of the Underground Railroad.* University of Kentucky Press, 1961.

Garrison, Wendell Phillips, and Francis Jackson Garrison, *William Lloyd Garrison, 1805-1879,* Vols. 1-4. Arno Press, 1969.

Genovese, Eugene D., *The Political Economy of Slavery: Studies in the Economy and Society of the Slave South.* Random House, 1961.

Gilbert, Olive, *Narrative of Sojourner Truth.* Arno Press, 1968.

Greene, Dana, ed., *Lucretia Mott: The Complete Speeches and Sermons.* E. Mellon, 1980.

Gunderson, Robert Gray, *Old Gentlemen's Convention: The Washington Peace Conference of 1861.* University of Wisconsin Press, 1961.

Halsey, Ashley, *Who Fired the First Shot?* Hawthorne Books, 1963.

Hamilton, Holman, *Prologue to Conflict.* University of Kentucky Press, 1964.

Harrison, Lowell, *The Antislavery Movement in Kentucky.* University of Kentucky Press, 1979.

Heckmen, Richard Allen, *Lincoln vs. Douglas.* Public Affairs Press, 1967.

Heitman, Francis B., *Historical Register and Dictionary of the United States Army.* University of Illinois Press, 1965.

Helper, Hinton R., *The Impending Crisis of the South: How to Meet It.* Ed. by George M. Frederickson. Harvard University Press, 1968.

Henry, Robert Selph, *The Story of the Confederacy.* Peter Smith, 1970.

Holmes, Emma, *Diary of Miss Emma Holmes, 1861-1866.* Ed. by John F. Marszalek. Louisiana State University Press, 1979.

Holzman, Robert S., *Adapt or Perish: The Life of General Roger A. Pryor, C.S.A.* Archon Books, 1976.

Jenks, William (Williamson Jahnsenykes), *Memoir of the Northern Kingdom.* Boston, 1808.

Jenson, Merrill, *The New Nation.* Random House, 1965.

Johansen, Robert W., *Stephen A. Douglas.* Oxford University Press, 1973.

John Brown's Raid. National Park Service (Government Printing Office), 1973.

Jordan, Winthrop D., *White over Black: American Attitudes toward the Negro.* University of North Carolina Press, 1968.

Keller, Allan, *Thunder at Harper's Ferry.* Prentice-Hall, 1958.

Ketchem, Richard, ed., *The American Heritage Picture History of the Civil War.* American Heritage Publishing Company, 1960.

King, Alvy L., *Louis T. Wigfall, Southern Fire-Eater.* Louisiana State University Press, 1970.

Klein, Philip S., *President James Buchanan.* Pennsylvania State University Press, 1962.

Long, E. B. and Barbara, *The Civil War Day by Day: An Almanac, 1861-1865.* Doubleday and Company, 1971.

Lossing, Benson, *Pictorial History of the Civil War.* G. W. Childs, 1866.

Luthin, Reinhard H., *The First Lincoln Campaign.* Harvard University Press, 1944.

McCardell, John, *The Idea of a Southern Nation.* W. W. Norton & Company, 1979.

McPherson, James M., *Ordeal by Fire: The Civil War and Reconstruction.* Alfred A. Knopf, 1982.★

McReynolds, Edwin C., *Missouri.* University of Oklahoma Press, 1962.

Malin, James C., "John Brown and the Legend of Fifty-Six," American Philosophical Society, Vol. 17, 1942.

May, Samuel J., *Some Recollections of Our Anti-Slavery Conflict.* Arno Press, 1968.

Meier, Peg, ed., *Bring Warm Clothes: Letters and Photos from Minnesota's Past.* Minneapolis Tribune, 1981.

Mitchell, Betty L., *Edmund Ruffin.* University of Indiana Press, 1981.

Monaghan, Jay, *Civil War on the Western Border, 1854-1865.* Little, Brown and Company, 1955.

Moore, Frank, ed., *The Rebellion Record*, Vols. 1-12. G. P.

Putnam, 1861-1868.

Moore, Glover, *The Missouri Controversy, 1819-1821.* University of Kentucky Press, 1966.

Neely, Mark E., Jr., *The Abraham Lincoln Encyclopedia.* McGraw-Hill, 1982.

Nevins, Allan:
The Emergence of Lincoln:
Vol. 1, *Douglas, Buchanan, and Party Chaos, 1857-1859.* Charles Scribner's Sons, 1950.★
Vol. 2, *Prologue to Civil War, 1859-1860.* Charles Scribner's Sons, 1950.★
Frémont: Pathmarker of the West. Frederick Ungar, 1961.
The Improvised War, 1861-1862 (The War for the Union, Vol. 1). Charles Scribner's Sons, 1959.
Ordeal of the Union:
Vol. 1, *Fruits of Manifest Destiny, 1847-1852.* Charles Scribner's Sons, 1947.★
Vol. 2, *A House Dividing, 1852-1857.* Charles Scribner's Sons, 1947.★

Nichols, Alice, *Bleeding Kansas.* Oxford University Press, 1954.

Nichols, Roy Franklin, *The Disruption of American Democracy.* The Free Press, 1967.★

Nicolay, John J., *Abraham Lincoln.* The Century Company, 1890.

Northup, Solomon, *Twelve Years a Slave.* Louisiana State University Press, 1968.

Oates, Stephen B.:
To Purge This Land with Blood: A Biography of John Brown. Harper Torchbooks, 1970.
With Malice toward None: The Life of Abraham Lincoln. Harper & Row, 1977.

Parrington, Vernon L., *The Romantic Revolution in America (Main Currents in American Thought*, Vol. 2). Harcourt, Brace, Jovanovich, 1955.

Pease, William H. and Jane H., eds., *The Anti-Slavery Argument.* Irvington, 1965.

Pfister, Harold Francis, *Facing the Light: Historic American Portrait Daguerreotypes.* Smithsonian Institution Press, 1978.

Phillips, Ulrich Bonnell, *American Negro Slavery.* Louisiana State University Press, 1969.

Population of the United States in 1860: The Eighth Census. Government Printing Office, 1864.

Potter, David M., *The Impending Crisis, 1848-1861.* Harper Torchbooks, 1976.★

Quarles, Benjamin:
Black Abolitionists. Oxford University Press, 1969.
Frederick Douglass. Associated Publishers, 1948.

Randall, J. G., *Lincoln the President: Springfield to Gettysburg.* Peter Smith, 1976.

Randall, J. G., and David Donald, *The Divided Union.* Little, Brown and Company, 1961.

Rawley, James A., *Race and Politics: "Bleeding Kansas" and the Coming of the Civil War.* Lippincott, 1969.

Roland, Charles P., *The Confederacy.* The University of Chicago Press, 1960.

Rudisill, Richard, *Mirror Image.* University of New Mexico Press, 1971.

Russell, William Howard, *My Diary: North and South.* Harper & Brothers, 1954.

Scarborough, William K., ed., *The Diary of Edmund Ruffin.* Louisiana State University Press, 1972.

Schaff, Morris, *The Spirit of Old West Point, 1858-1862.* Houghton, Mifflin and Company, 1907.

Sewell, Richard H., *Ballots for Freedom: Antislavery Politics in the United States, 1837-1860.* Oxford University Press, 1976.

Shaw, Albert, *Abraham Lincoln: His Path to the Presidency.* The Review of Reviews Corporation, 1929.

Sobieszek, Robert A., and Odette M. Appel, *The Spirit of Fact: The Daguerreotypes of Southworth and Hawes, 1843-1862.* David R. Godine, 1976.

Sorin, Gerald, *Abolitionism: A New Perspective.* Praeger Press, 1972.

Stampp, Kenneth M.:
And the War Came: The North and the Secession Crisis. Louisiana State University Press, 1980.★
The Peculiar Institution. Random House, 1956.★

Strode, Hudson, *Jefferson Davis, American Patriot.* Harcourt Brace, 1955.

Swanberg, W. A., *First Blood: The Story of Fort Sumter.* Charles Scribner's Sons, 1957.★

Swift, Lindsay, *William Lloyd Garrison.* G. W. Jacobs and Company, 1911.

Thomas, Benjamin P., *Abraham Lincoln.* Alfred A. Knopf, 1952.

Thomas, John L., ed., *Slavery Attacked: The Abolitionist Crusade.* Prentice-Hall, 1965.

Thomason, John W., Jr., *Jeb Stuart.* Charles Scribner's Sons, 1930.

Thompson, Robert M., and Richard Wainwright, eds., *Confidential Correspondence of Gustavus Vasa Fox.* DeVinne Press, 1918.

Thompson, William Y., *Robert Toombs of Georgia.* Louisiana State University Press, 1966.

United States Congress, *Congressional Globe*, 36th Congress, 1st Session, Vol. 1.

United States War Department, *The War of the Rebellion: A Compilation of the Official Records of the Union and Confederate Armies.* Government Printing Office, 1880.★

Villard, Oswald G., *John Brown, 1800-1859.* Doubleday, 1910.

Warner, Ezra J.:
Generals in Blue. Louisiana State University Press, 1964.
Generals in Gray. Louisiana State University Press, 1959.

Weiss, John, *Life and Correspondence of Theodore Parker*, Vols. 1 and 2. Arno Press, 1969.

Weitenkampf, Frank, *Political Caricature in the United States.* The New York Public Library, 1953.

Williams, Ben Ames, ed., *A Diary from Dixie.* Houghton Mifflin Company, 1949.

Williams, T. Harry:
P.G.T. Beauregard: Napoleon in Gray. Louisiana State University Press, 1955.
The Union Restored, 1861-1876 (The Life History of the United States, Vol. 6). Time-Life Books, 1980.
The Union Sundered, 1849-1865 (The Life History of the United States, Vol. 5). Time-Life Books, 1980.

Wilson, Forrest, *Crusader in Crinoline: The Life of Harriet Beecher Stowe.* Greenwood Press, 1972.

Wiltse, Charles M., *John C. Calhoun*, Vols. 1-3. Bobbs-Merrill Company, 1949.

Woodward, C. Vann, ed., *Mary Chesnut's Civil War.* Yale University Press, 1981.

Yearns, Wilfred Buck, *The Confederate Congress.* University of Georgia Press, 1960.

★ *Titles marked with an asterisk were especially helpful in the preparation of this volume.*

INDEX

159-161, 163, *168-169;* civilian workers in, 147, 152; Confederate government's role in reduction of, 132-141, 160, 163, *168-169;* damage to, 150, 152-156, 160, *162-167;* first Confederate shots, 3, 127, *140-141,* 146; first Union shots, 147-148; garrison flag, *162;* garrison officers, *148;* garrison strength, 147, 150-151, *map* 150; morale of garrison, 150-151; relief attempts and defense of, 121-128, 132-138, 146-150, *151,* 152-154, *155,* 156-157; surrender demanded, 138-141, 157-159; troops moved to, *123-125;* United States Navy at, 133-135, 147, 152-153, 156-157, 160-161. *See also* Anderson, Robert
Fort Taylor, Florida, 129
Forts seized by South, 128-129
Foster, J. G., *148*
Fox, Gustavus V., 133-135, 147, 152-157, 160
Franklin College, *14-15*
Freeport, Illinois, 106, 108
Frémont, John C., *103,* 104
Fugitive Slave Law, 45-46, 64, 119

G
Galesburg, Illinois, 106
Garner, Margaret, *44*
Garnett, James M., 36
Garrison, William Lloyd, 38-39, 62, *65,* 66, 68-69
Geary, John W., 79
Geography, effect on economy and society, 29
Georgia, secession by, 3, 128
Georgia, University of, *14-15*
Georgia Railway, 14
German immigrants, 16, 33, 100
Giddings, Joshua, 46
Gold resources, 9
Gray, Thomas, 99
Greeley, Horace: and Frémont as presidential candidate, 104; and Know-Nothings, 101; and Lincoln as presidential candidate, 108; as Oregon delegate, 111
Guadalupe Hidalgo Treaty, 42

H
Hale, John P., 42
Hall, Norman J., 156
Hammond, James H., 109
Harpers Ferry raid, 84-85, *86-87,* 88-89, *90-93. See also* Brown, John
Harriet Lane, 152
Harris, James, 71, 78-79
Hart, Peter, 156
Hartford, Connecticut, 114
Haynsworth, George E., 127
Helper, Hinton, 108-109
Henson, Josiah, *46*
Higginson, Thomas Wentworth, 84
Holmes, Emma, 132
Holt, George W., *143*
Holt, Joseph, 123-126

Hough, Daniel, 161
House of Representatives speakership, 108-109
Howe, Samuel Gridley, 85
Huntsville, Alabama, *14*

I
Immigrants: as political force, 16, 33, 101; prejudice against, 100
Immigration, 16
Impending Crisis of the South (Helper), 108-109
Indiana elections, 118
Industrial Revolution effect, 29
Industry: in Northern states, *18-19,* 29; in Southern states, 32-33; trends in, 9, 29
Interchangeable parts introduced, 18
Irish immigrants, 16, 100
Isabel, 161

J
Jack (slave), *48*
Jackson, Andrew, 39; on American government, 22; and nullification doctrine, 38
Jackson, Thomas J. "Stonewall," 97
James, George S., 141
James Island, 137, 147, 149
Jamison, David F., 24, 27
Jefferson, Thomas, 34, 101
Jones, Samuel, 76
Jonesboro, Illinois, 106

K
Kansas: Border Ruffians' depredations, *74,* 75-76, 82; emigration to, 74-75; statehood application, 80-83; violence in, 47, 70-71, *74, 75,* 76, *77,* 79, 80-82, *83*
Kansas-Nebraska Act, 71-74, 101
Kensel, George A., *145*
Kentucky Resolution, 37-38
Key West, Florida, 129
Kimmel, Manning M., *143*
Know-Nothings, 101, *102*

L
Lane, James, 76
Lawrence, Kansas, 75-76, *77*
Lawrence, Amos, 84
Lecompton (Kansas) Constitution, 82
Lee, Robert E., 87, *88*
Lee, Stephen D., 140, 159
Lee, Thomas J., *145*
Leslie's *Illustrated Newspaper, 81,* 139
Lexington (Kentucky) *Western Monitor,* 35
Liberator, The, 39, 62, 69
Liberia, emigration to, 38
Liberty Party, 62
Lincoln, Abraham, *99, 116;* on blacks' equality, 106; Cooper Union speech, 98-99; debates Douglas, 99, 105-107, *108;* elected President, 98, 118-119, 142; and Fort Pickens relief, 133; and Fort Sumter relief, 132-135, 137; house-divided speech, 105; inauguration address, 131-

132, *135,* 161; and Know-Nothings, 101; Philadelphia speech, *132;* political skill, 99; as presidential candidate, 98-99, 111, 113-114, *116-117,* 118; and Republican affiliation, 101-102; and secessionist movement, 118; on slavery, 98-99, 105, 113, 116, 118; as Senate candidate, 105, 108; on slavery, 98-99, 105, 113, 116, 118; as speaker, 116; vilified in South, 116-117, *118*
Livermore, Arthur, 35
Lloyd's Political Chart, *112*
Logan, John A., 109
Louisiana, secession by, 3, 128
Louisville, Kentucky, *12*

M
M'Cormick, T. B., 40
McCulloch, Ben, *131*
McLean, John, 113
McNeill, Henry C., *142*
Magruder, John T., 142
Maine, admitted into Union, 36
Mallory, Stephen R., 9
Manifest Destiny doctrine, 41
Manufactures. *See* Industry
Marmaduke, John S., *143*
Maryland, as Union slave state, 3
Maryland-Pennsylvania boundary, *36-37*
Mason, Charles, 37
Mason-Dixon line, *36-37*
Massachusetts antislavery campaign, 62, 74
Meade, Richard K., *142, 143, 148*
Melville, Herman, 16
Memminger, Christopher, 130
Metals industry production, 9
Mexico, war with, 41
Middlesex Anti-Slavery Society, 66
Miles, William Porcher, 159
Mineral resources, 9, 18
Minnesota Territory, emigration to, *32*
Mississippi: federal property seized by, 128; in secessionist movement, 3, 84, 128
Mississippi River as trade artery, 8-9
Missouri, as Union slave state, 3
Missouri Compromise, 34-37, 71-72, 79-80, 119
Mohawk, New York, 115
Monde Illustré, Le, 151
Montgomery, Alabama, 130, *134*
Morgan, Charles H., *144*
Morris Island, 127, 137, *139-141,* 146, 151-152
Mott, Lucretia, 67
Moultrieville, South Carolina, 121

N
Nashville convention, 43
Nebraska Territory Act, 71
New Mexico statehood application, 43
New Orleans, Louisiana: forts seized by state, 128; population, 14; port facilities, *8-9, 30*
New Orleans *Daily Crescent,* 24
New York City, *16-17, 114-115;* population, 16; port facilities, *31*

New York *Tribune,* 18, 78, 101
Newby, Dangerfield, 88
Newport, Indiana, *60-61*
Newspapers, partisanship among, 84
North Carolina, secession by, 3
North Star, The, 64
Northern states: abolitionist movement in, 30, 34-35, 38-39, 40-41, 46-47, 62-69, *70-76;* agricultural production, *20-21;* and blacks' equality, *100;* and Dred Scott ruling, 105; economic dependence on South, 9, 32-33; economic and industrial capacity, 18-19, 29, 101; emigration from, *32,* 74-75; and Fort Sumter, 127-128, *135,* 147; and fugitive slaves, 46-47; investments in South, 32-33; and John Brown, 78, 89, 109; militia musters by, 84; population, 16, 35; relations with South, 28-29; and secessionist movement, 27-28, 118; and slavery extension, 42-43, 71-76, 98, 101, 104-105, 110; Southern economic dependence on, 9, 32-33, 35-37; states remaining in Union, *map* 2-3
Nullification doctrine, 37-38

O
Oconee River, *14-15*
O'Connor, Michael P., 138
Ore resources, 9, 18
Osawatomie, Kansas, 79
Ottawa, Illinois, 106

P
Palfrey, John C., *144*
Palmetto Guard, *148,* 156
Parker, Richard, 91, *94-95*
Parker, Theodore, *64,* 84
Pawnee, 152, 156
Peck, Lafayette, *143*
Pennington, William, 109
Pennsylvania elections, 118
Pensacola, Florida, 128
Pensacola Bay, 129
Petigru, James, 25, 27
Philadelphia, Pennsylvania, *132*
Philadelphia Female Anti-Slavery Society, 67
Phillips, Wendell, 47, 68
Pickens, Francis, 126-127, 135, 161
Pierce, Franklin: as Democratic nominee, 100, 102; and Kansas elections, 74-75
Pittsburgh, Pennsylvania, *18-19*
Plantations: economic decline, 36-37; land-expansion need, 31-32; organization and work force, *10-11,* 29; social activities, *12-13,* 14
Pocahontas, 152, 156
Polk, James K., 22
Popular-sovereignty doctrine, 71-72, 106, 108, 113, 116
Population: national, 9; Northern states, 16, 35; Southern states, 14
Pottawatomie Massacre, 70-71
Powhatan, 152, 156
Propaganda, 47, 89, 108-109, 118

Time-Life Books Inc. offers a wide range of fine recordings, including a *Rock 'n' Roll Era* series. For subscription information, call 1-800-445-TIME, or write TIME-LIFE MUSIC, Time & Life Building, Chicago, Illinois 60611.